Protection of
HUMAN RIGHTS
AND THE POLICE
The Legal Imperatives

Protection of HUMAN RIGHTS AND THE POLICE

The Legal Imperatives

DR. H. ABDUL AZEEZ
BSc. (Hons.), LL.M. (Kerala), LL.M. (Europe), Ph.D.
Head of Department (Law)
Kerala Police Academy, Thrissur (Kerala)

Foreword

JUSTICE V.R. KRISHNA IYER
Former Judge, Supreme Court of India

REGAL

REGAL PUBLICATIONS
New Delhi

Protection of
HUMAN RIGHTS AND THE POLICE
The Legal Imperatives

ISBN 978-81-8484-428-3

Typeset by
RAHUL COMPOSERS
New Highway Apartments, Lakshmi Niwas
760, Pocket-D, Lok Nayak Puram, New Delhi - 110 041

Printed in India at
MAYUR ENTERPRISES
WZ Plot No. 3, Gujjar Market, Tihar Village, New Delhi - 110 018

Published by
REGAL PUBLICATIONS
F-159, Rajouri Garden, New Delhi - 110 027
Phone : 45546396, 25435369
E-mail : regalbookspub@yahoo.com, regaldeepbooks@yahoo.com

Dedicated
to
my Mother Smt. S. Ashya Beevi
and
Father Late Sri E. Habeeb Mustafa

Contents

V.R. Krishna Iyer
(Former Judge, Supreme Court of India)

Phone and Fax: 0484-2370088
"SATGAMAYA"
M.G. Road, Ernakulam-682011

Foreword

The term "human rights" is a dynamic concept and has attained a solemn premise and a powerful idea after the Second World War though the notion is as old as the coming into the existence of mankind. These rights were known by different names as basic rights, natural rights, inherent rights and fundamental rights. The protection of human personality and the dignity is the most important function of a modern State, and human rights, today, represent a powerful discourse against atrocities committed against human personality and human dignity. However, the Police as the State agency who are bequeathed with the power to protect the life and liberty of the people commit innumerable violations of human rights making the protection of human rights a fantasy. The unfettered powers vested with the police for the protection of human rights and human dignity of the people are abused to their detriment.

No doubt, the police as protectors of society play vital role in the administration of criminal justice by preventing and detecting crimes. While ensuring safety and security of the people it must also be ensured that no member of the society is put in peril and no person's human rights and dignity are violated. Police investigation, interrogation, arrest, detention and torture have been controversial in India for long and continue to be so. Attempts have always been made to make the investigations, interrogation, arrest and detentions free from coercion and "third degree" influences so that the minimum protection could be guaranteed. Nonetheless, police commit large number of human rights violations irrespective of all the measures that are taken to protect the human rights of persons.

Dr. H. Abdul Azeez, the author of the book "Protection of Human Rights and the Police : The Legal Imperatives" is the Head of the Department (Law) of Kerala Police Academy, Thrissur. He has earlier worked as Judicial First Class Magistrate and as Law College Professor in India and abroad. His vast experience has reflected in bringing out this book.

Dr. Azeez attempts to explore the extent of violation of human rights by the police in India and the level of protection of human rights from the police. He makes a systematic assessment of historical perspective of growth and evolution of human rights protection in India and globally, international legal framework related with protection of human rights, Constitutional and statutory protection available in India. He has also analyzed the working of the National Human Rights Commission and State Human Rights Commissions in protecting human rights violations by the police. A comparative scrutiny of the protection of human rights from the police in Regional systems of the World such as European, Inter-American, African systems, *etc.*, and an effective assessment of the United Nations' international standards of human rights and policing have also been made in this book. Towards the end of the book, Dr. Azeez makes valuable recommendations and suggestions to improve the mechanism of protection of human rights from being violated by the police. I find that Dr. Azeez has succeeded in bringing out a clear picture of extent of violation of human rights by the police in India and the problems and perspectives of protection of human rights from the police. I hope this book will be an eye opener not only for the police but for the Legislatures, executive and judicial officers also.

JUSTICE V.R. KRISHNA IYER

Preface

Human rights are significant for every Man ever since he came into existence in this world until he breaths the last. It has emerged as solemn legal premise after the Second World War. Law has been framed to protect the human rights due to its significance both nationally and internationally. Police is entrusted with the duty of protecting the life, liberty and security of persons in a State. However, the protectors, many a times, turn out to be violators. The Police in India are known for their violations of human rights. There is always hue and cry about violation of human rights by the police in India.

An attempt has been made to unravel the extent of the human rights violation by the police in India generally, and in Kerala particularly. Focus is made to find the reasons for the violations, the adequacies of the existing law to protect human rights from being violated by the police, the problems related with prevention of the violations by the law effectively.

The book reveals that there takes place a large number of human rights violations by the police. The existing law, to a certain extent, attempts to prevent the violations of human rights by the police. However, more additions to the existing laws are necessary. The lack of proper implementation of the existing law intensifies the problem. There should be clear mechanisms for the proper implementation of the law.

With special laws, both substantive and procedural, in dealing with violation of human rights by the police can reduce the extent of violation. However, proper monitoring, speedy and effective redressal mechanism, training on human rights, training on new technique for investigations and interrogations can improve the system and reduce the human rights violations by the police.

I must express my thanks to my Professor Dr. A. Prasanna, the Principal of Government Law College, Kozhikode, on deputation as associate Fellow at the Institute of Management in Government, Thiruvananthapuram who guided me to write this book. My thanks are also due to Justice R. Natarajan and Advocate K.E. Gangadharan, Members of Kerala State Human Rights Commission; Justice A. Lekshmi Kutty, Prof S. Varghese, former Members of the Kerala State Human Rights Commission; Mr. S. Pulikesi, Additional Director General of Police (Training), Kerala; K. Mohan Kumar, Advocate, Thiruvananthapuram and C.D. Anil, Retired Additional Chief Judicial Magistrate for their cooperation in collecting information and data on various aspects related with the subject.

I must record my gratitude to renowned former Supreme Court Judge and an authority in human rights jurisprudence Justice V.R. Krishna Iyer, who has pleasingly given a "Foreword" to this book.

I must also extend my appreciation to Mrs. Hairnesa, Miss. Alisha, Miss. Ansha, Miss. Afsana, Miss. Aleena, Mrs. Nasia and Miss. Asia for spending their valuable time for proof reading.

Finally, I express my gratitude to the renowned Publisher, Regal Publications who induced me to write this book and for their painstaking cooperation and efforts in bringing it out in this admirable form.

DR. H. ABDUL AZEEZ

Abbreviations

AAPP	-	Association of Asian Parliament for Peace
ACHPR	-	African Charter on Human and Peoples' Rights
ACHR	-	American Convention on Human Rights
ACtHPR	-	African Court of Human and Peoples' Rights
AIG (PG)	-	Assistant Inspector General (Public Grievances)
APA	-	Asian Parliamentary Assembly
AU	-	African Union
CEADAW	-	Convention on Elimination of All forms of Discrimination Against Women
CoE	-	Council of Europe
CRC	-	The Convention on the Rights of the Child
DEADAW	-	Declaration on Elimination of All forms of Discrimination Against Women
ECHR	-	European Convention on Human Rights and Fundamental Freedoms
ECtHR	-	European Court of Human Rights
ICCPR	-	International Covenant on Civil and Political Rights
ICESCR	-	International Covenant on Economic, Social and Cultural Rights
KSHRC	-	Kerala State Human Rights Commission
NHRC	-	National Human Rights Commission
OAS	-	Organization of American States
OAU	-	Organization of African Unity

PGC	-	Public Grievance Cell (Against Police)
POTA	-	Prevention of Terrorism Ordinance
SAARC	-	South Asian Association for Regional Cooperation
SHRC	-	State Human Rights Commission
TADA	-	Terrorist & Disruptive Activities (Prevention) Act
UDHR	-	Universal Declaration of Human Rights
UN	-	United Nations Organisation

1

Introduction

The concept of "human rights" is as old as the coming into existence of human beings on the earth. These rights are inherent in every person by virtue of his birth. However, these rights were referred to as natural rights until recently. In the eighteenth and nineteenth centuries in Europe, several philosophers such as Thomas Paine,[1] John Stuart Mill[2] and Henry David Thoreau[3] proposed the concept of "natural rights", the rights belonging to a person by nature by virtue of being born as a human being. The concept of human rights emerged as a solemn premise after the Second World War due to the barbarous atrocities and massacre committed by Nazi Germany prior to and during the War. Although the expression "human rights" came into general use after the Second World War,

1. Thomas Pine, *Rights of Man*, Reprint (1792), p. 25; In part 4 of 16 entitled "Being an Answer to Mr. Burke's Attack on the French Revolution" Pine claims "..... that all men are born equal, and with equal natural right, in the same manner as if posterity had been continued by creation instead of generation.... Natural rights are those which appertain to man in right of his existence".
2. John Stuart Mill, *Essays on Liberty*, Reprint (1973), pp. 15-17, John Stuart Mill though not directly using the term "natural rights", but he claims that a set of rights that must be protected by society as they are natural or God-given and also ultimate utility of individuals.
3. Henry David Thoreau, *On the duty of Civil Disobedience*, Reprint (1842), p. 14.

yet Henry David Thoreau is considered to first use the expression "human rights" in the previous century.[4] The concept of human rights can be traced from Western Philosophy to Stoic natural law doctrines.[5] The ideas that originated with Zeno of *Citium* and the Stoics teachings that there were pervasive laws of nature and hence, the Man's conduct should be measured in accordance with those laws had roots in the development of the concept of human rights.[6]

Human rights can generally be defined as those fundamental and natural rights that are attached with human beings and are essential to consider a Man as a human being. They are not the creation of any State or law. They are inherent in every Man by virtue of being human and are ascribed naturally by virtue of being born as a Man.[7] It is equal in every human being. The Universal Declaration of Human Rights 1948 declares that "all human beings are born free and equal in dignity and rights."[8] They are endowed with reason and conscience, and should act towards one another in a spirit of brotherhood. This profound proposition is central to the Charter of the United Nations which affirms its faith in fundamental human rights and in the dignity and worth of human person.[9]

Human rights are universal across all nations. They are based upon the belief that each individual should be treated with dignity and respect to which, as human being, they are entitled. Human rights are part of what each person needs to be human. Human rights, defined in Constitutions and legislations are the attempt to express how people's humanity should be respected by those with power over them, particularly the Governments and their law enforcement agencies like the police.[10]

There is no exaggeration to submit that generally, the police in India do not hesitate to violate human rights to any extent. The behaviour of Indian police is colonial and dreadful towards common man. No doubt, the police as protectors of society play a vital role in

4. Peter Halstead, *The Comprehensive Guide to All Facts: Human Rights* (2010), p. 16.
5. Stoics is a group of philosophers founded in Athens by Zeno of *Citium* in early 3rd century and existed until 529 AD when it was closed down by order of the Emperor Justinian I.
6. See *supra* n. 4, at p. 17.
7. Brian Orend, *Human Rights : Concept and Context* (2002), p. 38
8. Universal Declaration of Human Rights, Art. 1.
9. See Preamble of the United Nations Charter 1945.
10. Gopal Bhargava, *Meaning and Source of Human Rights* (2003), p. 15.

the administration of criminal justice by preventing and detecting crimes. While ensuring safety and security of the people police must also ensure that no member of the society is put in peril and no person's human rights and dignity are curtailed. It has always been a difficult task for the police to identify the culprit and set justice in motion to punish the delinquent without tampering the interest and dignity of human beings and the rights appended therewith. Police investigation, interrogation, arrest and detention have always been controversial for the non-compliance of the procedural requirement which put the accused and other persons in difficulty, violating their human rights and dignity. Attempts have always been made to make the investigations, interrogation, arrest and detentions fair and free from coercion and "third degree" influences so that the minimum protection could be guaranteed. Nonetheless, police commit large number of human rights violations irrespective of all the measures taken to protect the human rights of the people.

One of the important functions of the State in modern times is the protection of life, liberty and property of its citizens by maintaining law and order in the State. Rule of law comes to an end when the police who are bestowed with the authority to protect the common man turn out to be the violators of their human rights. There is no exaggeration in submitting that the police quite often violate the human rights of people in India. The magnitude and dimension of violation of human rights by the police in India are so painstaking that a common man or woman, whether as victim or witness would seldom approach the police for the redressal of their grievance without the aid of a politician or a lawyer or a bureaucrat. The police in India are more known for their violations of human rights than their protection.

I. MEANING OF THE TERM "HUMAN RIGHTS"

The Encyclopedia Britannica defines the term "human rights" as "rights that belong to an individual as a consequence of being human."[11] Oxford Advance Learner's Dictionary defines the term as "one of the basic rights that everyone has to be treated fairly and not in a cruel way, especially by their government".[12] Amnesty International defines human rights as "basic rights and freedoms that all people are entitled to regardless of nationality, sex, national or

11. Britannica Ready Reference Encyclopedia, Vol. 5 (2005), pp. 82-83.
12. Oxford Advanced Learners Dictionary (2010).

ethnic origin, race, religion, language, or other status".[13] The term came into wider use after the Second World War. As understood today, human rights refer to a wide variety of values and capabilities reflecting the diversity of human circumstances and history. They are conceived as universal, applying to all human beings everywhere. The definition "a human right is a universal moral right, something which all men, everywhere, at all times ought to have, something of which no one may be deprived of without a grave affront to justice, something which is owing to every human simply because he is human"[14] clearly expresses the meaning of human rights in modern times.

1.1. Three Generation of Human Rights

A right is an entitlement to certain kinds of treatment; while positive rights grant people the ability to demand the performance of some action, as for example, ability to vote, negative rights entitle people to demand that others refrain from certain kinds of action, as for example, not being tortured.[15] Human rights exist as a basic moral rights that all human beings are entitled to and high priority moral reasons demanding decent treatment for such rights just by virtue of its existence with human beings, and hence, cannot be denied on the basis of race, creed, ethnicity, or gender.[16] The Czech jurist Karel Vasak divides the human rights into three generations of rights. The first generation rights are the basic human rights that protect individuals from slavery, torture, and arbitrary arrest, and ensure freedom from arbitrary intrusions into their privacy.[17] Such rights include the rights set forth as civil and political rights, the most basic of which are the right to life, liberty, and personal security.[18] The second generation rights include the economic, social, and cultural rights to which all human beings are entitled.[19] The third generation provides solidarity rights which include the right to a social and

13. Amnesty International USA, Basics of Human Rights.
14. Mridushi, National Human Rights Commission—Role in Human Rights Protection, Legal Information to Knowledge, Jurisonline (2010).
15 David Little, The Nature and Basis of Human Rights, United States Institute of Peace.
16. *Ibid.*
17. The United Nations Publication, Human Rights Today: A United Nations Priority (2000), p. 3.
18. Call Wellman, Solidarity, the Individual and Human Rights, Human Rights Quarterly, Vol. 22 (2000), p. 639.
19. *Id.*, p. 641.

international order that allows for the exercise of fundamental freedoms.[20]

1.2. Definition under the Protection of Human Rights Act

The Section 2 (d) of the Protection of Human Rights Act, 1993 defines "human rights" as "the right relating to life, liberty, equality and dignity of individuals guaranteed by the Constitution or embodied in the International Covenants and enforceable by courts in India." However, before the 2006 Amendment to the Protection Human Rights Act, Section 2(c) provided that "international covenants" included only "the International Covenant on Civil and Political Rights" and "the International Covenant on Economic, Social and Cultural Rights".[21] This definition was very restrictive one before the 2006 Amendment. This lacuna has been resolved by the 2006 Amendment which now includes all conventions to which India is a party.

In summary, today, the term human rights refer to a wide variety of values and capabilities reflecting the diversity of human circumstances and history and are conceived of as universal, applying to all human beings everywhere, and as fundamental, referring to basic human needs.[22] Thus, the human rights are the most fundamental of all rights enjoyed by human beings and are essential for the up keep of the dignity as human being.

2. WHO ARE "POLICE"?

The term "police" have neither been defined in the Criminal Procedure Code nor in the Police Act 1881 nor in any State Police Acts. The State Police Acts provides only the structure and organisation of police force in the States. Black's Law Dictionary defines "police" as (1) "the governmental department charged with the preservation of public order, the promotion of public safety, and the prevention and detection of crime" and (2) "the officers or members of this department."[23] The police force as an organized body

20. *Id.*, p. 642.
21. Adopted by the General Assembly resolution 2200A (XXI) of the 16th December, 1966.
22. Mridushi, *National Human Rights Commission—Role in Human Rights Protection, Legal Information to Knowledge*, Jurisonline (2010); *available at*: http://jurisonline.in/2010/03/national-human-rights-commission-role-in-human-rights-protection/(Visited on June 3, 2011).
23. The Black's Law Dictionary, (8th Ed. 1999).

came into being in England in the 1820s when Sir Robert Peel established London's first municipal force.[24] Before that, policing had either been done by volunteers or by soldiers in the military service.[25] The U.N. Code of Conduct for Law Enforcement Officials[26] defines "law enforcement official" as including all officials whether they are elected or appointed who exercise police powers, especially the powers of arrest or detention[27] and also include military personnel who exercise police powers whether they are clothed with police uniform or not, and personnel of State security forces whether they are named as police or not.[28] This definition seems to be wider in as much as it takes within its sweep all those who are exercising police powers. As per this definition the criteria to determine whether a personnel is a law enforcement official or not is to look for the nature of the power that is exercised by the personnel. Thus, the term "Police" can, simply, be defined as any person or body of persons created by the authority of the State, obligated and empowered to maintain law and order, prevention and investigation of crimes. In this book, the term 'police' is confined only to local police discharging police functions within the State such as police (law and order), reserve police aiding local police in the maintenance of law and order, crime branch, etc. Military, prison or forest officials are not included in the category of police for this study.

3. TORTURE

Torture is the most aggravated form of violation of human rights committed by the police. It varies from simple beating to causing death in custody. Police in India are generally blamed of employing methods of torture for different reasons.

3.1. Reasons for Torture

The police department is entrusted with the task of investigation, and collection of evidences to prove the crime. The easiest method to collect evidence is to extract information from the

24. David H. Bayley, *Police for the Future* (1994), p. 27.
25. *Id.*, p. 27.
26. The Code of Conduct for Law Enforcement Officials was adopted by the General Assembly by Resolution 34/169 of 17 December 1979.
27. *See* The UN Code of Conduct for Law Enforcement Officials, Commentary (a) to Art. 1.
28. *Id.*, Art. 1, Commentary (b).

accused himself. The police employ different methods of torture to collect evidences from the accused. These methods are popularly called as "third degree methods". But the evidence collected by torturing human beings is not justifiable from the human rights point of view, and often violates norms of human rights protection. Some police officers are rough and rude by nature and find pleasure in torturing his fellow beings who are caught in their net. Pre-set offensive attitudinal behavioral pattern developed through the training or the years of rough experience by the police also results into torture. Some Police officials have the false notion that they can keep their dignity and obtain respect from people only when they horrify people by showing rude behavior or undignified attitudes towards accused or witnesses or even to general public. Corruption, political nexus or personal bias in particular cases under investigation may also cause violation of human rights by torture by the police. Police also employ torture on individuals who stand against the police officer's abuse of power.

3.2. Death in Police Custody

The extreme form of torture in custody is causing death of a person by the police. In spite of the Constitutional guarantee, statutory protections, Supreme Court directives, and institutional supervision by the National Human Rights Commission and the State Human Rights Commissions, a considerable number of deaths occur in police custody all over India. The statement made in the *Lok Sabha* by Shri Ajay Maken, Minister of State for Home Affairs[29] on 01-12-2010 and the Statement of Minster for Home in February 2013 shows in Table 1.1 the data of death in police custody. Year 2002-03 is taken as base year for calculating percentage increase.

The statement of the Minister in the *Lok Sabha* revealed that 126 cases of deaths in Police custody were registered by the National Human Rights Commission in 2012-13 against 128 cases in 2011-12 and 146 cases in 2010-11.[30] It is also significant to note that the majority of complaints received by the National Human Rights

29. Unstarred Question No. 1890 answered by Mr. Ajay Maken, Minister of State for Home Affairs, on 1.12.2009 in the *Lok Sabha*.
30. Statement of Minister of Home in the Lok Sabha in February 2013 and the Report of the Asian Centre for Human Rights Report, Torture in India 2010 (2010), p. 5.

Commission after its establishment in 1993 were against police personnel.[31]

TABLE 1.1

Death in Police Custody during 2002-03 to 2012-13

Year	*No. of Deaths*	*% of Increase*
2002-03	183	—
2003-04	162	-11.49
2004-05	136	-25.68
2005-06	139	-24.04
2006-07	119	-34.97
2007-08	187	2.19
2008-09	127	-30.60
2009-10	124	32.24
2010-11	146	-20.22
2011-12	128	-30.05
2012-13	126	-31.15
Overall	—	-21.65

Source : Statement of Minister for Home in the Lok Sabha and Torture in India, 2011, Asian Centre for Human Rights.

As per the Crime in India Report 2012 of the National Crime Records Bureau, New Delhi, 205 cases of human rights violation by the police were reported throughout the country during 2012.[32] This figure was much higher than the total number of cases of human rights violation by the police reported in 2011 and 2012 which stood at 72 and 37 respectively.[33] However, according to the Crime in India Report 2008 of the National Crime Records Bureau, 253 cases of human rights violation by the police were reported throughout the

31. Joshi, G.P., *Police Accountability in India: policing contaminated by politics*, Commonwealth Human Rights Initiative (2005), available at: http://www.hrsolidarity.net/mainfile.php/2005vol15no05/2448/(Visited on Feb. 22, 2011).
32. Crimes in India Report 2012, National Crime Records Bureau, Ministry of Home Affairs, Government of India, p. 5.
33. First Post India, Human Rights Violation cases against Police Tripled in 2012, October 25, 2013.

country during 2008.[34] The reported violations pertain mainly to 'Illegal Detentions', 'Fake Encounters', 'Extortion', and 'Torture'. Out of the 205 cases reported, 19 policemen were charge-sheeted and none of them were convicted during the year.[34] 5 out of 205 cases of 'Torture', 8 cases of 'Extortion' and one case of 'False implication' were reported in 2012.[35] However the data of the Asian Centre for Human Rights is different. The Asian Centre for Human Rights in its report "Torture in India 2011" claims that in the last ten years (from April 2001 to March 2010), an estimated 14,231 persons were killed in police custody in India.[36] Most of the victims were killed as a result of torture within the first 48 hours of being taken into custody. From the inception of National Human Rights Commission until 2008, in all, 2560 cases of police encounters have been brought to the notice of the National Human Rights Commission.[37] Of them, 1224 cases have been found by the Commission to be fake encounters. It means that, roughly, every 2nd police encounter is a fake one in the country. 555 cases of fake encounters were reported between 2009 and 2013.[38] From the above data, it can easily be identified that there takes place a number of human rights violations by the police throughout the country.

Human rights, today, refer to a wide variety of values and capabilities reflecting the diversity of human circumstances. They are conceived as universal, applying to all human beings everywhere. These rights are inherent in every human being. Hence, State is under obligation to protect the human rights. However, the Police, chief organ of State in protecting life and liberty of people commit numerous violations of human rights. Torture is employed quite often by the police. Chiefly, the police employ torture to extract information from the accused. However, it is not a correct method to torture and extract information from the accused. The police official should not underestimate the rights of their fellow human beings. They should adopt scientific method to investigate the case rather than torturing. Extraction of evidence by torture reveals the inefficiency of the police.

34. R.N. Mangoli and Ganapati, M. Tarase, *A Study of Human Rights Violation by Police in India,* International Journal of Criminology and Sociological Theory, Vol. 3, No. 2, December 2010, p. 401.
35. See *Supra* note 32.
36. Asian Centre for Human Rights, Torture in India, 2011 Report, p. 1.
37. See *Supra* note 32.
38. The Economic Times, 555 Alleged Fake Encounters Reported between 2009-13, July 28, 2013.

2

Protection of Human Rights

Historical Retrospective

The concept of "human rights" is deeply rooted in the historical past, though it came to lime light only after the Second World War. Justice V.R. Krishna Iyer, thus, remarked that "the humanity has a commitment to the history to make the human rights a viable reality".[1] Hence, an examination of the historical foundations of human rights would throw light into the concept and protection of human rights in the historical past.

I. PROTECTION OF HUMAN RIGHTS IN ANCIENT INDIA

Protection of human rights was known in ancient India. The rights of Man were found in *Rig veda*. It provided for the regulation of the behaviour of the ordinary persons as well as the Sovereign. It prescribed two norms, *viz.*, *Dharma* (moral order) and *Danda* (coercive power) which were provided in the administration of criminal justice.[2] The social responsibility of the King was fixed to perform a supreme duty of protecting his subject from disorder and

1. V.R. Krishna Iyer, *Human Rights and Inhuman Wrongs*, (1990), p. 36.
2. G.S. Bajwa, *Human Rights in India: Implementation and Violations* (1995), p. 27.

anarchy, and the King was very much subordinate to the law.[3] Further, there are evidences that in 1367 B.C., *Bahamani*[4] and *Vijayanagar*[5] Kings entered into an agreement for the humane treatment of prisoners of war and the sparing of lives of the enemy's unarmed subjects.[6] References pertaining to human rights can be found even in ancient Indian Scripture. *Atharva veda* provides that "Man is not an individual. He is a social organism. God loves him only who serves other beings: men, cattle and other creature".[7] This shows that the protection of human rights is part and parcel of human life in India and King had the duty to take care of that the human rights are not violated. Torture and inhuman treatment of prisoners were prohibited under Ashoka's administration.[8] Therefore, the traces of protection of human rights were prevalent in ancient India.

2. ANCIENT FOUNDATION OF HUMAN RIGHTS

The traces of the protection of the rights of man can be found in ancient Babylonian laws. When the Babylonian King Hammurabi issued a set of laws to his people in the form of Code in 1780 B.C., popularly known as Code of Hammurabi, it provided rights on a variety of matters, including women's rights, man's rights, children's rights, and slave's rights.[9] What is more significant is that it also provided punishments for the violation of those rights.[10] This kind of precedent and legal rules protected people from arbitrary persecutions in those days. After the conquest of the city of Babylon in 539 B.C. by Cyrus the Great, the first King of ancient Persia, his significant steps for the advancement of humanity were to free the slaves, to establish racial equality, and to provide all people the right to choose their own religion.[11] The well-known "Cyrus Cylinder"[12] is

3. T.S.N. Sastry, *India and human Rights: refection* (2005), p. 31.
4. One of the South Indian Kingdoms.
5. One of the South Indian Kingdoms.
6. Asish Kumar Das and P.K. Mohanty, *Human rights in India*, (2007) p. 4. *See* also Krishna Mohan Mathur, *Police, Law and Internal Security* (1994), p. 158.
7. *Ibid.*
8. Yogesh K. Tyagi, *Third World Response to Human Rights*, I.J.L.I., Vol. 21 (1981).
9. Hammurabi, *Code of Hammurabi* (2009) pp. 27-29.
10. *Id.*, pp. 34, 36.
11. Janey Levy, *Iran and the Shia* (2009) p. 11.
12. The basic decrees and orders of Cyrus the Great were recorded on a baked-clay cylinder in the *Akkadian* language with cuneiform script.

the ancient record which has now been recognized as the world's first Charter of Human Rights.[13] Its provisions are analogous with the first four Articles of the Universal Declaration of Human Rights.[14] Hence, Cyrus Cylinder is considered as sacrosanct even today.

In ancient Greece and Rome, the concept of human rights was deeply rooted in the notion of "Natural Law" and "Natural Rights". The Concept of "Natural Law" and "Natural Rights" generally advocate that some laws and rights are basic and fundamental to human nature and are discoverable by human reason without reference to specific legislative enactments or judicial decisions. It was in ancient Greece where the concept of natural law and natural rights originated to take a greater meaning. Later, human rights became synonymous with natural rights-rights that spring from natural law. According to the Greek tradition of Socrates and Plato, natural law is the law that reflects the natural order of the universe, essentially the will of the God who controls the nature.[15] From this, it inevitably follows that natural rights are inherent in Man when God created him and it is immutable. The Stoics believed that the natural rights are bound by natural law and grounded in a particular conception of natural human reasons and a natural impulse to community.[16] The idea of natural law and natural rights continued in ancient Rome, where the Roman jurist Ulpian believed that natural rights belonged to every person, whether they were a Roman citizen or not.[17] This idea became particularly important in Roman legal theory, which eventually came to recognize a common code regulating the conduct of all people. Christian philosophers such as St. Thomas Aquinas perpetuated this idea, asserting that natural law was common to all people—Christian and non-Christian alike— and hence, natural rights were universal for all.[18]

The concept of natural rights underwent several transformations during the Middle Ages in the Continental Europe and in England before it came to justify firmly the natural rights.[19]

13. It is translated into all six official languages of the United Nations and its provisions parallel the first four Articles of the Universal Declaration of Human Rights.
14. PrakashTalwar, *Human Rights* (2006), p. 19.
15. Jebagnanam Cyrill Kanmony, *Human Rights Violation* (2010), p. 4.
16. Ierodiakonou, *Topics in Stoic Philosophy* (1999), 155.
17. Clemens Neumann Nathan, *The Changing Face of Religion and Human Rights: A Personal Reflection* (2009), p. 26.
18. David Braybrook, *Natural Law Modernized* (2001), p. 32.
19. *Ibid.*

However, a real concept of protection of human rights started emerging from England after the signing of the Great Charter or the *Magna Carta* in 1215.

3. MAGNA CARTA

Magna Carta, popularly known as the Great Charter of Freedoms,[20] was signed by King John of England at Runnymede in 1215. The two most important legal clauses of *Magna Carta* that are relevant for the protection of human rights of man from the arbitrariness of State are:

(i) Clause 40 which affirms that *"to no one will we sell, to no one will we deny or delay, right of justice"*, and
(ii) Clause 39 which promises that *"no freeman shall be taken or imprisoned or dismissed except by lawful judgment of his peers or by the law of the land"*.

These clauses establish the principle of equal access to justice for all citizens without discrimination, and that the King would follow the legal procedure before His officials arrest, detain or punish a person.[21] Thus, the *Magna Carta* explicitly protects, *inter alia,* the above rightsof the people and, hence, considered to be the genesis of protection against arbitrariness of human rights of individuals.

4. THE PETITION OF RIGHTS 1628

When the British Parliament refused to finance the uneconomic policy of King Charles I, the King exacted forced loans and, as an economy measure, quartered troops in subjects' houses. Arbitrary arrest and imprisonment for opposing these policies had produced a violent hostility in the Parliament against King Charles I and George Villiers, the Duke of Buckingham. In 1628, the Parliament sent the

20. *Magna Carta*, also called *Magna CartaLibertatum* (Great Charter of Freedom), is an English legal Charter, originally issued in the year 1215 and was written in Latin.
21. Though the term writ of 'Habeas Corpus does not appear in the body of Magna Carta, yet this provision is an oblique reference to it. The writ of '*Habeas Corpus ad subjiciendum*' is a legal action through which a person can seek relief from the unlawful detention of him or herself, or of another person. The practice and right of Habeas Corpus was settled practice and law at the time of Magna Carta and was, thus, a fundamental part of the unwritten common "law of the land" as was expressly recognized by *Magna Carta.*

petition in the form of statement of civil liberties to King Charles I. Due to the inimical attitude of parliamentarians, the King had no option but to accept the Petition of Rights. The Petition of Rights is considered another mile stone in the history of development of human rights protection. The Petition of Rights initiated by Sir Edward Coke[22] had roots in the earlier Statutes and Charters including the *Magna Carta*. The Petition of Rights asserted that: (1) No subject may be imprisoned without cause shown;[23] (2) No soldiers may be quartered upon the citizenry; and (3) Martial law may not be used during the time of peace. The (1) above is, in fact, the origin of the concept that the arrested person shall be informed of the grounds of arrest. Thus, the Petition of Rights provided protection against arbitrary arrest and detention by affirming that no person may be imprisoned without showing a cause for the arrest and detention.

5. THE VIRGINIA DECLARATION OF RIGHTS 1776

The Virginia Declaration of Rights is a document drafted in 1776 to proclaim the inherent rights of men, including the right to rebel against "inadequate" Government. It influenced a number of later documents, including the U.S. Declaration of Independence (1776), and the French Declaration of the Rights of Man and of the Citizen (1789). Section 1of the Virginia Declaration provides: "all men are by nature equally free and independent, and have certain inherent rights, of which, when they enter into a state of society, they cannot, by any compact, deprive or divest their posterity; namely, the enjoyment of life and liberty, with the means of acquiring and possessing property, and pursuing and obtaining happiness and safety." Thus, the Virginia Declaration affirms that all people have certain inherent rights such as right to life and liberty which they enjoy as human beings.

6. THE AMERICAN DECLARATION OF INDEPENDENCE 1776

The American Declaration of Independence, 1776 is not

22. Sir Edward Coke was a prominent parliamentary adversary of the Crown, Speaker of the House of Commons, Attorney General, Chief Justice of the Court of Common Pleas and Chief Justice of the King's Bench.
23. Petition of Rights 1628, Art. V.

remembered for giving independence to thirteen colonies of America from the British King, George III,[24] but it is remembered for its recognition, acceptance and respect for human dignity and human rights. The Declaration contains the progressive socio-legal-political language of human rights, namely: (a) the natural equality of man and certain inalienable rights of life, liberty and pursuit of human happiness; (b) the purpose of the government is to secure those inalienable rights, and (c) of man the government gets the power, *i.e.* from the consent of the governed people.[25] The Declaration played a major role not only in the history of mankind, but in growth and development of the concept of the basics of human rights. The Declaration also inspired the French to undertake a similar revolt to achieve freedom in the pursuit of human happiness, which ultimately became the perambulatory language of the French Constitution and subsequently, a guiding model for the constitutional democracy globally.

7. DECLARATION OF THE RIGHTS OF MAN AND OF THE CITIZEN 1789

The Declaration of Rights of Man and of the Citizen, popularly known as "the French Declaration", was approved on August 26, 1789 by the National Assembly of France in consequence of the French Revolution.[26] The declaration, *inter alia*, stated that men are born free,[27] equal with the rights to liberty, property and security,[28] guaranteed equality before the law,[29] and granted of freedom from unlawful arrest or imprisonment.[30] The declaration also guaranteed protection against unlawful arrest and detention.

---

24. The intolerable Acts of the British Parliament by which the King restricted, among others, the natural and basic human rights of people in the colonies of America that cumulatively contributed to the American War of Independence during 1775-76.
25. American Declaration of Independence was adopted by the Congress on July 4, 1776.
26. French Revolution is also called the revolution of 1789. French revolution took place between 1787 and 1789 and reached the peak in 1789 overthrowing the monarch in France.
27. The Declaration of Rights of Man and of the Citizen, Art. 1.
28. *Id.*, Art. 2 and 4.
29. *Id.*, Art. 6.
30. The Declaration of Rights of Man and of the Citizen, Art. 7.

8. U.N. CHARTER

The global system established after the Second World War had a number of underlying principles, ideals and motivations including the need for an urgent response to atrocities against human beings that were taking place during the War. It was felt that these violations occur due to the lack of effective mechanisms to restrain such violations of human rights and human dignity at international level. Though the League of Nations came into existence after the First World War, it failed to address issues related with human rights and its violations.[31] The emerged extent of Nazi holocaust and atrocities against human beings during Second World War called for the definition of new crimes against humanity and human rights, and also, machineries to tackle with such crimes effectively globally. While there were deliberations to outline a United Nations Charter[32] at Sans Francisco, there were also proposals to incorporate a Bill of Rights in the U.N. Charter, though not materialized for want of consensus among the Nations due to the factors such as Communist, Capitalist and Islamic religious blocks of countries.[33] Although there were no consensuses on the incorporation of Bill of Rights into the U.N. Charter, yet the Charter contained a number of important references to the promotion and protection of Human Rights, which are worth considering here.

The preamble of the U.N. Charter expresses the avowed faith of the Member Nations in furtherance of human rights and human dignity, and unequivocally declares: *We the people of the United Nations determined...to reaffirm faith in fundamental human rights, in the dignity and worth of the human person, in the equal rights of men*

---

31. The Covenant of the League of Nations 1924 did not contain any provision effectively dealing with human rights.
32. The Charter of the United Nations was signed on 26 June 1945, in San Francisco, at the conclusion of the United Nations Conference on International Organization, and came into force on 24 October 1945.
33. Susan Waltz, *Who Wrote the Universal Declaration of Human Rights?*, e Journal, USA (2008), p. 219; It was Ricardo Alfaro, former president of Panama, who made the proposal of inclusion of a bill of human rights into the United Nations Charter. As Panama's representative to the United Nations' inaugural meeting in 1945, Alfaro brought with him a draft bill of international rights and formally proposed that it be incorporated into the U.N. Charter. *See* <www. Heinonline.org> accessed on 28-03-2010.

and women and of nations large and small, and...to promote social progress and better standards of life in larger freedom.[34]

The preamble, thus, discerns the U.N.'s clearer vision and mission of its intention to uphold and protect human rights, human dignity and worth of the human personality.

More substantive provisions dealing with human rights under the U.N. Charter include Article 1(3) which expresses some of the broad purpose of the U.N., including promotion and encouragement of human rights and fundamental freedoms without distinction as to race, sex, language or religion, Article 62(2) enables Economic and Social Council to make recommendations to promote human rights based on studies or reports to be presented to the General Assembly, Member States, and specialized agencies, and Article 68 empowers Economic and Social Council to set up Commissions in the economic and social fields to promote human rights, and such other commissions as may be required for the performance of its functions.

In fact, there were no agreements among the States for the incorporation of Bill of Rights into the U.N. Charter. However, the representatives of the States could reach an agreement to establish a Commission on Human Rights in order to provide protection of human rights at international level.[35] Thus, Article 68 was incorporated empowering the Economic and Social Council to establish Commissions for promoting human rights, and consequently, the Commission on Human Rights was established in 1946 to achieve the ends envisaged under the U.N. Charter related to human rights protection.[36]

It is submitted that the spirit envisioned in the preamble of the Charter in relation to upholding the human rights does not appear in the same vigor in the substantive provisions particularly in relation to the protection of civil and political rights. This could seem to be due to the flock of the communist countries led by Russia opposing to incorporate such civil and political rights in the body of the U.N. Charter, perhaps because of their obsession with respect to

34. U.N. Charter 1945, *Preamble.*
35. *Ibid.*
36. The functions of the Economic and Social Council included making 'recommendations for the purpose of promoting respect for, and observance of, human rights and fundamental freedoms for all'; *See*Mashood A. Baderin, *International Human Rights and Islamic Law* (2nd Ed., 2005), p. 19.

'individual' human rights and human dignity.[37] However, one of the main objectives of the establishment of the U.N. was to avoid recurrence of atrocities against human beings by upholding human dignity and human rights. After the inception of the U.N., the first main task was to initiate for a globally acceptable human rights document and this led to the birth of Universal Declaration of Human Rights.

9. UNIVERSAL DECLARATION OF HUMAN RIGHTS

Immediately after the coming into force of the U.N. Charter, the Economic and Social Council by the authority vested with it under Article 68 of the U.N. Charter established the Commission on Human Rights[38] in 1946 for the preparation of the International Bill of Rights.[39] The Commission on Human Rights headed by Eleanor Roosevelt[40] consisted of eighteen members.[41] The Human Rights Commission along with the Canadian human rights expert Dr. John Peters Humphrey, the principal drafter, prepared a draft declaration and submitted it to the General Assembly through the Economic and

37. Johannes Morsink, *the Universal Declaration of Human Rights: Origins, Drafting and Intent* (1999), p. 17.
38. The United Nations Commission on Human Rights has been replaced by the United Nations Human Rights Council as per United Nations General Assembly resolution A/RES/60/251 adopted on 15 March 2006. Thus, the Commission on Human Rights ceased to exist with effect from 16 June 2006.
39. Amnesty International U.S.A., *A Short History of Human Rights*, Human Rights Educators' Network, (1997) p. 19.
40. The widow of former U.S. President Franklin Delano Roosevelt served as chair of the U.N. Human Rights Commission from 1946 to 1951.
41. Eleanor Roosevelt, *The Promise of Human Rights*, in Allida M. Black (Ed.), What I Hope to Leave Behind: The Essential Essays of Eleanor Roosevelt (1995), p. 473; In the Economic and Social Council it was recommended by majority vote that since the Economic and Social Council consisted of representatives of governments, the members of the Commission on Human Rights should be elected by the Economic and Social Council from a list of nominees submitted by governments to serve in an individual capacity. The only dissenting opinion was from Union of Soviet Socialist Republic which insisted that they should be appointed as government representatives. Finally, the Council decided to leave it to the governments concerned to decide whether to appoint government officials or independent persons.

Social Council.[42] The Declaration was adopted by General Assembly on 10th December 1948 at *Palais de Chaillot*, Paris and it became the historic Universal Declaration of Human Rights.[43] The Guinness Book of Records describes the Universal Declaration of Human Rights as the "Most Translated Document" in the world.[44] The Universal Declaration of Human Rights is the first ever international document produced with the term "human rights" in the title. It is, now, considered to be the soul of human rights and human dignity.

The Universal Declaration of Human Rights, however, is not an overnight product, but is a cumulative historic acts of many treaties that had come into existence long before 1948 such as the *Magna Carta*, the Petition of Rights, Virginia Declaration of Rights, American declaration of Independence, French Declaration, etc. The historic words "all human beings are born free and equal in dignity and rights" that appear in Article 1 of Universal Declaration of Human Rights itself was taken from French Declaration which states that all "men are born, and always continue, free and equal in respect of their rights."[45] This shows that the drafters of the Universal Declaration of Human Rights relied on the previous historic humanistic declarations and covenants in drafting the Declaration.

---

42. The Commission on Human Rights headed by Eleanor Roosevelt assumed its first task of drafting of Bill of Rights in three parts, *viz.*, (i) a Declaration, (ii) a Convention containing legal rights and obligations, and (iii) measures of implementation—a system of international supervision and control. Canadian human rights expert Dr. John Peters Humphrey was called upon by the U.N. Secretary to work on the project and he later became the Declaration's principal drafter.
43. Adopted by the U.N. General Assembly, Resolution 217 (III), with forty eight votes in favor, none against and eight abstentions.
44. At present, there are 379 different translations of Universal Declaration of Human Rights.
45. *Supra n. 27.*

3

Protection of Human Rights and the Police

International Legal Framework

The protection of human rights has been a central issue for the U.N. ever since it had come into existence, as the main idea for the very inception of the U.N. was to restrain the recurrence of World War and of the vindictive acts of annihilation and carnage committed by Nazi Germany against human beings during the Second World War. Hence, the protection mechanisms afforded under the U.N. scheme assumes significance. An examination of the protection of human rights from its violation by the police under the international legal framework requires a systematic analysis of the provisions of the Universal Declaration of Human Rights (UDHR), the International Covenant on Civil and Political Rights (ICCPR), The Declaration Against Torture, the Convention Against Torture, etc. These fundamental documents on the protection of human rights are critically analysed with a view to identify the international system, the scheme of protection, the enforceability and the effectiveness of the protection mechanism. Further, India's obligation towards such international instruments and the extent of commitment for the compliance of such instruments by the Indian Government is also evaluated here. This evaluation is made with a view to identify how far the international legal framework is practical under the Indian context in relation to the protection of human rights from being violated by the police. A Systematic analysis of international instruments is made below.

I. PROTECTION OF HUMAN RIGHTS FROM THE POLICE

The preamble of the Universal Declaration of Human Rights recognizes the inherent dignity and inalienable rights of all human beings which are the foundation of freedom, justice and peace. It also sets out the past experience of consequence of the disregard and contempt for human rights as the result of the barbarous acts which outraged the conscience of mankind during the Second World War.[1] The inclusion of "past experience" in the preamble seems to be a reminder that such events shall not be repeated, and regards and honours are essential for the enjoyment of human rights.

After the adoption of the Universal Declaration of Human Rights, the Human Rights Commission embarked on the preparation of a Convention that has the authority of enforcing the human rights contained therein against its violations.[2] This lead the General Assembly for the adoption of a separate document, the International Covenant on Civil and Political Rights, with a mechanism for enforceability of the rights contained therein.

Even after the adoption of the International Covenant on Civil and Political Rights, one of the major concerns of the U.N. was how to combat with the torture, and other cruel and inhuman practices that takes place within domestic jurisdictions of National States. Though the Universal Declaration of Human Rights and International Covenant on Civil and Political Rights contained specific provisions regarding the right against torture or other cruel, inhuman and degrading treatment or punishment, they did not provide a precise definition as to what amounts to torture and how to embark upon with such crimes effectively.[3] In order to have effective protection against torture, it was felt that there must be a

1. *See* Preamble of the Universal Declaration of Human Rights.
2. Rhona K.M. Smith, *Textbook on International Human Rights* (2007), p. 47; United States of America and some other Western Countries were of the view that there should be two separate documents whereas the Union of Soviet Socialist Republics and the so called Communist bloc were of opinion that social, economic and cultural rights are of the same footing as that of civil and political rights.
3. Universal Declaration of Human Rights, Art.5; International Covenant on Civil and Political Rights, Art. 7.

separate instrument at least in the form of a declaration. This led to the birth of the Declaration against torture or other cruel, inhuman and degrading treatment or punishment in 1975,[4] and subsequently to the Convention against Torture or other Cruel, Inhuman and Degrading Treatment or Punishment in 1987 (Convention Against Torture).[5] Thus, the three documents, *viz.*, the Universal Declaration of Human Rights, International Covenant on Civil and Political Rights and Convention Against Torture, are the major international instruments which safeguards persons against arbitrary arrest, illegal detention, torture, etc.

1.1. Protection from Arbitrary Arrest or Detention

Arrest and detention by the police in the pre-trial stage procedure is controversial in almost every country as it inevitably affects the deprivation of liberty of a person. The police abuse the powers of arrest and detention against innocent persons, even at the instance of State machineries. Considering this situation, the Universal Declaration of Human Rights prohibits arbitrary arrests. Though the Universal Declaration of Human Rights does not define the term "arrest", Article 9 declares that "no one shall be subjected to arbitrary arrest, detention or exile". Thus, the Universal Declaration of Human Rights provides a right against arbitrary arrest or illegal detention to any individual person.

Regarding arrest and detention, the International Covenant on Civil and Political other law enforcement agencies. Article 9 provides:

(i) No person shall be subjected to arbitrary arrest or detention;

(ii) No person shall be deprived of his liberty except on such grounds and in accordance with such procedure as are established by law.

(iii) Arrested person shall be informed of the reasons for his arrest at the time of arrest, and also, the charges levelled against him.[6]

4. G.A. Res. 3452 (XXX), passed on December 9, 1975; Hereinafter referred as "Declaration Against Torture".
5. G.A. Res. 39/46, adopted by the General Assembly on December 10, 1984 and entered into force on June 26, 1987; Hereinafter referred as "Convention against Torture".
6. International Covenant on Civil and Political Rights, Art.10, Sub-Art. (1).

(iv) Any person arrested or detained shall be brought before a judicial official and shall be entitled to trial within a reasonable time or to be released.[7]

(v) Anyone who is deprived of his liberty by arrest or detention shall be entitled to take proceedings before a court.

(vi) The court may decide, without delay, on the lawfulness of his detention, and order his release, if the detention is not lawful.[8]

(vii) Arrested or detained persons shall be treated with humanity and with respect for the inherent dignity of the human person.[9]

(viii) Accused persons shall be segregated from convicted persons and shall be subject to separate treatment appropriate to their status as un-convicted persons."[10]

The International Covenant on Civil and Political Rights is more elaborate than the Universal Declaration of Human Rights with regard to protection from arbitrary arrest and detention. A careful observation of the International Covenant on Civil and Political Rights shows that it has been drafted very carefully for the protection of persons from arbitrary arrest and detention by providing excessive provisions. The Covenant also takes care of juvenile accused persons as well, and it provides that they shall be separated from adults and brought as speedily as possible for adjudication.[11] If the police arrests any person unlawfully or detain illegally, the victim shall have an enforceable right to compensation.[12] Thus, the International Covenant on Civil and Political Rights sets out broader protection from arbitrary arrest and detention of persons than that of the Universal Declaration of Human Rights.

1.2. Protection from Arbitrary Interrogation

Interrogation is the stage at which police questions persons acquainted with the facts of the crime, elicit facts and gather information for detecting the commission of crime and to prove the guilt of the accused before the court. The police officials may extract

7. *Id.*, Sub-Art. (3).
8. *Id.*, Sub-Art. (4).
9. *Id.*, Art. 10, Sub-Art. (1).
10. *Id.*, Sub-Art. (2)(a).
11. *Id.*, Sub-Art. (2)(b).
12. *Id.*, Art. 9, Sub-Art. (5).

information of crime from the suspect by employing torture or other cruel and inhuman methods. Considering such circumstances the Universal Declaration of Human Rights included the presumption of innocence of the accused person as a matter of right. Article 11 of the Declaration reads: *every one charged with a penal offence has the right to be presumed innocent until proved guilty according to the law in a public trial at which he has had all the guarantees necessary for his defence.*[13]

Similarly, the International Covenant on Civil and Political Rights also provides equivalent protection to a person accused of crime. Article 14 (2) provides that "Everyone charged with a criminal offence shall have the right to be presumed innocent until proved guilty according to law." Further, Article 14 (3) (g) prohibits a person to be compelled to testify against himself or to confess guilt. Article 14 (3) (g), in other words, sets out the accused person's right to remain silent in a crime.[14] In this context, it is worth noting the comment of the U.N. High Commissioner for Human Rights that the presumption of innocence has an important implication for the investigative process because all persons under interrogation are to be treated as innocent person, whether they have been arrested or detained, or whether they remain at liberty during the investigation.[15] Thus, the above guarantees under the Universal Declaration Human Rights and International Covenant on Civil and Political Rights are considered as significant control over the arbitrary interrogative process.

1.3. Protection from Torture

The Universal Declaration of Human Rights and the International Covenant on Civil and Political Rights categorically prohibits torture or other cruel, inhuman or degrading treatment or

13. The same presumption is provided under International Covenant on Civil and Political Rights, Article 14, paragraph 2; the European Convention on Human Rights, Article 6, paragraph 2; the American Convention on Human Rights, Article 8, paragraph 2; the African Charter on Human and People's Rights, Article 7 paragraph 1(b); *See also* High Commissioner for Human Rights, *Human Rights and Law Enforcement:Manual on Human Rights Training for the Police*, Professional Training Series No. 5, Center for Human Rights, Geneva, p. 59.
14. See *infra* Ch. 4 for details regarding 'right to remain silent'.
15. High Commissioner for Human Rights, *Human Rights and Law Enforcement : Manual on Human Rights Training for the Police*, Professional Training Series No. 5, Center for Human rights, Geneva p. 59.

punishment. Article 5 of the Universal Declaration of Human Rights provides that "no one shall be subjected to torture or to cruel, inhuman or degrading treatment or punishment". The same wordings are used in Article 7 of the International Covenant on Civil and Political Rights also. Article 7 thus provides "no one shall be subjected to torture or to cruel, inhuman or degrading treatment or punishment". Thus, both the documents unconditionally prohibit torture.

However, neither the Universal Declaration of Human Rights nor the International Covenant on Civil and Political Rights provide a definition for "torture". The Human Rights Committee constituted under International Covenant on Civil and Political Rights also does not define the term 'torture'. The Human Rights Committee in its General Comments[16] No. 20 which deals with torture expresses that the aim of the provisions of Article 7 of the International Covenant on Civil and Political Rights is to protect both the dignity and the physical and mental integrity of the individual and hence, it is the duty of the State party to afford to every person the protection through legislative and other measures as may be necessary against the acts of torture or cruel, inhuman treatment or punishment.[17]

The Convention Against Torture in Article 1 defines torture as:

(i) any act by which severe pain or suffering, whether physical or mental, is intentionally inflicted on a person for such purposes as obtaining from that person or a third person information or a confession; or

(ii) punishing by a public official or other person acting in an official capacity on a person for an act she/he or a third person has committed or is suspected of having committed of; or

(iii) intimidating or coercing him/her or a third person in connection with such commission or suspicious commission of the act; or

(iv) when such pain or suffering is inflicted by or at the instigation of or with the consent or acquiescence of a

16. Human Rights Committee constituted under the International Covenant on Civiland Political Rights publishes its interpretation of the content of human rights provisions in Covenant in the form of General Comments and it is considered to be an authoritative interpretation.

17. Human Rights Committee, General Comments, No. 20, Para 2.

public official of or other person acting in an official capacity.

The definition suffers from clarity as to what the term 'severe pain' means or implies. It seems that the intent was to give room for determining 'severity of pain' depending on the facts and circumstances of each case. The Working Group on Convention Against Torture interpreted the word "severe" to mean "prolonged coercive and abusive conduct which, in itself, is not severe but becomes so over a period of time".[18] Nevertheless, the definition seems providing wider import on the matters connected with torture inflicted by public officials. The definition takes within its sweep not only the actual torture inflicted by the public official but also, the torture inflicted at the instigation of or with the consent or acquiescence of a public official or any person acting in an official capacity. Thus, it is not only the police official's direct acts but their indirect acts are also included within the purview of the definition.

The Convention Against Torture not only totally prohibits torture but makes it further clear that no exceptional circumstances what so ever can be invoked to justify torture and refoulement.[19] It also provides that the States must make torture a domestic and extraditable crime.[20] It directs the States to arrest suspects who committed torture against any individual[21] and to investigate suspicious circumstances of torture.[22] This provision is included cautiously as, many a time, the torture is committed by officials of the State, and the Government may favour the suspects rather than victims of torture. The Convention Against Torture also provides that interrogation methods, practices and rules must be kept under review by the State parties. It also directs State Parties to make arrangements for the custody and treatment of persons subjected to arrest, detention or imprisonment for preventing cases of torture.[23] In sum, it is submitted that mostly the provisions are in the form of

18. V. Venkatesan, "Redefining Torture", *The Frontline*, January 29, 2011.
19. Sending or extraditing to a State where torture is likely to occur.
20. *See* Convention against Torture and other Cruel, Inhuman or degrading treatment or punishment (herein after referred as "Convention Against Torture"), Art. 5 and 8.
21. *Id.*, Art. 6.
22. *Id.*, Art. 12.
23. *See* Convention against Torture and other Cruel, Inhuman or degrading treatment or punishment (herein after referred as "Convention Against Torture"), Art. 11.

directions, suggestions and recommendations towards State parties. Obviously the torture, generally, takes place within the domestic jurisdiction, and State parties have a significant role in curbing the barbarous acts of torture.

1.4. Protection from Unlawful Search and Seizure

Right to privacy is quite often invaded by the police during the course of investigation and it is inevitable during investigation. However, there must be transparency during such process and must be within the legal framework. The Universal Declaration of Human Rights protects the Right to privacy, honour and reputation. Article 12 of the Declaration reads: No one shall be subjected to arbitrary interference with his privacy, family, home or correspondence, nor to attacks upon his honour and reputation. Everyone has the right to the protection of the law against such interference or attacks. Thus, the Universal Declaration of Human Rights provides protection against arbitrary search and/or seizure.

The International Covenant on Civil and Political Rights also provides a similar protection from arbitrary searches or seizures. Article 17 provides "no one shall be subjected to arbitrary or unlawful interference with his privacy, family, home or correspondence, nor to unlawful attacks on his honour and reputation". The Human Rights Committee under the International Covenant on Civil and Political Rights in General Comment No. 16 has interpreted that no interference with privacy can take place "except in cases envisaged by the law....which itself must comply with the provisions, aims and objectives of the covenant" and "reasonable in particular circumstances"[24] Thus, the Universal Declaration of Human Rights and the International Covenant on Civil and Political Rights protects people from unlawful searches or seizures by the police and other law enforcement agencies.

It is submitted that the Universal Declaration of Human Rights and the International Covenant on Civil and Political Rights provides protection from torture, illegal arrest or detention, unlawful search and seizure, and arbitrary interrogation of any person. Though many of the protections are the same in both the documents, the International Covenant on Civil and Political Rights provides elaborate safeguards in the event of arrest and detention. It also

24. Mashood A. Baderin, *International Human Rights and Islamic Law* (2003), p. 114.

provides for an enforceable right to compensation in the case of arbitrary arrest or detention. However, the crucial matter is how these rights are enforced in redressing the grievances of individuals.

2. ENFORCEABILITY OF THE RIGHTS UNDER THE UDHR

The Declaration is the first comprehensive instrument on International Human Rights which encompasses civil, political, economic, social and cultural rights in one document. However, as its name implies "the declaration", it was neither intended to impose legal obligations on States, nor does it establish any supervisory organ to enforce the rights. The major problem with Universal Declaration of Human Rights is that it does not possess a legally binding enforceability and as such cannot create any obligation on member States to enforce it. In other words, there are no mechanisms set forth for the implementation of the rights in the Universal Declaration of Human Rights in the event of any violation. The Declaration is simply a statement of intent and principles, nothing more; because it is merely a declaration, it is neither a Treaty nor a Covenant. As a result, some critics have questioned its significance.[25] Its defenders emphasize that since its unanimous adoption by the U.N. General Assembly without a dissenting vote reflects the international moral commitment of Member States to translate it through the mechanism of the language of respective State's Constitutional law.[26] In this way, the Universal Declaration of Human Rights imposes a moral obligation on the Member States not to ignore its effectuation. The operative part of the Preamble of Universal Declaration of Human Rights reads as follows:

> The General Assembly proclaims this Universal Declaration of Human Rights as a common standard of achievement for all peoples and all nations, to the end that every individual and every organ of society, keeping this Declaration constantly in mind, shall strive by teaching and education to promote respect for these rights and freedoms and by progressive measures, national and international, to secure their universal and effective

25. Richard A. Falk, *Human Rights Horizons: The Pursuit of Justice in a Globalizing World* (2000), p. 38.
26. With abstentions from the Byelorussia, Czechoslovakia, Poland, Saudi Arabia, South Africa, the Soviet Union, the Ukrainian, and Yugoslavia.

recognition and observance, both among the peoples of member states themselves and among the peoples of territories under their jurisdiction.

The Universal Declaration of Human Rights has attained significant recognition by the U.N. Member States by *jus receptum*.[27] It is true, the Universal Declaration of Human Rights has come out as an instrument of declaration and as such it did not contain any provision for its enforceability. But now, after 64 years, it is considered as a sacrosanct document setting the basic standards of human rights and human dignity, and over the years, it received greater recognition from all the countries and has, now, acquired the status of customary international law.[28] However, as customary international law theUniversal Declaration of Human Rights works on international sphere of human rights violations only, such as massacre, genocide, etc. It does not have the direct impact on the sporadic police atrocities unless the State is perpetrating the mass killings or tortures within the State. Nevertheless, it provides protection for people from illegal arrest, unlawful detention, torture, etc. Although the Universal Declaration of Human Rights did not contain enforceability mechanism, it, indeed, has contributed a lot to the birth, growth and development of global and national human rights instruments. Owing to the major lacuna of enforceability that the Universal Declaration of Human Rights suffered, there was felt that there, ought to be a document which provides some kind of enforcement mechanism, at least in the areas of civil and political rights. In fact, this led the U.N. to adopt two separate documents, *namely*,. the International Covenant on Civil and Political Rights and

27. Foreign laws are additions to a particular nation's domestic laws and in that respect are called *jus receptum*, *See*Black's Law Dictionary, (1990), p. 647.
28. Richard A. Falk, *Human Rights Horizons: The Pursuit of Justice in a Globalizing World* (2000), p.38. As long as international human rights treaties do not enjoy universal ratification, the treaties will be an incomplete means of attaining the goal of universal respect for human rights. Customary International Law fills the gap, as it fills those states not party to the treaty-provided that the relevant norm has become a rule of customary international law. A norm attains that status if it is a 'general practice accepted as law'. This means that the existence of such a rule has to be proven by demonstrating two elements, viz; state practice and *opinion juris; See* FransViljoen, *International Human Rights Law in Africa* (2007), p. 27.

the International Covenant on Economic, Social and Cultural Rights (ICESCR).

3. ENFORCEMENT MECHANISMS UNDER THE ICCPR

During the drafting process of the International Covenant on Civil and Political Rights, one of the controversial points was the mechanism of international remedy, control and supervision.[29] There were deliberations on the issues relating to inclusion of enforcement mechanisms in the International Covenant on Civil and Political Rights and, finally, a concurrence had been reached for the establishment of a Human Rights Committee.[30] Hence, International Covenant on Civil and Political Rights under Article 28 provides for the establishment of the Human Rights Committee which, thus, becomes the principal organ of implementation and enforcement of the International Covenant on Civil and Political Rights. The Human Rights Committee consists of eighteen Members from different State parties and the Members must have renowned competence in the field of Human Rights.[31] Article 28 (3) provides that the Members of the Committee shall serve in their personal capacity which implies that though they were nominated by the State parties, once they are elected Members of the Human Rights Committee, they are not Government (State) representatives. This is intended to ensure their independence, autonomous and impartiality in discharging the duties entrusted to them under the Covenant.

The enforcement mechanism under International Covenant on Civil and Political Rights can be categorized as follows:

1. State reporting
2. Communications/Complaints
   (i) Inter-State (State-to State) communications/ complaints
   (ii) Individual communications/complaints

3.1. State Reporting

As per the emergence of trans-national human rights jurisprudence, the States have the obligation to submit reports to

29. *Supra* n. 24, at p. 114.
30. Michael, J. Dennis, *Human Rights in 2002: The Annual Session of the UN Commission on Human Rights and the Economic and Social Council*, American Journal of International Law, Vol. 97, 2 (2003) p. 377.
31. International Covenant on Civil and Political Rights, Art. 28.

treaty monitoring bodies at prescribed intervals.[32] The ICCPR adopted the State reporting procedure as the principal means of implementation of the rights enshrined in it. Article 40 of the ICCPR imposes on the States the duty to submit initial and periodic reports. The report shall indicate:

(a) the measures the Member States have adopted to give effect to the rights recognized in the ICCPR,
(b) the progress made in the enjoyment of those rights, and
(c) the factors and difficulties, if any, affecting the implementation of the ICCPR.

These reports are to be transmitted to the Secretary General of the United Nations for consideration. The reporting procedure, in general, is criticized as not effective in as much as that reports prepared by State (Government) officials would not naturally give the real human rights situation in their countries. France Viljoen says "Governments are likely to paint a relatively positive picture of the situation for which they bear responsibility. Some State Reports even blatantly distort facts."[33] Besides, some States fail to submit reports properly and/or timely.[34] It is submitted that although these reporting systems by themselves do not constitute an effective measure of control, yet they open an opportunity for critical examination, for drawing attention to gaps or inaccuracies in the information provided, and for comparing official statements with other sources of information on the human rights situations in a State.

3.2. Communications

One of the mechanisms provided under the ICCPR for redressing the grievance of violation of human rights is communication procedure. This is a procedure by which one may submit communication of human rights violation to the Human Rights Committee with a view to obtain remedy from the appropriate organ alleging that a State party has not discharged its obligation in protecting the rights recognized in the ICCPR. In fact, the ICCPR doesn't use the word 'complaint' as the drafters seem to

32. Communication 869/1999, *Piandiong and Others* v. *The Philipines*, UN Doc a/56/40, Vol. II, 19 October, 2000; See*also* Frans Viljoen, *International Human Rights Law in Africa* (2007) p.37.
33. Frans Viljoen, *International Human Rights Law in Africa* (2007), p.38.
34. *Id.*, p. 38.

have deliberately avoided the use of the term at the instance of State parties. The State parties might have been sensitized by the fear of being accused for the violation of human rights before an international organ as the 'complaint' requires some kind of remedy. The ICCPR rather uses 'communications' as a moderating term. It recognizes two types of communications, namely:

(i) Inter-state Communications; and
(ii) Individual communications.

3.2.1. Inter-State Communications

The Inter-state communication is a process by which one State party directs a communication (complaint) to the Human Rights Committee against another State party in relation to the violation of human rights under ICCPR. The Committee examines communications only if (1) the State alleged to have committed violation of human rights has made a declaration recognizing the competence of the Human Rights Committee, and (2) the complaining State, the State that has submitted the communications, has made similar declaration.[35] When such communications are made, the first step is to enable the States concerned to resolve the matter themselves.[36] If the two States fail to solve the matter within six months, the matter may be referred to the Human Rights Committee by a notice.[37] The Committee, however, cannot pass its opinions on violations. It is to make its good offices available with a view to a friendly settlement, and if it is not possible, the Committee is required to submit a report to the U.N. setting out the facts, the steps taken by the Committee in resolving the matter, etc.[38] This mechanism is operative when there are mass violations of human rights at the instance of the State, and had gained international attention. This procedure is not applicable in the case of violation of human rights by the police in individual cases. Further, the solution by this process is conciliation, negotiation and settlement. The Human Rights Committee lacks authority for enforcement even if it finds violations of human rights. It is interesting to note that no interstate communication has been submitted under the U.N. human

35. *See* International Covenant on Civil and Political Rights, Art. 41 (1).
36. *Id.*, Art. 41, Sub-Art. (1) (a) and (b).
37. *See* International Covenant on Civil and Political Rights, Art. 41, Sub-Art. (1) (b)
38. *Id.*, Art. 41.

Rights treaties.[39] Thus, it is submitted that the mechanism is not an effective method in the case of violation of human rights by the police.

3.2.2. Individual Communication

Individual communication is a method by which individuals may submit communications directly to the Human Rights Committee with a view to obtain remedy, claiming that a State party has violated the rights recognized by the International Covenant on Civil and Political Rights. During the drafting process there were arguments for and against inclusion of a mechanism for enforcement of violation of human rights by individuals from the State Party.[40] However, it was difficult to reach a consensus when International Covenant on Civil and Political Rights was adopted in 1966 and hence, the provision for individual complaint mechanism was not included in the International Covenant on Civil and Political Rights. There were criticisms due to the lack of enforceability mechanism for individuals whose rights have been violated within a domestic jurisdiction of a State party. It has been commented that the real test of the effectiveness of an international system for the protection of human rights lies on the fact that whether it permits an individual, who believes that his rights have been violated, to seek a remedy from an international institution."[41] Thus, the First Optional Protocol to International Covenant on Civil and Political Rights was adopted separately allowing individuals to make communications directly to Human Rights Committee.[42] Since it is a separate instrument, separate ratification by the State parties is essential for its operation in domestic jurisdictions.

There are stipulations for the admissibility of the Individual complaints. One of the stipulations is the rule of exhaustion which dictates that all domestic remedies must have been explored by the

39. *Supra* n. 33, at p. 35.
40. Michael, J. Dennis and David, P. Stewart, Justiciability of Economic, Social, and Cultural Rights: Should There be an International Complaints Mechanism to Adjudicate the Rights to Food, Water, Housing, and Health?, 98 A.J.I.L. (2004), p. 462.
41. Steven, R. Ratner and Jason, S Abrams, *Accountability for Human Rights Atrocities In International Law: Beyond the Nuremberg Legacy*, (2nd Ed., 2001), p. 46.
42. First Optional Protocol was adopted separately but in the same year in 1976 when the International Covenant on Civil and Political Rights entered in to force.

individual before approaching the Human Rights Committee.[43] Another stipulation is that communications which are anonymous, abusive or incompatible with the provisions of the ICCPR are not admissible.[44] Article 1 of the First Optional Protocol to ICCPR stipulates that a State party to the ICCPR becomes a Party to the Protocol automatically recognizes the competence of the Human Rights Committee to receive and consider communications from individuals who claim to be victims of violation by that State party. The Human Rights Committee must communicate regarding the individual complaint to the State Party concerned, and the State party is required to submit written explanations or statements within six months clarifying the matter and the remedy, if any, that may have been taken by that State.[45] Article 5(4) provides that the Committee shall forward its views to the State Party concerned and to the individual.

International Covenant on Civil and Political Rights, no doubt, enlists a large number of human rights, particularly in relation to torture, custodial violence, arbitrary interrogation, arrest, detention, search and seizure, etc. However, it has only a weak mechanism for the enforceability of the rights in the event of violation of such rights. Even in the case of individual communication mechanism, after the conclusion of the complaint by the Human Rights Committee, it gives its opinion to the individual and the State concerned. The State may or may not comply with such opinion for lack of authority for enforcement by Human Rights Committee. State Reporting and Inter-State Communications have no much relevance as a mechanism for the enforceability of the rights. Hence, it is submitted that although the International Covenant on Civil and Political Rights guarantees a number of important rights for the protection of persons from police abuses, yet it suffers for want of effective enforceable mechanism.

4. ENFORCEMENT UNDER THE CONVENTION AGAINST TORTURE

Part II of the Convention Against Torture provides for the establishment of a Committee Against Torture comprising a body of

43. First Optional Protocol to International Covenant on Civil and Political Rights, Art. 2.
44. *Id.*, Art. 3.
45. *Id.*, Art. 4(2).

ten independent experts that monitors implementation of the Convention Against Torture.[46] Committee Against Torture is empowered to receive and consider communications for and on behalf of individuals who claim to be victims of torture by the State machineries, and the action or remedy given by the State is not satisfactory for the victim.[47] However, Committee Against Torture does not enjoy any authority to enforce its findings against any State. It is in the form of recommendation, suggestion or opinion only. To that extent, it is submitted that the enforcement mechanism under Convention Against Torture also suffers the same lacuna as the ICCPR mechanism of enforcement. It has also been made obligatory for the States parties to submit periodic reports to the Committee Against Torture indicating measures taken to fulfill their obligations under the Convention Against Torture.[48] The Committee Against Torture after examination of such reports, addresses its concerns and recommendations to the State party in the form of "concluding observations".[49] It may also conduct inquiries into the information of torture within a State Party jurisdiction and also consider inter-state complaints.[50] This way the U.N. makes the State parties responsible for torturous acts within their jurisdiction, and to deal with them separately as the acts of torture touch the very basis instinct of humanity and human dignity.

4.1. Monitoring under Optional Protocol to the Convention

In order to provide protection from torture and to monitor the commission of torture within the State jurisdictions, an Optional Protocol to the Convention Against Torture was adopted by the U.N. and it came into force in June 2006. Under the Optional Protocol to the Convention Against Torture, State Parties are obliged to establish an independent National Preventive Mechanisms for the prevention of torture at the domestic level and such National Preventive Mechanisms should have the mandate to inspect places of detention.[51] The Optional Protocol to the Convention Against

46. *Id.*, Art. 17.
47. *Id.*, Art. 22.
48. First Optional Protocol to International Covenant on Civil and Political Rights, Art. 19.
49. *Id.*, Art. 19.
50. *Id.*, Art. 20 (2).
51. *Id.*, Art. 17.

Torture also creates the Sub-committee on Prevention of Torture at the international level.[52] Sub-committee on Prevention of Torture makes recommendations to the State Parties regarding the working of National Preventive Mechanisms, and assists the State Parties for the establishment of effective preventive mechanisms within their domestic jurisdictions.[53] Sub-committee on Prevention of Torture has an unrestricted access to all places of detention and to all relevant information to visit places where persons deprived of their liberties are kept within the jurisdiction of States parties.[54] Thus, the Sub-committee on Prevention of Torture can visit any places of detention including police stations, prisons, pre-trial detention centres, juvenile homes and any other places where people deprived of their liberty are kept within a State.

However, the Sub-committee on Prevention of Torture has purely preventive mandate only. The mechanism provided for the Sub-committee on Prevention of Torture is only recommendations to the State Parties regarding the occurrence of torture, visits to places of detention and public reporting. The question that arises here is: Will those mechanisms be sufficient, or can be considered as efficient, to control the torture perpetrated by the State police? The answer, surely, is negative. It happens, frequently, that State Governments try to hush up the tortures in police custody. In such a situation, it is submitted that there should be a super-national body which could investigate into and bring about action against the culprits.

5. INDIA AND THE U.N. DECLARATIONS AND COVENANTS

Indian Constitution does not explicitly provide for the incorporation of international convention and treaties into the domestic legal system. However, Article 51(c) of the Constitution provides that "the State shall endeavour to foster respect for international law and treaty obligations in the dealings of organized people with another." This shows that India follows the

52. *Id.*, Part II.
53. First Optional Protocol to International Covenant on Civil and Political Rights, Art. 11 (1) (a).
54. *Id.*, Art. 11 (1) (a) and 12.

dualist pattern[55] pertaining to the implementation of the international declarations, treaties and covenants in the municipal legal system.[56] Hence, it is necessary for Indian Parliament to enact legislation incorporating the rights under such International covenants, treaties, etc., for its implementation in the Indian domestic jurisdiction. The Constitution of India exclusively empowers the Parliament to implement international treaties and conventions in India. Article 253 of the Constitution provides: "Parliament has power to make any law for the whole or any part of the territory of India for implementing any treaty, agreement or convention with any other country or countries or any decision made at any international conference, association or other body." Further, 'entry 14' of the Union List of the Seventh Schedule empowers Parliament to legislate in relation to "entering into treaties and agreement and implementing of treaties and agreement with foreign countries and implementing of treaties, agreements and conventions with foreign countries". Thus, in India, it is the Parliament which alone has the authority to implement the international treaties, covenants, conventions, etc.

5.1. The Supreme Court of India on the U.N. Covenants

The Supreme Court has reiterated the dualist approach by holding that an international treaty which India has signed does not become part of the *corpus juris* of India until Parliament makes implementing legislation incorporating those treaty provisions.[57] However, Supreme Court later has observed that non-conflicting treaties and covenants can be implemented into the domestic jurisdiction so long as they are not inconsistent with the sovereignty and integrity of India, and the supremacy of the legislative authority of the Parliament. The Supreme Court observed:

> The comity of Nations requires that Rules of International Law may be accommodated in the Municipal Law even without express legislative sanction

55. 'Dualist pattern' is one system whereby the international treaties, covenants etc. becomes part of the Municipal law by the act of Legislature in the State, on the other hand 'Monolist pattern' is one whereby the international treaties, covenants etc. becomes part of the Municipal law without any act of the Legislature in the State.
56. *State of Madras* v. *G.G. Menon*, A.I.R. 1954 S.C. 517.
57. *Jolly George* v. *Bank of Cochin*, A.I.R. 1980 S.C. 470; *See also* Reenu Paul, *National Human Rights Commission-An evaluation* (2003),Unpublished Master's Thesis, London School of Economics, London, p. 24.

> provided they do not run into conflict with Acts of Parliament. But when they do run into such conflict, the sovereignty and the integrity of the Republic and the supremacy of the constituted legislatures in making the laws may not be subjected to external rules except to the extent legitimately accepted by the constituted legislatures themselves. The doctrine of incorporation recognises the position that the rules of international law are incorporated into national law and considered to be part of the national law, unless they are in conflict with an Act of Parliament. Comity of nations or no, Municipal Law must prevail in case of conflict.[58]

Thus, the Supreme Court is demonstrating a harmonious construction between International treaties, declarations and conventions on the one hand and Indian laws on the other as long as there are no inconsistencies between them. It is only when there are inconsistencies that the domestic law shall prevail and requires an Act of Parliament for the implementation of such international treaties, covenants, declarations, etc.

However, in the case of implementation of rights guaranteed under the Universal Declaration of Human Rights and International Covenant on Civil and Political Rights, the Supreme Court has observed that those rights can be relied upon by courts and are enforceable in India even though implementing legislation has not been made by Parliament, since they are in tune with fundamental rights guaranteed by the Constitution of India. While dealing with handcuffing in *Prem Shankar Shukla* v. *Delhi Administration*[59] the Supreme Court reminded the relevance of the core principles of Article 5 of Universal Declaration of Human Rights and Article 10 of the International Covenant on Civil and Political Rights which speaks for humane treatment in arresting and detaining a person.[60] In *People's Union of Civil Liberties* v. *Union of India*[61] taking the experience of Common Law system the Supreme Court differentiated the status of International Covenant on Civil and Political Rights and other multilateral treaties by observing that in the case of International Covenant on Civil and Political Rights, even

58. *Gramophone Co. of India Ltd. v. Birendra Bahadur Pandey*, A.I.R. 1984 S.C. 667, p. 671.
59. 1980 S.C.R. (3) 855.
60. 1980 S.C.R. (3) 855, p. 864.
61. A.I.R. 1997 S.C. 1203.

though India has entered a specific reservation[62] while ratifying the Convention in 1979 on the application of Article 9 (5) and even in the absence of an Act of Parliament, rights guaranteed under International Covenant on Civil and Political Rights can operate into our legal system. Supreme Court observed:

> Apart from influencing the construction of a statute or subordinate legislation, an international convention may play a part in the development by the courts of the common law...it would suffice to State that the provisions of the covenant, which elucidate and go to effectuate the fundamental rights guaranteed by our Constitution, can certainly be relied upon by courts as facets of those fundamental rights and hence, enforceable as such. So far as multi-lateral treaties are concerned, the law is, of course, different -and definite.[63]

Thus, it is now settled matter that the Universal Declaration of Human Rights and the International Covenant on Civil and Political Rights are part of the Indian legal system, where as in the cases of multilateral treaties, it must get recognition from Indian Parliament.

In *Neelabati Behera* v. *State of Orissa,*[64] Supreme Court made a reference of Article 9 (5) of International Covenant on Civil and Political Rights which provides for an enforceable right to compensation for victims of unlawful arrest or detention, and observed "we may also refer to Article 9(5) of the International Covenant on Civil and Political Rights, 1966 which indicates that an enforceable right to compensation is not alien to the concept of enforcement of a guaranteed right *in India*."[65] Initially, the Supreme Court was also hesitant to provide compensation under Article 21 of the Constitution of India to victims of unlawful arrest, illegal detention or torture when it dealt with in *Khatri* v. *State of Bihar*[66]

62. India entered a specific reservation regarding Article 9(5) of the International Covenant on Civil and Political Rights at the time of ratification in 1979 stating that the Indian legal system did not recognise a right to compensation for victims of unlawful arrest or detention.
63. *Supra* n. 61, at 1206; *See also Visakha* v. *State of Rajasthan,* A.I.R. 1997 S.C. 3011.
64. 1993 S.C.R. (2) 581.
65. 1993 S.C.R. (2), p. 604; emphasis added.
66. A.I.R. 1981 S.C. 928; *See also* R. Venkata Rao, *Custodial Violence and Judicial Response*, Vol. 7, Journal of the National Human Rights Commission of India (2008), p. 88.

and *Veena Sethi* v. *State of Bihar.*[67] However, due to the continuous and unabated violation of human rights by the police and the State machineries, the Supreme Court, taking the spirit from Article 9 of International Covenant on Civil and Political Rights, evolved the compensation jurisprudence inherent in Article 21. *Rudal Shah* v. *State of Bihar*[68] was the first case whereby the Supreme Court ordered to pay compensation of Rupees thirty five thousand for illegally detaining a person without legal justification for fourteen years. The Supreme Court thereby opened a new horizon in the Indian human rights jurisprudence by making the State accountable for the violation of human rights by State machineries. Thereafter, in a number of cases, the Supreme Court has awarded monetary compensation for the violation of human rights for illegal detention, unlawful arrest, torture, etc.[69] Thus, though the Constitution does not expressly provide an enforceable right to compensation, taking the spirit from Article 9 (5) of International Covenant on Civil and Political Rights, now it has become a rule under Article 21 to provide compensation for the violation of human rights.

However, it is unfortunate to note that India has not ratified the First Optional Protocol to International Covenant on Civil and Political Rights which provide for individual communication mechanism for the individuals to directly approach the Human Rights Committee in connection with the violation of rights enshrined under the International Covenant on Civil and Political Rights where the complainant is not satisfied by the State action/

67. A.I.R. 1983 S.C. 339.
68. A.I.R. 1983 S.C. 1086.
69. *Sebastian M. Hongray* v. *Union of India*, A.I.R. 1984 S.C. 1026, where Supreme Court awarded Rupees One lakh each as exemplary cost for the wives of two person who were not been produced even after the writ issued by the Supreme Court; *Bheem Singh* v. *State of Jammu & Kashmir*, A.I.R. 1986 S.C. 494, where SC awarded Rupees fifty thousand for illegal arrest and detention; *Supreme Court legal Aid Committee* v. *State of Bihar*, (1990) 3 S.C.C. 482, where Supreme Court awarded Rupees twenty thousand for not providing medical treatment while in custody; *Peoples' Union for Democratic Rights* v. *State of Bihar*, A.I.R. 1987 S.C. 355, where the Supreme Court awarded Rupees twenty thousand each to the dependents of deceased and rupees five thousand to the injured in a brutal police firing; *Saheli* v. *Commissioner of Police*, (1990) 1 S.C.C. 422, where Supreme Court awarded compensation of Rupees twenty five thousand to the mother of the deceased who was tortured to death by police; *NeelabatiBehera* v. *State of Orissa*, (1993) 2 S.C.C. 746, where Supreme Court awarded Rupees one lakh fifty thousand to the mother for the torture to death of her son.

remedy.[70] It is submitted that Government of India is not very serious about the enormous human rights violations that takes place in many quarters including violations by the police. Moreover, the system of individual complaint/communication mechanism is much more intrusive than the State Reporting mechanism into the affairs of domestic jurisdiction. Hence, it may be embarrassing for India among international community by the unequivocal findings of the Human Rights Committee. It is further submitted that considering the significance of human rights and values, India should have ratified the First Optional Protocol to International Covenant on Civil and Political Rights giving opportunities for individual citizens to redress their grievances, if the action/remedy of the State Institutions is not satisfying to the individuals.

5.2. Adoption of Convention Against Torture in India

Regarding the Convention Against Torture, India was reluctant to adopt and ratify it ever since Convention Against Torture was passed by the U.N. General Assembly in 1984. After the establishment of National Human Rights Commission in 1993, one of the major tasks of the Commission was to persuade the Government of India to ratify the Convention Against Torture. The National Human Rights Commission, right from the beginning of its functioning, made a series of communications with the Prime Minister, Home Minister and External Affairs Minister for the adoption and ratification of the Convention Against Torture.[71] As a result of the relentless effort of the National Human Rights Commission, India has adopted the Convention Against Torture in 1997. Unfortunately, India has not ratified the Convention Against Torture so far. However, there is a move for the ratification of Convention Against Torture by India. In pursuance of this, the Central Government introduced the Bill against Torture in the *Lok Sabha* on April 26, 2010. The *Lok Sabha* passed it on May 6 and submitted to *Rajya Sabha. Rajya Sabha* adopted a motion on August 31,2010 referring the Bill to a Select Committee, comprising 13 of its members. The Select Committee has presented its report to *Rajya*

---

70. International Covenant on Civil and Political Rights has two optional Protocols; while the First Optional Protocol deals with allowing individual communication, the Second Optional Protocol is meant for abolition of death penalty in State Jurisdictions.
71. National Human Rights Commission, Annual Report, 1994-95 and 1995-96.

Sabha on December 6, 2010.[72] The Bill provides for punishment of torture inflicted by public servant or torture committed with the consent or acquiescence of a public servant. According to the Bill, "torture" means and includes any act that cause "grievous hurt "or "mental or physical danger to life, limb or health". There were criticisms about such a restrictive definition and, hence, the Select Committee consulted the Pre-Legislative Briefing Service, a group of legal experts, and obtained the advice from them. They suggested that the words "grievous hurt" and "danger to life, limb or health" be replaced with "severe pain or suffering" in line with Convention Against Torture.[73] The Select Committee has accepted its suggestion and recommended that the definition of torture be suitably enlarged so as not to exclude acts generally known to be committed on persons in custody which cause severe physical and mental injury, pain, trauma, agony, and so on.[74] The Bill provides for six months limitation period for making a complaint against torture. The Select Committee suggested that it should be extended for a period of two years from the date of alleged torture as this would give sufficient time to enable the victim of torture to initiate proceedings against those responsible for torture.[75] Another significant point to be noted is that the Clause 6 of the Bill provides for prior sanction from the Government in order to prosecute the public servant. It is submitted that this can be a bottleneck for the victim of torture in obtaining the prior sanction from the Government for taking action against erring Police officials. Police officials are already powerful and could influence the Government or even manipulate the case. However, it is provided in the Bill that if such sanction is not granted within three months, it would be deemed to have been granted. The Select Committee has recommended that sanction in blatant cases of torture should be the norm and where sanction to prosecute is declined, the said decision should be supported by reasons, and the decision must also be appealable.[76] It is hoped that India would ratify the Convention Against Torture sooner thereby upholding the rights against torture or cruel, inhuman treatment or punishment of the helpless individuals in the custody of police and other law enforcement agencies.

72. *Supra* n. 18.
73. Article 1 of Convention Against Torture provides definition of "torture".
74. *Supra* n. 18.
75. Clause 5 of Convention Against Torture Bill.
76. *Supra* n. 18.

6. CONCLUSION

The Universal Declaration of Human Rights provides protection from torture, arbitrary arrest and illegal detention. However, the Universal Declaration of Human Rights was made as a declaration having neither the force of International law nor any mechanism to enforce the violations of the human rights. The so called 'Cold War' that existed between the two prominent veto powers of the Security Council of the U.N., namely, U.S.A. and U.S.S.R., it was made further difficult to take concrete measures in protecting the human rights at the international level and the status of the Universal Declaration of Human Rights remained more or less the same as a declaration. However, over the years, due to the popular recognition and acceptance, the Universal Declaration of Human Rights has attained the position of international customary law which implies that where ever and whenever there is violation of the rights contained in the Universal Declaration of Human Rights, U.N. can follow such procedure as are used in the case of violations of international law and can even use such force as is provided in the matters of violations of any other international law to compel a State party to comply with it. However, the U.N. Charter confirms by virtue of Article 2(7) by reassuring its Member States that it lacked the authority to intervene in matters that were "essentially within the domestic jurisdiction" of States. This prohibition was subject only to qualification relating to the overriding responsibility of the U.N. acting under Chapter VII of the Charter to maintain international peace and security.[77] Thus, it is submitted that though there is no specific mechanism provided in the Universal Declaration of Human Rights, U.N. Security Council can invoke its power to maintain international peace and security and compel any State to comply with the protection of the human rights under Universal Declaration of Human Rights and can also use such force as are necessary depending on the gravity of the offence committed by the State. However, such measures taken by the U.N. are only in cases of gross human rights violations such as genocide or mass killings at the instances of State. Individual human rights violations are not dealt with under such mechanism too. Hence, individual Police atrocities, which are outrageous in India, cannot be dealt with under this mechanism.

77. *Supra* n. 25.

International Covenant on Civil and Political Rights gained significant credence over the years and it provides a number of protections in the cases of torture, arbitrary arrest, detention, search or seizure. However, the enforcement mechanisms provided such as State Reporting, Inter-State communication and Individual communication are not very effective in the event of violation of human rights by the police. Indian Supreme Court and High Courts which deal with enforceability of fundamental rights, tries to incorporate the spirit of Universal Declaration of Human Rights and International Covenant on Civil and Political Rights in its decisions, particularly in matters connected with unlawful arrest, illegal detention, torture, inhuman treatment, etc., committed by the police and other law enforcement agencies. In many cases, irrespective of the fact that Indian Constitution does not expressly provide for enforceable right to compensation for the violation of fundamental rights, the Supreme Court relying on Article 9 (5) of International Covenant on Civil and Political Rights and by interpreting Article 21 of Constitution of India, has awarded monetary compensation for the violation of human rights of individuals. Thus, the Supreme Court, rely on Universal Declaration of Human Rights and International Covenant on Civil and Political Rights provisions for giving vivid interpretation to fundamental rights guaranteed by the Constitution of India.

However, it is unfortunate to note that India, the largest democratic country in the world, is not a signatory for the First Optional Protocol to ICCPR[78] which provides with a mechanism for individual communication. This way, the Government of India limits the opportunity of individuals to complain to a super-national body to redress their grievances related with violations of human rights. It may be positively seen as that the Courts in India, particularly the apex Court, are known for impartiality, autonomy and upholding the fundamental human rights by way of judicial activism, judicial interpretation and judicial review, and has widened the scope of impartial remedy to the aggrieved person whose rights are violated by State machinery. However, this cannot be a valid justification for not accepting the First Optional Protocol to ICCPR thereby restricting the right to effective remedy of an individual.

---

78. Christ of Heyna and FransViljoen, *The Impact of the United Nations Human Rights Treaties on the Domestic Level*, Kluwer Law International(2002), p. 323.

The message of U.N. is serious in relation to physical harm by torture or other cruel, degrading, inhuman treatment or punishment that such acts of barbarous nature must be curbed. The Convention Against Torture, in addition to defining what amounts to torture, also provide by the Optional Protocol to the Convention Against Torture an enforcement mechanism of individual communication. It is submitted that the enforcement mechanism cannot be considered as very effective in as much as there is no mechanism for punishing the wrongdoer. However, the Convention Against Torture categorically provides that any excuse for the torture employed by the State machineries will not be considered as a defense. India has adopted the Convention Against Torture in 1997, but has not ratified it so far. It is welcome that India is now taking positive steps to ratify Convention Against Torture.

Thus, in summary, it can be submitted that the Universal Declaration of Human Rights, International Covenant on Civil and Political Rights and Convention Against Torture provide effective international legal framework for the protection of individuals from being subjected to torture, arbitrary arrest, unlawful interrogation, illegal detention or unlawful search and seizure by the police. The International Covenant on Civil and Political Rights and the Convention Against Torture provides mechanism for enforceability of such rights. However, the mechanism suffers for its binding effect on the State Parties. This can be considered as a major defect of the International Covenant on Civil and Political Rights and the Convention Against Torture.

4

Constitutional Protection of Human Rights and the Police

The Universal Declaration of Human Rights provides for a number of minimum guarantees that must be complied with under all circumstances during arrest, detention and interrogation of a person. The Constitution of India came into operation just two years after the adoption of Universal Declaration of Human Rights by the U.N. General Assembly in 1948. This had a great bearing on Part III of the Constitution of India which elaborates fundamental rights and freedoms. The Framers of the Indian Constitution had a crucial concern about the protection of accused, arrested and detained persons from the false inculpation, arbitrary arrest, unlawful detention and vexatious prosecution in criminal cases of the underprivileged, illiterate and ignorant masses by the State colonial police. This had, *inter alia*, influenced the framers to include provisions such as Article 20 dealing with protection from double jeopardy and self-incrimination; Article 21 dealing with right to life and personal liberty; and Article 22 dealing with rights of arrested and accused persons in criminal cases. Basically, these provisions are the constitutional safeguards available to any person as accused or arrested or detained by the police. Indeed, the areas of accusation, arrest and detention are the most controversial areas in connection with the police action on the one hand and the rights of arrested or detained persons on the other.

I. FUNDAMENTAL RIGHTS UNDER THE INDIAN CONSTITUTION

The Constituent Assembly which first met on December 9, 1946 deliberated to uphold the civil liberties of the people as a significant matter. The demand for a declaration arose from four factors : (i) lack of civil liberties in India during the British rule, (ii) deplorable socio-economic conditions particularly affecting the untouchables and women, (iii) existence of different religious, linguistic and ethnic groups encouraged and exploited by the British, and (iv) exploitation of the tenants by the landlords.[1] Considering these aspects the founding fathers of the Constitution gave a significant place for fundamental rights in the Constitution as an embodiment of the aspirations of the people for the Constitutional recognition of civil rights. The Fundamental Rights in the Indian Constitution have been grouped under seven heads as follows:

(i) Right to Equality comprising Arts. 14 to 18.
(ii) Right to Freedom comprising Arts. 19 to 22 which guarantee several freedoms such as freedom of speech and expression, right to life and personal liberty, freedom from arbitrary arrest and detention, etc.
(iii) Right against Exploitation consists of Arts. 23 and 24.
(iv) Right to Freedom of Religion is guaranteed by Arts. 25 to 28.
(v) Cultural and Educational Rights are guaranteed by Arts. 29 and 30.
(vi) Right to Property is now very much diluted and is secured to some extent by Arts. 31-A, 31-B, 31-C.
(vii) Right to Constitutional Remedies is secured by Arts. 32 to 35.

It is guaranteed under the Indian Constitution that these rights are available irrespective of race, place of birth, religion, caste, creed or gender. The Fundamental Rights are enforceable through court of law and hence, the concept of Fundamental Rights protects

1. Sunil Deshta and Kiran Deshta, *Philosophy of Right to life: A Movement from Rigidity to Flexibility*, Civil and Military Law Journal, Vol. 31, No. 3 (1995), p. 102.

individuals against excesses of the State and constitutes by and large, a limitation on the goverment.[2] In *A.K. Gopalan* v. *The State of Madras*,[3] Sastri J., said:

> It is true to say that, in a sense, the people delegated to the legislative, executive and judicial organs of the State their respective powers while reserving powers to themselves the fundamental rights which they made paramount by providing that the State shall not make any law which takes away or abridges the rights conferred by that Part.[4]

Thus, the Indian Constitution provides the fundamental rights of the people and safeguards from the arbitrary encroachment or abuse or abridgment of those rights by the State machineries.

2. FUNDAMENTAL RIGHTS ARE HUMAN RIGHTS

The Part III of the Constitution of India sets out a number of civil, political and cultural rights as fundamental rights. The rights provided in this part are made enforceable through court of law. Fundamental rights differ from ordinary rights in the sense that the former are inviolable. No law, ordinance, custom, usage, or administrative order can abridge or take them away. Any law which is violative of any of the fundamental rights, is void to the extent of its inconsistency. In *A.D.M. Jabalpur* v. *Shiv Kant Shukla*[5] Justice Beg observed "the object of making certain general aspects of rights fundamental is to guarantee them against illegal invasion of these rights by executive, legislative, or judicial organ of the State".[6] Earlier, Chief Justice Subba Rao in *Golak Nath* v. *State of Punjab*[7] had also observed that the fundamental rights are the modern name for what have been traditionally known as natural rights.[8]

The Supreme Court recognised these fundamental rights as "Natural Rights" or "Human Rights" while dealing with different

2. M.P. Jain, *Indian Constitutional Law* (2006), p. 6.
3. A.I.R. 1950 S.C. 27.
4. H. M. Seervai, *Constitutional Law of India: A Critical Commentary*, Vol. 1 (1991), p. 369.
5. A.I.R. 1976 S.C. 1207.
6. *Id.*, p. 1293.
7. A.I.R. 1967 S.C. 1643.
8. *Id.*, p. 1656.

cases. The Chief Justice Patanjali Shastri in *State of West Bengal* v. *Subodh Gopal Bose*[9] referred fundamental rights as those great and basic rights, which are recognized and guaranteed as the natural rights inherent in the status of a citizen of a free country.[10] Referring to the fundamental rights contained in Part III of the constitution, Sikri, the then Chief Justice of India in *Keshavananda Bharathi* v. *State of Kerala*,[11] observed, "I am unable to hold these provisions to show that rights are not natural or inalienable rights. As a matter of fact India was a party to the Universal Declaration of Human Rights... and that Declaration describes some fundamental rights as inalienable."[12] Thus, Fundamental rights under the Indian Constitution are nothing but a synonym of human rights and natural rights.

3. PROCEDURAL SAFEGUARDS AGAINST ARREST AND DETENTION

When Indian Constitution came into force in 1950, it provided three clear provisions in relation to rights of liberties and security of person, *namely,* Articles 20, 21 and 22. These provisions stand as pillars against the Governmental arbitrariness affecting life, liberty and security of persons. Article 20 of the Constitution of India provides three safeguards in respect of conviction of offences to a person accused of crimes, namely, *Ex post facto law* (clause 1), Double jeopardy (clause 2) and Prohibition against self-incrimination (clause 3). Since Clauses 1 and 2 of Article 20 are matters connected with conviction by a court, these provisions are not the subjects of discussion here. Since the Clause (3) of Article 20 deals with prohibition against self-incrimination, it affects a person ever since he is arrested because of the guarantee of 'right to remain silent' of an accused in a criminal case. Article 21 of the Constitution of India guarantees right to life and personal liberty, and Article 22 provides safeguards against arbitrary arrest and detention. Supreme Court of India played a vital role in elaborating the protection and safeguards implied in these rights. A brief account of the protection afforded by these provisions is made below.

9. A.I.R.1954 S.C. 92.
10. *Id.*, p. 96.
11. A.I.R. 1973 S.C. 1461.
12. *Id.*, p. 1536.

3.1. Right to Remain Silent

India follows adversarial system[13] of trial proceedings in which accused person is presumed to be innocent until the guilt is proved before the court beyond reasonable doubt. As the burden, in this system, lies on the prosecution and in turn, on the police to prove the case before the court to such an extent to remove the shadow of doubt, the police who follow colonial system of unscientific investigation import torture, threat, assault, harassment, *etc.* as methods to elicit confessions, facts and information from accused and witnesses of crimes. The right to self-incrimination is a privilege given to a person accused of crime as he is the one who has to fight against the mighty State and its machineries, and this right ensures that encroachment shall not be made against a person to extract facts from him if he is not willing to provide it.[14] By this privilege the accused can remain silent and, more importantly, it is an obligation of the police official interrogating the accused to inform him that he has a right to remain silent.

---

13. Criminal trials involve the risk of life and liberty of persons who may not have committed the crime and by the two known trial systems viz., Adversarial system (also known as accusatorial or the Common Law system) and the Inquisitorial system (also known as Continental or the Civil Law system) culprits are punished and innocents are set free. In adversarial system each side, acting in its self-interest, is expected to present facts and interpretations of the law in a way most favorable to its interests before an impartial tribunal and the Inquisitorial system, is characterized by a continuing investigation conducted initially by police and then more extensively by an impartial examining magistrate. The adversarial approach presumes that the accused is innocent (*See* Lord Sankey LC in *Woolmington v. D.P.P.*, (1935) AC462), and the burden of proving guilt rests with the prosecution. The Inquisitorial system assumes that an accurate verdict is most likely to arise from an exhaustive investigation and the examining magistrate serves also as investigator who directs the fact-gathering process by questioning witnesses, interrogating the suspect, and collecting other evidence. Due to the different operating styles of these two systems, there are differences in the role of the accused in the trial proceedings *viz.*, in adversarial proceedings the accused has great role in defending his case and in inquisitorial trials he has only limited role in defending his case.
14. John H Langbien, *The Privilege and Common Law Criminal Procedure: The Sixteenth to the Eighteenth Centuries* in Helmholz R.H. et al, *The Privilege against Self-Incrimination: Its Origins and Development* (1997), pp. 83-84.

The Fifth Amendment to the U.S. Constitution, 1791 protects persons from compelling to be witness against himself.[15] In *Miranda* v. *Arizona*,[16] a landmark case decided by the United States Supreme Court, the Court ruled that when a suspect is taken into police custody, prior to any interrogation by the police, the suspect must be informed of the rights available to him as per the Constitution of the U.S. secured through the 1st, 5th and 6th Amendments to the U.S. Constitution. These rights are often called as "Miranda Rights" or "Miranda Warning". The Miranda rights as laid down by the U.S. Supreme Court include:

(i) The accused have a right to remain silent,

(ii) It is the duty of the interrogating police official to inform the accused that

(a) as accused, he is not bound to say anything, but if he says anything it will be used against him during the trial before a court of law,

(b) as accused, he has a right to consult his lawyer, and

(c) If he is not able to afford a lawyer, one will be appointed for him.

In the U.S., failure to advise the suspect of these rights by the police results in the rejection of the statements made by the suspect as evidence and cannot be used at the trial. Under the U.S. Constitution the protection is available even to witnesses, whereas, in India, the protection is available only to the accused. From this, it can be seen that the position in India is much narrower than the U.S. Constitution.

However, the right to remain silent is not expressly provided under the Indian Constitution. Article 20 (3) protects persons from self-incrimination thereby avoiding to be witness against himself in a crime. By judicial interpretation of the Supreme Court, the right to remain silent is implied under Article 20 (3) which reads: "No person accused of any offence shall be compelled to be a witness against himself". Since the term used in Article 20 (3) "to be a witness", the

15. The Fifth Amendment to US Constitution provides "No person shall be........compelled in any criminal case to be a witness against himself, nor be deprived of life, liberty, or property, without due process of law; nor shall private property be taken for public use, without just compensation."

16. 384 U.S. 436 (1966).

question before the Supreme Court was that whether Article 20 (3) was applicable only during a trial before a court of law or was it available even before a trial when a person was arrested by the police as an accused. The Supreme Court dealt with the question in *M.P. Sharma* v. *Satish Chandra*[17] by holding that a person, whose name was mentioned as an accused in the First Information Report and an investigation was conducted by the police on the basis of that Report, could claim the protection as 'accused of an offence' under Article 20(3). The Supreme Court explained the meaning of the phrase "to be a witness" in this case as not only covering oral evidence but documentary and testimonial evidences also.

3.1.1. "To be a Witness" and "Furnishing Evidence"

The wider definition given by the Supreme Court for the phrase "to be a witness" created a lot of practical difficulties and confusions in applying provisions such as Section 27 of the Indian Evidence Act. However, the Supreme Court in *State of Bombay* v. *Kathi Kalu*[18] held that the interpretation given in *M.P. Sharma's* case for the phrase "to be a witness" was too broad and 'to be a witness" is not equivalent to "furnishing evidence".[19] The Court observed:

> "To be a witness" may be equivalent to "furnishing evidence" in the sense of making oral or written statements, but not in the larger sense of the expression so as to include giving of thumb impression or impression of palm or foot or fingers or specimen writing or exposing a part of the body by an accused person for the purpose of identification. "Furnishing evidence" in the latter sense could not have been within the contemplation of the Constitution-makers for the simple reason that-though they may have intended to protect an accused person from the hazards of self-incrimination, in the light of the English Law on the subject-they could not have intended to put obstacles in the way of efficient and effective investigation into crime and of bringing criminals to justice.[20]

The Court, thus, held that self-incrimination can only mean

17. 1954 S.C.R. 1077; (hereinafter referred as "M.P. Sharma's case").
18. 1962 S.C.R. (3) 10.
19. *Id.*, p. 29.
20. *Ibid.*

conveying information based upon personal knowledge of the person giving information and cannot include merely the mechanical process of producing documents in court which may throw light on any point in controversy, but which does not contain any statement of the accused based on his personal knowledge.[21] Thus, when a person gives his finger impression or specimen writing or signature, though, it may amount to furnishing evidence in the large sense, the same is not included within the expression "to be a witness". In these cases, he is not giving any personal testimony. What is forbidden under Article 20(3) is to compel a person to say something from his personal knowledge relating to the charge against him. However, the Court reiterated that "to be a witness" is not merely in respect of testimonial compulsion in the court room but may well extend to compelled testimony previously obtained from him. The Supreme Court observed:

> As was pointed out in Sharma's Case (1) the phrase used in Art. 20(3) is "to be a witness" and not "to appear as a witness". That by itself justifies the conclusion "that the protection afforded to an accused in so far as it is related to the phrase "to be a witness" is not merely in respect of testimonial compulsion in the court room but may well extend to compelled testimony previously obtained from him". If the protection was intended to be confined to being a witness in Court then really it would have been an idle protection. It would be completely defeated by compelling a person to give all the evidence outside court and then, having what he was so compelled to do, proved in court through other witnesses. An interpretation which so completely defeats the constitutional guarantee cannot, of course, be correct. The contention that the protection afforded by Art. 20(3) is limited to the stage of trial must therefore be rejected.[22]

Thus, the Supreme Court limited the scope and application of the phrase "to be a witness" in this case to the personal knowledge of the accused and not to extent to the documentary evidence or material objects or body parts. Nevertheless, the Court confirmed that so far as personal knowledge of the accused is concerned, the

21. *Id.*, p. 30.
22. *Id.*, p. 40.

protection extends not only to testimonial compulsion in the court proceedings but may well extend to the testimony obtained previously by compelling the accused even before a court proceeding. It means that the protection is available even during police investigation and interrogation. However, it must be noted that the Article 20(3) is operative as long as there is compulsion and if there is no compulsion and the person is providing information voluntarily, the information can be considered as valid.

3.1.2. Physical and Psychological Coercion

In *Nandini Satpathy* v. *P.L. Dani*[23] the Supreme Court has reiterated the protection afforded under Article 20(3) by unequivocally declaring that the protection afforded under Article 20 (3) is not only for the trial stage but it should start from the time the investigation is initiated by the police against a person accused of an offence. The Court has widened the scope of Article 20(3) by holding that the compulsion does not only mean physical torture or coercion but it also extends to psychic torture, atmospheric pressure, environmental coercion, tiring interrogatives, prolixity, overbearing and intimidatory methods and the like.[24] In this case, charges of corruption were levelled against the former Chief Minister of Orissa, Smt. Nandini Satpathi. In the course of investigation the appellant, a former Chief Minister of Orissa and one time Minister at the National level was directed to appear at the Vigilance Police Station, Cuttack, in September, 1977 for being examined in connection with the case registered against her by the Deputy Superintendent of Police, Vigilance, Cuttack under Section 5(2) read with Section 5(1) (d) and (e) of the Prevention of Corruption Act and under Sections 161, 165, 120-B and 109 of the Indian Penal Code. She was asked to answer written questions in connection with the corruption allegations, but she refused to answer the questions invoking the protection afforded under Article 20(3). As a result, a complaint was filed by the Deputy Superintendent of Police, Vigilance (Directorate of Vigilance) Cuttack, against the appellant, under Section 179 of the Indian Penal Code. Justice V.R. Krishna Iyer held in summary the following:

(a) Section 161 of the Criminal Procedure Code enables the police to examine the accused during investigation;

23. 1978 S.C.R. (3) 608; (hereinafter referred as "Nandini Satpathy's case").
24. *Id.*, p. 644.

(b) The prohibitive sweep of Art. 20(3) extends not only to the proceedings before a court but it extend to the stage of police interrogation also;

(c) The ban on self-accusation and the right to silence, while an investigation or trial is under way, goes beyond that case and protects the accused in regard to other offences pending or imminent, which may deter him from voluntary disclosure of incriminatory matter.

(d) A police officer is clearly a person in authority. Insistence on answering is a form of pressure especially in the atmosphere of the police station unless certain safe guards erasing duress are adhered to.

(e) "Self-incrimination or tendency to expose oneself to a criminal charge is less than 'relevant' and more than 'confessional'. Irrelevance is impermissible; while relevance is licit if the relevant questions are loaded with guilty inference in the event of an answer being supplied the tendency to incriminate springs into existence."

(f) The accused person cannot be forced to answer questions, merely because the answers thereto are not implicative when viewed in isolation and confined to that particular case. He is entitled to keep his mouth shut if the answer sought has a reasonable prospect of exposing him to guilt in some other accusation actual or imminent, even though the investigation under way is not with reference to that.[25]

From the above, the right to remain silent is implicit in Article 20(3) and the protection is available not only during the trial before a court but also during interrogation by the police. This right also extends not only with regard to the offence pending but with other offences pending or imminent which may deter him from voluntary disclosure of incriminatory matter.

3.1.3. Narco-analysis and Right to Remain Silent

Narco-analysis,[26] Poligraph,[27] and Brain Mapping[28] are the tests

25. *Id.*, pp. 609-10.
26. Narco-analysis is conducted by intravenously injecting Sodium Pentothal into the bloodstream; it is an ultrafast-acting anesthetic and acts within 45 seconds of being injected. There are 4 stages to this process of anesthesia. The aim in narco analysis is to keep the person in the second stage where an appropriate dose of the chemical is maintained where the person is partly conscious and loses his inbuilt inhibitions which could

that have been used by the police against the accused in certain crimes as an alternative to the third degree methods with a view to extract information. The investigative agencies have been using these tests even without the consent of the accused. In 2010, in a land mark judgment in *Selvi* v. *State of Karnataka*[29] the Supreme Court held that narco-analysis, brain mapping and polygraph tests carried out on the suspects by the investigative agencies for the interrogation was unconstitutional. A bench headed by Chief Justice K.G. Balakrishnan held that these tests are violation of the fundamental rights under Article 20(3) of the Constitution. The Court observed that forcing a person to undergo narco-analysis, brain-mapping, or polygraph tests itself amounted to the requisite compulsion, regardless of the lack of physical harm done to administer the test or the nature of the answers given during the tests.[30] Further, since the answers given during the test are not consciously and voluntarily given, and an

allow him to lie successfully. Therefore, under the effect of this chemical, the person is not only induced into a trance like state, but is also induced into speaking the truth. This is based on the fundamental assumption that the cortical portion of the brain is responsible for our ability to lie and Sodium Pentothal affects this portion thus successfully impairing the ability to lie; this assumption however, has no concrete scientific basis. The effects of the second stage are reversible; an overdose of the chemical form this stage could lead the victim to be unconscious and send him into the 3rd or 4th stage of anesthesia, the latter being irreversible and leading to a coma or death.

27. This is also known as Lie detector. In this, the Polygraphic machine records Blood Pressure, nerves, breathing speed, skin sensation at the time when continuous questioning is done on the suspect. Firstly, such questions are asked where suspect can't lie. During this, by polygraphic machine his blood pressure, heart beats, breathing speed and skin sensation is recorded. After that such questions asked, which investigators wanted to know. Actually, during right answer and wrong answer body language changes. Based on this results truth and lies are detected.
28. Brain Mapping is a test that maps the brain to reveal 'guilty knowledge'. The brain-mapping test is done to interpret the behaviour of the suspect and corroborate the investigating officers' observation and the suspect's statements. During the tests, forensic experts apply unique technologies to find out if a suspect's brain recognizes things from the crime scene that an innocent suspect would have no knowledge of.
29. Criminal Appeal Nos. 54, 55, 56-57, 58-59 of 2005, 1199 of 2006, 1471 of 2007, and 990 of 2010 (Arising out of SLP (Crl.) Nos. 10 of 2006 and 6711 of 2007), Supreme Court of India, available at: http://www.indiankanoon.org/doc/338008/(Visited on May 25, 2011).

individual does not have the ability to decide whether or not to answer a given question, the results from these tests amount to the requisite compelled testimony to violate Article 20(3).[31]

The court further observed that the results of these tests are not absolutely fool proof and hence, not completely reliable, and may not be admissible in court as evidence. In a narco test, the accused is injected with 'truth serums' that cause the person to become uninhibited and talkative. It is still possible for people to lie under the influence of truth serums, so it is not altogether reliable.[32] The Supreme Court comprising Chief Justice K.G. Balakrishnan, and Justices R.V. Raveendran and J.M. Panchal observed: *We hold that no individual should be forcibly subjected to any of the techniques in question, whether in the context of investigation in criminal cases or otherwise. Doing so would amount to an unwarranted intrusion into personal liberty.*[33]

The Court held that compelling public interest cannot justify the dilution of constitutional rights such as the "right against self-incrimination". Further, the Court observed that "compulsory administration of any of these techniques is an unjustified intrusion into the mental privacy of an individual. It would also amount to 'cruel, inhuman or degrading treatment' with regard to the language of evolving international human rights norms."[34] The judgment of the Supreme Court is appreciable as this decision prohibits the violation of right against self-incrimination, and consequently, right to remain silent of the accused which were violated by the investigative agencies under the pretext of narco-analysis, brain mapping and polygraph tests. However, the question is how far the judgment be respected by the police and investigating officials.

3.1.4. Justice Mallimath Committee on the Right to Silence

Since the accused is presumed to be innocent in adversarial legal systems, the accused has a right to remain silent and the burden is always on the prosecution. Hence, the police have to gather facts and information from other sources than the accused to support the prosecution to prove the case before the court of law. The Mallimath

30. *Id.* at paras 158, 165.
31. *Id.* at paras 161, 165.
32. *Id.* at para 28.
33. *Id.* at para 223.
34. *Id.* at para 218.

Committee on Criminal Justice Reforms[35] states that the accused is a valuable source of information.[36] Since India follows adversarial system of investigation and trial proceedings, the accused remains silent or even if he provides information to police during investigation, later he may disown it before the court of law. Hence, Mallimath Committee recommended that India should adopt a system which also appreciates the investigation by the police being supervised by a Magistrate as in the case of inquisitorial system that is prevalent in continental countries such as France, Germany, etc. This system will have the advantage of proving the statement of accused as valuable piece of evidence during trial, and hence, the proceeding would be more effective.[37] The Committee considered the right to remain silent available to the accused, but recommended that since the accused is the best source of correct information, without any kind of coercion such information must be gathered under the supervision of the Magistrate, and the Magistrate shall have the authority to question the accused and gather relevant information related with the crime.

However, the Law Commission has refused to accept the recommendations on the ground that the acceptance of such procedure under the Indian legal system would adversely affect the rights and liberties enshrined to the Individuals under the Constitution of India and hence, the Law Commission in its 180th report recommended that there is no need to dilute the existing right to remain silent.[38] The view of the Law Commission is acceptable as India follows predominantly a system which is not fully trustworthy as against developed civil law systems and, hence, in India, the

---

35. The Ministry of Home Affairs, Govt. of India constituted Justice V.S. Mallimath Committee on Reforms of Criminal Justice System (hereinafter referred as "Mallimath Committee") to make a comprehensive examination of all the functionaries of the Criminal Justice System, the fundamental principles and the relevant laws. The Committee, having given its utmost consideration to the grave problems facing the country, has made its recommendations in its final report in 2003.
36. Government of India, Report: Justice V.S. Mallimath Committee on Criminal Justice Reform (Ministry of Home Affairs, 2003), p. 39.
37. Mallimath Committee Report recommends for giving authority to Judges to supervise the investigating and prosecuting officials to gather evidences to make the criminal justice system effective in bringing the truth.
38. Government of India, Law Commission of India, 180th Report (2002), p. 2.

persons in authority can easily be influenced, evidences can easily be tampered, and the innocent persons may be put in peril. Considering the nature and attitude of the police from top to bottom towards the accused, the right to remain silent must be protected in all cases.

3.2. Right to Life and Personal Liberty

Article 21 which provides "right to life and personal liberty" is the most significant provision under the Indian Constitution in relation to protection of human rights. It provides that "no person shall be deprived of his life or liberty except according to procedure established by law". Article 21 of the Indian Constitution is equivalent to the 'due process' clause of U.S. Constitution.[39] Article 21 clearly provides two concepts, namely, the right to life and personal liberty.

3.2.1. Concept of "Right to Life"

The 'right to life' is the most fundamental of all rights that a person holds since without life there is no meaning of other rights. It is the natural right and is the basic human right. All other rights are supplemental to the right to life. 'Life' in Article 21 of the Constitution is not merely the physical act of breathing.[40] Judicial magnanimity of Supreme Court of India gave a heavenly interpretation to Article 21 by holding that the right to life does not connote mere animal existence.[41] The Court relied on the meaning given to the term 'life' by the U.S. Supreme Court in *Munn* v. *Illinois*,[42] in which Field J held that the term 'life' meant something more than mere animal existence and the prohibition against its deprivation extended to all those limbs and faculties by which the life was enjoyed. It has a much wider meaning which includes right to live with human dignity.[43] Right to life is fundamental to our very existence without which we cannot live as human being and includes all those aspects of life which go to make a man's life meaningful, complete and worth living.[44] After the wider interpretation given to Article 21 by the Supreme Court in *Maneka Gandhi* v. *Union of*

39. Fifth Amendment to the US Constitution provides "No person shall.....be deprived of life, liberty, or property, without due process of law".
40. P.M. Bakshi, The Constitution of India (2010), p. 55.
41. *Kharak Singh* v. *State of U.P*, 1964 S.C.R. (1) 332 at p. 345.
42. 94 U.S. 113 (1877).
43. *Maneka Gandhi* v. *Union of India*, 1978 SCR (2) 621.
44. *Maneka Gandhi* v. *Union of India*, 1978 SCR (2) at 662.

India,[45] a large number of human rights have been recognized under the umbrella of Article 21.

3.2.2. Concept of "Personal Liberty"

Individual freedoms and liberties has been a subject for struggle for long in the world as liberty is as important as life to an individual. The *Magna Carta*[46] in England, known as the Great Charter of Fundamental Rights, as back as 1215 provided that "no freeman shall be taken or imprisoned... but... by the law of the land". Article 21 has the greatest significance of providing the concept of liberty under the Constitution of India. The personal liberty under Article 21 has received a far more expansive interpretation at the hands of Supreme Court of India. The Supreme Court in A.K.*Gopalan* v. *State of Madras*[47] held that the liberty denotes merely freedom from bodily restraint. But in *Maneka Gandhi*'s case,[48] the Supreme Court has rejected this view and held that it encompasses those rights and privileges which have long been recognized as being essential to the orderly pursuit of happiness by free men.[49] Thus, the 'right to life and personal liberty' under Article 21 means to live with human dignity and enjoyable as a free man.

Article 21 has always been central for judicial scrutiny and interpretation after the adoption of the Constitution in 1950. Immediately after the coming into operation of Constitution of India, a crucial question of right to life and personal liberty of persons arose in *A.K. Gopalan* v. *State of Madras*[50] and the Supreme Court interpreted the provisions of Article 21 in a restrictive way. In this case, India's first preventive detention law, the Preventive Detention Act 1950, was challenged as violative of article 21 of the Constitution. A.K. Gopalan, a Communist leader, was detained under the Act and he challenged the Act mainly on the ground that the 'procedure' prescribed in the Act violated Article 21 by infringing upon the personal liberty of him. The Supreme Court, six Judges Bench headed by Chief Justice Kania held that the impugned Act is

45. *Id.*, at p. 696.
46. See *Supra* Ch.2 n.20.
47. (1950) S.C.R. 88. AIR 1950 SC 27; (hereinafter referred as "A.K. Gopalan's case"). Here, the Supreme Court gave a narrow interpretation holding that the Article 21 must be seen by the letter of the Article and principle of natural justice has no place under it.
48. 1978 S.C.R. (2) 621.
49. See supra n. 43 at p. 696.
50. *Supra* n 47.

not violative of the Article 21of the Constitution. The Court held that whatever may be the generally accepted connotation of the expression "personal liberty', it is used in Article 21 in a sense which excludes the freedom of movement dealt with in Article 19. Thus, the personal liberty in the context of part III of the Constitution is something distinct from the freedom to move freely throughout the territory of India.[51]

Justice B.K. Mukherjee concurring majority opinion observed that 'personal liberty' in Article 21 is the antithesis of physical restraint or coercion, and it means a personal right not to be subjected to imprisonment, arrest or other physical coercion in any manner that does not admit legal justification.[52]

Justice Murtaza Fazal Ali, delivering minority judgment, observed that the expression personal liberty and personal freedom have wider meaning and also a narrower meaning. In the wider sense, they include not only immunity from arrest and detention, but also freedom of speech, freedom of association, *etc*. In the narrower sense, they mean immunity from arrest and detention. He further observed that when these words are used in the sense of immunity from arrest, the juristic conception of personal liberty is that it consists in freedom of movement and locomotion.[53]

Thus, the majority judges in the Supreme Court gave a narrower interpretation to the concept of personal liberty. Four Judges, namely, Kania, CJ, Patanjali Shashtri, B.K. Mukherjee and Dass JJ held that "procedure prescribed by law' means procedure prescribed by the law of the State. According to them, these words are to be taken to refer to a procedure which has a statutory origin, for no procedure is known or can be said to have been established by such vague and uncertain concepts as "the immutable and universal principles of natural justice".[54] Hence, the majority rejected the connection of Article 21 with natural justice principles.

However, Justice Fazal Ali gave the minority judgment which attained far reaching consequences in later years in the concept of personal liberty and which ultimately proved correct.[55] In his dissenting opinion, Justice Fazal Ali had opined that 'law' in Article 21 means a valid law and 'procedure' means certain definite rules of

51. *Id.*, p. 195.
52. *Id.*, p. 262.
53. *Id.*, p. 150.
54. Dr. G.B. Reddy, Judicial Activism in India (1997), pp. 164-65.
55. *Id.* at pp. 164-65.

proceedings and not something which is a mere pretence for procedure.[56]

Thus, where the majority rejected the presence of the principles of natural justice in Article 21, the minority observed that the 'procedure' in Article 21 is meant a fair and just procedure.[57] This view was partially supported by the Supreme Court in *Kharak Singh's* case[58] and held that the right of personal liberty in Art. 21 as a right of an individual to be free from restrictions or encroachments on his person, whether those restrictions or encroachments are directly imposed or indirectly brought about by calculated measures.[59] However, the minority view has been fully accepted in terms and in spirit by the Supreme Court after twenty eight years in *Maneka Gandhi* v. *Union of India.*[60]

3.2.3. Right to Life and Personal Liberty and the Police Violation

Justice Bhagwati in *Maneka Gandhi's* case substantially widened the scope and ambit of the personal liberty under Article 21. In *Maneka Gandhi's* case, Supreme Court gave a dynamic interpretation to Article 21 and held that the law which deprives the life and liberty of the people must be "fair, just and reasonable" and not "arbitrary, oppressive and fanciful". The Supreme Court observed: "*the mere prescription of some kind of procedure cannot even meet the mandate of Article 21. The procedure prescribed by law has to be fair, just and reasonable, not fanciful, oppressive or arbitrary. The question whether the procedure prescribed by law which curtails or takes away the personal liberty guaranteed by Art. 21 is reasonable or not has to be considered not in the abstract or on hypothetical considerations like the provision for a full-dressed hearing as in a court room trial but in the contest, primarily, of the purpose which the Act is intended to achieve and of urgent situations which those who are charged with the duty of administering the Act may be called upon to deal with. Secondly, even the fullest compliance with the requirements of Art. 21 is not the journey's end because a law which prescribes fair and reasonable procedure for curtailing or taking away the personal liberty granted by Art. 21 has still to meet a possible challenge under the other provisions of the Constitution.*"[61]

56. 1950 S.C.R. 88 at p. 169.
57. *Id.*, pp. 165-66.
58. 1964 S.C.R. (1) 332.
59. *Id.*, p. 360.
60. *Supra* n.43.
61. See supra n.43 at p. 626.

Thus, a wider magnitude has been laid down for deprivation of personal liberty in *Maneka Gandhi*'s Case. Justice V.R. Krishna Iyer, speaking in *Sunil Batra* v. *Delhi Administaration*[62] has said that though our Constitution has no due process clause as available under the U.S. Constitution, after *Maneka Gandhi*'s case the consequence is the same, and as much as such Article 21 may be treated as counterpart of the due process clause which requires fair and reasonable procedure for depriving liberty under the U.S.Constitution.[63] The dynamic interpretation that has been given to Article 21 of the Indian Constitution in *Maneka Gandhi*'s case has widened the horizons of human rights jurisprudence in India and the Supreme Court has brought many rights under the umbrella of Article 21 such as right to live with human dignity,[64] right against delayed execution of death sentence,[65] right against inhuman treatment,[66] right against smoking in public places,[67] right to free legal aid,[68] right to livelihood,[69] right to privacy,[70] right against solitary confinement,[71] right to speedy trial,[72] right against hand cuffing,[73] etc. Thus, the *ratio* 'just, fair and reasonable' feature of law for depriving the liberty of a person in *Maneka Gandhi*'s case has widened the scope and ambit of "right to life and personal liberty" under Article 21 and the Supreme Court has opened new vistas for the growth and development of human rights protection in India including in the areas of protection of human rights from being violated by the police. The areas where the Supreme Court has acted for the protection of human rights from being violated by the police are investigation, interrogation, illegal arrest, unlawful detention, illegal search, unlawful seizure of properties, handcuffing, torture and inhuman treatment, death in police custody, fake encounter, *etc.* and are discussed below in detail.

62. 1979 S.C.R. (1) 392.
63. *Id.*, at 428.
64. *Francis Coralie* v. *Union Territory of Delhi*, A.I.R. 1981 S.C. 746.
65. *Sher Singh* v. *State of Punjab*, A.I.R. 1981 S.C. 625.
66. *Kishore Singh* v. *State of Rajasthan*, A.I.R. 1986 S.C. 180.
67. *Murli S. Deora* v. *Union of India*, A.I.R. 2000 S.C. 40.
68. *M.H. Hoskot* v. *State of Maharashtra*, A.I.R. 1978, S.C. 1548.
69. *Olga Tellis* v. *Bombay Municipal Corporation*, A.I.R. 1986 S.C. 180.
70. *R. Rajagopal* v. *State of Tamil Nadu*, (1985) 2 S.C.C. 431.
71. *SunialBatra (No. 1)* v. *Delhi Administration*, A.I.R. 1978 S.C. 1575.
72. *Hussainara Khatoon (No. 1)* v. *Home Secretary*, State of Bihar, A.I.R. 1979 S.C. 1360.
73. *Prem Shankar* v. *Delhi Administration*, A.I.R. 1980 S.C. 155

(i) Investigation

Police investigations are the basic method of collection of evidences in order to establish the guilt of the accused person before a court of law. Many a time, the manner of collection of evidence during investigation, the methods of interrogation, the arrest and the detention detrimentally affect the decency and dignity of persons; thereby infringing the human rights of individuals by the police. The Supreme Court of India, time and again, has assumed the mantle of saviours of innocent or accused persons from the hands of mighty police and has issued directives and guidelines that must be observed by the police during the course of investigation, interrogation, arrest or detention.[74] Delaying the investigation process is one of the tactics of the police in order to harass the party disfavoured by the police. Since the investigation is an integral part in the process of trial, delaying the investigation adversely affects speedy trial. Supreme Court has held in many cases that speedy trial is implicit in Article 21.[75] In *Abdul Rehman Antulay* v. *R.S. Nayak*, the Supreme Court emphasized that the "fair, just and reasonable"[76] procedure implicit in Article 21 of the Constitution creates a right in the accused to be tried speedily and that the right to speedy trial flowing from Article 21 encompasses all the stages, namely, the stage of investigation, inquiry, trial, appeal, revision and retrial. Thus, the speedy investigation is a prerequisite for speedy trial and hence within the purview of Article 21. Again, in *Vakil Prasad Singh* v. *State of Bihar*[77] the Supreme Court reiterated the same view and held that the right to speedy trial in all criminal prosecutions is an inalienable right under Article 21 of the Constitution and this right is applicable not only to the actual proceedings in court but also includes within its sweep the police investigations as well. There was an unreasonable delay of 17 years for investigating in this case. In *Nirmal Singh Kahlon* v. *State of*

74. *D.K. Basu* v. *State of West Bengal*, A.I.R. 1997 S.C. 610; *Joginder Singh* v. *State of UP*, (1994) 4 S.C.C. 260; *Arvind Singh Bagga* v. *State of U.P.*, AIR 1985 S.C. 117; *Prem Shankar Shukla* v. *Delhi Administration*, (1980) Cr L J 930; *Sunil Batra* v. *Delhi Administration*, (1978) 4 S.C.C. 494.
75. Supreme Court held in *Hussainara Khatoon* (No. 1) v. *Home Secretary, State of Bihar*, A.I.R. 1979 S.C. 1360, that 'right to speedy trial is implicit in Article 21; *In HussainaraKhatoon (No. 2)* v. *Home Secretary, State of Bihar*, A.I.R. 1979 S.C. 1369, and *Hussainara Khatoon (No. 3)* v. *Home Secretary, State of Bihar*, A.I.R. 1979 S.C. 1377 the Court reiterated the same view.
76. A.I.R. 1992 S.C. 1630.
77. A.I.R.2009 S.C. 1822.

Punjab[78] the Court had to consider the case of fairness of the investigation. The Court held that fair trial includes fair investigation and fair investigation is essential for the preservation of fundamental rights of an accused under Article 21. Again in *Babubhai* v. *State of Gujarat*[79] the Supreme Court reiterated that not only fair trial but fair investigation is also part of constitutional rights guaranteed under Articles 20 and 21 of the Constitution of India. Thus, from *Abdul Rehman Anthulay*'s case to *Babubhai*'s case the Supreme Court affirmed categorically that speedy investigation is an integral part of speedy trial, and hence, delaying investigation process by the police is against constitutional right of the accused. Otherwise the very purpose of Constitutional right of speedy trial would be meaningless.

(ii) Arrest

Arrest of a person by the police is yet another controversial area in the criminal justice process as a result of the wide discretionary powers enjoyed by the police and the practical misuse of those powers by them. According to the National Police Commission's Third Report, the power of arrest is one of the chief sources of corruption by the police and around 60 percent of the arrests made by the police are unnecessary and unjustified.[80] There lies the point of misuse of power to arrest by the police. Even when arrest is necessary, the police do not comply with the procedural requirements provided by the Constitution of India and the Criminal Procedure Code. This had come to the notice of the Supreme Court in different cases and the Court has been obsessive in the matters connected with unlawful arrest, illegal detention and non-compliance of the procedural requirements while effecting arrest and detention. In *Bhim Singh* v. *State of Jammu & Kashmir*[81] the petitioner, an MLA, was arrested and detained in Police custody and deliberately prevented from attending the session of the legislative assembly. The Supreme Court held that the police officials acted deliberately and hence, the court awarded compensation to the petitioner.

In *Joginder Kumar* v. *State of U.P.*[82] the Supreme Court has laid down guidelines governing arrest of a person during investigation. This has been done with a view to strike a balance between the needs

78. A.I.R. 2009 S.C. 984.
79. Supreme Court, Judgment delivered on 26 August, 2010.
80. *Joginder Kumar v. State of U.P.*, (1994) 4 S.C.C. 260, at para 12.
81. (1985) 4 S.C.C. 730.
82. (1994) 4 S.C.C. 260.

of police on the one hand and the protection of human rights of citizens from oppression and injustice at the hands of law enforcing agencies, on the other hand.[83] The court has held in *Joginder Kumar's* case that the police officer arresting a person must be able to justify the arrest apart from his power to do so. Arrest and detention in police lock-up of a person can cause incalculable harm to the reputation and self-esteem of a person.[84] A person is not to be arrested merely on the suspicion of complicity in an offence, but there must be reasonable justification in the opinion of the police officer making the arrest that such arrest was necessary and justified.[85] For effective enforcement of these fundamental rights, the Supreme Court has laid down that (i) an arrested person being held in custody is entitled to have one friend, relative or other person, informed, as far as is practicable, that such person has been arrested and where he is being detained; (ii) the police officer shall inform the arrested person when he is brought to the police station of this right; and (iii) an entry should be made in the diary as to who was informed of the arrest. The Court observed that these protections from the police powers must be held to flow from Articles 21 and 22(1) of the Constitution of India and must be enforced strictly. In fact, the guidelines of the Supreme Court in *Joginder Kumar*'s case were a foot step towards judicial activism of Supreme Court in the protection of human rights of persons from the hands of police. *Joginder Kumar*'s case has paved the way for Supreme Court to give judicial standing directives to police and law enforcement officials in *D.K. Basu v. State of West Bengal.*[86]

The judgment of the Supreme Court in *D.K Basu's* case is a milestone in matters of arrest, detention and interrogation by the police as in this case the Court gave a pragmatic as well as realistic approach to procedural requirement of arrest and detention. The Supreme Court laid down eleven directives to the Police and law enforcement officials to be followed in all cases of arrest and/ detention. The directives, as directed by the Supreme Court, must be complied with in all cases of arrest or detention till legal provisions are made in that behalf as preventive measures. The directives are:

(1) The police personnel carrying out the arrest and handling

83. See supra n.23. at p. 1032.
84. *Ibid.*
85. *Ibid.*
86. AIR 1997 S.C. 610.

the interrogation of the arrestee should bear accurate, visible and clear identification and name tags with their designations. The particulars of all such police personnel who handle interrogation of the arrestee must be recorded in a register.

(2) The police officer carrying out the arrest of the arrestee shall prepare a memo of arrest at the time of arrest and such memo shall be attested by at least one witness, who may be either a member of the family of the arrestee or a respectable person of the locality from where the arrest is made. It shall also be counter signed by the arrestee and shall contain the time and date of arrest.

(3) A person who has been arrested or detained and is being held in custody in a police station or interrogation centre or other lock-up, shall be entitled to have one friend or relative or other person known to him or having interest in his welfare being informed, as soon as practicable, that he has been arrested and is being detained at the particular place, unless the attesting witness of the memo of arrest is himself such a friend or a relative of the arrestee.

(4) The time, place of arrest and venue of custody of an arrestee must be notified by the police where the next friend or relative of the arrestee lives outside the district or town through the Legal Aid Organization in the District and the police station of the area concerned telegraphically within a period of eight to twelve hours after the arrest.

(5) The person arrested must be made aware of this right to have someone informed of his arrest or detention as soon as he is put under arrest or is detained.

(6) An entry must be made in the diary at the place of detention regarding the arrest of the person which shall also disclose the name of the next friend of the person who has been informed of the arrest and the names and particulars of the police officials in whose custody the arrestee is.

(7) The arrestee should, where he so requests, be also examined at the time of his arrest, and major and minor injuries, if any present on his/her body, must be recorded at that time. The "Inspection Memo" must be signed both by the arrestee and the police officer effecting the arrest and its copy provided to the arrestee.

(8) The arrestee should be subjected to medical examination by a trained doctor every 48 hours during his detention in custody by a doctor on the panel of approved doctors appointed by Director, Health Services of the concerned State or Union Territory. Director, Health Services should prepare such a penal for all *Tehsils* and Districts as well.

(9) Copies of all the documents including the memo of arrest, referred to above, should be sent to the *illaka* (local) Magistrate for his record.

(10) The arrestee may be permitted to meet his lawyer during interrogation, though not throughout the interrogation.

(11) A police control room should be provided at all district and State Headquarters, where information regarding the arrest and the place of custody of the arrestee shall be communicated by the officer causing the arrest, within 12 hours of effecting the arrest, and at the police control room, it should be displayed on conspicuous notice board.[87]

The Supreme Court made it clear that these requirements are in addition to the constitutional and statutory safeguards and do not detract from various other directions given by the courts from time to time in connection with the safeguarding of the rights and dignity of the arrestee.[88]

In effect, *D.K. Basu*'s case is a drive far ahead of *JoginderKumar*'s case in relation to arrest, detention and interrogation by the police officials. *D.K. Basu*'s case is significant in as much as it is almost a legislation made by the Supreme Court. The judgment in *D.K. Basu*'s case is landmark as it was the need of the hour and the Government was not positive enough to formulate legislation to this effect despite growing atrocities of the police.

It is significant to note that in this case the Court, after setting out the directives, made it clear that failure to comply with such directives will not only attract the departmental action but also the contempt of court proceedings. *D.K. Basu*'s case occupied the field due to the absence of clear legislation related with arrest and detention of persons. The Parliament has amended the Code of

87. *Id.*, para 36.
88. *Id.*, para 39.

Criminal Procedure thrice (in 2005, 2008 and 2010) after *D.K. Basu*'s case in order to incorporate the directives into the Code of Criminal Procedure. However, *D.K. Basu*'s case is a clear illustration of judicial activism in the protection of human rights of arrested persons.

(iii) Handcuffing

The Police, at large, believe that handcuffing is a necessity in effecting the arrest and they, quite often, do not take into consideration the humiliation and embarrassment suffered by the handcuffed person and the disrepute of his family. At times, the police handcuff persons intentionally in order to tarnish the image, esteem and dignity of the arrestee or the family of the arrestee even though there is no danger of accused escaping from the custody. In the landmark case of *Sunil Batra* v. *Delhi Administration*[89] the Supreme Court pronounced that the indiscriminate use of handcuffs is illegal. The Court observed : *where an under trial has a credible tendency for violence and escape a humanely graduated degree of 'iron' restraint is permissible if only if-other disciplinary alternatives are unworkable. The burden of proof of the ground is on the custodian. And if he fails, he will be liable in law.*[90]

This decision has influenced subsequent judgments on the use of handcuffs and has been heavily relied on. In *Prem Shankar* v. *Delhi administration*[91] the Supreme Court held that hand cuffing is *prima facie* inhuman, unreasonable and over harsh, and it is permitted only in exceptional circumstances where there is a reasonable apprehension of escape of the detainee.[92] The court observed: *handcuffing is prima facie inhuman and, therefore, unreasonable, is over harsh and at the first blush, arbitrary. Absent fair procedure and objective monitoring to inflict "irons" is to resort to zoological strategies repugnant to Article 21. Surely, the competing claims of securing the prisoner from fleeing and protecting his personality from barbarity have to be harmonized. To prevent the escape of an under-trial is in public interest, reasonable, just and cannot, by itself be castigated. But to bind a man hand and foot, fetter his limbs with hoops of steel, shuffle him along in the streets and stand him for hours in the courts is to torture him, defile his dignity, vulgarise society and foul the soul of our Constitutional culture.*

89. 1979 S.C.R. (1) 392.
90. *Id.*, p. 489.
91. 1980 S.C.R. (3) 855.
92. *Id.*, p. 859.

In *State of Maharshtra* v. *Ravikant S. patil*[93] a detainee was handcuffed and paraded on streets. The Bombay High Court held that hand cuffing and parading was violative of article 21 and directed the police official who was responsible for hand cuffing and parading to pay Rupees ten thousand by way of compensation and directed that this act of violation of Article 21 should also be entered in his service record. Although the Supreme Court upheld the judgment of the High Court, directing a payment of compensation yet held that the police officer was not personally liable as he acted as an official in the discharge of his official function. It is submitted that the decision of the High Court must be accepted as the police official was acting in excess of his authority and hence, he must be made personally liable.

Though the Supreme Court gave verdict that the hand cuffing could genuinely be used only in extreme cases of danger of escape of detainee, police may not follow it because they are either unaware of it or just ignore it. In one such case, *Citizen for democracy* v. *State of Assam*[94] the Supreme Court expressed its great concern when the police officials hand cuffed under-trial prisoners ignoring the Supreme Court guideline in *Prem Shankar Shukla's* case. The Supreme Court gave direction to the State Government that stringent measures must be taken against erring police officials. This verdict itself shows the intolerance of the Supreme Court against such acts of disgrace as it viewed the same as a very grave and offending act of demeaning a person *sans* dignity.

(iv) Torture and Death in Police Custody

The Constitution of India does not contain an express prohibition of torture. However, the Supreme Court has construed Article 21 of the Constitution as including a prohibition of torture. The Supreme Court in *Fancis Coralie Mullin* v. *Union Territory of Delhi*[95] held:

> Now obviously, any form of torture or cruel, inhuman or degrading treatment would be offensive to human dignity and constitute an inroad into this right to live and it would, on this view, be prohibited by Article 21 unless it is in accordance with procedure prescribed by law, but no

93. (1991) 2 S.C.C. 373.
94. (1995) 3 S.C.C. 743.
95. 1981 S.C.R. (2) 516.

> law which authorizes and no procedure which leads to such torture or cruel, inhuman or degrading treatment can ever stand the test of reasonableness and non-arbitrariness: it would plainly be unconstitutional and void as being violative of Articles 14 and 21.[96]

The "third degree" methods are the barbarous weapon in the hands of police for various purposes such as eliciting hidden facts, to compel a person to falsely admit guilt, to retaliate favouring the other party, to coerce a person in custody, *etc.* In a landmark judgment, *Kishore Singh* v. *State of Rajasthan*[97] the Supreme Court plainly laid down that the use of "third degree" method by the police is violative of Article 21. In this case the detainees were brought before the Court as per the direction of the Court. While they were brought, in transit, violence had been used by the escort police on the person of one of the petitioners resulting in deep wounds on his person. The Court observed "Article 21 would become dysfunctional unless the agencies of the law in the police and prison establishments have sympathy for the humanist creed of that Article."[98] The Court in this case directed the State to re-educate the police and inculcate a respect for the human person and to punish the escort police who misconducted with the prisoner. Precisely, a human rights course has been prescribed for police in Police Academies in the country to impart training on human rights.

In *Sheela Barse* v. *State of Maharashtra*,[99] the petitioner, a journalist, in her letter addressed to the Supreme Court stated that five women prisoners interviewed by her in the Bombay Central Jail alleged that they had been assaulted by the police in the police lock-up and two of them in particular alleged that they had been assaulted and tortured in the lock-up. The Supreme Court gave detailed instructions to the concerned authorities for providing security and safety in police lock-up, particularly to women suspects and the Court directed that the female suspect should be kept in separate police lock-ups and not in the same in which male accused are detained and should be guarded by female constables.[100]

96. *Id.*, p. 539.
97. 1981 S.C.R. (1) 995.
98. *Id.*, p. 999.
99. 1983 S.C.R. (2) 337.
100. *Id.*, p. 345.

Custodial violence and atrocities portray the extent of flagrant violation of human rights and brutal attitude of police. There are many instances of custodial death and violence by the police. *In Nilabati Behera@ Lalita Behera* v. *State of Orissa,*[101] petitioner's son was arrested and taken in custody from his home by the Assistant Sub-Inspector of Police in connection with the investigation of a theft and the petitioner came to know that the dead body of her son was found on the railway track. There were multiple injuries on the body and his death was unnatural, caused by those injuries. The Supreme Court directed the District Judge to hold an inquiry into the matter and to submit a report to the Supreme Court. The District Judge found that petitioner's son died on account of multiple injuries inflicted to him while he was in police custody.The Supreme Court awarded compensation of Rupees one lakh fifty thousand to the mother of the deceased and directed the State government to take appropriate action against each erring police personnel. While awarding the compensation the Court observed:

> Article 21 which guarantees the right to life and liberty will be denuded of its significant content if the power of this Court were limited to passing orders to release from illegal detention. One of the telling ways in which the violation of that right can reasonably be prevented and due compliance with the mandate of Article 21 secured, is to mulct its violators in the payment of monetary compensation.[102]

The Court further observed that the violation of fundamental rights attracts strict liability for which the Supreme Court or High Court has the authority to compensate the victim or dependents of the victim.[103]

In *Smt. Shakila Abdul Gafar Khan* v. *Vasant Raghunath Dhoble,*[104] the complainant's husband was taken in custody by the police and was beaten up in public for more than an hour in front of the complainant (wife), deceased's mother and sister with hockey sticks. Later, he was released from the custody and admitted in a hospital where he died. The Supreme Court ordered for compensation of

101. 1993 S.C.R. (2) 581.
102. *Id.*, p. 597.
103. *Id.*, p. 596
104. A.I.R. 2003 S.C. 4567.

Rupees one lakh to the mother and children of the deceased and expressed great concern over the defect of the present criminal law due to which the police atrocities and custodial crimes go unpunished. The Apex Court further directed the State Government to conduct a detailed enquiry to find out who are the police personnel responsible for the injuries caused on the body of the deceased and to take appropriate action against the culprit. In yet another glaring example of police atrocities, in *Peoples' Union for Democratic Rights* v. *Police Commissioner, Delhi Head Quarter*[105] where a labourer who was engaged to work for police for wages when demanded his wages was beaten to death. The Supreme Court awarded compensation of Rs. 75,000 to the family of the deceased. In *Saheli* v. *Commissioner of Police*[106] a nine year old child was beaten up by the police and later succumbed to injuries inflicted on him by the police. The Supreme Court awarded compensation of Rs. 75,000 to the mother.

How cruel and barbaric are our police can be found in *C.B.I.* v. *Kishore Singh,*[107] where a police constable chopped off the genital organ of an arrested person due to the suspected illicit relationship with the wife of the relative of the police constable. The Supreme Court observed that the case reveals how some policemen in our country have not got over their old colonial mentality and are still persisting in barbaric acts in a free country which claims to be run by a democratic Constitution and the rule of law. The Court held that the policemen who commit such acts of criminal nature deserve harsher punishment than other persons who commit such acts, because it is the duty of the policemen to protect the people, and not break the law themselves.

Custodial violence against women very often includes rape and other forms of sexual violence such as threats of rape, touching, virginity testing, being stripped naked, invasive body searches, insults and humiliations of a sexual nature, *etc. Tukaram* v. *State of Maharashtra*[108] notoriously known as *Mathura rape case* in which a 16 year old girl was raped in a police station. The Session's Judge acquitted the accused but the High Court, on appeal, convicted the

105. (1989) 4 S.C.C. 730.
106. A.I.R. 1990 S.C. 513.
107. S.L.P. (Criminal) Nos. 8485-87 of 2009, Supreme Court Judgment delivered on 25 October, 2010, available at: http://www.indiankanoon.org/doc/1473938/(Visited on January 7, 2011).
108. (1979) 2 S.C.C. 143.

accused but the Supreme Court reversed the conviction of the High Court saying that there was no mark of injury on her body and there was no stiff resistance on the part of the girl in custody. This judgment attracted much criticism and public outcry for the amendment of the rape laws. The most important factor in this case was in relation to consensual sex and rape. In this case the Supreme Court did not take into consideration of a girl of 16 years during night in the hands of dreadful intoxicated policemen where she would fearfully submit herself for whatever they demand from her. This decision, however, made way for making amendments in the Indian Evidence Act and the Indian Penal Code. The Indian Evidence Act was amended by inserting Sec.114-A drawing a conclusive presumption as to the absence of consent of the woman in the case of prosecution of rape under Sec. 376(2) clauses (a) to (g) and shifting the burden of proof of innocence on the accused. The Criminal Law (Amendment) Act 1983, incorporated custodial rape as a new offence by including Sections 376-B to D to the Indian Penal Code making custodial rape by police as an aggravating offence. *Ram Kumar* v. *State of Himachal Pradesh*[109] is yet another glaring instance of custodial rape and the Supreme Court upheld the sentence awarded by the State High Court to the two policemen in this case with seven years and two years rigorous imprisonment.

Criminal Law Amendment 2013 changes the definition of rape and the law altogether. Section 376 (2) (a) now provides that where a policeman committing rape shall be punished with rigorous imprisonment for a term which shall not be less than ten years, but which may extend to imprisonment for life which shall mean imprisonment for the reminder of that person's natural life and shall also liable to fine. Surely, the intention of the legislature to incorporate such a severe punishment is to deter the like-minded offenders and to protect women.

(v) Fake Encounter

"Fake Encounter" is another area where the police commit glaring human rights violations by way of atrocities and arbitrary killings against persons. In *People's Union for Civil Liberties* v. *Union of India* [110] the Supreme Court held that killing of two people in fake encounter by Imphal Police was clear violation of right to life guaranteed by Article 21 of the Constitution of India and defence of

109. A.I.R. 1995 S.C. 1965.
110. A.I.R. 1990 S.C. 513.

sovereign immunity does not apply in such cases. The Court awarded Rs. 1,00,000 as compensation for the dependants of each of the deceased. People's Union for Civil Liberties, an NGO committed for protecting human rights, demanded for Central Bureau of Investigation enquiry on all encounters that took place in Chattisgarh since 2005.[111] Mangoli and Ganapati, Criminologists, study reveals that every 2nd police encounter in the country is fake.[112] Thus, fake encounter is enormous in many parts of India either under the pretext of terrorist or Maoist or Naxalite or dacoit killing and flagrantly violating the human rights of individuals by the police.

3.3. Protection against Arbitrary Arrest and Detention

In the Constituent Assembly, there had been a heated discussion about the exception clause of Article 15 (now Article 21) which ends with the proviso"except according to the procedure established by the law". The discussion centered on the issue that Parliament could take away the life and liberty by a mere Act of Parliament due to the reason that Article 15 gives very wide powers to the Parliament to restrain the right to life and personal liberty by making a simple law.[113] It was, therefore, felt necessary to limit the authority of the Parliament from taking away such rights unless there are exceptional circumstances so warrants. This led to the incorporation of another Article 15-A (now Article 22). Thus, Article 22 was "brought in as a compensation" to provide extra safeguard to the proviso "procedure established by law" in Article 21.[114] The Framers had taken the experience of colonial feudalism that persisted in a wide spread abuse of power in the case of arrest and detention of persons arbitrarily without proper investigation and trial.[115] Article 22 in Sub-articles (1) and (2) expressly provides the rights and protections of the arrested and detained persons. The Article 22 (1) reads, "no person who is arrested shall be detained in custody without being informed, as soon as may be, of the grounds

111. Press Release, People's Union for Civil Liberties, 9th May 2007.
112. See supra Ch.1 n.33, pp. 401-418.
113. Constituent Assembly of India, Volume IX, September15, 1949, available at : <http://parliamentofindia.nic.in/ls/debates/vol9p35a.htm> (Visited on December 17, 2010).
114. *Ibid.*
115. Kolsky, E, Codification and the Rule of Colonial Difference: Criminal Procedure In British India, (2005), 23 law & hist. rev. p. 631; See also Kalhan. A et al, Colonial Continuities: Human Rights, Terrorism, And Security Laws in India, (2006), 20 Colum. J. Asian L. 93, fall 2006.

for such arrest nor shall he be denied the right to consult, and to be defended by, a legal practitioner of his choice." Article 22 (2) further provides:

> Every person who is arrested and detained in custody shall be produced before the nearest Magistrate within a period of twenty-four hours of such arrest excluding the time necessary for the journey from the place of arrest to the court of the Magistrate and no such person shall be detained in custody beyond the said period without the authority of a Magistrate.

Thus, the Constitution has guaranteed certain rights to the arrested and detained persons such as: (i) the right to be informed of the ground of arrest 'as soon as possible'; (ii) the right to consult a lawyer and to be defended by a lawyer of his choice; (iii) the right to be produced before a Magistrate within twenty four hours; and (iv) the right to be released from custody beyond the period of twenty four hours if not produced before a Magistrate.

3.3.1. Right to Know the Grounds of Arrest

It is important for an arrested person to know the grounds of depriving his liberty immediately on arrest so that he can assess whether the arrest is arbitrary or not, and, he can prepare for his defence. The Article 22 requires the arresting officials to disclose the grounds of arrest "as soon as may be" to the arrested person. In *re Madhu Limaye*,[116] the Supreme Court held that the requirements of Article 22(1) are meant to afford the earliest opportunity to the arrested person to remove any mistake, misapprehension or misunderstanding on the part of the authorities who made the arrest.[117] The provision is essential so that the arrested person may know the accusations that have been levelled against him before hand and will not take it as a surprise.[118] He also gets opportunity to prepare himself and to engage a lawyer to defend his side before a court of law. Thus, article 22(1) embodies the fundamental safeguards of the personal liberty of an arrested person.

Since the words used in Article 22(1) are "as soon as may be", the question arises as to what exactly the term "as soon as may be"

116. 1969 Cri.L.J. 1440.
117. *Id.*, p. 1452.
118. P. Ramanatha Aiyer, Code of Criminal Procedure (1999), p. 262.

implies. In *D.P. Ghosh* v. *State of West Bengal*[119] the Supreme Court held that while the object of communicating the grounds of arrest is to enable the concerned person to make a representation against the arrest, communicating the grounds of arrest 'as soon as may be' must be interpreted in the correct context. The Court held that it implies that the ground of arrest must be conveyed as early as practicable and without delay.[120]

The question, at times, arises is as to whether oral communication is sufficient or written communication is mandatory. In *Ajithkumar* v. *State of Assam*[121] the Supreme Court held that the details of particulars of the offence must be communicated in a way understandable by the arrested person and should also be in a language understandable by him.[122] Thus, the communication may be oral or written, but what is important is that it must be understood by the arrested person regarding the grounds of his arrest. In *Joginder Kumar*'s case[123] and *D.K. Basu*'s case[124] the Supreme Court has laid down detailed procedures to be complied with in making the arrest such as to inform about the arrest to a friend, relative or other person who is known to him or likely to take an interest in his welfare as far as is practicable that he has been arrested and where he is being detained. Further, it has been made an obligation to the arresting officer to inform the arrested person about this right.

The Criminal Procedure Code contains analogous provision in Section 50(1) which provides that "Every police officer or other person arresting any person without warrant shall forthwith communicate to him full particulars of the offence for which he is arrested or other grounds for such arrest." The Supreme Court in *re Madhu Limaye*[125] explained the reasons of analogous provisions under the Code of Criminal Procedure and under the provisions of the Constitution as that the Constitution-makers were anxious to make these safeguards an integral part of fundamental rights. The Supreme Court observed that Dr. B.R. Ambedkar said while moving for insertion of Article 15-A (as numbered in the Draft Bill of the Constitution) which corresponded to present Article 22:

119. (1972) 2 S.C.C. 656.
120. *Id.*, at 662.
121. 1976 Cri.L.J. 1303.
122. *Id.*, p. 1316.
123. 1994 S.C.C. (4) 260, at p. 268.
124. See supra n.74.
125. *Supra* n. 116 at 1448.

> "Article 15-A merely lifts from the provisions of the Criminal Procedure Code two of the most fundamental principles which every civilised country follows as principles of international justice. It is quite true that these two provisions contained in clause (1) and clause (2) are already to be found in the Criminal Procedure Code and thereby probably it might be said that we are really not making any very fundamental change. But we are, as I contend, making a fundamental change because what we are doing by the introduction of Article 15-A is to put a limitation upon the authority both of Parliament as well as of the Provincial Legislature not to abrogate the two provisions, because they are now introduced in our Constitution itself."

Further, in *Govind Prasad* v. *State of West Bengal*[126] the Supreme Court held that the provisions of Section 50 of the Code of Criminal Procedure are material and cannot be overlooked as it brings the law in conformity with Article 22(1) of the Indian Constitution.[127] The Court further observed that this Section confers a valuable right to the arrested person and non-conformity with its mandatory provision would lead to non-conformity with the "procedure established by law" in article 21.[128]

Hence, the Article 22(1) of the Constitution provides safeguards against arbitrary arrest. A duty is caste on the arresting official to make known the arrested person the grounds of arrest at the earliest possible time. If the arresting official is not complying with this mandate, he would be liable for unlawful arrest of the person.

3.3.2. Right to Consult a Lawyer

The right to consult a lawyer is a constitutional safeguard guaranteed to arrested persons by the Constitution under Article 22 (1). In fact, the Original Draft Constitution initially contained only a right to "consult" lawyer. In the Constituent Assembly, there was a strong argument for the incorporation of "to be defended" by a legal practitioner of his choice in Article 15-A. Dr. B.R. Ambedkar[129]

126. 1975 Cri.L.J. 1249.
127. *Id.*, at 1261.
128. *Ibid.*
129. Chairman, The Drafting Committee for the Constitution of India after its independence in 1947.

was of the opinion that the words "to consult" included also the right to be defended because he observed that 'consultation' would be utterly purposeless if it was not for the purpose of defense.[130] However, in order to provide clarity and remove any ambiguity he added the words "and be defended by a legal practitioner" after the words "to consult".[131] The Supreme Court in *Nandini Satpathy*'s case[132] made a clear departure from its earlier decisions[133] and held that Article 22 (1) does not mean that persons who are not strictly under arrest or custody can be denied the right to counsel. The Supreme Court widened the scope of right "to consult" to include right to counsel to any accused person coming within the purview of interrogation by a police official.[134] The Supreme Court went further in *Joginder Kumar*'s case[135] and took a pulsating approach in relation to right "to consult" by holding that right to consult implies right to consult *privately* with his lawyer.[136] The Supreme Court in *D.K. Basu*'s case issued directives that in the event of arrest, the arrestee can ask the police to allow him to consult his lawyer. It provides that "the arrestee may be permitted to meet his lawyer during interrogation though not throughout the interrogation".[137]

In a recent case, the Supreme Court affirmed its position once again. In *Shukur Ali* v. *State of Assam*[138] the Supreme Court held that the "right to consult and to be defended by a lawyer of choice" should be given widest possible construction to effectuate the intention of the Founding Fathers of the Indian Constitution. The Supreme Court observed :

> The Founding Fathers of our Constitution were themselves freedom fighters who had seen civil liberties of

---

130. See *supra* n.113, 16 September, 1949.
131. *Ibid.*
132. See supran 23.
133. The Supreme Court in JanardhanReddi v. State of Hyderabad, A.I.R. 1951 S.C. 217, held that "the right to be defended by a legal practitioner of his choice could only mean a right of the accused to have the opportunity to engage a lawyer and does not guarantee an absolute right to be supplied with a lawyer by the State. This in fact is a literal interpretation of Article 22 (1).
134. *Supra* n. 5.
135. 1994 S.C.C. (4) 260.
136. *Id.*, p. 268.
137. *Supra* n. 74, para 10.
138. (2011) INSC 195 (24 February 2011); In the Supreme Court, Crl. App. No. 546 of 2011 (arising out of S.L.P. (CRL.) No(s). 679 of 2011), available at: http://www.indiankanoon.org/doc/1470346/(Visited on May 22, 2011.).

> our people trampled under foreign rule, and who had themselves been incarcerated for long period under the formula "*Na vakeel, na daleel, na appeal*" (No lawyer, no hearing, no appeal). Many of them were lawyers by profession, and knew the importance of counsel, particularly in criminal cases. It was for this reason that they provided for assistance by counsel under Article 22 (1), and that provision must be given the widest construction to effectuate the intention of the Founding Fathers.[139]

It is worth noting that a similar provision to Article 22(1) can be found under Article 303 of the Criminal Procedure Code. Section 303 of Code reads "any person accused of an offence before a Criminal Court, or against whom proceedings are instituted under this Code, may of right be defended by a pleader of his choice". While it may seem superfluous to have the same provision in the Constitution as well as in the Criminal Procedure Code, Dr. B.R. Ambedkar stated that by introducing this provision in the constitution, there would be a limitation upon the authority of the Parliament as well as the Provincial Legislatures not to abrogate the rights guaranteed under this provision.[140]

3.3.3. Right to be Produced Before a Magistrate

After the arrest of a person by the police officer, judicial recourse is important to determine the legality of the arrest and detention. Article 22 (2) provides that the arrested person must be produced before a Magistrate within twenty four hours. Within the period of twenty four hours, the investigation has to be completed by the investigating officer. Even if the investigation cannot be completed, arrested person must be produced before the Magistrate immediately. Right to be brought before a Magistrate within twenty-four hours of arrest has been provided under the Constitution so that the arrest and detention are not carried out for extracting confessions or compelling information by means of duress or terror.[141] Supreme Court in *State of Punjab* v. *Ajaib Singh*[142] held that the arrests without warrants require more protection than those with warrants. The Court observed:

---

139. *Ibid.*
140. *Supra* n.116 at 1448.
141. R.V. Kelkar, Criminal Procedure (1998), p. 53.
142. 1953 S.C.R. 254.

> ...arrests without warrants issued by a court call for greater protection than do arrests under such warrants. The provision that the arrested person should within 24 hours be produced before the nearest Magistrate is particularly desirable in the case of arrest otherwise than under a warrant issued by the court, for it ensures the immediate application of a judicial mind to the legal authority of the person making the arrest and the regularity of the procedure adopted by him. In the case of, arrest under a warrant issued by a court, the judicial mind had already been applied to the case when the warrant was issued and, therefore, there is less reason for making such production in that case a matter of a substantive fundamental right.[143]

Thus, the provision for compulsorily producing the arrested person within twenty-four hours before a Magistrate ensures the immediate application of a judicial mind to the legal authority of the person making the arrest and legality of the arrest made by him.

The twenty-four hours' time excludes the time taken for travel to bring the arrestee before the Magistrate. Failure to comply with the requirement will attract the police officer liable under section 340 of the Indian Penal Code for wrongful detention.[144] In the case of *Khatri (II)* v. *State of Bihar*[145] the Supreme Court observed that the State and its police authorities must see that this constitutional and legal requirement to produce an arrested person before a Judicial Magistrate within 24 hours of the arrest must be scrupulously observed.[146] The Court further observed that "the provision inhibiting detention without remand is a very healthy provision which enables the Magistrates to keep check over the police investigation and it is necessary that the Magistrates should try to enforce this requirement and where it is found to be disobeyed, come down heavily upon the police".[147] A question arose was whether the protection is available to the arrests made on the order of legislative bodies. In *Gunupati Keshavram* v. *Nafisul Hasan*[148] it was held that the

143. *Id.*, p. 268.
144. D.D. Basu, Criminal Procedure Code (1973), p. 143.
145. 1981 S.C.R. (2) 408.
146. *Id.*, p. 414.
147. *Ibid.*
148. A.I.R. 1954 S.C. 636.

protection conferred by clauses : (1) and (2) of Article 22 extends to arrest and detention in pursuance of an order of the Speaker of a Legislature on a charge of breach of privilege.

Thus, the right to be produced before the Magistrate is a safeguard available to the arrested person under Article 22(2), even if the investigation cannot be completed within twenty-four hours. It is illegal for the police to keep a person in custody beyond the period of twenty-four hours without producing before a Magistrate. Though the Constitutional mandate is like this, but in reality there is always hue and cry of illegal arrest and detention by the police.

3.4. Preventive Detention

Detentions can be broadly divided into punitive and preventive detentions. While the former is applicable when a person is alleged to have committed an act in due disregard of law, the latter is aimed at preventing a person from doing anything that may be detrimental to the public order or national security. Though preventive detention is a curse to rule of law, it is a necessary evil to maintain public order and safety. Since it is a repugnance to human rights and liberty of common man, the principle is that the preventive detention is to be used sparingly when there is an imminent danger of public order and safety. However, the wielders of power frequently and grossly misuse preventive detention to suppress the opponents who stand against them. The danger of preventive detention lies on the fact that it is an administrative order and hence, the scope of judicial review is limited. In other words, the court will have the power only to the extent of examining the legality of the decision-making process and not to the legality of the order *per se*. As the phrase "preventive detention" suggests, it is meant for preventing the commission of crimes and hence, this measure cannot be considered as a punitive measure. Article 22 (3) (b) provides that nothing in sub Article (1) and (2) shall apply to any person who is arrested or detained under any law providing for preventive detention. Thus, preventive detention is exempted from the purview of the operation of Article 22 (1) and (2). However, clauses (4) to (7) of Article 22 provides procedures that have to be followed in the event of the arrest and detention under preventive detention laws.

Article 22 was inevitably included in the constitution due to the anxiety of the exception clause under article 21 which provides "except according to the procedure established by law". Thus, there was an apprehension during the constituent Assembly debate that the liberty can be deprived of by any arbitrary law in accordance with the whims and fancies of the ruling government. This led to the incorporation of additional Article 15-A (now Article 22) providing certain procedural requirements and safeguards to the accused and arrested persons under Clause (1) and (2). Article 22 (3) dealing with preventive detention denies the safeguards provided under Clause (1) and (2). The reason for denying such safeguards for the preventively detained persons were explained by Dr. B.R. Ambedkar as the then prevailing circumstances of aftermath of partition of the country that led to the turmoil and communal violence resulting in huge loss to life and property.[149] This shows that the Framers of the Constitution had in their mind the emergence of untoward disturbances to public order and safety and thought of having some guiding principles that could possibly prevent the commission of such disturbances and communal violence before its occurrence. Dr. B.R. Ambedkar argued that in such a state of situation the Parliament must be able to pass laws arming the executive with adequate powers to check these forces of violence, anarchy and disorder.[150] He contended that the interest of the State is of paramount importance over the individual liberty. Nevertheless, he explained that this power of preventive detention had been enclosed in by two limitations : (i) power is limited by three months period of time for detaining a person and if further extension of period is inevitable, the Government must obtain positive report from the Advisory Board constituted for this purpose justifying the continuing of the detention; and (ii) in other cases, the three months period can be extendable for more than three months period only by Parliament by making a legislation in this regards.[151]

3.4.1. Protection against Arbitrary Detention

Article 22 (4) provides that no preventive law shall authorizes a person to be detained for more than three months. However, exception to this general prohibition also is provided under Clause (4). The exceptional situations for exceeding detentions for more than three months are (i) obtaining an opinion from an advisory body consisting of Judges of High Court; or (ii) such person is detained in accordance with the provisions of any law made by Parliament under sub-clauses (a) and (b) of clause (7).[152] It is also made clear that the advisory body shall, in no case, authorize the detention

149. See supra n.113, Constituent Assembly Debate, 15 September, 1949.
150. *Ibid.*
151. *Ibid.*
152. Article 22, Clause (7) provides that the Parliament may by law prescribe- (a) the circumstances under which, and the class or classes of cases in

of any person beyond the maximum period prescribed by any law made by Parliament under sub-clause (b) of clause (7).

Though Clause (1) and (2) of the Article 22 is exempted from the purview of preventive detention, Clause (5) of Article 22 provides certain safeguards even in the case of preventive detention. Article 20 (5) reads:

> When any person is detained in pursuance of an Order made under any law providing for preventive detention, the authority making the Order shall, as soon as may be, communicate to such person the grounds on which the Order has been made and shall afford him the earliest opportunity of making a representation against the Order.

Thus, Article 22(5) of the Constitution provides two categories of protection, namely, (i) the grounds on which the detention Order is passed must be communicated to the detenue as soon as possible; and (ii) earliest opportunity of making representation against the detention Order shall be provided.

A person who has been detained under preventive detention law shall have a right to be supplied copies of all documents, statements and other materials relied upon in the grounds of detention without any delay. The predominant object of communicating the grounds of detention is to enable the detenue at the earliest opportunity to make effective representation against his detention. In *Dr. Ram Krishan Bhardwaj* v. *State of Delhi*[153], the Supreme Court while interpreting Clause (5) held that "preventive detention is a serious invasion of personal liberty and such meager safeguards as the Constitution has provided against the improper exercise of the power must be jealously watched and enforced by the Court".[154] In *Shalini Soni* v. *Union of India*[155] the Supreme Court

---

which, a person may be detained for a period longer than three months under any law providing for preventive detention without obtaining the opinion of an Advisory Board in accordance with the provisions of sub-clause (a) of clause (4); (b) the maximum period for which any person may in any class or classes of cases be detained under any law providing for preventive detention.

153. 1953 S.C.R. 708.
154. *Id.*, p. 713.
155. 1981 S.C.R. (1) 962.

considered the significance of 'communication' and 'representation' in the event of preventive detention of a person. The Court observed:

> Article 22(5) has two facets: (i) communication of the grounds on which the order of detention has been made; (ii) opportunity of making a representation against the order of detention. Communication of the grounds presupposes the formulation of the grounds and formulation of the grounds requires and ensures the application of the mind of the detaining authority to the facts and materials before it, that is to say, to pertinent and proximate matters in regard to each individual case and excludes the elements of arbitrariness and automatism.[156]

While in *Shalini Soni*'s case the Supreme Court was explaining the significance of the right to communication and representation in the case of preventive detention, in *Vijay Kumar* v. *State of J& K*[157] the Supreme Court has elaborated the words used as "earliest opportunity" and held:

> The word "earliest" which qualifies the term "opportunity" must equally qualify the corresponding obligation of the State to deal with the representation if and when made as expeditiously as possible. The jail authorities who are merely a communicating channel have to move with promptitude so that sufficient guarantee of affording earliest opportunity of making the representation and the same reaching the Government is translated into action. The corresponding obligation of the State to consider the representation cannot be whittled down by merely saying that time was lost in transit.[158]

The Supreme Court in this case has reminded of the obligation of the State in affording the earliest opportunity for a person detained under the preventive detention law for making his representation in a court of law.

Thus, the Constitution provides certain safeguards for protecting persons from preventive detention laws. When a preventive detention law authorizes to detain a person, the

156. *Id.*, p. 966.
157. 1982, S.C.R. (3) 522.
158. *Id.*, p. 523.

Constitution provides two important safeguards to the detenue, i.e., (i) the right to know the grounds of detention and (ii) right to make representation. The Supreme Court has also been cautious to extent the safeguards provided under Article 22 relating to preventive detention in protecting the interest of detained persons.

4. CONCLUSION

The Constitutional safeguards that are provided for the arrested or detained persons are set out under the provisions of Articles 20 (3), 21 and 22. Article 20 (3) provides the right against self-incrimination which includes the right to remain silent also. The crucial question before the Supreme Court was whether these rights are available to an accused only during trial before a court or it was available from the stage of investigation by the police. The Supreme Court settled the matter by affirming that these rights are available to the accused from the time the First Information Report is registered by the police.[159] The Supreme Court has broadened the scope of this right in *Nadini Satpathy's* case by holding that this right is available to an accused even when the investigation is initiated by the police. In a very recent case the Supreme Court held that *narco* analysis, polygraph and brain mapping tests are violative of Article 20(3) as the information are obtained without the consent of the accused and are not conclusively reliable.[160] However, Mallimath Committee on Criminal Justice Reform recommended that the accused person is a valuable source of information in a crime, and hence, India should adopt a system where in the statement made to the higher ranking police officer or under the supervision of a Magistrate shall be made valid. However, the Law Commission of India rejected the recommendation of Mallimath Committee as a dilution of 'right to remain silent' which will jeopardize the accused persons.[161]

Right to life and personal liberty is an important safeguard provided under the Indian Constitution. Article 21 of the Constitution of India provides that right to life and personal liberty shall not be curtailed to any person except according to the procedure established by law. Initially, in *A.K. Gopalan's* case[162] the Supreme

159. See *supra* n. 17.
160. See *supra* n. 29.
161. Law Commission of India, 180th Report on Article 20(3) of the Constitution of India and the Right to Silence (2002), p. 2.
162. See *supra* n. 47.

Court interpreted the provision narrowly and held that the liberty denotes merely freedom from bodily restraint, any law passed by parliament can take away the personal liberty as provided under Article 21. However, Fazal Ali J delivering minority judgment ruled that 'law' which curtails the liberty must be valid and the 'procedure' that takes away the liberty must be fair. The Supreme Court took a different view from *A.K. Gopalan*'s case in *Maneka Gandhi*'s case,[163] and held that the law which takes away or abridges the liberty must be "just, fair and reasonable" and not "arbitrary, oppressive and fanciful". The Court observed that Article 21 encompasses those rights and privileges which have long been recognized as being essential to the orderly pursuit of happiness by free men. The *ratio* in *Maneka Gandhi*'s case has played a vital role in the growth and development of human rights in India including the protection of human rights from being violated by the police.

Article 22 provides safeguards against arbitrary arrest and detention. Article 22 (1) an (2) provides that the arrested person has a right to know the grounds of arrest, to consult and to be defended by a lawyer, to be produced before a Magistrate within twenty-four hours. Clauses (4) to (7) of Article 22 provides procedures that have to be followed in the event of the arrest and detention under preventive detention laws. The Article 22(5) of the Constitution provides two categories of protection in the event of preventive detention, namely, (i) the grounds on which the detention order is passed must be communicated to the detenue as soon as possible; and (ii) earliest opportunity of making representation against the detention order shall be provided. The Supreme Court held that preventive detention is a serious invasion of personal liberty and such meager safeguards as the Constitution has provided against the improper exercise of the power must be jealously watched and enforced by the courts.

Thus, the analysis above clearly reveals that the Constitution of India provides a number of safeguards against arbitrary arrest and illegal detention. The interpretations of Article 20 (3), 21 and 22 by the Supreme Court has added strength and meaning to these safeguards of the rights of arrested and detained persons. However, there have always been hue and cries about human rights violations by police.

163. See *supra* n. 43.

5

Statutory Protection of Human Rights and the Police

Apart from the Constitutional safeguards, the Indian legal framework provides elaborate provisions in relation to the protection of human rights of accused, arrested or detained persons and the procedural formalities that are to be complied with in the event of arrest, detention or interrogations. These provisions can be found primarily in the Code of Criminal Procedure, 1973 as amended in 2005, 2008 and 2010, Indian Evidence Act, 1872, and Indian Penal Code, 1860. In addition to these laws, Indian Police Act, 1861 and State Police Acts provide organization and structure of police force in India and the States respectively. Protection of Human Rights Act, 1993 is a special Act which was enacted to create institutions such as National Human Rights Commission and State Human Rights Commissions for the protection of human rights of the persons from various spheres including from the police. The legislature intended to make such laws with a view to avoid arbitrary interrogation, arrest and detention by the police and unnecessary intrusion into the privacy of persons. Though the legal framework envisions protecting the innocent and accused persons from the high handedness of police, yet there take place many violations of human rights of people by the police. Illegal arrest, arbitrary interrogation, unlawful detention, torture, custodial violence, false implication, fake encounters, extortions, etc., are the chief violations of human rights perpetrated by the police. An analysis of relevant provisions of these Codes and Acts would enlighten how far and to what extent the statutory ptovisions could protect the human rights of persons, and the merits and demerits of following such provisions.

I. SAFEGUARDS FROM ARREST AND DETENTION

Procedural aspect of arrest, detention, search and seizure by the police affect liberty, dignity and human rights of individuals. It is essential to provide effective procedural requirements and proper control of exercise of power by the police in making arrest, detention, search and seizure for effective administration of criminal justice in any country. Code of Criminal Procedure in India provides a large number of provisions in order to control arbitrary arrest, capricious interrogation, illegal detention, unlawful search and seizure, etc.

Arrest and Detention are the procedures by which an offender is taken into custody thereby depriving his liberties. It becomes essential for either the prevention of commission of crime or the continuance of commission of crime, or enabling investigation to be carried out without interruption, or producing the evading offender before the judicial or other authorities. It, then, becomes indispensable to empower the police with ample powers to arrest and detain a person and in case of resistance from the offender, even to use force or firearms in appropriate cases. Vesting of such discretionary powers with the police is justified in any democratic set up of the country for the safety and security of the members of the society. However, arrest and detention are those areas which attract much criticism due to the abuse of power by the police on the one hand and its necessary effect on the deprivation of liberty of persons on the other hand.

I.I. Report of Commissions on Arrest and Detention

Irrespective of procedural requirements for carrying out arrest and detention, there takes place large number of arbitrary arrests and illegal detentions. As mentioned earlier, the National Police Commission in its Third Report, suggested that by and large nearly 60 percent of the arrests were either unnecessary or unjustified and that such unjustified police actions accounted for 43.2 percent of the expenditure of the prison department.[1] Thus, the National Police Commission recommended for reducing the arresting and detaining power of the police.

Generally, the police making the arrest and detention do not take into consideration the personal and psychological aspects of the arrestee. How the arrest affects the persons psychologically, personally and the attitudes of the police are depicted by the Mallimath Committee in the following words :

> Power of arrest is often misused. The person arrested apart from suffering considerable inconvenience, also suffers by loss of his image in the society. Even if ultimately he is found to be innocent that damage done to the arrested person cannot be undone. There is an erroneous impression in the minds of the police that the first thing for him to do is to arrest the suspected person even without making any inquiry. It may be necessary to arrest the person when the offence involved is fairly serious and the accused is likely to abscond or evade the process of law or there is reasonable apprehension of the accused committing offences or when he would be a serious threat to the victim, or witnesses, or is likely to tamper the evidence, or when it is necessary in the circumstances to restore a sense of security in the locality and similar other considerations as pointed out by the Law Commission in its 154th report.[2]

The Law Commission in its 152nd report made recommendations to make the arrest more transparent by intimating relatives or friends by the police officer arresting the person.[3] Further, in its 154th report the Law Commission recommended that when an arrest of women is to be made, it shall be done by a female police officer only, and if male officer is making arrest, he shall not touch the body of the woman.[4]

Arrest is a major area where police commit breach of human rights violations in total disregard of the arrestee's personal, physiological, physical conditions and status. Different Commissions and Committees recommended for the reform of the arrest and detention laws and procedures. Recently, Code of Criminal Procedure has been amended in 2005, 2008 and 2010 to incorporate

1. Government of India, Third Report : National Police Commission (Ministry of Home Affairs, 1980), pp. 30-31.
2. *Id.*, p. 115.
3. Law Commission of India, 152nd Report (1994), p. 172.
4. *Id.*, 154th Report (1996), p.13.

many of the recommendations and also the directions of the Supreme Court in different cases such as *Sheela Barse*,[5] *Joginder Kumar*[6] and *D.K Basu*[7] on arrest and detention.

1.2. Protection from Arbitrary Arrest and Detention

The Code of Criminal Procedure does not define the term ''arrest'', though Section 46 details "arrest how made". Arrest ordinarily coveys the meaning of depriving of the liberty by virtue of legal authority. Thus, if the arrest is not made under a legal authority or misuse the legal authority for making arrest, it cannot be considered as an "arrest" in the legal sense. It can only be considered as illegal confinement in accordance with the provisions of Indian Penal Code or as a subject matter of tort. Sections 41-50, 53-60, 76, 89, and 151 deal with powers to arrest a person and the procedure to be complied with in the event of making an arrest of a person.

The Code Criminal Procedure (Amendment) Act, 2010[8] has made substantial amendments in Section 41 of the Criminal Procedure Code relating to the power of police officer to arrest without warrant. The Amendment intended that the powers of arrest

5. See supra Ch. 4 n.99.
6. See supra Ch. 5 n.82.
7. See supra Ch. 5 n. 86.
8. In the light of recommendations of the National Police Commissions, Law Commission of India, the Mallimath Committee on Criminal Justice reform and in the wake of the guidelines issued by the Supreme Court in Joginder Kumar's and D.K Basu's cases, the Parliament made Amendments in the Code of Criminal Procedure in 2005, 2008 and in 2010. The Criminal Procedure Code (Amendment) Act, 2005 and 2008 provided comprehensive changes for making the criminal justice system more effective. However, there was stiff opposition from lawyers relating to arrest (Section 5 of Amendment Act, 2008), notice of appearance before a police officer (Section 6 of Amendment Act, 2008) and adjournments (Section 21 (b) of the Amendment Act, 2008), and urged the government not to notify these amended laws and hence, the Government decided not to notify Sections 5, 6 and 21 (b) then (See Code of Criminal Procedure (Amendment) Act, 2010, Statement of Objects and Reason, p. 3.). The other amended provisions of the Code of Criminal Procedure (Amendment) Act 2008 came into effect from December 31, 2009. The matter related with Sections 5, 6 and 21 (b) was then referred to the Law commission of India to take the initiative to bring about a consensus on the issues. Law Commission recommended certain changes and the changes recommended were incorporated into the Amendment Act of 2010 and the Code of Criminal Procedure (Amendment) Act, 2010 came into effect from 1st November 2011.

conferred upon the police officer must be exercised after reasonable care and justification. The major change that is made in relation to arrest is in sections 41, 41-A, 41-B, 41-C and 41-D. One of the important changes is that it is now compulsory for the police to record the reasons both for making as well as for not making an arrest on the basis of a complaint or information or reasonable suspicion in respect of a cognizable offence for which the maximum punishment prescribed is 7 years or less. Hence, no person can be arrested for a complaint or suspicion of involvement in such an offence without a warrant. However, there are certain exceptions to this rule where in the police officer can arrest a person without a warrant and the circumstances are provided in the substituted Section 41(1)(b) which provides that when a person commits a cognizable offence in the presence of a police officer; or the police officer has reason to believe that such person has committed the offence and is satisfied that such arrest is necessary in the following situations:

(i) to prevent such person from committing any further offence; or
(ii) for proper investigation of the offence; or
(iii) to prevent such person from causing the evidence of the offence to disappear or tampering;
(iv) to prevent such person from making any inducement, threat or promise to any person acquainted with the facts of the case; or
(v) to ensure his presence before the court as and when required;

However, the provision provides that the reasons for the arrest should be sound and recorded in writing by the police officer. In all cases where the arrest of a person is not required, the police officer shall record the reasons in writing for not making the arrest. Section 41-A provides that in all cases where the arrest of a person is not required under the provisions of Sub-section 1 of Section 41, the police officer shall, issue a notice directing the person to appear before him and to comply with the terms of notice. He can be arrested if such person fails to comply with such direction. No arrest will be made in a non-cognizable offence except under a warrant or order of a Magistrate. Section 41-B provides that the police officer while making the arrest shall : (a) bear an accurate, visible and clear identification of his name for easy identification, (b) prepare a memorandum of arrest which shall be attested by at least one witness and counter signed by the person arrested, (c) inform the person arrested that he has a right to have a relative or a friend named by him to be informed of his arrest. Section 41-D provides that when any person is arrested for any offence and interrogated by the police, he shall be entitled to meet an advocate of his choice during interrogation, though not throughout the interrogation.

The Amended provisions of arrest and detention are humanistic and afford reasonable protection from the police by loosening the power of arrest by police in crimes carrying upto seven years imprisonment. However, it can be misused over its discretionary powers to shield the culprits by the police department as well as politicians and could give a free hand to gangsters, anti-socials and habitual offenders without any fear of being arrested. It would remove the fear or deterrence from the minds of criminals who will misuse the provisions under the cover of personal liberty. However, it must be appreciated that the Amended provisions of arrest and detention aim at reducing arbitrary arrests and illegal detentions by the police. The Amendment is expected to reduce corruption and extortions in police stations and will also decrease the number of false complaints.

As per Section 46, a police officer is empowered to use all means necessary to effect the arrest in case of a person forcibly resists the arrest of him, or attempts to evade the arrest. In the event of arrest, Section 50 of the Code of Criminal Procedure casts a duty on police officer making arrest to inform the arrestee of the ground of his arrest and of the right to be released on bail on arrest if the case is one of bailable offence. Similarly, Section 56 of the Code of Criminal Procedure expressly provides that on arrest, a person shall be produced before the nearest Magistrate within 24 hours of his arrest, excluding time taken for journey in bringing him before the Judicial Magistrate.[9] This provision corresponds to Article 22 (2) of the Constitution of India. Section 49 further casts a responsibility on the police that the arrested person shall not be subjected to more restraint than what is necessary to prevent his escape.

Section 167 provides safeguards to accused person when investigation cannot be completed within twenty-four hours. It provides that whenever the investigation cannot be completed in twenty-four hours and there is reasonable ground for believing that the accusations are well founded, the accused person shall be brought

9. Code of Criminal Procedure, S. 57 and 76.

to the Magistrate and the Magistrate, if necessary, may authorize to keep the accused person in custody under detention. This provides a judcial control over the rights of arrested person where the investigation is prolonged beyond twenty-four hours.

1.3. Special Procedure for Arrest and Detention of Woman

The Code of Criminal Procedure (Amendment) Act, 2005 and 2008 provides a number of safeguards and special treatments that have to be made in arresting or detaining women. After the Amendment in 2005, Section 46 of the Code of Criminal Procedure provides that no woman shall be arrested after sunset and before sunrise. If such exceptional circumstances exist to arrest a woman during this period, the woman police officer shall, by making a written report, obtain the prior permission of the Judicial Magistrate within whose local jurisdiction the offence is committed or the arrest is to be made. Section 46 further provides that where a woman is to be arrested, unless the circumstances indicate to the contrary, her submission to custody on an oral intimation of arrest shall be presumed. The provision prohibits the touching of the body of the women by a male police officer in making an arrest, unless the circumstances otherwise require. This provision has been incorporated on the basis of the recommendations of the 154th Report of the Law Commission of India. Further, Section 167 now provides that in case of arrest of a woman under eighteen years of age, the detention shall be authorized to be in the custody of a remand home or recognized social institution. The new Amendment also incorporates the Supreme Court guidelines in *Sheela Barse* v. *State of Maharashtra*[10] in arresting and detaining women. The Code of

10. In Sheela Barse's case, the Supreme Court has provided guidelines to be followed if arrested person is a woman such as : (i) when the circumstances so requires that she shall be kept in police station under detention, she must be kept in a separate lock-up separated from male suspects, (ii) if separate lock-ups are not available in a police station and the circumstances so warrants that she is required to be kept in police lock-up, she may be transferred to the nearest police station where separate women lock-up is available, (iii) the interrogation of a woman suspect shall be carried out only in the presence of a female police officer or constable, (iv) if, at any time during interrogation, she needs or wants to consult a lawyer, she shall be given the opportunity to do so.

Criminal Procedures provides that every woman who is a suspect and is required to be searched shall be searched by a female only and in strict regard to decency.[11]

Thus, the Criminal Procedure Code, now, after the amendments provides elaborate safeguards in relation to arrest and detention. It provides special treatment and precautions to women in the event of being arrested by the police. After the Amendments, the Code of Criminal Procedure makes the arrest and detention more transparent and tries to avoid arbitrary arrest and illegal detention. It makes the police officials more accountable in the making of arrest and detention.

2. SAFEGUARDS FROM ARREST AND DETENTION OF CHILDREN

The Safeguards from Arrest and Detention of Children[12] was made repealing the earlier Juvenile Justice Act of 1986. The Act was made in compliance with the U.N. Convention on the Rights of the Child 1989. The Act provides for a special approach towards the prevention and treatment of juvenile delinquency and affords a framework for the protection, treatment and rehabilitation of children within the purview of the juvenile justice system. The Juvenile Justice (Care and Protection of Children) Act, 2000 was amended in 2006.[13] In the case of arrest and detention of juveniles, normal criminal procedures of arrest and detention are not applicable. Special procedures are laid down in the Juvenile Justice (Care and Protection of Children) Act.

Section 18 of the Juvenile Justice (Care and Protection of Children) Act specifically provides that no child shall be kept in police lock-up or jail, what ever may be the crime committed by the child. Children shall be dealt with by specially trained Juvenile Police officer only.[14] The Act further provides that when any juvenile is accused of a bailable or non- bailable offence and is arrested by a police officer, the police officer arresting the juvenile shall produce him immediately to the Magistrate.[15] If it is not possible for the police

11. *Id.*, S. 51.
12. Act 56 of 2000.
13. The Juvenile Justice (Care and Protection of Children) Act, 2000 was amended by the Juvenile Justice (Care and Protection of Children) Amendment Act, 2006 (33 of 2006).
14. Juvenile Justice (Care and Protection of Children) Act, S. 63(1).
15. *Id.*, S. 18 (1).

officer to bring the juvenile to the Magistrate immediately, the police officer shall cause him to be kept in an observation home or a place of safety until he can be brought before a Juvenile Court.[16] The juvenile shall not be kept in police station or jail in any circumstances. Section 19 states that where a juvenile is arrested, the officer-in-charge of the police station to which the juvenile is brought shall, as soon as may be after the arrest, inform : (a) The parent or guardian of the juvenile, if he can be found, of such arrest and direct him to be present at the Juvenile Court before which the juvenile will be brought; and (b) The probation officer in order to enable him to obtain information regarding the antecedents and family history of the juvenile and other material circumstances likely to be of assistance of the Juvenile Court for making the inquiry. The law is made children-friendly due to the vulnerability and their feeble mind by which they are easily susceptible to any circumstance-good or bad. However, there are number of incidents of violating the procedure of handling of juveniles by the police. Though the law is as above, many a times, the police officer making the arrest of juvenile, while preparing First Information Report, may bring the age of juvenile into adult.

3. PROTECTION BY PENALISING VIOLATIONS

The Indian Penal Code does not explicitly provide provisions for criminal offence of arbitrary arrest or illegal detention or torture committed by the police officers. However, the Indian Penal Code contains many criminal provisions that could be utilized against police in the case of illegal arrest, unlawful detention, torture, assault, etc. The Indian Penal Code provides certain provisions that might have relevance in taking criminal action against the police who commit violation of human rights and these provisions are:

(i) Public servant concealing design to commit offence which it is his duty to prevent (Section 119).[17]

16. *Id.*, S. 18 (2).
17. Section 119 of the Indian Penal Code provides that " whoever, being a public servant intending to facilitate or knowing it to be likely that he will thereby facilitate the commission of an offence which it is his duty as such public servant to prevent, voluntarily conceals, by any act or illegal omission, the existence of a design to commit such offence, or makes any representation which he knows to be false respecting such design; and-shall, if the offence be committed, be punished with imprisonment of any description provided for the offence, for a term

(ii) Public servant disobeying law, with intent to cause injury to any person (Section 166).[18]

(iii) Prohibition of public servant requiring attendance of persons (Section 166-A).[19]

(iv) If the policeman causes death of a person in custody, it may amount to either culpable homicide (Section 299);[20] or, murder (Section 300)[21] or causing death by negligence

---

which may extend to one-half of the longest term of such imprisonment, or with such fine as is provided for that offence, or with both"; or if the offence be punishable with death or imprisonment for life, with imprisonment of either description for a term which may extend to ten years; or, if the offence be not committed, shall be punished with imprisonment of any description provided for the offence for a term which may extend to one-fourth part of the longest term of such imprisonment or with such fine as is provided for the offence.

18. Section 166 of the Indian Penal Code provides "whoever, being a public servant, knowingly disobeys any direction of the law as to the way in which he is to conduct himself as such public servant, intending to cause, or knowing it to be likely that he will, by such disobedience, cause injury to any person, shall be punished with simple imprisonment for a term which may extend to one year, or with fine, or with both".

19. Inserted by the Criminal Law Amendment Act, 2013. Section 166A makes liable the police officer knowingly disobey any direction of law which prohibits him from requiring the attendance at any place of any person for the purpose of investigation into an offence or any other matter or knowingly disobeys, to the prejudice of any person, any direction of the law regulating the manner in which he shall conduct such investigation or fails to record any information given to him under Sub-section (1) of 154 of the Code of Criminal Procedure in relation to congnizable offence punishable under Section 326A, Section 326B, Section 354, Section 354B, Section 370, Section 376, Section 376A, Section 376B, Section 376C, Section 376D, Section 376E or Section 509. The punishment prescribed for such offence is rigorous imprisonment for a term which shall not be less than six months but which may extend to two years and shall be liable to fine.

20. Section 299 of the Indian Penal Code provides "whoever causes death by doing an act with the intention of causing death, or with the intention of causing such bodily injury as is likely to cause death, or with the knowledge that he is likely by such act to cause death, commits the offence of culpable homicide".

21. Section 300 of the Indian Penal Code provides "except in the cases hereinafter excepted, culpable homicide is murder, if the act by which the death is caused is done with the intention of causing death, or 2ndly. If it is done with the intention of causing such bodily injury as theoffender knows to be likely to cause the death of the person to whom the harm is caused, or 3rdly. If it is done with the intention of causing bodily

(Section 304-A).[22]

(v) Voluntarily causing "hurt" (Section 319).[23]

(vi) Voluntarily causing "grievous hurt" (Section 320).[24]

(vii) Voluntarily causing "hurt" to extort confession or to compel restoration of property (Section 330).[25]

(viii) Voluntarily causing "grievous hurt" to extort confession or to compel restoration of property (Section 331).[26]

---

injury to any person and the bodily injury intended to be inflicted is sufficient in the ordinary course of nature to cause death,....and commits such act without any excuse for incurring the risk of causing death or such injury as aforesaid".

22. Section 304-A of the Indian Penal Code provides "whoever causes the death of any person by doing any rash or negligent act not amounting to culpable homicide shall be punished with imprisonment of either description for a term which may extend to two years, or with fine."
23. Section 319 of the Indian Penal Code defines hurt as "whoever causes bodily pain, disease or infirmity to any person is said to cause hurt"
24. Section 320 of the Indian Penal Code defines "grievous hurt" as emasculation or permanent privation of the sight of either eye, or Permanent privation of the hearing of either ear, or Privation of any member or joint,or permanent impairing of the powers of any member or joint or Permanent disfiguration of the head or face or Fracture or dislocation of a bone or tooth or any hurt which endangers life or which causes the sufferer to be during the space of twenty days in severe bodily pain, or unable to follow his ordinary pursuits".
25. Section 330 of the Indian Penal Code provides "Whosoever voluntarily causes hurt for the purpose of extorting from the sufferer, or from any person interested in the sufferer, any confession or any information which may lead to the detention of any offence or misconduct, or for the purpose of constraining the sufferer or any person interested in the sufferer to restore or to cause the restoration of any property or valuable security or to satisfy any claim or demand, or to give information which may lead to the restoration of any property or valuable security, shall be punished with imprisonment of either description for a term which may extend to seven years, and shall also be liable to fine."
26. Section 331 of the Indian Penal Code provides "Whoever voluntarily causes grievous hurt for the purpose of extorting from the sufferer or from any person interested in the sufferer any confession or any information which may lead to the detection of an offence or misconduct, or for the purpose of constraining the sufferer or any person interested in the sufferer to restore or to cause the restoration of any property or valuable security, or to satisfy any claim or demand or to give information which may lead to the restoration of any property or valuable security shall be punished with imprisonment of either description for a term which may extend to ten years, and shall also be liable to fine".

(ix) Wrongful confinement (Section 340).[27]

(x) Wrongful confinement to extort confession, or compel restoration of property (Section 348).[28]

(xi) Criminal force (Section 350).[29]

(xii) Assault (Section 351).[30]

(xiii) Assault or criminal force in attempt to wrongfully confine a person (Section 357).[31]

(xiv) Assault or criminal use of force with intent to dishonour a person (Section 356).[32]

---

27. Section 340 of the IPC provides "Whoever wrongfully restrains any person in such a manner as to prevent that person from proceeding beyond certain circumscribing limits, is said "wrongfully to confine" that person".
28. Section 348 of the Indian Penal Code provides "Whoever wrongfully confines any person for the purpose of extorting from the person confined, or any person interested in the person confined, any confession or any information which may lead to the detection of an offence or misconduct, or for the purpose of constraining the person confined or any person interested in the person confined or restore or to cause the restoration of any property or valuable security.or to satisfy any claim or demand, or to give information which may lead to the restoration of any property or valuable security, shall be punished with imprisonment of either description for a term which may extend to three years, and shall be liable to fine."
29. Section 350 of the Indian Penal Code provides "Whoever intentionally uses force to any person, without that person's consent, in order to the committing of any offence, or intending by the use of such force to cause, or knowing it to be likely that by the use of such force he will cause injury, fear or annoyance to the person to whom the force is used, is said to use criminal force to that other.
30. Section 351 provides" whoever makes any gesture, or any preparation intending or knowing it to be likely that such gesture or preparation will cause any person present to apprehend that he who makes that gesture or preparation is about to use criminal force to that person, is said to commit an assault.
31. Section 357 of the Indian Penal Code provides "whoever assaults or uses criminal force to any person, in attempting wrongfully to confine that person, shall be punished with imprisonment of either description for a term which may extend to one year, or with fine which may extend to one thousand rupees, or with both"
32. Section 356 of the Indian Penal Code provides "whoever assaults or uses criminal force to any person, intending thereby to dishonour that person, otherwise than on grave and sudden provocation given by that person, shall be punished with imprisonment of either description for a term which may extend to two years, or with fine, or with both".

(xv) Rape Committed in police custody (Section 376 (2) (a)).[33]

(xvi) Assault or criminal force to woman with intent to outrage her modesty. (Section 354).[34]

3.1. The Punishments for the Violations

The above Penal Code provisions are generally applicable in the cases connected with illegal arrest, unlawful detention, assault, torture, causing death, rape in custody by the police, etc. The punishments prescribed for public servant concealing design to commit offence which it is his duty to prevent under Section 119 of the Indian Penal Code are classified into three categories, namely, (i) if the offence is committed, the offender public servant shall be punished with imprisonment of any description provided for the offence for a term which may extend to one-half of the longest term of such imprisonment, or with such fine as is provided for that offence, or with both; or (ii) if the offence be punishable with death or imprisonment for life, the offender public servant shall be punished with imprisonment for a term which may extend to ten years; or (iii) if the offence is not committed, the offender public servant shall be punished with imprisonment of any description provided for the offence for a term which may extend to one-fourth part of the longest term of such imprisonment or with such fine as is provided for the offence, or with both.[35] Similarly, public servant disobeying law with intent to cause injury to any person is punished with simple imprisonment for a term which may extend to one year and/or with fine.[36] The punishment prescribed for voluntarily causing hurt to extort confession or to compel restoration of property is seven years and with fine.[37] If the hurt caused is grievous

33. Section 376(2) (a) of the Indian Penal Code provides "whoever being a police officer commits rape-(i) within the limits of the police station to which he is appointed; or(ii) in the premises of any station house whether or not situated in the police station to which he is appointed; or(iii) on a woman in his custody or in the custody of a police officer subordinate to him".

34. Section 354 of the Indian Penal Code provides "Whoever assaults or uses criminal force to any woman, intending to outrage or knowing it to be likely that he will there by outrage her modesty, shall be punished with imprisonment of either description for a term which may extend to two years, or with fine, or with both".

35. *See* Indian Penal Code, S. 119.

36. *Id.*, S. 166.

37. *Id.*, S. 330.

one to extort confession or to compel restoration of property, the maximum punishment is ten years imprisonment and fine.[38] Wrongful confinement to extort confession or compel restoration of property carries a maximum punishment of three years imprisonment and liability to pay a fine.[39]

The police officers are generally known for using assault or criminal use of force to intimidate the accused or witnesses to elicit information. Assault or criminal force is attempted wrongfully to confine a person carries imprisonment for a term which may extend to one year and/or with fine which may extend to one thousand rupees.[40] Assault or criminal force with intent to dishonour a person under section 356 prescribes punishment with imprisonment for a term which may extend to two years and/or fine. Culpable homicide, depending on the circumstances, carries punishment ranging from various terms of imprisonment up to imprisonment for life and fine.[41] Murder which covers acts where the offender intended to cause death or inflicted bodily injury or committed other acts sufficient or likely to cause death is punishable with death or life imprisonment and a fine.[42] However, culpable homicide is not murder if the offender, being a public servant or aiding a public servant acting for the advancement of public justice, exceeds the power given to him by law, and causes death by committing an act which he, in good faith, believes to be lawful and necessary for the due discharge of his duty.[43] If death is caused by negligence, the maximum punishment is imprisonment for two years and/or a fine.[44]

---

38. *Id.*, S.331.
39. Section 348 of the Indian Penal Code provides "whoever wrongfully confines any person for the purpose of extorting from the person confined, or any person interested in the person confined, any confession or any information which may lead to the detection of an offence or misconduct, or for the purpose of constraining the person confined or any person interested in the person confined or restore or to cause the restoration of any property or valuable security or to satisfy any claim or demand, or to give information which may lead to the restoration of any property or valuable security, shall be punished with imprisonment of either description for a term which may extend to three years, and shall be liable to fine".
40. *See* Indian Penal Code, S. 357.
41. *Id.*, S. 299 and 304.
42. *Id.*, S. 300 and 302.
43. *Id.*, S. 300, exception 3.
44. *Id.*, S. 304.

3.1.1. Punishment for Custodial Violence against Woman

Assault or criminal force to a woman with intent to outrage her modesty is punishable with imprisonment which may extend to two years and/or with fine.[45] Rape carries a punishment ranging from seven years to life imprisonment.[46] After the controversial *Mathura rape* case,[47] an amendment was brought about in Sec. 376 of the Indian Penal Code. Sec. 376(2) (a) now penalizes custodial rape committed by police officers. This has been made after a hue and cry raised by public aftermath of acquittal of police officials who committed rape on a 16 year old girl named Mathura in police custody taking the advantage of police authority. After the amendment, rape in custody is considered to be an aggravating circumstance carrying a heavier punishment. The new amendments of Code of Criminal Procedure, 2005 incorporated into it the recommendations of the National Police Commission (Fourth Report) and the amendment to Section 176 now provides for mandatory judicial inquiries in all incidents of custodial rapes.

The provisions in the Indian Penal Code which specifically deal with police atrocities and human rights violations committed by police in custody are very few. The general provisions dealing with hurt, murder, culpable homicide, assault, wrongful confinement, etc., is used for the purpose of prosecuting the erring police personnel. This, sometimes, creates anomaly due to the fact that the police generally commit atrocities in the custody where there are no independent witnesses. When the normal provisions are made applicable, it may not be easily proved before a court of law and the police will always be in an advantageous position due to the lack of witnesses and evidences. Hence, there requires special laws to tackle the situations of human rights violations committed by the police.

4. CONFESSION TO POLICE: JUDICIAL APPROACH

The areas that come in touch with the Indian Evidence Act, 1872 and human rights violations by the police are 'confessions' made to police and 'presumptions' in the case of custodial violence against women. Custodial confessions are always controversial, though presumption as to consent of the woman sparingly comes for decision. The Indian Evidence Act does not define the term

45. *See* Indian Penal Code, S. 354.
46. *Id.*, S.375 and 376 (2).
47. *Id.*, S.375 and 376 (2).

'Confession". Nevertheless, the Act provides generally that the confession made under threat, promise or undue influence as inadmissible.[48] Further, the confession made to a police officer is altogether inadmissible. Section 25 provides: "confession made to a police officer is not admissible in evidence". It is also provided by the Act that confession made to any person while in the custody of the police is also not admissible.[49] However, any recovery made on the basis of information given by the accused is proved in trial against him.[50] Thus, in India, the confessions made to a police officer or to any other person while in the police custody, are inadmissible. But this is not the position in other parts of the World. Singapore, which virtually follows the same system as ours, has empowered the Sergeant-level officers to record confessional statements.[51] Indian legal system does not admit the validity of confession made to the police due to the apprehension that police may use force, threat or torture to extract confession.

However, confessions made to certain law enforcement agencies are made admissible in evidence in India such as (i) Section 9 of the Railway Property (Unlawful Possession) Act, 1996[52] (ii) Section 108 of the Customs Act, 1962;[53] and (iii) Section 32 of POTA, 2002.[54]

4.1. Supreme Court on the Admissibility of Confession to the Police

Terrorist and Disruptive Activities (Prevention) Act, 1987

48. (1979) 2 SCC 143.
49. Indian Evidence Act, S. 24.
50. *Id.*, S. 26.
51. Michael Hor, The Confessions Regime in Singapore, Malayan Law Journal (1991), p. 3.
52. Section 9(3), the Railway Property (Unlawful Possession) Act, 1996 provides"..... all persons so summoned shall be bound to state the truth upon any subject respecting which they are examined or make statements and to produce such documents and other things as may be required".
53. Section 108(3), The Customs Act, 1962 provides "... all persons so summoned shall be bound to state the truth upon any subject respecting which they are examined or make statements and produce such documents and other things as may be required".
54. Section 32(3)(a), Prevention of Terrorism Act, 2002 provides "any person who has been convicted of a conspiracy to commit any of the offences under sections 3, 4, 5, 6, 7, 11, 12, 14, or 15 shall be exempted from penalty as specified in subsection (1) and absolutely discharged if, having revealed the conspiracy to the police or to the Court, he has made it possible to prevent the commission of the offence and to identify the other persons involved in the conspiracy".

(TADA)[55] also contained provisions for the admissibility of the confession, but TADA expired on May 23, 1995. However, it is worth noting that section 18 of the TADA provided for the admissibility of confessional statements made to police officers. The constitutionality of the section 18 was challenged in *Kartar Singh* v. *State of Punjab.*[56] The Supreme Court while upholding the validity of section 18 laid down guidelines so as to ensure that the confession obtained in the pre-indictment interrogation by a police officer not lower in rank than a Superintendent of Police is not tainted with any vice but is in strict conformity of the well-recognized and accepted aesthetic principles and fundamental fairness. The guidelines laid down by the Supreme Court are:

(i) The confession should be recorded in a free atmosphere in the same language in which the person is examined and as narrated by him;

(ii) The person from whom a confession has been recorded under section 15(1) of the Act, should be produced before the Chief Metropolitan Magistrate or the Chief Judicial Magistrate to whom the confession is required to be sent under Rule 15(5) along with the original statement of confession, written or recorded on mechanical device without unreasonable delay;

(iii) The Chief Metropolitan Magistrate or the Chief Judicial Magistrate should scrupulously record the statement, if any, made by the accused so produced and get his signature, and in case of any complaint of torture, the person should be directed to be produced for medical examination before a Medical Officer not lower in rank than of an Assistant Civil Surgeon;

(iv) Notwithstanding anything contained in the Code of Criminal Procedure, no police officer below the rank of an Assistant Commissioner of Police in the Metropolitan

55. The Terrorist and Disruptive Activities (Prevention) Act was enacted on May 23, 1985 to combat disruptive and terrorist activities posing a serious threat to the integrity of the country initially for a period of two years applicable to Punjab only. However, in the context of continued terrorist violence and disruption in the country, a new legislation, Terrorist and Disruptive Activities (Prevention) Act was enacted in 1987 for the whole of India.

56. (1994) 3 S.C.C. 569.

cities and elsewhere of a Deputy Superintendent of Police or a Police Officer of equivalent rank, should investigate any offence punishable under this Act of 1987;

(v) In case, the person, taken for interrogation, on receipt of the statutory warning that he is not bound to make a confession and that if he does so, the said statement may be used against him as evidence, asserts his right to silence, the police must respect his right of assertion without making any compulsion to give a statement of disclosure.[57]

Thus, the Supreme Court favoured for admitting the statement made to higher ranking police officers in certain cases of complex nature, but, at the same time, the Court insisted that the right to silence of the accused should be respected and the police should make sure that there was no compulsion to make the statement. This view has been taken due to the growing organized terrorist and disruptive acts that take place frequently in the country.

4.2. Law Commission on Confession to the Police

The Law Commission in its 48th Report had recommended that the confession recorded by a Superintendent of Police or a higher ranking police officer should be made admissible in evidence subject to the condition that the accused is informed of his right to remain silent and to consult a legal practitioner.[58] Justice Mallimath Committee has also made recommendations in its Report that officers of the level of Superintendents of Police or higher level police officers shall be entrusted to record confessions fairly and without subjecting the accused to duress or inducement. If the confession is audio/video recorded, it would lend further assurance that the accused was not subjected to any form of compulsion. Hence, Mallimath Committee recommended that section 25 of the Indian Evidence Act may suitably be substituted by a provision rendering the confessions made before a police officer of the rank of Superintendent of Police and above as admissible. It also recommended that provisions should also be made to enable audio/video recording of statements made to police as admissible in evidence. However, the Law Commission of India in its 180th Report changed its earlier stand in 48th Report and rejected the recommendation of Mallimath Committee that confession made to

57. See supra Ch. 4 n. 35 p.,222.

58. Law Commission of India, 48th Report (1972), p. 4.

high ranking police officer should be made admissible on the ground that it adversely affect the accused person's civil liberties.

It is to be noted that Mallimath Committee, it seems, did not give due consideration of the fact that in India, even higher police officials are also not absolutely free from corruption and/or have secret political nexus which may be used for harrassment of innocent persons. If the recommendation of the Mallimath Committee is accepted, police may use the power for trapping innocent persons. Though the custodial torture is not expressly prohibited by law in India, the evidence collected by illegal means such as extraction of confession by torture, threat, etc., is not accepted and is not admissible. At the same time, judicial confessions are admissible and considered as a valid piece of evidence. It seems that the existing position is better from the point of view of human rights of accused, arrested or detained persons.

5. TORTURE AND CRIMINAL LAW

Police use torture for various purposes such as extraction of confession, means of retaliation, bribery by the opposite party, political influence by the opposite party, etc. Since the police notoriously use torture as a means to extract confession, the Indian Evidence Act makes the confessions made to police as inadmissible.[59] The Indian Penal Code does not contain a definition of "torture" nor uses the term "torture". However, the Indian Penal Code contains provisions such as hurt,[60] grievous hurt,[61] hurt or grievous hurt to extract confession,[62] a public servant disobeying the law with intent to cause injury,[63] assault,[64] etc., as amounting to torture and can be used against a police official who import torture against a person. The Supreme Court has, though not defined the term torture, but attempted to provide in general phrase the impact of torture on human beings. Justice Dr. A.S. Anand quoting Adriana P. Bartow in *D.K. Basu* observed:

59. *See* Ss. 25 and 26 of the Indian Evidence Act and S. 164 of the Code of Criminal Procedure.
60. *See* Indian Penal Code S. 319.
61. *Id.*, S. 320.
62. *Id.*, S. 330 and 331.
63. *Id.*, S. 166.
64. *Id.*, S. 357.

> "Torture" has not been defined in the Constitution or in other penal laws. "Torture" of a human being by another human being is essentially an instrument to impose the will of the 'strong' over the 'weak' by suffering. The word *torture* today has become synonymous with the darker side of human civilization. "Torture" is a wound in the soul so painful that sometimes you can almost touch it, but it is also so intangible that there is no way to heal it. Torture is anguish squeezing in your chest, cold as ice and heavy as a stone paralyzing as steep and dark as the abyss. Torture is despair and fear and rage and hate. It is a desire to kill and destroy including yourself.
>
> —Adriana P. Bartow[65]

Sections 46 and 49 of the Criminal procedure Code protect persons under custody from torture who are not attempting to evade lawful arrest or not accused of an offence punishable with death or imprisonment for life.[66] After the new Amendment of Criminal Procedure Code in 2008, the police officer is required to make the accused person medically examined immediately after the arrest. Section 54 (1) now provides:

> When any person is arrested, he shall be examined by a medical officer in the service of Central or State Governments and in case the medical officer is not available by a registered medical practitioner soon after the arrest is made: Provided that where the arrested person is a female, the examination of the body shall be made only by or under the supervision of a female medical officer, and in case the female medical officer is not available, by a female registered medical practitioner.

65. *Supra* Ch. 4, n. 86, D.K. Basu's case, para.10.
66. S. 46 (2) of theCode of Criminal Procedure provides: "If such person forcibly resists the endeavour to arrest him, or attempts to evade the arrest, such police officer or other person may use all means necessary to effect the arrest"; and 46 (3) provides: "Nothing in this section gives a right to cause the death of a person who is not accused of an offence punishable with death or with imprisonment for life". Section 49of the Code of Criminal Procedure provides: The person arrested shall not be subjected to more restraint than is necessary to prevent his escape.

This indicates that in the event of torture by the police in custody, the medical examination can prove it and the Magistrate shall verify the record of the result of the examination. It affords an opportunity to the arrestee or detainee to bring to the attention of the Magistrate's notice of any torture or assault committed against him during the custody. But in practice, the police may intimidate the arrestee not to disclose to the Magistrate, if he was tortured in custody. Further, Section 176 of the Criminal Procedure Code expressly provides inquiry by a Magistrate into the cause of death in custody. It provides that when any person dies while in the custody of the police, the nearest Magistrate empowered to hold inquest shall conduct inquiry into the cause of death. Thus, in the case of death in police custody, an immediate magisterial inquiry is provided under the provisions of Criminal Procedure Code to determine the cause and circumstances of death.

In summary, the Indian Penal Code does not use the term "torture" nor does it prescribe punishment for torture as such, though it contain provisions which can operate for criminalizing police official who commit torture. The Criminal Procedure Code takes certain measures under sections 46, 49, 50, 56 and 167 to ensure that torture is not committed against arrested or detained persons. Guidelines are given by the Supreme Court in *D.K. Basu*'s case with respect to procedure to be followed when a person is arrested or under detention. The significant procedure in connection with torture is that the arrestee should be subjected to medical examination every 48 hours during his detention by a doctor from the approved panel of doctors and copies of all prescribed documents should be sent to the concerned Magistrate. This directive is now incorporated into the Criminal Procedure Code by the Amendment in 2008. This provision is intended to assess the health condition of arrested or detained person and to ensure that torture is not employed on him by the police.

6. PROTECTION OF HUMAN RIGHTS ACT, 1993

With a view to provide effective protection and promotion of human rights, the Parliament has enacted the Protection of Human Rights Act, 1993. The Section 2 (1) (d) of the Protection of Human Rights Act provides that "human rights" means the rights relating to life, liberty, equality and dignity of the individual guaranteed by the Constitution or embodied in the International Covenants and enforceable by courts in India. The same Section in Sub-section (1) (f) states what includes the international covenants and it provides that "International Covenants" means the International Covenant on Civil and Political Rights and the International Covenant on Economic, Social and Cultural rights adopted by the General Assembly of the United Nations on the 16th December, 1966 and such other Covenant or Convention adopted by the General Assembly of the United Nations as the Central Government may, by notification, specify. Originally, when the Protection of Human Rights Act was adopted in 1993, the Act included only two international covenants, *viz*., the International Covenant on Civil and Political Rights and International Covenant on Economic, Social and Cultural Rights. After the Amendment in 2006 the words "and such other Covenant or Convention adopted by the General Assembly of the United Nations as the Central Government may, by notification, specify" were added to it. The Protection of Human Rights Act provides for the establishment of National Human Rights Commission, State Human Rights Commissions and the Human Rights Courts. It also elaborates the constitution, composition, powers and functions of National Human Rights Commission and State Human Rights Commissions. Accordingly, on October 12, 1993, National Human Rights Commission was established. Invoking section 21 of the Protection of Human Rights Act, the Kerala State Government established Kerala State Human Rights Commission in December 1998.[67] The powers and functions of the State Human Rights Commissions are the same as those of National Human RightsCommission.[68]

The Protection of Human Rights Act also provides for the establishment of Human Rights Courts. Section 30 states that for the purpose of providing speedy trial of offences arising out of violation of human rights, the State Government may, with the concurrence of the Chief Justice of the High Court, by notification, specify for each district a Court of Session to be a Human Rights Court to try the said offences. Section 31 further provides that for every Human Rights

---

67. The Kerala State Human Rights Commission was set up by the Government of Kerala in December 1998 under Section 29 of Protection of Human Rights Act, 1993 vide G.O. (P) No. 523/98/Law dated 11th December 1998 and published as S.R.O. No. 1065/98 in the Kerala Gazette Extraordinary No. 2036 on 11th December 1998; *See* Ch. 7 for details.
68. Protection of Human Rights Act 1993, S. 29; See Ch. 7 for details.

Court, the State Government shall specify a Public Prosecutor or appoint an advocate who has been in practice as an advocate for not less than seven years as a Special Public Prosecutor for the purpose of conducting cases in that Court.

7. THE POLICE ACT, 1861

India has the credit of accommodating the largest number of Police men in the world with around 1.03 million. The second country in the world to have largest police force is USA with around 0.94 million. UK and France stands ninth and tenth position respectively. However, considering the population of the country, India has only 0.956207 per 1,000 people and comes 47th in the world countries, while, UK with 2.04871 per 1,000 people stands at 34th position. Each State in India has its own police force, whose top officials are filled by officers of Indian Police Service recruited by the Central Government. The Police Act, 1861 was enacted during the colonial period of British rule immediately after the First World War in1857. Many States in India are also following the same Police Act of 1861. Even after sixty six years of attaining independence, the basic attitude and behaviour of the police did not change much. There has always been criticism about following such a colonial Act which was made because of distrust of Indian officers and for the purpose of suppressing the people by force and intimidation during the British rule.

There were long persuasions for the police reforms in India. The discussions and deliberations went on regularly ever since independence of India. However, it was only in 1976, the Government of India came forward to set up a National Police Commission (NPC) under the chairmanship of Mr. Dharma Vira for submitting recommendations for reform of the police in India. The Commission submitted eight reports with its recommendations and a model Police Act. The Government of India did not adopt the recommendations submitted by the commission nor taken any steps to reform the police for decades. Disheartened by the pathetic situation of the police in the country, two former Director Generals of Police in 1996 brought the matter before the Supreme Court by way of Public Interest Litigation in the case *Prakash Singh* v. *Union of India*.[69] In compliance with the direction of the Supreme Court in

69. (2006) 8 S.C.C. 1; (hereinafter referred as "Prakash Singh' scase").

this case the Ministry of Home Affairs in May 1998 set-up the Ribeiro Committee to review the action taken to implement the recommendations of the National Police Commission and the National Human Rights Commission, to suggest ways and means to implement the pending recommendations and to make any other recommendations which it considered necessary. The Ribeiro Committee submitted its report on October 28, 1998 and a supplementary report on March 18, 1999 diluting the National Police Commission's recommendation regarding setting up of a State Security Commission in so far as it said that the State Security Commission may be "non-statutory, advisory and recommendatory body". Since there were many objections regarding the recommendations of the Ribeiro Committee, the Ministry of Home Affairs. Government of India constituted another Committee, the Padmanabhaiah Committee on Police Reforms in January 2000. The report was submitted by the Committee to the Central Government in October 2000". The Police Act Drafting Committee or popularly the Soli Sorabjee Committee that drafted a new model Police Act in 2006 to replace the colonial 1861 Police Act.

Mallimath Committee on Criminal Justice Reform stated the need for reform of Police Act in the following words:

> The police system in the Country is functioning under the archaic Indian Police Act which was enacted in 1861 for the perpetuation of the British Empire. The police now have an obligation and duty to function according to the requirements of the Constitution, law and democratic aspirations of the people. Further, the police is required to be a professional and service-oriented organization, free from undue extraneous influences and yet be accountable to the people. Besides, it is necessary to have the police force which is professionally controlled and is politically neutral, non-authoritarian, people friendly and professionally efficient. The National Police Commission had recommended enactment of a new Police Act for achieving the above objectives about two decades back. The Central Govt., however, has not taken any action. The Committee strongly feels that a new Police Act may be enacted by the Central Govt. on the pattern of the draft prepared by the National Police Commission.[70]

70. *Id.*, para 11.

Sections 7 and 29 of the Act provide for dismissal, penalty or suspension of police officers who are negligent in the discharge of their duties or unfit to perform the same. Apart from the general provision of negligence, the Act is silent about the atrocious acts committed by the police on people and an impartial mechanism to redress the grievance against police atrocities.

The Supreme Court, considering the growing atrocities, police excesses and absence of proper mechanism for redressal of police excesses, gave its verdict in 2006 in *Prakash Singh*'s case directing the reform of Police Acts at the Centre, the States and Union Territories in India. The Supreme Court observed that there has been no reform of archaic Police Acts even after many Committee's and Commission's Reports. The Supreme Court further observed the need for giving directives in the following words:

> Having regard to (i) the gravity of the problem; (ii) the urgent need for preservation and strengthening of Rule of Law; (iii) pendency of even this petition for last over ten years; (iv) the fact that various Commissions and Committees have made recommendations on similar lines for introducing reforms in the police set-up in the country; and (v) total uncertainty as to when police reforms would be introduced, we think that there cannot be any further wait, and the stage has come for issue of appropriate directions for immediate compliance so as to be operative till such time a new model Police Act is prepared by the Central Government and/or the State Governments pass the requisite legislations.[71]

The Supreme Court has observed that the time was already over for police reform in Central, State and Union Territories Governments, and issued seven directives that may be considered for police reform by the Governments. The directives are as follows:

7.1. State Security Commission

Constitute a State Security Commission in every State to ensure that the State Government does not exercise unwarranted influence or pressure on the State police and for laying down the broad policy guidelines so that the State police always act according to the laws of the land and the Constitution of the country. This watchdog body

71. *Id.*, para 11.

shall be headed by the Chief Minister or Home Minister as Chairman and have the DGP of the State as its ex-officio Secretary. The other members of the Commission shall be chosen in such a manner that it is able to function independent of Government control. For this purpose, the State may choose any of the models recommended by the National Human Rights Commission, the Ribeiro Committee or the Sorabjee Committee, which are as under:

(a) National Human Rights Commission (NHRC) Model : 1. Chief Minister/Home Minister as Chairman; 2. Lok Ayukta or, in his absence, a retired Judge of High Court to be nominated by Chief Justice or a Member of State Human Rights Commission. 3. A sitting or retired Judge nominated by Chief Justice of High Court. 4. Chief Secretary 5. Leader of Opposition in the Lower House; 6. Director General of Police as ex-officio Secretary.

(b) Ribeiro Committee Model: 1. Minister in charge of Police as Chairman; 2. Leader of Opposition. 3. Judge, sitting or retired, nominated by Chief Justice of High Court. 4. Chief Secretary 5. Three non-political citizens of proven merit and integrity. 6. Director General of Police as Secretary.

(c) Sorabjee Committee Model : 1. Minister in charge of Police (ex-officio Chairperson); 2. Leader of Opposition. 3. Chief Secretary; 4. Director General of Police (ex-officio Secretary); 5. Five independent Members.

7.2. Selection and Minimum Tenure of the Director General of Police

The Director General of Police of the State shall be selected by the State Government from amongst the three senior-most officers of the Department who have been empanelled for promotion to that rank by the Union Public Service Commission on the basis of their length of service, very good record and range of experience for heading the police force. And, once he has been selected for the job, he should have a minimum tenure of at least two years irrespective of his date of superannuation unless any action taken against him under the All India Services (Discipline and Appeal) Rules or following his conviction in a court of law in a criminal offence or in a case of corruption, or if he is otherwise incapacitated from discharging his duties.

7.3. Minimum Tenure of Inspector General of Police and Other Officers

Police Officers on operational duties in the field like the Inspector General of Police in-charge Zone, Deputy Inspector General of Police in-charge Range, Superintendent of Police in-charge district and Station House Officer in-charge of a Police Station shall also have a prescribed minimum tenure of two years unless it is found necessary to remove them prematurely following disciplinary proceedings against them or their conviction in a criminal offence or in a case of corruption or if the incumbent is otherwise incapacitated from discharging his responsibilities.

7.4. Separation of Investigation

The investigating police shall be separated from the law and order police to ensure speedier investigation, better expertise and improved rapport with the people. It must, however, be ensured that there is full coordination between the two wings. The separation, to start with, may be effected in towns/urban areas which have a population of ten lakhs or more, and gradually extended to smaller towns/urban areas also.

7.5. Police Establishment Board

There shall be a Police Establishment Board in each State which shall decide all transfers, postings, promotions and other service related matters of officers of and below the rank of Deputy Superintendent of Police. The Establishment Board shall be a departmental body comprising the Director General of Police and four other senior officers of the Department. The State Government may interfere with the decision of the Board in exceptional cases only after recording its reasons for doing so. The Board shall also be authorized to make appropriate recommendations to the State Government regarding the posting and transfers of officers of and above the rank of Superintendent of Police, and the Government is expected to give due weight to these recommendations and shall normally accept it. It shall also function as a forum of appeal for disposing of representations from officers of the rank of Superintendent of Police and above regarding their promotion/ transfer/disciplinary proceedings or their being subjected to illegal or irregular orders and generally reviewing the functioning of the police in the State.

7.6. Police Complaints Authority

There shall be a Police Complaints Authority at the district level to look into complaints against police officers of and up to the rank of Deputy Superintendent of Police. Similarly, there should be another Police Complaints Authority at the State level to look into complaints against officers of the rank of Superintendent of Police and above. The district level Authority may be headed by a retired District Judge while the State level Authority may be headed by a retired Judge of the High Court/Supreme Court. The head of the State level Complaints Authority shall be chosen by the State Government out of a panel of names proposed by the Chief Justice; the head of the district level Complaints Authority may also be chosen out of a panel of names proposed by the Chief Justice or a Judge of the High Court nominated by him. These Authorities may be assisted by three to five members depending upon the volume of complaints in different States/districts, and they shall be selected by the State Government from a panel prepared by the State Human Rights Commission/Lok Ayukta/State Public Service Commission. The panel may include members from amongst retired civil servants, police officers or officers from any other department, or from the civil society. They would work whole time for the Authority and would have to be suitably remunerated for the services rendered by them. The Authority may also need the services of regular staff to conduct field inquiries. For this purpose, they may utilize the services of retired investigators from the CID, Intelligence, Vigilance or any other organization. The State level Complaints Authority would take cognizance of only allegations of serious misconduct by the police personnel, which would include incidents involving death, grievous hurt or rape in police custody. The district level Complaints Authority would, apart from above cases, may also inquire into allegations of extortion, land/house grabbing or any incident involving serious abuse of authority. The recommendations of the Complaints Authority, both at the district and State levels, for any action, departmental or criminal, against a delinquent police officer shall be binding on the concerned authority.

7.7. National Security Commission

The Central Government shall also set up a National Security Commission at the Union level to prepare a panel for being placed before the appropriate Appointing Authority, for selection and placement of Chiefs of the Central Police Organisations (CPO), who should also be given a minimum tenure of two years. The Commission would also review from time to time measures to upgrade the effectiveness of these forces, improve the service conditions of its personnel, ensure that there is proper coordination between them and that the forces are generally utilized for the purposes they were raised and make recommendations in that behalf. The National Security Commission could be headed by the Union Home Minister and comprise heads of the CPOs and a couple of security experts as members with the Union Home Secretary as its Secretary.

In fact, the direction of the Supreme Court to the Central, State & Union Territory Governments is a very welcome step for reforming the Police Acts. Significance of the directives lies in the fact that the Central, State & Union Territory Governments have taken serious steps in reforming their respective Police Acts which the Governments could have done within the last sixty six years of Independence. It clearly indicates that the popular Governments of Indian States greatly rely on brutal police force for suppressing the opponents. Finally, the interference of the apex judiciary became inevitable to reform the Police Acts which would insulate the police from external pressure, enable it to secure to all citizens their rights under the Constitution, ensure rule of law and equality for everyone.

8. STATE POLICE ACTS

Article 246 read with entries 1 and 2 in the State list under the Seventh Schedule of the Indian Constitution, the "public order" and "police" are the subjects coming under the State List. The States in India are entrusted with the maintenance of law and order and hence, the organisation of police force within a State jurisdiction is primarily the responsibility of the concerned State. However, from 1950 until the verdict of Supreme Court in *Prakash Singh*'s case in 2006, only four Police Acts have been enacted in the independent India and these Acts are Bombay Police Act 1951, Kerala Police Act 1960, Karnataka Police Act 1963 and Delhi Police Act 1978. Most Indian States followed Indian Police Act, 1861. Each State has its own police force, whose top level officials are filled by officers of Indian Police Service. The hierarchical structure of the police in the State follows a vertical alignment consisting of senior officers drawn from the Indian Police Service who do the supervisory work. The subordinates, i.e. the inspectors, sub-inspectors, and asst. sub-inspectors, work generally at the police station. The police constabulary are delegated the patrolling, surveillance, guard, and law and order duties.

In the backdrop of Supreme Court direction in *Prakash Singh*'s case to reform the Police Acts in Union and States, and considering the growing cry of the general public and human rights activists, new Police Acts have been either enacted or, at least, initiated for its enactment at the Central level and in many States and Union Territories in India. In 2007, a year after the Supreme Court direction in *Prakash Singh*'s case, as many as eleven States have enacted new Police Acts. These States are Assam, Bihar, Chhattisgarh, Gujarat, Haryana, Himachal Pradesh, Punjab, Rajasthan, Sikkim, Tripura and Uttar khand. Kerala has enacted new Police Act in 2011, Karnataka amended it earlier Police Act in 2012 and Tamil Nadu enacted the Police Act in 2013. Delhi is getting on with the old Delhi Police Act 1978. Ministry of Home affairs has proposed to replace Delhi Police Act 1978 and as a result, a bill was drafted in 2010. However, it still waits to be an Act. Goa has drafted new police bill in 2008, but so far it did not become a law in the State. There were many attempts to make a new Police Act but it still remains a dream.

It can certainly be stated that positively responding to the direction of the Supreme Court in *Prakash Singh*'s case, many States came forward to reform the police Act in their respective States and many have taken initiative to reform the Police Act in their State domain. The most significant aspect of these new Acts is that they attempt to incorporate the directives of the Supreme Court in *Prakash Singh*'s case and also the protection of human rights and human dignity of persons. It would better to analyze the some of the State Acts here.

8.1. The Assam Police Act 2007

The Preamble of the Assam Police Act 2007 makes it clear that the Act is intended to redefine the role of the police taking into account the emerging challenges of policing and security of the State, the imperatives of good governance, and respect for human rights. Further, the object and reasons part in the Act also stresses this aspect which provide "to make the Police force function in accordance with good governance and respect for human rights". Thus the protection of human rights by the police has been made the spirit of Act. Further, Section 47 (a) provides that the role and functions of the police shall broadly be to uphold and enforce the law impartially, and to protect life, liberty, property, human rights, and dignity of the members of the public. Thus, the Act aims to attain the protection and promotion of human rights from others as well as from the police.

8.1.1. Selection and tenure of Director General of Police

Section 6 (2) provides that the empanelment for the rank of Director General of Police shall be done by the State Security Commission. The Director General of Police may only be transferred from the post before the expiry of his tenure by the State Government consequent upon:

- (a) conviction by a court of law in criminal offence or corruption or moral turpitude; or
- (b) punishment of dismissal, removal, or compulsory retirement from service or of reduction to a lower post,
- (c) suspension from service in accordance with the provision of the rules; or
- (d) incapacitation by physical or mental illness or otherwise becoming unable to discharge his function as the Director General Police; or
- (e) promotion to a higher post under either the State or the Central Government, subject to the officer's consent to such a posting;
- (f) inefficiency or negligence or misdemeanour *prima facie* established after preliminary enquiry.[72]

However, the *proviso* to Section 6(2) provides that the State Government, on the ground of public interest, may transfer the Director General of Police as may be deemed appropriate to meet any contingency. This shows that the ultimate power of transfer of the Director General of Police is vested with the Government. If the Director General of Police is not acting in accordance with the whims and fancies of the ruling Government he can be transferred under the mask of public interest. In fact, this was not envisaged by the Supreme Court.

8.1.2. State intelligence and Criminal Investigation

The Act provides for State intelligence and Criminal Investigation as separate departments. Section 17(1) provides that the State Police Organization shall have a State Intelligence Department

72. Section 6(3), Assam Police Act 2007.

for collection, collation, analysis and dissemination of intelligence, and a Criminal Investigation Department for investigation inter-state, inter-district crimes and other specified crimes. Thus, there shall be separate crime investigation department different from state intelligence and law and order as envisaged by the Supreme Court in the *Prakash Singh*'s case.

8.1.3. State Security Commission

The Act provides for the constitution of State Security Commission under Section 34. It provides that the State Government shall establish a State Security Commission within six months of the coming into force of this Act. The State Security Commission shall be composed of (a) the Chief Minister as the Chairperson; (b) a retired High Court Judge; (c) the Chief Secretary; (d) the Secretary in charge of the Home Department as its Member Secretary; (e) the Director General of Police of the State; and (f) three non-political persons of high integrity, expertise and competence in administration, law enforcement and security related matters nominated by the State Government. Out of these, one shall be a police officer superannuated in the rank not below the Director General of Police, another a retired Civil Service officer not below the rank of Commissioner and Secretary to the State Government with experience in public administration, and the third member will be from the fields of public service, legal profession or social organization with at least fifteen years' experience in the field.[73] The provision for composition of State Security Commission seems to be in tune with the directives of the Supreme Court.

8.1.4. Police Establishment Board

The Act further provides for the constitution of Police Establishment board. Section 44 provides that the State Government shall constitute a Police Establishment Board with the Director General of Police as its Chairperson and two other senior officers not below the rank of Inspector General of Police within the police organization of the State as members. The Police Establishment Board shall perform the following functions:

(i) accept and examine complaints from the police officers about being subjected to illegal orders;
(ii) make appropriate recommendations for necessary action;

73. Section 35, Assam Police Act 2007.

(iii) forward such report to the State Security commission if the matter under report involves any authority above the ranks of the members of the Police Establishment Board;

(iv) recommend annually a panel of names of suitable officers to the State Government for posting in the rank of Assistant/Deputy Superintendent of Police.

(v) recommend the names of officers up to the rank of Sub-Inspector for posting to a Police District on initial appointment, or for transfer from one Police District to another, where such transfer is considered expedient for the Police Force.

(vi) recommend posting and transfer of officers in the rank of Inspector to the Director General of Police of the State.

8.1.5. Police Accountability Commission

Police Accountability Commission is same as that of Police Complaint Authority as given in the directives by the Supreme Court in *Prakash Singh*'s case. This is intended to redress the grievances against police personnel. Section 70 of the Act provides that the State Government shall establish a State-level Police Accountability Commission within three months of the coming into force of this Act. The State Accountability Commission shall consists of a Chairperson, Members and such other staff as may be necessary, to enquire into public complaints against the police personnel for serious misconduct and perform such other functions as are entrusted with the police by this Act.

The State Accountability Commission shall have a Chairperson and three members with a credible record of integrity and commitment to human rights and shall consist of:

(a) a retired High Court Judge, who shall be the Chairperson of the Commission.

(b) a retired police officer superannuated in the rank of Director General of Police or Additional Director General of Police;

(c) a person with a minimum of 10 years of experience either as a judicial officer, public prosecutor, practicing advocate, or a professor of law, or a person of repute and standing from the civil society; and

(d) a retired officer with experience in public administration, not below the rank of Commissioner or Secretary to the State Government.[74]

74. Section 71, Assam Police Act 2007.

The Act also provides for the establishment of District Accountability Authority in each Police District or a group of districts in a police range to enquire into cases of complaints of 'serious misconduct' against police personnel[75], either *suo moto* or on a complaint received from (a) a victim or any person on his behalf; or (b) the National or the State Human Rights Commission; or (c) the police; or (d) any other source.[76] Explanation to Section 78 further provides that serious misconduct shall mean any act or omission of a police officer that leads to or amounts to:

(a) death in police custody;
(b) grievous hurt, as defined in Section 320 of the Indian Penal Code.
(c) molestation, rape or attempt to commit rape;
(d) arrest or detention without due process of law;
(e) forceful deprivation of a person of his rightful ownership or possession of property;
(f) blackmail or extortion;
(g) non registration of First Information Report.

Thus, it can be stated that the Assam Police Act attempts to comply with the directives of the Supreme Court in *Praksh Singh*'s case, in many aspects such as constitution of security Commission, Police Establishment Board, Police Accountability Commission at State and District level, etc.

8.2. The Bihar Police Act 2007

The Bihar Police Act 2007 in its preamble states, *inter alia*, the promotion and respect for the human rights of individual and protection of their civil, political, social, economic and cultural rights as the first responsibility of the law. It further states that "keeping in view the challenges emerging before the police and the security of the state, administration of good governance and the respect of the human rights, it is necessary to redefine the role of the police, their duties and responsibilities". Thus, the Act aims to attain the protection, promotion of and respect for human rights.

8.2.1. Selection and tenure of Director General of Police

Section 5 of the Bihar Police Act 2007 deals with the appointment of Director General, Additional Director General,

75. Section 84, Assam Police Act 2007.
76. Section 78 (1), Assam Police Act 2007.

Inspector General, Deputy and Assistant Inspector General of Police. Section 5(1) provides that the Government shall appoint Director General of Police who shall exercise such powers and perform such functions, duties and responsibilities as are determined by the Government. Section 5(2) provides that the Government may appoint one or more Additional Director Generals and such number of Inspector Generals, Deputy and Assistant Inspector Generals as it may deem fit. The tenure of the Director General of Police shall normally be two years. However, the Director General of Police may be transferred from his post before the completion of his tenure by the Government on the reasons which are as follows:

(a) he has been convicted by any court for any punishable crime or has been charge sheeted by any court for being involved in any case of corruption, or of moral turpitude; or,

(b) if he is incapable due to any physical or mental ailment or due to any other reason and is not able to discharge the duty of the Director General of Police; or

(c) promotion to higher post under the State or the Union Government, subject to the consent of the officer so promoted; or

(d) any other administrative reason in respect of effective discharge of the duty.

Thus, generally the term of the Director General of Police is for two years. As in the case Assam Police Act 2007, the Bihar Act does not provide that the government can remove him at any time during the tenure in the public interest. It can be stated that the Bihar Police Act, to that extent, intends to give non-transferable position for the Director General of Police within the period of his tenure unless for the stated defects or disabilities.

8.2.2. State Police Board

Section 23 of the Act provides that the Government shall establish a State Police Board within six months of the implementation of the Act. The Police Board shall be composed of : (i) Chief Secretary as Chairman; (ii) Director General of Police as Member; and (iii) Secretary in charge of Home Department as Member Secretary. The State Police Board shall discharge the following duties:

a) formation of comprehensive Policy Guidelines, for making police administration efficient, affective, sensitive and accountable according to the law.
b) identification of Performance Indicator for Assessment of the working of police service, the Performance Indicator, *inter alia*, shall contain the police research and response, accountability, maximum utilisation of amendments, operative efficiency, public satisfaction, and satisfaction of the victims in comparison to the compliance of norms of human rights.
c) review and assessment of organisational work of district wise police service in the State in comparison to the Performance Indicator identified and determined and the resources available to and under the control of the police.[77]

Thus, Bihar Police Act 2007 provides for the stablishment of State Police Board for giving guidelines, performance evaluation, review and assessment of work of police.

8.2.3. Complaint of Violation of Human Rights

Bihar police Act separately provides a section dealing with human rights violation by the police. Section 26 provides that complaints against police personnel and officers in connection with (i) violation or abetment for violation of human rights; and (ii) Negligence in prevention of such violations shall be investigated by the State Human Rights Commission. Thus, Bihar Police Act takes into consideration of the possible human rights violations by the police and, in the event of such violations, for the remedial mechanism. The Act, by entrusting investigative powers to the State Human Rights Commission, envisages an impartial investigation in the cases of human rights violations by the police.

8.2.4. Tenure, Transfer and Posting of Police Officers

Section 30 of the Act provides that the transfer and posting of police officers and police personnel of the supervisory grade shall be governed by the conduct rule and other rule formulated by the government from time to time. It further provides that the tenure of such officers shall normally be of two years.

8.2.5. Crime investigation department

By section 43, the Act provides for the constitution of separate

77. Section 25, Bihar Police Act 2007.

crime investigation department in the State. Such department shall initiate investigation of inter-state, inter-district and other offences of serious nature as notified by the Government from time to time or specially handed over to it by the Director General of Police in accordance with the prescribed process and norms.

8.2.6. District Accountability Authority

The Bihar Police Act 2007 provides only for the constitution of District Accountability Authority. There is no provision for the State Accountability Authority as given in the directives of the Supreme Court. Section 59 provides that the Government shall set up District Accountability Authority. The District Magistrate shall be the head of the District Accountability Authority, the Superintendent of Police and the Senior Additional District Magistrate shall be the Members and the Additional District Collector shall be the Member Secretary. The District Accountability Authority shall perform the following work:

(a) It shall monitor the departmental enquiry or actions related to the complaints of "misbehaviour" against officers below the rank of Assistant/Deputy Superintendent of Police on the basis of quarterly report received from time to time from the District Superintendent of police.

(b) If the authority is of the view that unnecessary delay is being made in the conduct of enquiry in any case, it shall give proper advice to the District Superintendent of Police to speedily complete the enquiry.

However, the above provisions shall not be deemed to dilute disciplinary, supervisory or administrative control of the District Superintendent of Police.

The Bihar Police Act does not strictly follow the directives given by the Supreme Court in reforming the Police Act. It does not provide for the constitution of the Police Establishment Board. In the Constitution of the State Security Commission or the State Police Board, Government did not follow the directives of the Supreme Court. There are wide spread criticism that the commission should have been headed by the Chief Minister in which Leader of Opposition in the State Assembly, a sitting judge of the Patna High Court, Chief Secretary and Director General of Police should have been made members and the same committee should have been empowered to frame the rules to control and regulate the police. But, under the present act, the State Police Board would be headed by Chief Secretary to which State Home Secretary and Director General of Police would be the members.

8.3. The Bombay Police (Gujarat Amendment) Act, 2007

The Gujarat made amendments in 2007 to the existing Bombay Police Act, 1951 operational in Gujarat by the Bombay Police (Gujarat Amendment) Act, 2007. The Amendment Act 2007 makes the following changes in the existing Act.

8.3.1. Selection and tenure of Director and Inspector Generals of Police

Section 5A (2) provides that the Director General and Inspector General of Police shall be selected by a screening committee from a panel of Director General of Police already working in the rank or of the officers in the rank of Additional Director General of Police. The appointment shall be made by the Government. The Director General and Inspector General of Police so appointed shall ordinarily hold the office for a minimum tenure of two years unless for specified reasons (a) conviction by a court of law in criminal offence or corruption or moral turpitude; or (b) punishment of dismissal, removal, or compulsory retirement from service or of reduction to a lower post, (c) suspension from service; or (d) incapacitation by physical or mental illness or otherwise becoming unable to discharge his function as the Director General Police.

8.3.2. State Security Commission

Section 32A (1) of the Act provides that the Government shall establish a State Security Commission. The State Security Commission shall consist of the following members:

(a) the Chief Minister of the State, *ex-officio*, as the Chairperson;
(b) the Home Minister of the State, *ex-officio*;
(c) the Chief Secretary to the Government of Gujarat, *ex-officio;*
(d) the Home Secretary to the Government of Gujarat, *ex-officio;*
(e) the Director General of Police, *ex-officio*, who shall be the Member Secretary; and
(g) two non-official members to be appointed by the State

Government of persons having reputation for integrity and competence in the field of academia, law, public administration or media.

8.3.3. Police Establishment Board

Section 32D (1) of the Act provides to constitute a Police Establishment Board. The Board shall consist of the following members:

(1) the Director General and Inspector General of Police, *ex-officio*, who shall be the Chairman;
(2) additional Director General of Police (Administration), *ex-officio*;
(3) an officer not below the rank of the Deputy Secretary to the Government of Gujarat, Home Department, *ex-officio*; and
(4) an officer not below the rank of Inspector General of Police to be nominated by the State Government, *ex-officio*, who shall be the Member Secretary.

The Police Establishment Board shall exercise the following powers and perform the following functions and duties:

(a) transfer of officers in the rank of Police Inspector and Sub-Inspectors;
(b) prescribe guidelines and instructions for transfer of Subordinate ranks from one Police District to another;
(c) analyse the grievances of the police personnel below the rank of Deputy Superintendent of Police and suggest remedial measures to the State Government;
(d) grant promotion to higher post from the cadre of constable and *Lok Rakshak.*

8.3.4. Police Complaints Authorities

Section 32F (1) provides that the State Government shall constitute the State Police Complaints Authority. The Authority shall consist of the following members:

(a) a retired Judge of the High Court or a retired officer not below the rank of Principal Secretary to the Government of Gujarat who shall be the Chairperson;
(b) the Principal Secretary to the Government of Gujarat, Home Department, *ex-officio*;

(c) an officer not below the rank of an Additional Director General, nominated by the State Government, *ex-officio,* who shall be the Member Secretary; and

(d) a person of eminence appointed by the State Government.

The State Police Complaints Authority shall exercise the following powers and perform following functions:

(1) look into complaints against police officers of the rank of Deputy Superintendent of Police and above, in respect of serious misconduct, dereliction of duty, misuse of powers, or any other matter specified by the Government, not covered by the Vigilance Commission, National Human Rights Commission, State Human Rights Commission, Commission for Minorities, Commission for Scheduled Castes and Scheduled Tribes, Commission for Women and Commission for Backward Communities, or any other Commissions as may be appointed from time to time either by the Central Government or by the State Government;

(2) require any person to furnish information relevant to the subject matter of the inquiry;

(3) enforce attendance of any person and take evidence on oath in the manner of a civil court.

(4) make appropriate recommendations to the State Government on any case required into by it.

The Act further provides under Section 32H (1) to constitute the District Police Complaints Authority for each District. The District Police Complaints Authority shall consist of the following members:

(a) the Superintendent of Police of the District, *ex-officio*, who shall be the Chairperson;

(b) the Additional District Magistrate of the District, to be appointed by the State Government, *ex-officio*;

(c) two members of the Gujarat Legislative Assembly elected from the concerning District, to be appointed by the State Government;

(d) the Deputy Superintendent of Police, *ex-officio,* who shall be the Member-Secretary.

The Bombay Police (Gujarat Amendment) 2007 Act is

attempting to incorporate the directives given by the Supreme Court in reforming the Police Act. The major changes are in the selection procedure and tenure of Director General and Inspector General of Police, constitution of State Security Commission, Police Establishment Board and State and District Police Complaint Authorities or the State Police Board.

8.4. The Rajasthan Police Act 2007

The Rajasthan police Act 2007 provides in its preamble the respect and promotion of human rights of people, and protection of their civil, political social, economic and cultural rights.

8.4.1. Appointment and Tenure of Police Officers

Section 19 of the Rajasthan police Act provides for the appointment of Director General of Police for the overall control and supervision of the police in the State. His minimum tenure is fixed as two years before which he shall not be removed. Similarly, subordinate police officer in the field duty is also normally fixed as two years. Any police officer from subordinate to the Director General of police can be removed from the office for the reasons (i) his conviction by criminal court; (ii) his punishment of dismissal, removal, etc.; (iii) his suspension; (iv) his physical or mental incapacity; (v) his own request; (vi) an administrative exigency which shall be recorded in writing.

8.4.2. State Police Commission

Sec. 21 provides for the establishment of State Police Commission for the State. The Commission shall consist of Minister in charge of Home department as the Chairman and Leader of Opposition in the Assembly, Chief Secretary, Home Secretary, Director General of Police and three persons of eminence as Members. The State Government may appoint a police officer not below the rank of Additional Director General of Police to act as Secretary to the Commission. The Commission would ensure enhancement in the efficiency, capability and accountability of the State police force.

8.4.3. Police Establishment Board

Sect 28 provides for the constitution of Police Establishment Board. The Board shall perform functions such as the recruitment of constables, promotion of subordinate officers, transfer of subordinate officers, redressing the grievances of police personnel. The Board shall perform functions such as:

(i) recruitment of constables;
(ii) promotion in the subordinate ranks;
(iii) prescribe guidelines for transfer of subordinate ranks;
(iv) transfer of subordinate ranks from one range to another;
(v) prepare proposals for transfer of police officers in the rank of Additional Superintendent of police.
(vi) analyse the grievances of police personnel and suggest remedial measures to the State Government

8.4.4. Crime Investigation Units

Section 42 prescribes to create a separate investigation units in such police stations which the Government may decide from time to time. The investigation unit shall be headed by a police officer not below the rank of Sub-Inspector of Police. The State Government may also create one or more special crime investigation units in the office of Director General of Police or in any police districts headed by an officer not below the rank of Inspector of Police for investigation of cyber-crimes, organised crimes and such other crimes as may be specified by the Director General of Police.

8.4.5. Police Accountability Committees

Section 62 prescribes for the constitution of Police Accountability Committees. It provides that the State Government may establish a State Police Accountability Committee for the State and District Accountable Committee for each district. The State Accountability Committee shall consist of four independent persons of eminence, one Additional Director General of Police as its Member-Secretary. The Government shall appoint one independent Member as Chairman of the State Committee. The Committee shall inquire into the allegations of serious misconduct and make recommendations to the State Government on any case inquired into by it. Section 67 provides that the District Committee shall consist of four independent persons of eminence and one Additional Superintendent of Police as its Member-Secretary. The Government shall appoint one independent Member as Chairman of Committee. The functions of the State Committee are to enquire into allegations of serious misconduct against police officers in the supervisory rank and to make recommendations to the state government on any case enquired into by it. The functions of the District Committee are to enquire into allegations of serious misconduct against police personnel in the subordinate rank, to monitor departmental enquiries against police officer in the subordinate ranks and to refer to the State Committee complaints received by it against police officer in the supervisory rank.

8.5. The Haryana Police Act 2007

The preamble of the Haryana Police Act 2007 states to attain good governance, security and protection of human rights as its objective. It also aims to provide a new State police law to enable the police to function as an efficient, professional, effective, accountable, people friendly and responsive agency by taking into account the emerging challenges of policing, and enforcement of rule of law.

8.5.1. Appointment of Director General of Police

Section 5(1) provides that for the overall direction and supervision of the police service, the State Government shall appoint a Director General of Police. The State Government may appoint one or more Director Generals of Police, Additional Director Generals of Police, and as many Inspector Generals, Deputy or Assistant Inspector Generals of Police as may be necessary. The State Government shall appoint the Director General of Police of the State from amongst the officers holding the rank of Director General of Police. The Director General of Police so appointed shall have a minimum tenure of one year.

8.5.2. State Police Board

Section 25 provides that the State Government shall establish a State Police Board within three months of the coming into force of this Act. The State Police Board shall consist of following members:

(a) the Chief Minister as its Chairperson;
(b) the Home Minister as Vice-Chairperson;
(c) the Leader of the Opposition in the State Assembly;
(d) a retired High Court Judge or Advocate General of Haryana;
(e) the Chief Secretary;
(f) the Secretary in charge of the Home Department;
(g) the Director General of Police as its Member-Secretary;
(h) three non-political independent persons to be nominated by the State Government.

The State Police Board shall perform the functions such as: (i) aid and advise the State Government in discharge of its functions and responsibilities under this Act; (ii) frame broad policy guidelines for promoting efficient, effective, responsive and accountable policing in accordance with the law; and (iii) review and evaluate organizational performance of the service in the State.

8.5.3. Police Establishment Committee

The State Government may constitute a Police Establishment Committee for the State.[78] The Director General of Police shall be the Chairperson and two other senior officers not below the rank of Inspector General of Police posted within the police organization of the State as Members for administrative matters. The establishment committee may prepare an action plan for improving the infrastructure facilities, professionalism, general discipline in the service, modernization, training, welfare of the police personnel and any other work assigned by the State Government.

8.5.4. Crime Investigation

Section 43 provides that the State Government shall create a specialised crime investigation unit in every Police district. Such units shall be headed by an officer not below the rank of Inspector with an appropriate strength of officers and staff for investigating economic and heinous crimes. The Personnel posted to this unit shall not be diverted to any other duty, except under very special circumstances with the written permission of the Director General of Police.

8.5.5. Police Complaint Authority

The State Government shall establish a Police Complaint Authority at the State Level, within three months of the commencement of this Act.[79] The State Level Police Complaint Authority shall be either a retired Judge or a retired civil servant, not below the rank of Secretary to the State or a lawyer well versed with criminal law and with an experience of at least twenty years in the relevant field, for inquiries and investigations into the complaints against the police officers and officials of the State. The term of office of the Authority shall be for three years. Section 65(1) provides that the Authority shall inquire into allegations of serious misconduct against police personnel either *suo motu* or on a complaint received from: (a) a victim or any person on his behalf on a sworn affidavit; or (b) the National or State Human Rights Commission. Explanation to Section 65 provides "serious misconduct" shall mean any act or omission of a police officer that leads to or amounts to : (a) death in

78. Section 34 (1), Haryana Police Act 2007.
79. Section 59, Haryana Police Act 2007.

police custody; or (b) rape or attempt to commit rape; or (c) grievous hurt in police custody. The Authority may also inquire into any other case referred to it by the Director General of Police or the State Government. Section 68 provides that the State Government may notify and constitute a District Police Complaint Authority for each district as and when required.

Haryana followed the Police Act of 1861 and the Punjab Police Rules, 1934. It can be seen that the Haryana Police Act has complied with the Supreme Court Directives to a greater extend in the appointment of Director General of Police, separation of crime investigation, constitution of State Security Commission, Police Establishment Board and Police Complaints Authority. However, the minimum tenure of Director General of Police is lowered to one year.

8.6. The Kerala Police Act, 2011

The Kerala Police Act 2011 totally replaces the earlier Kerala Police Act 1960. One of the most significant aspects to be noted in the new Act is that it expressly incorporates, *inter alia,* the protection human rights and dignity of all persons as the function of the police.[80] The Act introduces several provisions with a view to protect the human rights of people from being violated by the police.

8.6.1. State Police Chief

The State Police Chief shall be appointed by the Government from among those officers of the State Cadre of Indian Police Service Officers who have been promoted to the rank of Director General of Police. While appointing the State Police Chief, the Government will take into account the ability to lead the police force of the State, the overall history of service, professional knowledge and experience.

8.6.2. Reception at the Police Station

The Act ensures that all citizens shall have the right to efficient police services from any Police Station.[81] It provides for peaceful entry and reception at any time at any Police Station and to receive lawful services as a matter of right of the public.[82] It is to be noted that this provision intents to remove the dreadful image of the police and the police stations in the State. It also provides for facility for women

80. Kerala Police Act, S. 4 (b).
81. *Id.*, S. 7.
82. Kerala Police Act, S. 8 (1).

to submit complaints with privacy and in the presence of women police. The general trend in police stations is not to give any receipt of the complaint. The new Kerala Police Act now makes it as a matter of right of the complainant to receive mandatorily a receipt acknowledging the complaint given by him, and also to know the stage of the police action or investigation in respect of the complaint.[83]

Another significant aspect is the provision relating to the whereabouts of detained person. Section 8 (6) provides that 'any citizen shall have the right to know whether any particular person is in custody at the police station'. This has been made with a view to reduce illegal detentions in police custody, and as a matter of right any citizen can require the police to give information about a person in custody. Section 13 provides that all Chairpersons and Members of the State Human Rights Commission or the State Women's Commission or the State Scheduled Caste/Scheduled Tribe Commission or the State or District Police Complaints Authorities may enter in a Police Station and directly verify the entries in any General Diary and also the condition of any person kept in custody. It further provides that any such person visiting the police station shall make a contemporaneous record of his visit in the diary, and also communicate to the District Police Chief the summary of his observations. The District Police Chief shall take, as soon as possible, further actions as may be necessary on such observations. It is submitted that this measure can provide effective supervision and control mechanism on the situation of the police stations and also on the police.

8.6.3. Behaviour of the Police

There have always been grumblings and controversies regarding the police behaviour and use of abusive language of police towards accused, victims or witnesses of crime. Section 26 of the new Kerala Police Act bans such indecent behaviour and use of filthy languages of the police. It provides:

(i) all Police officers on duty, in their dealings with the public, shall exhibit courtesy, propriety and compassion appropriate to the occasion and use polite and decent language.

(ii) the police officers shall not use force against anybody or

83. *Id.*, S. 8 (4).

threaten that force be will used, or any adverse police or legal action will be taken unless it is necessary to carry out any lawful purpose.

(iii) the police officers shall exhibit special sympathy in their dealings with the victims of crimes and give due consideration to the special needs of women, children, senior citizens and the disabled.

(iv) the police officer shall give up unnecessary show of aggression and avoid intemperate behaviour even on provocation.

(v) the police officer shall not misbehave or use indecent language to anyone in their care or custody.

Where any person is arrested and kept in the custody of the Police, he shall be permitted to wear the dress which is decent and appropriate under the circumstances and which he is used to wear.[84] Regarding handcuffing, the Act makes the general rule that handcuffs shall not be used on an arrested person. However, in exceptional circumstances where the Police Officer arresting the person has sufficient ground to believe that the arrested person shall escape from custody or injure himself or others if not handcuffed.[85]

Thus, the Kerala Police Act attempts to change the behavioural pattern and use of language of the police. It is submitted that only the time can determine how far, by law, the behaviour and attitude of the police can be changed. However, the move of the Government for the incorporation of such a provision in the Act must be appreciated.

8.6.4. Audio, Video or Other Electronic Records

The Act, as part of making the police actions transparent and non-arbitrary, provides certain measures such as that the police may make and keep audio or video or electronic records of any activity performed by them during the discharge of their duties and such records may be used in any proceedings in which the correctness of the police action is called in question.[86] Further, no Police Officer shall prevent any member of the public from lawfully making any audio or video or electronic record of any police action or activity carried out in a public or private place.[87]

84. Kerala Police Act, S. 46 (3).
85. *Id.*, S. 46 (2).
86. *Id.*, S. 33 (1).
87. Kerala Police Act, S. 33 (2).

8.6.5. Crime Investigation

Section 23 provides for the separation of investigation from law & order. The Government is empowered to separate these two wings of police taking into consideration of the population of an area or the circumstances prevailing in a particular area to ensure speedy, affective and professional investigation. The District Police Chief shall ensure the full co-ordination between the two wings.

8.6.6. Vexatious Arrest, Search, Seizure, Violence, etc.

The Act also makes vexatious arrest, search, seizure, violence, etc., as offences punishable with three year imprisonment and/or with fine. Section 116 provides:

> Whoever, being a police officer—
>
> (a) enters into or conducts unnecessary searches or causes to be searched without lawful authority or reasons in any building, vessel, tent or place for causing annoyance; or
>
> (b) seizes the property of any person or detains a person in custody or conducts search or arrests any person illegally for causing annoyance and without reasonable cause; or
>
> (c) deliberately subjects, any person in custody or with whom he comes into contact in the course of his duties, to torture or any kind of inhuman or unlawful personal violence or grave misconduct; or
>
> (d) deliberately, knowingly and maliciously with intent to implicate an innocent person in a criminal offence records a false statement or make a forged document or raises a false allegation of attack on the police; or
>
> (e) deliberately and directly aids or abets for the commission of an offence which, as a police officer, he is bound to prevent, shall on conviction, be punished with imprisonment for a term which may extend to three years or fine or with both.

Thus, the Act punishes the acts of arbitrary arrest, search, seizure, violence, etc., committed by the police. At the same time, the Act does not restrict the operation of any other laws for punishing offender, if the same matter is an offence under the provisions of that law.

8.6.7. State Security Commission

Section 24 of the Kerala Police Act provides for the

establishment of State Security Commission. The Act provides that the State Security Commission shall consist of members, namely, (i) the Minister in-charge of Home Department who shall be the Chairman; (ii) the Minister in-charge of Law; (iii) the Leader of Opposition; (iv) a retired Judge of the High Court nominated by the Chief Justice of the High Court of Kerala; (v) the Chief Secretary-ex-officio; (vi) the Secretary to Government, Home Department-ex-officio; (vii) the State Police Chief- ex-officio; (viii) three non-official members, who shall be persons of eminence in public life with wide knowledge and experience in maintenance of law and order, administration, human rights, law, social service, management of public administration, nominated by the Governor of whom one shall be a woman.

The Commission shall have the functions, such as: (a) to frame general policy guidelines for the functioning of the Police in the State; (b) to issue directions for the implementation of crime prevention tasks and service oriented activities of the Police; (c) to evaluate, from time to time, the performance of the Police in the State in general; (d) to prepare an annual report of the activities of the Commission and submit it to the Government; (e) to prepare the guidelines for the changes to be carried out, from time to time, in the state police; and (f) to discharge such other functions as may be assigned to it by the Government.

The Commission is required to submit annual report and the annual report submitted by the Commission shall be placed before the Legislative Assembly. The Act empowers the Commission to evaluate the performance of the police every year. It is submitted that this is a welcome step in as much as police performance is evaluated periodically and, hence, the police will have an apprehension that an extra departmental oversight mechanism is working over their head.

8.6.8. Police Establishment Board

The Kerala Police Act authorizes the Government to constitute a department level Police Establishment Board with the Director General of Police as Chairman and other four senior police officers, not below the rank of Additional Director General of Police of the Department, as members.[88] The Board shall discharge the following functions, namely: (a) to decide on complaints and appeals in respect of service matters like transfer, promotion, etc., of police officers of and below the rank of Inspector after detailed examination of related

88. Kerala Police Act, S.105 (1).

Acts and rules or submit suitable recommendations in this regard; (b) to study the particular problems in respect of women police officers, decide on grievances in respect of the same and submit recommendations in necessary matters; (c) to review the activities of State Police in general or in respect of special subjects; and (d) such other functions as may be entrusted to the Board by Government from time to time.[89]

The Act provides that the Government shall give due consideration to the recommendations of the Board. However, the Government may, either *suo motu* or on a complaint by the person concerned, for reasons to be recorded in writing, modify or cancel any decision or order of the Board.[90] The State Police Establishment Board shall nominate an officer of the rank of Deputy Superintendent of Police in each district and such nominated officer shall set apart one day in a week to hear or receive complaints from police officers of and below the rank of Sub Inspector.[91] Such officer shall examine and study the complaints and give recommendations in respect of appropriate redressal measures to the District Police Chief and if the matter is beyond the jurisdiction of the District Police Chief then to the State Police Establishment Board through the District Police Chief.

8.6.9. Police Complaints Authorities

In order to redress the grievances against police effectively, the Kerala Police Act now provides for the establishment of Police Complaints Authorities at State and District levels. The establishment of Police Complaints Authority is a significant change that has been brought about by the new Kerala Police Act in the human rights perspective.

Section 110 sets out that the Government shall constitute a State Police Complaints Authority for examining and inquiring the—

(i) complaints on all types of misconduct against police officers of and above the rank of Superintendent of Police;
(ii) grave complaints against officers of other ranks in respect of sexual harassment of women in custody or causing death of any person or inflicting grievous hurt on any person or rape, etc.[92]

89. *Id.*, S. 106(1).
90. *Id.*, S. 106(3).
91. *Id.*, S. 107(1).
92. Kerala Police Act, S. 110 (1).

The State Police Complaints Authority shall consist of (i) a retired Judge of a High Court who shall be the Chairperson of the Authority; (ii) an officer not below the rank of Principal Secretary to Government; (iii) an officer not below the rank of Additional Director General of Police; (iv) a person as may be fixed by the Government, in consultation with the Leader of Opposition, from a three member panel of retired suitable officers not below the rank of Inspector General of Police furnished by the Chairman of the State Human Rights Commission; and (v) a person as may be fixed by the Government, in consultation with the Leader of Opposition, from a three member panel of retired District Judges furnished by the State *Lok Ayuktha*.[93]

The Act further authorizes the Government to constitute the District Police Complaints Authority at district level for examining and inquiring the complaints against police officers of and up to the rank of Deputy Superintendent of Police. The District Police Complaints Authorities shall consist of : i) a retired District Judge, who shall be the Chairperson; ii) the District Collector; and iii) the District Superintendent of Police.[94]

The State Authority and the District Level Authorities shall have all the powers of a Civil Court for conducting inquiries in respect of the following matters, namely, (a) summoning and enforcing the attendance of any person and examining him on oath; (b) requiring the discovery and production of any document; (c) receiving evidence on affidavit; and (d) any other matter as may be prescribed.[95]

All concerned officers shall be bound to carry out the recommendations given by the authority in respect of matters of initiation of department level inquiry, registration of criminal case, etc., against a police officer.[96] Thus, the Kerala Police Act authorizes the State Government to constitute an impartial high power State Police Complaints Authority and district level District Police Complaints Authorities for redressing the grievances against police. It is submitted that the constitution of State and District Police Complaints Authorities is an effective mechanism for the protection of human rights of accused, arrested or detained persons.

---

93. *Id.*, S. 110 (2).
94. Kerala Police Act, S. 110 (3) and (4).
95. *Id.*, S. 110 (7).
96. *Id.*, S. 110 (9).

The Act also authorizes the people's representatives and others to make complaints against police officers directly to the Police Complaints Authorities. Section 111 provides that the Presidents of Three-tier-Panchayats, Chairpersons of Municipal Councils, Members of Legislative Assemblies, Members of Parliament, Mayors of the Corporations, etc., may give all types of complaints against the police officers that have come to their notice or have been brought to their notice, to the Police Complaints Authority and the Authority shall, after conducting necessary inquiry, inform the result of such inquiry to the representative concerned.

8.6.10. Community policing

The Act also provides for constitution of "community policing". Section 64 empowers the District Police Chief to constitute Community Contact Committees for each Police Station under his jurisdiction. The Community Contact Committee shall comprise the representatives of the local residents of the area and will give general assistance to the Police in the discharge of their duty. The Committee may also formulate programmes for promoting security awareness, safety awareness, prevention of crimes and legal literacy, etc.

Justice K.T. Thomas Commission, appointed by the Government of Kerala to suggest Police Reforms submitted its report in 2006. The report recommended that the Government should implement Community Policing on an experimental basis. Accordingly, the Government with the help of police launched *Janamaithri Suraksha* in March 2008. By *Janamaithri*, it is meant that the relationship of police and public should come closer and help each other. By April 2011, *Janamathri* has been implemented in 41 police stations. In fact, this is a welcome step that this can reduce the dreadful image of the police by maintaining closer relationship between the police and the public. However, the success of *Janamaithri* depends on how far the egocentric police would be viable to such schemes.

8.7. The Tamil Nadu Police Reforms Act 2013

The Preamble of the Tamil Nadu Police Reforms Act 2013 States that the Act is made to provide for law to carry out the directions of the Hon'ble Supreme Court in *Prakash Singh*'s case regarding police reforms and for matters connected therewith.

8.7.1. Selection and tenure of the Director General of Police

The Government shall appoint the Director General of Police from amongst five senior most police officers of the department empanelled by the Union Public Service Commission. The Director General of Police shall hold minimum period of two years or till the date of superannuation unless : (i) he is convicted by a court of law in a criminal case or corruption case; or (ii) he is punished with dismissal, removal, or compulsory retirement from service or of reduction to a lower post; or (iii) he is incapacitated by physical or mental illness or otherwise become unable to discharge his function as the Director General Police; or (iv) he is appointed to any other post with his consent; or (v) he is removed on any administrative grounds to be recorded in writing.

8.7.2. State Security Commission

Section 5 provides that the Government shall establish a security commission for the state. It shall consist of (a) the Minster for home, *ex officio;* (b) Leader of Opposition in the Assembly (c) Chairperson, Tamil Nadu Public Service Commission, *ex officio*; (d) Chairperson, Tamil Nadu State Human Rights Commission, *ex officio*; (e) Chairperson, State Women's Commission, *ex officio;* (f) Chairperson, State Minorities Commission, *ex officio;* (g) Chief Secretary, *ex officio;* (h) Home Secretary, *ex officio;* and (i) Director General of Police, *ex officio.* The Commission shall perform the functions such as (i) to frame broad guidelines for promoting efficient, effective, responsive and accountable policing in accordance with law; (ii) to identify performance indicators to evaluate the functioning of the police force; (iii) to review and evaluate the organizational performance of the police force; and (iv) such other functions that may be entrusted by the Government. The Commission shall submit an annual report to the Government at the end of every year.

8.7.3. Crime Investigation Wing

Section 9 provides for separate wings of law and order from crime investigation in every Police Station. The section further provides that both the wings will work under the control of the Station House Officer who shall ensure co-ordination between the two wings. The investigation wing shall be responsible for investigation and prosecution of all cases registered in the station including cases detected by law and order wing.

8.7.4. Police Establishment Board

Section 8 provides for the constitution of Police Establishment Board. It shall consist of Director General of Police as Chairperson and four senior police officers in the rank of Additional Director General of Police. The Board shall consider and recommend transfer and posting of Superintendent of Police and above up to Inspector General of Police. There shall be a State Police Establishment Committee to consider matters relating to promotion, transfer and posting of officers of and below the rank of Additional Superintendent of Police.

8.7.5. Police Complaints Authority

Section 10 provides that the Government shall establish at the State level a Police Complaints Authority. The Authority shall have the Secretary in charge of the Home department as its Chairperson. The Director General of Police and Additional Director General of Police (Law and Order) shall be the members of the Authority. The State Police Complaints Authority shall inquire into allegations of "serious misconduct" against the police Personnel in the supervisory ranks, on a complaint received from a victim or, in the case of death in custody, form legal heirs of the victim. Section 14 provides for constitution of District Police Complaints Authority. The District Police Complaints Authority shall have District Collector/District Magistrate as Chairperson. Superintendent of Police/Commissioner of Police, as the case may be, and Additional Superintendent of Police/Deputy Commissioner, as the case may be, shall be Members. District Police Complaints Authority shall enquire into allegations of misconduct or serious misconduct against police personnel in the subordinate rank.

In conclusion, it can be stated that there is place for upholding the human rights and human dignity of persons in the above detailed State Police Acts. They also generally attempt to provide accountability and impartiality by fixing minimum tenure of the Director General of Police and by providing provision for the constitution of State Security Commission, Police Establishment Board and Police Complaints Authorities. However, the Assam Police Act provides that even before the tenure of the Director General of Police the State Government can transfer him on the ground of public interest. This shows that the ultimate power of control and transfer of the Director General of Police is in the hands of the Government and the Government can transfer the Director

General of Police under the mask of public interest. While the Bihar, Gujarat, Rajasthan and Tamil Nadu Police Acts fixes the minimum tenure of the Director General of Police as two years, Haryana fixes it as one year, but Kerala does not fix the minimum tenure of State Police Chief.

The above State Police Acts provides for separation of crime investigation from law and order. The Assam Police Act provides for setting up of Criminal Investigation Department for investigation of inter-state, inter-district crimes and other specified crimes. The Bihar Police Act also provides for the creation of crime investigation units more or less in the similar way as provided by the Assam Police Act. The Haryana Police Act provides to create a specialised crime investigation unit in every Police district. The Rajasthan Police Act separates investigation units in such police stations which the Government may decide from time to time. Similarly, Kerala Police Act provides for separation of crime investigation in such areas which may be determined by the Government. Bombay Police (Gujarat Amendment) Act does not mention of separation. The Tamil Nadu Police Reforms Act clearly demarcates separation of law & order and crime investigation.

The State Police Acts detailed above provides for setting up of State Security Commissions, Police Establishment Boards and Police Complaints Authorities as directed by the Supreme Court. However, some State Police Acts deviate from the direction of the Supreme Court or the models suggested by the National Human Rights Commission or Ribeiro Committe or Soli Sorabjee Committee. The Bihar Police Act provides for setting up of State Police Board which shall be composed of three officials, namely, the Chief Secretary, the Director General of Police and the Home Secretary. This does not suit with the directives of the Supreme Court.

In Addition to the the above State Acts, Punjab, Chattisgarh, Uttarkhand, Sikkim and Tripura have also enacted new Police Acts in 2007 for their respective States. These State Police Acts provide two year's tenure for the Director Generals of Police in their respectives States. All these State Acts provide for seperate investigation units for crime investigation. They also provide for the constitution of State Security Commission, Police Establishment Board and Police Complaints Authorities as per the directives of the Supreme Court. While Punjab and Sikkim provide for constitution of State Police Board which will function as State Security Commission with Chief Minister as Chaiperson. Chattisgarh,

Uttarkhand and Tripura makes Home Minister of the State as Chairperson of the State Security Commission. Chief Secretary, Secretary in charge of Home department and Director Generals of Police are Members in all these Security Commissions. All these State Police Acts provide for constitution of Police Establishment Boards or Committees with the Director General of Police as the Chairperson and four or five senior police officers as the Members. In order to redress the grievances against police Chattisgarh Police Act provides for the constitution of Police Accountability Authority, Sikkim and Tripura Police Acts for the constitution of Police Accountability Commissions in their respective States with retired High Court Judge as Chairman. Uttarakhand Police Act provides for the constitution of State Police Complaint Authority with a Chairperson and four other Members. Four members shall be persons of eminence with experience in public dealing and having credible record of integrity and commitment to human rights as independent members and a police officer superannuated not below the rank of Inspector General of Police. Punjab Police Act provides that the State Government may, by notification, constitute State and District Police Complaint Authorities. The Act does not provide the composition of Chairperson and Members.

Thus, pursuant to the Supreme Court verdict in *Praskash Singh*'s case many States have come forward either to reform their existing police Act or to enact new police act in accordance with the guidelines of the Supreme Court. This is indeed an appreciable step on the part of States and Union Territories. The State Police Acts detailed above provides many provisions which are in agreement with human rights aspect of accused, victims and witnesses. The constitution of State Security Commission, Police Establishment Board and Police Complaints Authorities will have far reaching effects in the police-public relationship and prevention of torture, arbitrary arrest, illegal detention, unwanted search and seizure, false implication, failure to take action, etc. However, it shall be the primary responsibility of the respective State Governments and Union Territories to implement the provisions of the respective Police Acts effectively to ensure a more efficient but people friendly police for the State.

9. DEPARTMENTAL DISCIPLINARY ACTIONS

The service and disciplinary rules are State affairs in relation to State police establishments. However, the Indian Police Service is controlled by the Central Civil Service Rules that apply to the employees of the Government of India and the All India Service Rules that apply to All India Services such as Indian Administrative Service (IAS), Indian Police Service (IPS) and Indian Foreign Service (IFS). Members of the Indian Police Service are subject to disciplinary sanctions ranging from censure to dismissal.[97] However, in any case, the departmental mechanisms for dealing with police misconduct do not always inspire public confidence. There are allegations that police departments, many a times, suppress the incidents of criminality or misconduct by police officers because the revelation of the facts could damage the image of the organization or due to fraternity relationship within the department. There have always been allegations of partisanships and manipulations on the investigation of complaints against police officers.

Police officials as public servant enjoy some protection under Section 197 of Code of Criminal Procedure in the case of prosecution proceedings against them. Section 197 provides that Court shall not take cognizance of an offence except with the previous sanction of Government when any person who is or was a public servant not removable from his office save by or with the sanction of the Government is accused of any offence alleged to have been committed by him while acting or purporting to act in the discharge of his official duty. However, Supreme Court in *Surjeet Singh* v. *Jit Singh*[98] in 1997 held that the protection of Section 197 will not be available in the case of custodial death. Supreme Court relying on its earlier decision in *S.P. Saha* v. *M.S. Kochar*[99] observed that the investigation of an offence is certainly the duty of the police, but it can never be stated that during the course of investigation, the police

97. Section 311 of the Constitution and The All India Services (Discipline and Appeal) Rules, 1955, as well as the Central Service Rules of India and the individual States, the Police Act, 1861 and the provisions of the Police Acts of the individual Union States.
98. 1998 Cri.L.J. 3562.
99. 1979 Cri.L.J. 1367; In this case the customs officials dishonestly misappropriated the goods which they had seized and as such were holding in trust to be dealt with in accordance with law. The SC held that section 197 of the Code of Criminal Procedure cannot be construed too narrowly, in the sense that since the commission of offence is never a part of the official duty of a public servant, an act constituting an offence can never be said to have been done or purportedly done in the discharge of official duty, as such a narrow construction, will render the section entirely otiose.

are entitled to torture a person who was in their custody and thereby cause his death. In such circumstances, it cannot at all be said that they were acting only in the discharge of their duties while they allegedly tortured and caused the death of a person and hence, prosecution for the commission of such offences can never attract the provisions of Section 197 of the Code of Criminal Procedure.

9.1 Recommendations of the National Police Commission

In order to enhance the image of the police and to increase the trust of general public on the investigation against police atrocities, the National Police Commission, by departmental authorities and also by an independent authority outside the police. The National Police Commission felt that a large number of complaints against police should be looked into and disposed of by the supervisory ranks in the police hierarchy, but a judicial inquiry should be made mandatory in the following categories of complaints against the police:

(i) alleged rape of a woman in police custody;
(ii) death or grievous hurt caused while in the police custody; and
(iii) death of two or more persons resulting from police firing in the dispersal of unlawful assemblies.[100]

The response of the Government to these recommendations had been very cold for long. However, the Government has incorporated Magisterial enquiry into the rape or death cases in police custody by the new Amendment to the Code of Criminal Procedure in 2005.[101]

9.2. Departmental Actions

The Police Acts provides elaborate provisions for departmental actions and for departmental enquiry Proceedings. Any police officer, who commits any misconduct or offence may be subjected to departmental enquiry proceedings under the State Police Departmental Enquiries, Punishment and Appeal, Rules notified by the Government. The State Police Chief may order initiation of action against any police officer before the Court in accordance with the provisions of the Code of Criminal Procedure, in addition to the

100. See supra Ch. 1, p. 6, n. 1.
101. Code of Criminal Procedure, S. 176.

Departmental Enquiry Proceedings. However, the official found guilty of disciplinary proceedings shall not be considered as a criminal nor be sentenced to any punishment under the Criminal law. The penalties that may be imposed on a police officer found guilty on completion of the departmental inquiry generally are:

(a) fine;
(b) extra duty including drill and physical training;
(c) recovery of loss caused to Government from salary;
(d) recovery of loss sustained to the concerned party from salary;
(e) giving training to improve work and conduct;
(f) prohibit from performing fixed particular duties or assigning fixed particular rank;
(g) warning;
(h) censure;
(i) barring increment without cumulative effect;
(j) barring increment with cumulative effect;
(k) withholding of promotion;
(l) reducing pay without cumulative effect;
(m) reducing pay with cumulative effect;
(n) reduction in seniority or rank;
(o) compulsory retirement;
(p) removal;
(q) dismissal.

Department level enquiry proceedings may be initiated against any police officer for the same matter even though he was exonerated by a criminal court after trial. A police officer if convicted for an offence involving moral turpitude or serious misconduct, the disciplinary authority concerned or the State Police Chief or the Government may, after considering the nature of the offence, make him compulsorily retire or remove or dismiss that officer from service.

9.3. Departmental Inquiries, Punishment and Appeal

Since it is vital for the police to maintain higher level of discipline than any other governmental department the disciplinary proceedings of the proceedings of the police department are of prime significance. The rules relating to the award of punishments to the members of the police service are provided under the State Police Departmental Inquiries, Punishment and Appeal rules maintained by each State. The procedure prior to awarding punishments can be split into three categories.

a. Minor defaults where formal charge need not be framed
b. Defaults where no oral inquiry is necessary, but a charge is framed
c. Defaults where a charge is framed and an oral inquiry or personal hearing is held[102]

Thus, in summary, if either the IPS officers or the State police officers commit misconduct, the same shall attract disciplinary proceedings. However, the disciplinary punishments are not considered as criminal sanctions. Nonetheless, there is no restriction to bring other criminal or civil action against the erring personnel. It is to be noted that when a police officer commits excess, most of the time, unless there is a hue and cry from public and media, departmental enquiries are not ordered and are not carried out properly due to political pressure or partisanship. Even where the police officer is found culprit, now the practice is that the State takes the responsibility of making the payment of compensation to the victims. In all cases where the police commit human rights violations against common man, the State should make the erring police officer to be personally liable for paying the compensation. This may considerably reduce human rights violations by the police.

10. CONCLUSION

The Indian legal system provides a number of provisions and procedures to protect persons from arbitrary arrest, unlawful detention, interrogation, false implication, vexatious searches and seizures, torture, etc., from the police. The Code of Criminal Procedure provides provisions that are to be followed in making arrest, detention, seizures etc. These procedures are considered to be inadequate to tackle the police excesses. Hence, the Supreme Court made guidelines and directives in *Joginder Kumar* and *D.K. Basu* cases as a temporary measure until the new legislation has been made by the Government to this effect.

The Indian Penal Code does not provide an exclusive definition of "torture" nor does it prescribe punishment as such for torture committed by the police. However, there are various general

102. N.R. Madhava Menon, Criminal Justice India Series: Kerala, Vol. 6 (2002), p. 42.

provisions such as hurt, grievous hurt, assault, public servant concealing design to commit offence which it is his duty to prevent, public servant disobeying law with intent to cause injury to any person, criminal use of force, unlawful confinement, unlawful restraint, etc., which may be used against police atrocities. Nonetheless, the Indian Penal Code provides very few specific provisions such as Sections 330 and 331 which provide for punishment for causing hurt or grievous hurt to extort confession or to compel restoration of property respectively and Section 376(2)(a) which provides punishment for committing rape in police custody. Since police commit torture and other atrocities in custody where there are no witnesses other than police personnel, the general provisions of the Indian Penal Code have proved to be inadequate in order to bring the erring police officer to justice.

Indian Police Act which was enacted in 1861 during the period of British rule to coerce and suppress people who stood against the rule is still followed in India. This has been criticized by National Police Commission, Law Commission of India, Mallimath Committee, etc. Many Commissions and Committees such as Dharma Veera Commission (National Police Commission), Reibero Commission, Soli Sorabjee Committee and Justice Mallimath Committee were constituted, from time to time, for making recommendations to the reform of law relating to the police. However, the recommendation of these Commissions and Committees were not implemented by the Government of India. Considering the lethargic attitude of the Government in reforming Police Act even after recommendations of the various Commissions and Committees, the Supreme Court in *Prakash Singh*'s case gave directions to the Government to reform police Acts at the Centre, States and Union Territories with specific guidelines.

Consequent to the directives of the Supreme Court, the Governments of many States have passed new Police Acts in their respective States. Assam, Bihar, Punjab, Rajasthan, Gujarat, Haryana, Sikkim, Tripura, Chhattisgarh and Uttarakhand passed the new Police Act in 2007. Kerala enacted the Police Act in 2011, Karnataka in 2012 and Tamil Nadu in 2013. Many States and Union Territories are still attempting to reform the Police Acts. The new State Police Acts contain provisions for protection of human rights and human dignity of individuals. These Acts also attempts to change the colonial dreaded attitudinal behaviour of police with polished and civilized behaviour. These Acts also ensure increased autonomy for the police department by providing provisions for establishing a Police Establishment Board for posting, promotion and transfer of employment of police with a view to minimize political and Governmental interference at minimal level. Another significant features of these State Acts are the complaint redressal mechanisms against the police personnel by providing for the establishment of State Police Complaint Authority and the District Police Complaint Authorities. The Authority with retired High Court Judge as Chairperson at State level and retired District Judge at District level can ensure more impartial mechanism for redressing the complaints/ grievances against police atrocities. The mechanism may be considered as a milestone in the protection of human rights in the years to come. However, there are criticisms about the form and content of the Security Commission and Complaint Authorities in many States. Despite the fact of criticism, these State Police Acts are a lead ahead for reformation of the police in India. Above all, the success of the Acts lies on the fact that the public, the Government, the Police Department, the concerned professional groups, the human rights groups and the media must closely monitor police practices to see that provisions are upheld.

6

National Human Rights Commission

The Constitution and the Statutes in India provided various provisions related with human rights protection. However, the only available impartial method of redressal of grievance against violation of human rights was through the tiresome, expensive and lengthy process of court proceedings. So the effective monitoring of the human rights protection was a major concern for India for long. Enactment of Protection of Human Rights Act in 1993 was a milestone in the history of protection of human rights in India. The Act provides for the establishment of human rights Commissions at National and State levels and for the constitution of human rights Courts at Sessions level in the State for the effective protection and promotion of human rights. The preamble of the Protection of Human Rights Act mirrors the purpose as "an Act to provide for the constitution of a National Human Rights Commission, State Human Rights Commission in States and Human Rights Courts for better protection of Human Rights and for matters connected therewith or incidental thereto."

Thus, the Protection of Human Rights Act provides for the institutionalized monitoring and protection through the establishment of National and State level Human Rights Commissions and Human Right Courts. In accordance with the Protection of Human Rights Act, the Government of India established National Human Rights Commission on October 12,

1993.[1] India is the first country to establish the National Human Rights Commission among the South Asian countries, and also few among the National Human Rights Institutions in the world which were established as early as 1990s.[2]

I. COMPOSITION OF NATIONAL HUMAN RIGHTS COMMISSION

The National Human Rights Commission consists of a Chairperson and four Members.[3] The Chairpersons of the National Commission for Minorities, the National Commission for the Scheduled Castes,[4] the National Commission for Scheduled Tribes[5] and of the National Commission for Women are ex-officio Members of the National Human Rights Commission. Only a person who has been a Chief Justice of the Supreme Court can be appointed as the Chairperson of the National Human Rights Commission. Two other Members must also be persons who held positions in Higher Judiciary.[6] Other two Members are persons having knowledge of, or practical experience in, matters relating to human rights.[7] Thus, out of five members of the National Human Rights Commission, three are from the higher judiciary.

There are criticisms on the scheme of the selection of members as it is mainly limited to persons belonging to judiciary who may not

1. S. 3 of the Protection of Human Rights Act empowers the central government to constitute the National Human Rights Commission and also sets out the composition of office bearers and members of the Commission.
2. The Human Rights Commission of Sri Lanka was established under the Human Rights Commission of Sri Lanka Act, No. 21 (1996) and became operational in September 1997. The National Human Rights Commission of Nepal is an independent statutory body established in the year 2000 under the Human Rights Commission Act 1997. See Also Manoj Kumar Sinha, Role of the National Human Rights Commission of India in Protection of Human Rights, available at: http://www.rwi.lu.se/pdf/seminar/manoj05.pdf (Visited on January 12, 2011).
3. Protection of Human Rights Act, S. 3(2).
4. Substituted by Amendment Act 43 of 2006 for "The National Commission for the Scheduled Castes and Scheduled Tribes".
5. Substituted by Amendment Act 43 of 2006 for "The National Commission for the Scheduled Castes and Scheduled Tribes".
6. S. 3 (2) of the Protection of Human Rights Act states that one Member shall be a person who is a sitting or a retired judge of the Supreme Court and another Member, a sitting or a retired Chief Justice of a High Court.
7. Protection of Human Rights Act, S. 3(2).

have proficiency in or commitment for human rights. In this way, the National Human Rights Commission is "restricted from getting the plurality of perspectives, vocations and diverse experiences from the civil society."[8] It is to be noted that since the three Members are from higher judiciary who have proven track record of impartiality and judicious decision making can ensure high fortitude of objectivity and deep sense of responsibility in settling the disputes and recommending the Governments to take appropriate measures to protect the human rights as the matter concerned is human rights, its violation and protection.

2. APPOINTMENT OF CHAIRPERSON AND MEMBERS

The appointment of the Chairperson and others Members of the National Human Rights Commission are made by the President of India upon the recommendation of a high level Committee under the Chairmanship of Prime Minister of India. The Selection Committee shall consist of Speaker of the *Lok Sabha*, Minister in-charge of the Ministry of Home Affairs in the Government of India, Leaders of the opposition in the *Lok Sabha* and *Rajya Sabha*, and Deputy Chairman of the *Rajya Sabha* as Members.[9] Thus, in the matters of appointment of the Chairperson and Members of the National Human Rights Commission, the leaders of the opposition in the *Lok Sabha* and *Rajya Sabha* are included to ensure impartiality and fairness. Here again, there are criticisms on the selection process, and also about the Selection Committee itself. The first criticism is that the committee recommending selection of the Chairperson and the Members consists solely of politicians. It does not consist of high profile experts or experienced personalities in the areas of human rights. Secondly, the process of selection is not transparent because the composition of the National Human Rights Commission is generally decided through "noting in secret files or during closed door meetings between the politicians and their favourite bureaucrats."[10] However, the inclusion of opposition leaders in the appointment process of the National Human Rights Commission

8. Joshi G.P., National Human Rights Commission—Need for Review, Commonwealth Human Rights Initiative Publications, New Delhi, available at : http://www.humanrightsinitiative.org/programs/aj/police/papers/gpj/national_human_rights_ commission.pdf (Visited on July 12, 2010).
9. Protection of Human Rights Act, S. 4(1).
10. *Supra* n. 8.

may be seen as making the selection on an impartial method rather than as a partisan process of Government.

3. INDEPENDENCE OF CHAIRPERSON AND THE MEMBERS

The Protection of Human Rights Act makes the office of the Chairperson and the Members impartial and autonomous. The Chairperson and the Members are made ineligible to hold any office under the Central or State Government after retirement from the Commission.[11] This way, to a considerable extent, the Act ensures autonomy and independence of the National Human Rights Commission in as much as they can act impartially without being ambitious to get into any governmental position after retirement. Another significant aspect that makes the office of the Chairperson or Members of the National Human Rights Commission independent is that it explicitly prohibits the varying of the salary or allowances or other terms and conditions of service of a Member to his disadvantage after his appointment and during the tenure of office.[12] So the Chairperson and Members can function without the apprehension of reducing the salary, allowances or term of service by the Government if the decisions of the Commission are adverse to the interest of the Government. Thus, the Protection of Human Rights Act takes possible measures in order to make the office of the Chairperson and its Members to be impartial and autonomous, free, and independent of Governmental interference.

4. POWERS AND FUNCTIONS OF THE COMMISSION

The National Human Rights Commission enjoys a large number of powers for the promotion and protection of human rights. The powers and functions of the National Human Rights Commission are elaborately provided under Chapter III of the Protection of Human Rights Act.

4.1. Power to Inquire into the Violations of Human Rights

The most important power that has been entrusted with the Commission is the power to inquire *suo motu* or on a petition

11. Protection of Human Rights Act, S. 6 (3).; The Chairperson shall hold office for a period of five years or until he attains seventy years of age, whichever is earlier and the Members also hold office for a period of five years or until he attains seventy years of age, whichever is earlier. However, Members can be reappointed for one more term of five years.
12. *Id.*, S.8.

presented to it by a victim or any person on his behalf, into the complaint registered against a public servant on charges of violation of human rights.[13] This power can equally be exercised by the Commission even in the case of abetment, or for negligence in the prevention of such violation by a public servant. The Commission has been extensively using *suo motu* power to inquire into the violation of human rights committed by the police. Invoking such powers the National Human Rights Commission has taken action in many cases right from its establishment in 1993. Some of the significant cases where the Commission took cognizance *suo motu* are the death of two persons in police firing in Meghalaya,[14] custodial death of Shri. Madan Lal in Delhi,[15] amputation of male organ of Shri Jugta Ram in police custody in Barmer, Rajasthan,[16] beating up of Mr. Suseel Kumar and his wife by the Police of Gautam Budh Nagar,[17] firing by security forces in Bijbehara, Jammu & Kashmir killing 60 persons,[18] firing by Armed Forces killing at least 5 persons including a minor in Manipur,[19] killing of innocent citizens in the wake of post Godhra violence in Gujarat,[20] shooting and injuring 21

13. Protection of Human Rights Act 1993, S.12 (a).
14. National Human Rights Commission, Annual Report 1993-94 (1994), para 5.6; the inquiry was made by the National Human Rights Commission on the basis of a broadcast over All India Radio on 5 November 1993.
15. *Ibid.* The inquiry was made by the National Human Rights Commission on a report published in a newspaper dated 30 November 1993 captioned "Two Cops Suspended for Custody Death".
16. *Ibid.* The inquiry was made by the National Human Rights Commission on a Newspaper report dated 10 February 1994 and captioned "Cops Cut off Man's Penis".
17. National Human Rights Commission, Annual report 2007-08 (2008), p. 44; The inquiry was made by the National Human Rights Commission on a news report published in the "Times of India" on the 16th September 2006 under the headline: "Brutal Cops Batter Noida Couple".
18. National Human Rights Commission, Annual Report 1993-94 (1994), p.13; The inquiry was made by the National Human Rights Commission on the press report.
19. National Human Rights Commission, 2001-02 Annual Report (2002), p. 175; the inquiry was made by the National Human Rights Commission on Press report.
20. National Human Rights Commission, 2007-08 Annual Report (2008), p.52; cognizance was taken by the National Human Rights Commission on the basis of a programme, "Operation Kalank" telecast on TV channel 'Aajtak' on 25th October 2007, accusing the State functionaries of Gujarat, including the Chief Minister, Minister of State for Home Affairs

scheduled castes by the police in a land dispute in Allahabad, U.P.[21] There are numerous other instances where the Commission has *suo motu* taken action. The National Human Rights Commission has been expansively using the power to inquire and take cognizance of cases of the violation of human rights by the State functionaries.

4.2. Power to Intervene in Court Proceedings

Another significant power enjoined by the National Human Rights Commission is the power to intervene under Section 12 (b) in any proceeding involving any allegation of violation of human rights pending before a court with the approval of such court. Invoking the power of intervention the Commission has intervened in many cases in the legal proceedings. The Commission had intervened in a case which was pending proceedings in the Punjab & Haryana Court relating to the disappearance of Harjit Singh.[22] The infamous *Best Bakery case*[23] is another best illustration of it. This case is a vivid illustration of human rights violations committed in the State of Gujarat during the 2002 riots.[24] Fourteen persons were brutally killed by a mob in the presence of the police and the policemen were reluctant to take any action to prevent the killings. Investigation was not properly conducted by the Gujarat State Administration. The National Human Rights Commission had recommended the State Government and State officials to provide securities for the victims and witnesses for attending the trial, but the recommendations were not seriously taken by the authorities, and as a result, the witnesses turned hostile and accused were acquitted.[25] The Commission, on receiving reports from its own investigation team and deeply

---

and Police Officers, for abetment of killing of innocent citizens in the wake of post Godhra violence.

21. National Human Rights Commission, 2007-08 Annual Report (2008), p. 58; the inquiry was made by the National Human Rights Commission on a distressing report captioned "21 SCs Shot due to Land Dispute", which appeared in a publication by the 'Indian People's Tribunal on Untouchablity".
22. National Human Rights Commission, Human Rights Newsletter, Vol. 2, n.7 (1995), p. 1.
23. *National Human Rights Commission v. State of Gujarat*, Crl.M.P. No.10719/2003 in WP (Crl.) No. 109/2003, available at : www.indiankanoon.org/doc/168922/?type=print (Visited on August 12, 2010).
24. *Zahira Habibulla v. State of Gujarat*, A.I.R. 2004 S.C. 3114; shortly known as "Best Bakery Case".
25. Case No. 1150/6/2001/2002, National Human Rights Commission, Annual Report, 2002-03 (2003), p. 188.

concerned with the truth being buried at the hands of human rights violators, took a remarkable step in filing a Special Leave Petition for a separate investigation by an independent agency and for retrial of the case to be conducted outside of Gujarat State as there were serious human rights violations involved in the case. The Supreme Court accepted the plea of the Commission and issued orders in connection with re-investigation and retrial.[26] Thus, the Commission enjoys power to intervene in legal proceedings before a court or to approach a court for appropriate orders.

4.3. Power to Make Surprise Visits

The Protection of Human Rights Act empowers the National Human Rights Commission to make surprise visits to police stations, jails or other institutions under the control of the State Government where persons are detained or lodged.[27] In exercise of such power, the National Human Rights Commission or its officials have visited a number of jails and lock-ups in Andhra Pradesh and Bihar the same year and made a series of observations which were attended to in consultation with the competent State authorities.[28] The Commission continues the periodical visits in many jails and lock-ups in other States and Union Territories.[29] The periodic and surprise visits by the National Human Rights Commission works as an oversight mechanism for the police and other detention authorities.

---

26. The other notable incidence where the National Human Rights Commission involved in bringing protection of human rights are Starvation death case in Orissa Case No. 37/3/97-LD, National Human Rights Commission, 2002-03 Annual report (2003), p.197; and the Mass Cremation case in Punjab and protection of Mentally disabled persons (Case No. 1/97/NHRC; Two writ petitions, Writ Petition (Crl.) No. 497/95, ParamjitKaur v. State of Punjab, and Writ Petition (Crl.) No. 447/95, Committee for Information and Initiative on Punjab v. State of Punjab were filed before the Supreme Court containing serious allegations about large-scale cremations resorted to by the Punjab Police of persons allegedly killed in what were termed as "encounters".
27. Protection of Human Rights Act, S.12 (c); Inserted by Protection of Human Rights (Amendment) Act 43 of 2006.
28. National Human Rights Commission, Annual Report 1998-99, para.3.26; See also Annual Reports of 1999-2000, 2000-01, 2001-02, 2002-03, 2003-04, 2004-05, 2005-06, 2006-07, 2007-08.
29. Visited Thihar jail on 14th June, 2007, (See, National Human Rights Commission, Annual Report 2007-08 (2008) p. 26); Visited District jail at Shillong and Jowai from 6-8 June, 2006, (See National Human Rights Commission, Annual Report 2006-07 (2006), p. 15); Visited Central jail,

4.4. Power of Review of the Laws and Policies

It is one of the functions of the National Human Rights Commission to conduct a systematic review of the human rights policies of the Government in order to identify shortcomings in the human rights observance and to suggest ways of improvements.[30]

Invoking this authority, the Commission has vehemently criticized the Terrorist & Disruptive Activities (Prevention) Act (TADA)[31] and also questioned the need for the Prevention of Terrorism Ordinance, 2001 (POTO).[32] A number of laws and policies have been received the attention of the Commission, in accordance with sub-sections (d) and (f) of Section 12 of Protection of Human Rights Act. On the basis of requests from Governments, the Commission made comments on the draft legislation of Freedom of Information Bill 2000, the Protection from Domestic Violence Bill 2002; the Prevention of Terrorism Act, 2002; draft of Model Prison Manual, Food Safety and Standard Bill, 2005, the draft bill for ratification of Convention against Torture, Copy Right (Amendment Bill), 2010.[33] Thus, the Commission plays a vital role in the reviews of the laws, policies, regulations and draft legislations from the point of human rights perspective and provide comments/ recommendations to the Governments.

Raipur, Chattisghar on 14th February, 2006 (See National Human Rights Commission, Annual Report 2005-06 (2006), p. 18); Visited jails in Tripura, Kerala, Andhra Pradesh, Goa and Chandigarh during the year 2004-05 (See National Human Rights Commission, Annual Report 2004-05 (2005), pp. 17-18).

30. Kaur Jaskaran, *A Judicial Blackout: Judicial Impunity for Disappearances in Punjab, India*, Harvard Human Rights Journal, Vol. 15 (2002) p. 269; Seealso Reenu Paul, National Human Rights Commission of India: A Human Rights Evaluation, (2003), (Unpublished MA thesis, London School of Economics, London).
31. National Human Rights Commission, Annual Report 1993-94 (1994), Para 7.3.
32. *Id.*, Annual Report 2001-02 (2002), p. 48.
33. National Human Rights Commission, Annual Reports 2007-08, p. 143, 2005-06, p. 205, National Human Rights Commission, Human Rights Newsletter (May 2003); National Human Rights Commission: India, Office of the High Commission for Human Rights publication, 2010; the other functions, inter alia, include to review the factors, including acts of terrorism that inhibit the enjoyment of human rights and recommend appropriate remedial measures; study treaties and other international instruments on human rights and make recommendations for their effective implementation; undertake and promote research in the field of

4.5. Power of a Civil Court

While inquiring into the complaints, the National Human Rights Commission enjoys all the powers of a civil court trying a suit in respect of the following matters, *namely*:

(a) summoning and enforcing the attendance of witnesses and examine them on oath;
(b) discovery and production of any document;
(c) receiving evidence on affidavits;
(d) requisitioning any public record or copy thereof from any court or office;
(e) issuing commissions for the examination of witnesses or documents;
(f) any other matter which may be prescribed.[34]

Besides, the National Human Rights Commission shall have power to require any person to furnish information on matters that may be useful for/relevant to the subject matter under inquiry. and any person so required shall be deemed to be legally bound to furnish such information within the meaning of Section 176[35] and Section

---

human rights; spread human rights literacy among various sections of society and promote awareness of the safeguards available for the protection of these rights through publications, the media, seminars and other available means; encourage the efforts of non-governmental organizations and institutions working in the field of human rights; and any other functions as it may consider necessary for the protection of human rights.

34. Protection of Human Rights Act, S.13(1).
35. Section 176 of the Indian Penal Code, provides "Whoever, being legally bound to give any notice or to furnish information on any subject to any public servant, as such, intentionally omits to give such notice or to furnish such information in the manner and at the time required by law, shall be punished with simple imprisonment for a term which may extend to one month, or with fine which may extend to five hundred rupees, or with both; or, if the notice or information required to be given respects the commission of an offence, or is required for the purpose of preventing the commission of an offence, or in order to the apprehension of an offender, with simple imprisonment for a term which may extend to six months, or with fine which may extend to one thousand rupees, or with both; 2*[or, if the notice or information required to be given is required by an order passed under sub-section (1) of section 565 of the Code of Criminal Procedure, 1898 (5 of 1898), with imprisonment of either description for a term which may extend to six months, or with fine which may extend to one thousand rupees, or with both.]".

177[36] of the Indian Penal Code.[37] Further, the Commission or any officer authorized by the National Human Rights Commission, may enter any building or place where the National Human Rights Commission has reason to believe that any document relating to the subject matter of the inquiry may be found, and may seize any such document or take extracts or copies there from subject to the provisions of section 100[38] of the Code of Criminal Procedure, 1973, in so far as it may be applicable.[39] Thus, wide powers are given to the National Human Rights Commission in the matters of summoning persons or public servants, searching for finding documents and seizing of such materials.

4.6. Power to Initiate Criminal Proceedings in Certain Cases

The National Human Rights Commission is generally deemed to be a civil court. However, when wilful omissions are committed by the public servant in the view or presence of the Commission, it can, after recording the facts constituting the offence and the statement of the accused as provided for in the Criminal Procedure Code, forward the case to a Magistrate having jurisdiction to try the same.[40] The Magistrate to whom any such case is forwarded shall

36. Section 177 of the Indian Penal Code, provides Furnishing false information: Whoever, being legally bound to furnish information on any subject to any public servant, as such, furnishes, as true, information on the subject which he knows or has reason to believe to be false shall be punished with simple imprisonment for a term which may extend to six months, or with fine which may extend to one thousand rupees, or with both; or, if the information which he is legally bound to give respects the commission of an offence, or is required for the purpose of preventing the commission of an offence, or in order to the apprehension of an offender, with imprisonment of either description for a term which may extend to two years, or with fine, or with both.
37. Protection of Human Rights Act, S.13(2).
38. Section 100 (1) of the Criminal procedure Code 1973 provides "Persons in charge of closed place to allow search: Whenever any place liable to search or inspection under this Chapter is closed, any person residing in, or being in charge of, such place, shall, on demand of the officer or other person executing the warrant, and on production of the warrant, allow him free ingress thereto, and afford all reasonable facilities for a search therein."
39. Protection of Human Rights Act, S.13(3).
40. Protection of Human Rights Act, S.13 (4); such offences are described in the S. 175, 178-180 and S.228 of the Indian Penal Code. S. 175 of the Indian Penal Code deals with Omission to produce document to public servant by person legally bound to produce it; S. 178 of the Indian Penal

proceed to hear the complaint against the accused as if the case has been forwarded to him under Section 346[41] of the Criminal Procedure Code.[42] These provisions reveal that the National Human Rights Commission has no independent prosecuting powers.

4.7. Power of Investigation

When the National Human Rights Commission gets reports of human rights violations, it can make necessary inquiries with the help of its independent investigative agency. The Protection of Human Rights Act casts an obligation on the Central Government to make available an officer not below the rank of a Director General of Police and other necessary staff for the purpose of the investigation.The Investigating Officer submits a report to the Commission within the specified period after the investigation.[43] The Commission may verify the correctness of the report of such investigation.[44] It is to be noted that the assistance form the investigating experts is advantageous for the Commission to gather information directly from the spot where violations of human rights took place.

Code deals with Refusing oath or affirmation when duly required by public servant to make it; S. 179 of the Indian Penal Code deals with Refusing to answer public servant autho rized to question; S. 180 of the Indian Penal Code deals with Refusing to sign statement; S. 228 of the Indian Penal Code deals with Intentional insult or interruption to public servant sitting in judicial proceeding.

41. S. 346 of the Criminal Procedure Code provides that "if the court in any case considers that a person accused of any of the offences referred to in section 345 (Section 345 of the Criminal Procedure deals with certain offences of contempt as described in section 175, section 178, section 179, section 180 or section 228 of the Indian Penal Code, 1860) and committed in its view or presence should be imprisoned otherwise than in default of payment of fine, or that a fine exceeding two hundred rupees should be imposed upon him, or such Court is for any other reason of opinion that the case should not be disposed of under section 345, such Court, after recording the facts constituting the offence and the statement of the accused as hereinbefore provided, may forward the case to a Magistrate having jurisdiction to try the same, and may require security to be given for the appearance of such person before such Magistrate, or if sufficient security is not given shall forward such person in custody to such Magistrate. The Magistrate to whom any case is forwarded under this section shall proceed to deal with, as far as may be, as if it were instituted on a police report".
42. Protection of Human Rights Act, S.13(4).
43. *Id.*, S.14 (4).
44. *Ibid.*

5. ENFORCEABILITY OF DECISIONS AFTER INQUIRY

The following steps may be taken by the Commission after the completion of an inquiry :[45]

(1) where the inquiry discloses violation of human rights or negligence in the prevention of violation of human rights by a public servant, the Commission may recommend to the concerned Government or authority the initiation of proceedings for prosecution or such other action as the Commission may deem fit against the concerned person or persons;

(2) approach the Supreme Court or the High Court concerned for such directions, orders or writs as the Court may deem necessary;

(3) recommend to the concerned Government or authority for the grant of such immediate interim relief to the victim or the members of his family as the Commission may consider necessary;

(4) provide a copy of the inquiry report to the petitioner or his representative (subject to the provisions of clause (5) of section 17;

(5) the Commission shall send a copy of its inquiry report together with its recommendations to the concerned Government or authority and the concerned Government or authority shall, within a period of one month, or such further time as the Commission may allow, forward its comments on the report, including the action taken or proposed to be taken thereon, to the Commission;

(6) the Commission shall publish its inquiry report together with the comments of the concerned Government or authority, if any, and the action taken or proposed to be taken by the concerned Government or authority on the recommendations of the Commission.

In fact, the National Human Rights Commission is established primarily as a recommendatory body. The Commission submits an annual report to the Central Government, and to the State

45. Section 18 has been substituted after the amendment in the Protection of Human Rights Act in 2006 for providing the course of action that is required to be taken by the Commission after the completion of the inquiry.

Government concerned.[46] It may, at any time, submit special reports on any matter which, in its opinion, is of such urgency or importance that it should not be deferred till submission of the annual report.[47] The reports of the Commission are required to be placed in the Parliament or to the State Legislature, as the cases may be, with the memorandum of action taken or proposed to be taken by the Government. Article 20 sub-section (2) further provides that if the Government considers that the recommendations of the Commission cannot be complied with, it must furnish reasons for non-acceptance of the recommendations.

6. COMPLAINTS RECEIVED BY THE COMMISSION

After the establishment in 1993, the National Human Rights Commission has started functioning actively bringing out many cases that wouldn't have come to lime light but for the efforts of the Commission. In the beginning, the number of complaints received was very less. However, the number of complaints gradually increased over the years. During 1993-94, the very year of inauguration of the National Human Rights Commission, and immediately thereafter, the Commission received 496 complaints of violation of human rights.[48] Over the years, the number of complaints has increased progressively and during the period from 1st April 2009 to 31st April 2010, it received 82,022 complaints.[49] Whereas the number of complaints received during 2003-04 was 71,427.[50] There is an increase of 14.83 per cent between 2003-04 and 2009-10. The Table 6.1 shows a gradual increase from the year 2003-04 to 2009-10. However, in the year 2008-09 and 2009-10 there was slight decrease in the number of complaints/intimations received by the Commission. The Commission claims that "the phenomenal increase in the number of complaints is indicative of growing awareness amongst the people in the country as well as the increased trust in the Commission".[51]

---

46. Protection of Human Rights Act, S.20.
47. *Id.*, S.20 (1).
48. National Human Rights Commission, Annual Report 2009-10 (2010), p. 14.
49. Asia Pacific Forum, Activities of the National Human Rights Commission-India 2009-10, Report to 15th Annual Meeting (2010), p. 8.
50. National Human Rights Commission, Annual Report 2003-04 (2004), p. 138.
51. 13th Asia Pacific Forum Meeting at Kuala Lumpur, Report of National Human Rights Commission of India (2008), p. 3.

TABLE 6.1

Number of Complaints Received by the NHRC from April 2003 till March 2010

Year	*2003-04*	*2004-05*	*2005-06*	*2006-07*	*2007-08*	*2008-09*	*2009-10*
Complaints received	71,427	72,775	74,444	82,233	100,616	90,942	820,22
Complaints disposed of/ concluded	57,694	64,369	80,923	93,421	102,848	103,996	85587

Source : NHRC, Annual Reports 2003-04 to 2009-10.

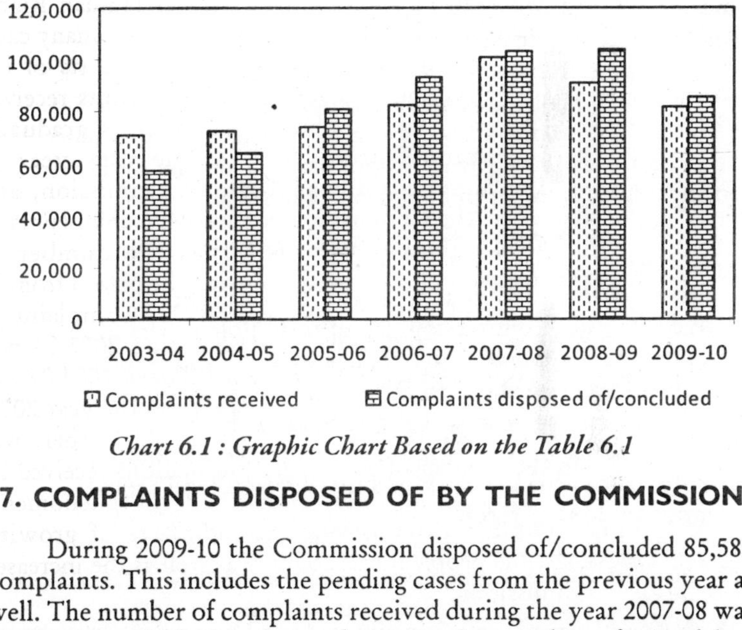

Chart 6.1 : Graphic Chart Based on the Table 6.1

7. COMPLAINTS DISPOSED OF BY THE COMMISSION

During 2009-10 the Commission disposed of/concluded 85,587 complaints. This includes the pending cases from the previous year as well. The number of complaints received during the year 2007-08 was 82,022. The Table 6.1 shows the year wise number of complaints received and complaints disposed of/concluded cases from 2003-04 to 2009-10. Form the Table 6.1, on an average the disposal rate is higher than the complaints received. Further, Table 6.1 shows that there is a gradual increase in the number of cases disposed of by the Commission from 2003-04 to 2009-10 except for the year 2009-10 where there is slight decrease. Comparing complaints received and complaints disposed of, the more the number of complaints received the more the number of disposal of cases. Thus, the Commission is very quick and active in disposing off the complaints/intimations received by it.

8. INTERIM RELIEF

During the year 2009-10, the National Human Rights Commission recommended to Rs. 63,483,000.[52] In 2007-08, the amount recommended by the Commission was only Rs. 32,000,000 to be paid in 199 cases.[53] There was an increase almost twice the amount of interim relief and twice the number of complaints within a span of two years. While in the year 2002-03 the Commission recommended for compensation amounting to Rs. 3,140,000 to be paid in 39 cases.[54] These figures show the dramatic increase in the amount of interim relief recommended by the Commission in appropriate cases. In addition to recommending interim reliefs, the Commission also recommends for disciplinary actions. In 2007-08 it recommended for the disciplinary action in 11 cases and prosecution in 2 cases.[55] From the above, it can be understood that the work of the National Human Rights Commission is on the right direction settling a large number of complaints annually.

9. COMPLAINTS AGAINST POLICE

It is pathetic to state that the majority of the complaints received by the Commission are against police personnel.[56] The Commission is subdued about police excesses and atrocities and it recommends for taking stern action against erring police personnel. The complaints against police can broadly be classified into two heads depending on the seriousness of offence committed, namely, (i) custodial death/rape cases, and (ii) torture/illegal arrest/unlawful detention and other cases.

---

52. National Human Rights Commission, Annual Report 2001-02 (2002), p. 138.
53. National Human Rights Commission, Annual Report for 2007-08 (2008), p. 184.
54. National Human Rights Commission, Annual Report for 2002-03 (2003), p. 170.
55. National Human Rights Commission, Annual Report for 2007-08 (2008), p. 184.
56. Joshi, G.P., Police Accountability in India, Commonwealth Human Rights Initiative, New Delhi, available at : www.humanrightsinitiative.org/.../police/...police_accountability_ in_india.pdf (Visited on May 14, 2010).

9.1. Custodial Death/Rape Cases

The National Human Rights Commission has been taking serious measures against custodial violence in the cases of deaths or rapes by the police ever since its commencement of functioning. Immediately after the establishment, one of the significant steps that was taken by the Commission was directing all the States and the Union Territories requiring District Magistrates and Superintendents of Police to report directly to the Commission any instance of death or rape in police custody within twenty four hours of its occurrence.[57] It was also made clear by the Commission that failure to send such reports would lead to a presumption that an effort was being made to suppress the facts.[58] The communication stated: "*in view of the rising number of incidents (custodial deaths/rapes)*[59] *and reported attempts to suppress or present a different picture of these incidents with the lapse of time, the Commission has taken a view that a direction should be issued forthwith to the District Magistrates and Superintendents of Police of every district that they should report to the Secretary General of the Commission about such incidents within 24 hours of occurrence or of those officers having come to known about such incidents. Failure to report promptly would give rise to presumption that there was an attempt to suppress the incident.*"[60]

Another significant step that has been taken by the Commission is in relation to *post mortem*. Since there is no credible and reliable witnesses or evidences in the custodial death cases, the only important evidence is the *post mortem* report. As the officials involved in the custodial death crime are police/jailors, there are all possibilities of manipulation in such *post mortem* reports either by influence or by coercion of surgeons conducting the *post mortem*. Anticipating such manipulations, the Commission had recommended to the State Governments to video-film all *post-mortem* examinations and to send the cassettes to the Commission.[61] Thus, the Commission made solemn designs to make the higher officials of the Government responsible for the acts of death in custody.

---

57. Letter No. 66/SG/NHRC/93, dated 14th December 1993, National Human Rights Commission, Annual Report 1993-94 (1994), Annexure IV.
58. *Ibid.*
59. *Emphasis added.*
60. Letter No. 66/SG/NHRC/93, dated 14th Dec. 1993, NHRC, AR 1993-94 (1994), Annexure IV.
61. National Human Rights Commission, Annual Report 1997-98 (1998), p. 53.

There were 2222 complaints of deaths in police custody received by the National Human Rights Commission from 1-9-1993 to 31-3-2008 and all these deaths were reported within 24 hours to the Commission.[62] Out of the above 2222 deaths reported, 1485 deaths in police custody were turned out to be deaths due to natural causes but 158 deaths were due to police brutality. The Commission recommended for interim relief, prosecution and departmental action against defaulting personnel in these 158 cases.[63] From 1st April 2009 to 31st March 2010 the Commission received 124 cases of death in police custody.[64] A comparison of compliance of death received by National Human Rights Commission from 2003-04 to 2009-10 on all India with that of most literate State in India, Kerala, which irrespective fact of highest literacy is still perpetrating the barbarous acts of torture and killing in the police custody. The Table 6.2 shows the number of complaints of deaths in police custody received by the National Human Rights Commission from all over India and from Kerala during the period from 2003-04 to 2009-10.

From the Table 6.2, it can be understood that there were decrease in the complaints of deaths in police custody received by the Commission for the period 2003-04 to 2009-10, though there was slight increase in the year 2007-08 than its previous year. It is, however, unfortunate that in 2007-08, number of complaints of deaths in police custody rose up to 188 than the number of 119 in the previous year 2006-07. This shows there was a steep increase of 63 per cent. This is astonishing that irrespective of the stringent measures that were being taken by the Commission, there takes place a number of incidents of custodial deaths.The national average[65] of number of complaints of deaths in police custody was twenty-eight during the period from 2003-04 to 2009-10. However, the number of complaints received from Kerala State by the National Human Rights Commission during the same period was thirty two (Table 6.2). This indicates that the number of complaints from Kerala State is above the national average. Surely, it is pain staking to

62. Asia Pacific Forum, Activities of the National Human Rights Commission-India 2009-10, Report to 15th Annual Meeting (2010), p. 9.
63. National Human Rights Commission, Annual Reports from 1993-94 to 2007-08.
64. National Human Rights Commission, Annual Report 2009-10 (2010), p. 175.
65. Total number of complaints of deaths during 2003-04 to 2009-10 i.e., 995. divided by thirty five (twenty eight States and seven union territories)

note that Kerala, the most literate state in India, is also perpetrating the torture and deaths in police custody.

TABLE 6.2
Number of Complaints of Deaths in Police Custody from April 2003-04 till March 2009-10

Custodial Death/Rape	*2003-04*	*2004-05*	*2005-06*	*2006-07*	*2007-08*	*2008-09*	*2009-10*
Complaints received on All India	162	136	139	119	188	127	124
Complaints received from Kerala	4	6	5	3	6	2	6

Source : NHRC, Annual Reports 2003-04 to March 2009-10.

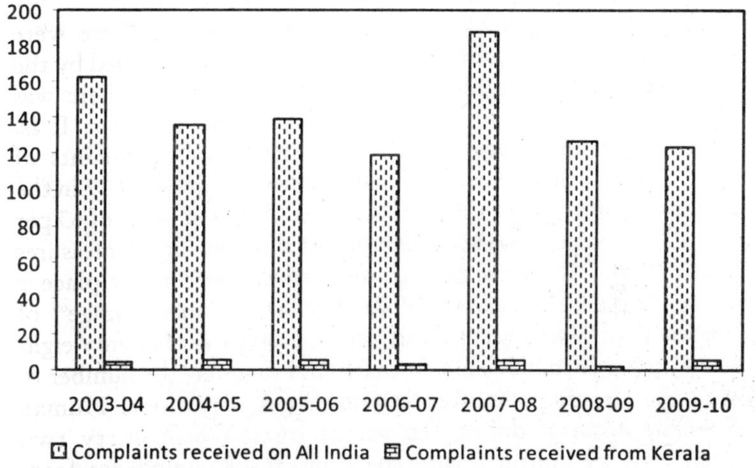

Chart 6.2: Graphic Chart based on the Table 6.2

9.2. Torture/Unlawful Arrest/Detention and Other Cases

Besides causing death or rape in custody, the police generally indulge in torture, unlawful arrest, illegal Detention, false Implication, etc. In relation to prevention of torture in custody, the National Human Rights Commission took major efforts to eradicate such practices in India. The major initiation by the National Human

Rights Commission was to make India sign the U.N. Convention against Torture. The Commission wrote a number of letters to this effect to the Prime Minister of India and, as a result, on October 14, 1997 the Government of India signed the Convention against Torture.[66] But, unfortunately, India has not ratified the convention. However, there is a move for the ratification of the Convention by the Government of India in this regard. As part of it, the Prevention of Torture Bill, 2010 has been passed by the *Lok Sabha* and is now pending before the *Rajya Sabha* for approval. The bill provides up to 10 years imprisonment for public servants responsible for torturing any person.[67] Surely, it can be stated that the Bill will act as a deterrence for the police and other public servants indulging in custodial violence. The National Human Rights Commission played a vital role in bringing the bill into the Parliament.

The Commission categorizes complaints against police into eight categories, namely, Custodial Violence, Illegal Arrest, Unlawful Detention, False Implication, Failure in Taking Action, Fake Encounter, Disappearances and Other Police Excesses. The Table 6.3 provides the number of complaints registered against police before the National Human Rights Commission during the period from 2003-04 to 2009-10.

The Table 6.3 shows that there is intermittent decrease and increase in the number of complaints before the National Human Rights Commission against police excesses during the period 2003-04 to 2009-10. In the year 2003-04, the number of complaints were 5230, but it shot up to 15744 in 2004-05, and then gradually decreased to 9246 and 7779 in 2005-06 and 2006-07 respectively. Again in 2007-08, it increased to 9246, but slightly decreased to 9176 in 2008-09. However, there is an all-time low of 3912 in 2009-10. It is significant to note that in the case of death in police custody, there was considerable decrease during the period from 2003-04 to 2009-10, where as in the case of torture, unlawful arrest, illegal detention, etc., there is decrease during the same period. It is stated that the decrease in the number of cases of torture, unlawful arrest, illegal detention, etc., may be due to the reason that police personnel are becoming cautious about the consequences of the matter if it reaches to the

66. National Human Rights Commission, Annual Report, 1994-95 (1994), para 4.27; However, India has not ratified the Convention; See also The UN General Assembly Res. A/53/150, 17 August 1998.
67. P.T.I., "Bill for Prevention of Torture in Introduced in LS", The Hindu, April 26, 2010; The Bill was passed by the Lok Sabha on May 6th 2010.

Table 6.3

Number of complaints against police registered before the NHRC from April 2002 to March 2008

Sl. No.	*Category of Complaints*	*2003-04*	*2004-05*	*2005-06*	*2006-07*	*2007-08*	*2008-09*	*2009-10*
	(1)	*(2)*	*(3)*	*(4)*	*(5)*	*(6)*	*(7)*	*(8)*
1.	Custodial Violence	1	16	7	4	2	11	10
2.	Illegal Arrest	188	210	183	155	318	1027	639
3.	Unlawful detention	472	876	741	605	675	1500	696
4.	False implication	420	1213	606	489	254	427	109
5.	Failure in taking action	1766	6833	3397	2682	1589	2269	1012
6.	Alleged Fake encounters	34	84	45	89	57	84	47
7.	Alleged disappearance	5	24	19	15	32	35	25
8.	Other Alleged Police Excesses	2344	6488	4248	3740	4248	3823	1374
	Total	5230	15744	9246	7779	9246	9176	3912

Source : NHRC, Annual Reports 2003-04 to 2009-10.

National Human Rights Commission. Earlier, complaints against the police could have been manipulated with the help of political influence or abuse of power, but now, the National Human Rights Commission is entirely a different body, devoid of political pressure. The policy of the National Human Rights Commission is very vivid and it calls for "*stringent action against those who are responsible for perpetrating inhuman treatment and torture*" against persons while in custody.[68]

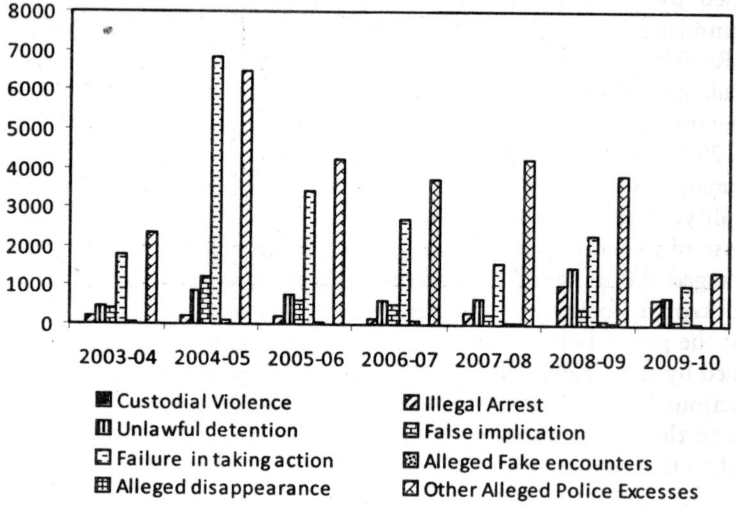

Chart 6.3: Graphic Chart based on the Table 6.3

10. REMEDY AND RELIEF AGAINST POLICE EXCESSES

Since the National Human Rights Commission is a recommendatory body, it cannot enforce its decisions. It can only recommend to the Central or State Governments to implement its decision.[69] The Governments may implement its decision. However, the Commission, in a large number of cases, has recommended interim relief where there occurred police torture, false implication, and illegal arrest. In many appropriate cases the Commission

68. Naresh Mahipal, The Protection of Human Rights Act 1993 (No. X of 1994), Expert Column (2009), available at : *http://expertscolumn.com/content/protection-human-rights-act-1993-no-x-1994* (Visited on January 14, 2011).
69. Protection of Human Rights Act, S.18 (a).

recommended for disciplinary action and prosecutions. The space may not be enough to mention the cases in which the Commission had recommended for interim relief. Very few instances are given to make known the diversified areas where the Commission awarded interim relief. In the case of illegal detention and torture by the police of three persons by the Rajasthan police, the Commission recommended the State of Rajasthan to pay interim compensation for all the three victims.[70] A young girl was tortured first and then gang raped by three police officers in Tripura on 26/5/2003. The Commission directed the Government of Tripura to pay an amount of Rs. 50,000 as immediate interim relief to the victim.[71] In a daring incident of beating of Mr. Suseel Kumar and his wife by the Police of Gautam Budh Nagar, U.P., the Commission recommended to pay Rs. 25,000 to Suseel and Rs. 50,000 to his wife.[72] A *dalit* (Lower caste) woman made a complaint to the police against a person in her locality. The Police colluding with the opposite party raided the house of the complainant during night, abused the family members, outraged the modesty of the complainant who was stripped naked and kept in lock-up by the police officer. The Commission found that the police helped the opposite party and in a show cause notice issued by the Commission, the Home Secretary of the State of Bihar sanctioned Rs. 50,000 to the victim.[73] The instances are many where due to the intervention of the Commission the interim reliefs were paid to the victims of police atrocities.[74]

70. National Human Rights Commission, Annual Report, 1997-98 (1998), p. 47.
71. Case No.5/23/2003-2004-WC, National Human Rights Commission, Annual Report, 2003-04 (2004), p. 36.
72. Case No.28117/24.2006, National Human Rights Commission, Annual Report 2007-08 (2008), Para 6.74.
73. Case No.1375/13/2006, NHRC, 2007-08 Annual Report (2008), p. 82.
74. Illegal detention/abduction of Rama Rao by Andhra Police, Case No.5828/95-96/NHRC; Illegal detention and torture of Anil Kumar: Maharashtra, Case No.517/13/98-99; Illegal detention and torture of D.M. Rege: Maharashtra, Case No.1427/13/98-99; Illegal detention by Police: Uttar Pradesh, Case No.13161/24/98-99; Unlawful Detention of Manoharan: Tamil Nadu, Case No.213/22/2001-2002; Illegal Detention and Torture in Police Station, Shikarpur: Uttar Pradesh, Case No.17171/24/1999-2000; Illegal detention and torture of ShriZamir Ahmed by the police at *Sayana*, *Bulandshahr*, Uttar Pradesh, Case No: 14071/24/2001-2002; False implication and torture of Rajiv Rattan by the Police, Case No. 9302/95-96; False Implication of the Complainant and Others and

The Commission has been actively interfering for protecting human rights and recommending for remedial action in the event of human rights violations, particularly in the matters of police atrocities and inaction against common man. Interference by the Commission in the infamous Gujarat Communal violence cases is a best illustration for its credit. It was because of the active involvement of the Commission that many police officials and culprits involved in the Gujarat communal riots in 2002 was brought before justice. The Commission issued as many as 11 orders in relation to the human rights situations after the Gujarat riots in 2002 and in "Best Bakery case".[75] Thus, it is to be noted that the Commission takes serious steps towards unearthing the police excesses either *suo motu* or on the basis of complaints made to it. The Commission is only a recommendatory body and within its jurisdiction, it recommends the Governments to provide remedies and reliefs to people. It is appreciable that the Commission disposes off the cases quickly affording speedy remedy to the people.

11. CONCLUSION

When the National Human Rights Commission was established, though there were some hopes for the protection of human rights, it was doubtful in many quarters regarding the effective enforceability of its decisions, because the Commission is created primarily as a recommendatory body. Now, it will not be wrong to state that the National Human Rights Commission is working actively solving many human rights violations. The National Human Rights Commission has dealt with many death and torture cases in police custody which would not have come to lime

Torture by police, Delhi, Case No. 3069/30/1999-2000; False implication of Madhukar Jetley: Uttar Pradesh, Case No.2385/24/2000-2001; False implication of Rajinder Singh: Haryana, Case No.810/7/98-99; False implication of Manoj Kumar Tak and NarenderTak, Madhya Pradesh, Case No. 667/12/98-99-FC; False implication of Navi Ullah under NDPS Act, Uttar Pradesh, Case No. 13501/24/2000-2001.

75. *Suo motu* case taken by National Human Rights Commission in Case No: 1150/6/2001-2002 orders dated 1st March, 2002; 1st April, 2002; 1st May, 2002; 31st March, 2002, 10th June, 2002;
1st July,2002; 25th September 2002; in "Best Bakey case" 30th June 2002; 3rd July 2002 and 11th July 2002; "In re. Custodial death of Samir Khan Sarfaraz Khan Pathan", Case Number: 452/6/2002-2003 dated 28th October, 2002.

light but for the involvement of the Commission. It will not be out of place to state that the National Human Rights Commission, due to its impartial and commendable activities in the protection of human rights, and as a defender of violation of human rights gained credibility among the people. Hence, the recommendations submitted by the Commission to the Governments are also generally complied with. This is evident from the fact that the number of cases pending for compliance of the recommendations by State Governments was only 266 for the payment of monitory relief/ disciplinary action/prosecution during the year 2009-10.[76] Mr. Sharma, a Member of the National Human Rights Commission, in an interview stated that 99% of the recommendations of the Commission are complied with by the Governments.[77] It can, thus, be stated that the recommendations of the Commission operate as forceful as an order of it. The follow-up mechanisms of the Commission on the implementation of its recommendation by the Governments are also praise worthy. When the Commission recommends for monetary relief to be paid by the Government to the person affected by the violation of human rights, it demands the compliance report from the Government along with a payment receipt. In this way the Commission ensures that its recommendations are complied with in a time bound manner.

76. National Human Rights Commission, Annual Report 2009-10 (2010), p. 144.
77. Rahman, Azera, U.P. police: The biggest violator of human rights, Human Rights published, iGovernment, 2010, available at : *http://www.igovernment.in/site/police-biggest-violator-human-rights 99-37465* (Visited on June 7, 2011).

7

State Human Rights Commissions

The Protection of Human Rights Act, besides establishing National Human Rights Commission, provides for the establishment of State level Human Rights Commissions also.[1] Chapter V of the Act provides for the composition, appointment, removal and the term of office of Chairperson and Members. It also provides the powers and functions of the State Human Rights Commissions. The State level Human Rights Commissions have the power, functions, procedure for investigation, inquiry and reporting after inquiry same as that of National Human Rights Commission.[2] However, the Act provides for transfer of cases from National Human Rights Commission to State Human Rights Commissions. Section 13 subsection (6) of the Act provides that National Human Rights Commission may transfer a complaint filed or pending before it to the State Human Rights Commissions where the former considers it necessary or expedient to do so for the disposal.[3] However, the National Human Rights Commission shall not transfer such complaint unless the State Human Rights Commissions has authority to entertain the same.[4] In respect of the jurisdiction, Section 21

1. Protection of Human Rights Act, S.21.
2. *Id.*, S.29.
3. *Id.*, S.13 (6).
4. *Id.*, S.13, proviso to Sub-section (6); inserted by the Protection of Human Rights (Amendment) Act 43 of 2006.

subsection (5) provides that a State Human Rights Commission may inquire into the violation of human rights only in respect of matters relatable to any of the entries enumerated in List II[5] and List III[6] in the Seventh Schedule to the Constitution of India. Nevertheless, the State Human Rights Commissions should not inquire into a complaint which is already inquired into by the National Human Rights Commission or any other Commission constituted by law.[7] However, it is doubtful whether the National Human Rights Commission has authority to inquire into a case which has already been taken up by the State Human Rights Commission.

I. COMPOSITION OF STATE HUMAN RIGHTS COMMISSIONS

The State Human Rights Commissions shall consist of one Chairperson and two Members.[8] The Chairperson or a Member of one State Human Rights Commission may be appointed as Chairperson or Member of the State Human Rights Commissions of another State with the consent of such Chairperson or Member, and with the prior approval of the Selection Committee as per Section 22.[9] Only a person who has been a Chief Justice of the High Court can be appointed as Chairperson.[10] One Member of State Human Rights Commissions shall be a person who held position as High Court Judge or as District Judge with seven years' experience in that position.[11] Another Member is to be appointed from amongst persons having knowledge of, or practical experience in, matters relating to human rights.[12] Thus, out of three Member Commission, two persons are from Judiciary who do not require any back ground in human rights for their appointment as Chairperson or Member of

5. List II sets out the subject matter of State jurisdiction.
6. List III sets out subject maters where Union and States have Concurrent jurisdiction.
7. Protection of Human Rights Act, S.21, proviso to Sub- section (5).
8. *Id.*, S.21(2); inserted by the Protection of Human Rights (Amendment) Act 43 of 2006.
9. *Id.*, S.21(6); inserted by the Protection of Human Rights (Amendment) Act 43 of 2006.
10. *Id.*, S.21(2)(a); inserted by the Protection of Human Rights (Amendment) Act 43 of 2006.
11. *Id.*, S.21(2)(b); inserted by the Protection of Human Rights (Amendment) Act 43 of 2006.
12. *Id.*, S.21(2)(c); inserted by the Protection of Human Rights (Amendment) Act 43 of 2006.

the State Human Rights Commissions. The same criticism that usually forwarded against National Human Rights Commission may again be significant here as the selection is limited to a narrow band of persons who, just by belonging to judiciary, need not reflect any particular expertise in or commitment to human rights.[13]

2. APPOINTMENT OF CHAIRPERSON AND MEMBERS

The appointment of the Chairperson and Members are made by the Governor of the State, upon the recommendation of a high level Selection Committee under the Chairmanship of the Chief Minister of the State. The Selection Committee shall consist of Speaker of the Legislative Assembly, Minister in-charge of the Ministry of Home in the State, Leader of the opposition in the Legislative Assembly.[14] Thus, in the matters of appointment of the Chairperson and Members of the State Human Rights Commissions, the leader of the opposition in the Legislative Assembly has a role to play. Here again there are criticisms same as in the case of National Human Rights Commission that the Selection Committee consist only of politicians which may yield to political bias, the selection is not transparent as public has "no say" in the selection process, etc.[15] However, the inclusion of opposition leader in the selection process of the State Human Rights Commissions ensures some degree of impartiality in the selection process.

The Protection of Human Rights Act makes the office of the Chairperson and the Members as impartial and independent as possible. The Chairperson and the Members of the State Human Rights Commissions are made ineligible to hold any office under the Central or State Government after the retirement from the State

13. See supra Ch.6, Joshi, G.P., *National Human Rights Commission—Need for Review*, Commonwealth Human Rights Initiative Publications, New Delhi.
14. Protection of Human Rights Act, S.23 (1); Where there is a Legislative Council in a State, the Chairman of that Council and the Leader of the Opposition in that Council shall also be members of the Committee, and also that no sitting Judge of a High Court or a sitting District Judge shall be appointed except after consultation with the Chief Justice of the High Court of the concerned State.
15. See Supra Ch.6, Joshi, G.P., *National Human Rights Commission—Need for Review*, Commonwealth Human Rights Initiative Publications, New Delhi.

Human Rights Commissions.[16] This way, to a considerable extent, it ensures the independence of the State Human Rights Commissions in as much as they can act impartially without being ambitious to get into any governmental position after their retirement. Another significant aspect in order to make the office of the Chairperson or Members of the State Human Rights Commissions independent and autonomous is that Protection of Human Rights Act specifically prohibits the varying of the salary or allowances or other terms and conditions of service of the Chairperson or of a Member to his disadvantage after his appointment and during the tenure of office.[17] Thus, in the case of State Human Rights Commissions also the Act takes possible measures in order to make the office of the Chairperson and Members to be impartial and independent of Governmental interference.

3. POWERS AND FUNCTIONS OF THE SHRCs

Regarding the powers and functions of State Human Rights Commissions, Section 29 provides that the provisions of Sections 12 (Functions), 13 (Powers relating to inquiries), 14 (Investigation), 15 (Statement made by persons to the Commission), 16 (Persons likely to be prejudicially affected to be heard), 17 (Inquiry into complaints), and 18 (Steps during and after inquiry) applicable to National Human Rights Commission, shall apply to a the State Human Rights Commissions as well. Thus, the powers, functions, inquiry, investigation and procedure of the State Human Rights Commissions are the same as that of the National Human Rights Commission. Hence, the State Human Rights Commissions has also the power to inquire *suo motu* on a complaint registered against a public servant on charges of violation of human rights, its abetment or the negligence in preventing such violation.

4. ENFORCEABILITY OF THE DECISIONS

Like in the case of National Human Rights Commission, State Human Rights Commissions also functions as a recommendatory

16. Protection of Human Rights Act, S.24 (3); The Chairperson shall hold office for a period of five years or until he attains seventy years of age, whichever is earlier and the Members also hold office for a period of five years or until he attains seventy years of age, whichever is earlier.However, Members can be reappointed for one more term of five years.
17. *Id.*, S.26.

body and submits its annual report or special reports, in case of urgency, to the State Government concerned.[18] The State Government is required to place such reports before the State Legislative Assembly along with memorandum of action taken/ proposed to be taken.[19] However, if the Government considers that the recommendations of the State Human Rights Commission cannot be complied with, it must furnish reasons for non-acceptance of the recommendations.[20] Thus, the concerned State Government is required to give a memorandum on the action taken/or proposed to be taken on the recommendations of concerned State Human Rights Commission. In this way, the Protection of Human Rights Act ensures that the recommendations of the State Human Rights Commissions are complied with to the possible extend.

5. JURISDICTIONAL ISSUE BETWEEN NATIONAL AND STATE COMMISSIONS

Section 36 of the Protection of Human Rights Act provides that the National Human Rights Commission "shall not inquire into any matter which is pending before a State Commission or any other Commission duly constituted under any law for the time being in force". However, this provision has created a confusion regarding the jurisdiction of National and State Human Rights Commissions. The question was whether the National Commission has authority to enquire into a matter (i) which has not been initiated by the State Commission, and (ii) which has not been properly inquired into by the State Commission. It was because of this confusion that the National Human Rights Commission has been demanding for the amendment of section 36 of the Protection of Human Rights Act with a view to establish a clear functional relationship between National and State Commissions.

It would be of significance to consider a case that relates to a conflict about jurisdiction between National Human Rights Commission and West Bengal State Human Rights Commission.[21] In the Case No.624/25/2000-2001, the National Human Rights Commission took cognizance of a complaint received from an

18. Protection of Human Rights Act, S.28 (1).
19. *Id.*, S.28 (2); The report shall be laid to each Houses of the State legislature where the House consists of two Houses.
20. Protection of Human Rights Act, S.28 (2).
21. Case No.624/25/2000-2001;National Human Rights Commission, Annual Report 2001-02 (2002), p. 183.

advocate, Tamali Sengupta of West Bengal, alleging that atrocities had been committed by the police in the villages in Midnapore district on 29th December 2000. The National Human Rights Commission called for an investigation report from the State Government, and directed on 3rd January 2001 that a team of officers of the National Commission proceed to the area for an on-the-spot investigation and collection of facts in respect of the allegations made in the complaint.

On 22nd January 2001, the National Human Rights Commission received a resolution from the West Bengal Human Rights Commission stating that since the matter was pending before the West Bengal State Human Rights Commissions, the National Human Rights Commission is prevented from inquiring into the matter by virtue of section 36(1) of the Protection of Human Rights Act. The resolution of the West Bengal Human Rights Commission was considered by the National Human Rights Commission in its proceedings on 24th January 2001 and it did not agree with the view of the West Bengal Human Rights Commission. National Human Rights Commission observed that:

"(i) the opinion required to be formed for the purpose of Section 36(1) is of the National Human Rights Commission itself which is not obliged to act on the view taken by the State Commission and the National Human Rights Commission is not to be governed merely by the view of the State Commission in formation of its opinion; and

(ii) the Protection of Human Rights Act does not exclude any part of India from the jurisdiction of the National Human Rights Commission nor does it prohibit any person from approaching the National Human Rights Commission in respect of violation of human rights anywhere in the country, simply because a State Commission exists for that area. Prior clearance of the State Commission is also not needed by the National Human Rights Commission to exercise its functions in any part of India."[22]

The National Commission further observed that the overall purpose of Section 36(1) of the Act is to empower the National

22. Case No.624/25/2000-200, National Human Rights Commission, Annual Report 2000-01 (2001).

Human Rights Commission to avoid multiplicity of proceedings where another Commission is fully seized of the matter.[23]

Though the West Bengal Human Rights Commission did not respond to the above observation of the National Human Rights Commission, it didn't mean the matter is settled there as the wording of Section 36 (1) is not clearly demarcating the jurisdictions of the Commissions. Thus, though the Protection of Human Rights Act provides for the establishment of National Human Rights Commission and State Human Rights Commissions, but their jurisdictions are not clearly defined. It is also not clear from the Act that where a complainant who is not satisfied with the inquiry conducted by the State Human Rights Commissions, if approached National Human Rights Commission what course of action would be taken by the National Human Rights Commission. Thus, there needs further review with regard to working relationship, power and functional sharing between National Human Rights Commission and State Human Rights Commissions for the smooth and effective functioning.

6. CONCLUSION

The greater advantage of approaching the Human Rights Commissions than on Courts in relation to human rights violation committedby the police is that there is speedy remedy. Earlier, the police could have violated the human rights and the only effective and impartial remedy available was from the Courts. The problem with the court system is that there is no independent investigative team for courts and, hence, in majority of the cases, the police and other violators used to hush up or manipulate the case and escaped from the justice system. So the people who suffer at the hands of police normally keep silence as there can be further revenge from the police due to the complaint made to the court. Even it took longer times to determine such cases by courts. Due to the prolonged struggle in getting "unsure" justice, people, often, do not approach the courts unless there is a compelling and grave circumstance.

Whereas the National and State Human Rights Commissions have its own investigative teams and, in appropriate cases, send its own investigative team to probe the case in order to find the truth and, hence, the investigation cannot be sabotaged or manipulated by State or other Governmental agencies. In this way the Human Rights

23. *Ibid.* (Case No.624/25/2000-200).

Commissions get first-hand information about the happenings and conclude its findings quickly even in complex cases and recommends the matters to the Governments for appropriate action and interim relief. There are also no procedural hurdles of formal court procedure and lawyerings in the case of Human Rights Commissions.

Nevertheless, the works of National Human Rights Commission and State Human Rights Commissions have suffered due to certain infirmities and deficiencies in the law governing its functioning.[24] The power of the National Human Rights Commission and State Human Rights Commissions to inquire in to the complaints against violation of human rights committed by Armed forces is restricted by Section 19 of Protection of Human Rights Act. What is more aggravating is that the definition of "armed forces" not only includes the naval, military and air force but "any other armed forces of the Union", such as Border Security Force, Central Reserve Protection Force, etc.[25] This may be seen as a major lacuna of the Protection of Human Rights Act.

Further, under the Act, the National Human Rights Commission and State Human Rights Commissions have no power to enforce its decisions.[26] According to the Act, where the enquiry conducted by the National Human Rights Commission and State Human Rights Commissions discloses a violation of human rights, it can only advise or recommend the Government concerned to take action against the guilty person or grant relief to the victim.[27] If any State government refuses to accept the advice, there is no provision in the law which empowers the National Human Rights Commission and State Human Rights Commissions to force the Government to implement its advice.[28] Nevertheless, it is a fact that the State Governments, generally, comply with the recommendations of National Human Rights Commission and State Human Rights Commissions.[29] If any State Government does not comply with its

24. *Supra*, Ch. 6, Joshi, G.P., *National Human Rights Commission—Need for Review*.
25. S.2(1) (a) of the Protection of Human Rights Act defines "armed forces" as "armed forces" means the naval, military and air forces and includes any other armed forces of the Union.
26. See *Supra* Ch.6, Joshi, G.P., *National Human Rights Commission—Need for Review*.
27. Protection of Human Rights Act, S. 18, 1993.
28. See *Supra* Ch.6, Joshi, G.P., *National Human Rights Commission—Need for Review*.
29. *Supra* Ch. 6 n. 77, Azera Rahman.

recommendations, the only mechanism available to National Human Rights Commission and State Human Rights Commissions is to approach the Supreme Court or the concerned State High Court seeking directions to enforce it. Hence, the National Human Rights Commission and State Human Rights Commissions are, sometimes, described as "toothless" or a "paper tiger" or a "pen pusher."[30] However, it is to be noted that the reliability and esteem that has been achieved by the National Human Rights Commission over the years has produced cautiousness on the Government and officials that non-compliance to the recommendations of the National Human Rights Commission creates a disturbing image on the political face of the Government. The National Human Rights Commission could penetrate and come out from the clutches of political/Governmental interference due to the prominent leaderships of Justice Ranganatha Mishra, Justice A.S. Anand, Justice M.N. Venkatachellaya, Justice J.S. Varma, and Justice S. Rajendra Babu. The working of the National Human Rights Commission, from its inception, was attractive. National Human Rights Commission, over the period of its splendid activities, established a trust and goodwill among the people as a protector and defender of human rights by affording quick remedy.

30. *Ibid.*

8

Protection of Human Rights and the Police

Position in Regional Systems

When the domestic institutions fail to protect human rights, or when they themselves are the violators of human rights, it may become necessary to seek redress beyond national boundaries. Regional legal frameworks give victim of violations of human rights in a nation within the region a chance to bring his case before a regional body provided that the country in question is a Member State of the Regional Treaty such as European Union, African Union, etc. Regional systems can further help strengthen the protection of human rights. The known regional systems that exist for the protection of human rights now are the European, American, African systems. There are some countries such as former Soviet Russian member countries which are not part of European Union, Arab countries in the Middle East, South Asian Countries, etc., which do not have an effective mechanism to check the violation of human rights on national or international basis. However, these countries are now emerging with new system of regional mechanisms for the protection of human rights within their region which, in turn, intends to protect individuals within their nations in the region. However, the protection of the human rights in European, American, African, Arab and Asian countries are not uniform due to factors such as the difference in economic and ideological diversity that determines the status of nations as developed/developing, democratic/communist, and also the diverse religions that is adopted as State religion in many countries within the regions e.g. Saudi Arabia, Qatar, Iran. A detailed analysis is made on how the human rights protection mechanism works in regional systems.

1. EUROPEAN SYSTEM

When the League of Nations was formed, the human rights issues were not given much significance due to which there were large numbers of human rights violations by nations which ended up in Second World War. When Second World War was about to end the allies determined to set up a new global regime, the United Nations Organization which would, *inter alia*, protect human rights violations. As both world conflicts originated in Europe, many European States believed that in addition to the United Nations Organization, there had to be a specific European regional response concentrating on human rights. As a result Europe had developed different documents in order to protect human rights. The principal document that relates with human rights protection especially in relation to civil and political rights is the European Convention on Human Rights and Fundamental Freedoms, 1950.

1.1. European Convention on Human Rights, 1950

The European Convention on Human Rights and Fundamental Freedoms or shortly, the European Convention on Human Rights (ECHR), is an international regional treaty under which the Member States of the Council of Europe (CoE) promise to secure fundamental civil and political rights, not only to their own citizens but also to everyone within their jurisdiction.[1] The Convention that came into existence as a result of the establishment of the Council of Europe for a number of reasons, *inter alia*, as a reaction to Second World War atrocities and determination to avoid future repetition; to encourage co-operation rather than conflict between European States; and to avoid the dangers that arose from the punishment and humiliation inflicted on Germany after the First World War.[2] The Convention, which was signed on 4th November 1950 in Rome, came into force on

1. In 1949, the Treaty of London established the Council of Europe based on principles of pluralist democracy, human rights, and the rule of law.
2. See *supra* Ch. 1, Peter Halstead.

3rd September 1953 and the emphasis is on individual and political rights rather than collective economic, social and cultural rights.

Among the existing regional mechanisms for the protection of human rights, the Europe has the most advanced system in terms of the scope, influence and enforceability. The preamble of the European Convention on Human Rights provides that considering the Universal Declaration of Human Rights which aims at securing the universal and effective recognition and observance of the human rights this enactment is made for the effective protection and promotion of the human rights. The provisions of the convention are more or less similar to that of earlier Universal Declaration of Human Rights in relation to protection of civil and political rights.[3] The convention contains 66 Articles in five sections. Any Member of the European Council can be a party to the Convention and Article 65 (2) makes it clear that any Member country which shall cease to be a member of the Council shall also cease to be a party to the Convention.

European Convention on Human Rights provides specific protection for the right to life[4], liberty and security of person[5], freedom from unlawful arrest and detention[6] and right against torture and inhuman treatment.[7] These are categorized as absolute rights and cannot be derogated even in the case of national emergency.[8] Article 5 of the Convention specifically guarantees for the liberty and security of persons. It provides :

1. Everyone has the right to liberty and security of person. No one shall be deprived of his liberty save in the following cases and in accordance with a procedure prescribed by law :
   (a) the lawful detention of a person after conviction by a competent court;
   (b) the lawful arrest or detention of a person for non-compliance with the lawful order of a court or in

3. However, it did not contain some provision that were provided under International Covenant on Civil and Political Rights in relation to right to self-determination or minority group rights.
4. Art. 2.
5. Art. 5.
6. *Ibid.*
7. Art. 3.
8. Art. 15.

order to secure the fulfillment of any obligation prescribed by law;

(c) the lawful arrest or detention of a person effected for the purpose of bringing him before the competent legal authority on reasonable suspicion of having committed an offence or when it is reasonably considered necessary to prevent his committing an offence or fleeing after having done so;

(d) the detention of a minor by lawful order for the purpose of educational supervision or his lawful detention for the purpose of bringing him before the competent legal authority;

(e) the lawful detention of persons for the prevention of the spreading of infectious diseases, of persons of unsound mind, alcoholics or drug addicts or vagrants;

(f) the lawful arrest or detention of a person to prevent his effecting an unauthorized entry into the country or of a person against whom action is being taken with a view to deportation or extradition.

2. Everyone who is arrested shall be informed promptly, in a language which he understands, of the reasons for his arrest and of any charge against him.

3. Everyone arrested or detained in accordance with the provisions of paragraph 1(c) of this Article shall be brought promptly before a judge or other officer authorized by law to exercise judicial power and shall be entitled to trial within a reasonable time or to release pending trial. Release may be conditioned by guarantees to appear for trial.

4. Everyone who is deprived of his liberty by arrest or detention shall be entitled to take proceedings by which the lawfulness of his detention shall be decided speedily by a court and his release ordered if the detention is not lawful.

5. Everyone who has been the victim of arrest or detention in contravention of the provisions of this Article shall have an enforceable right to compensation."

The Article 5 protects persons from arbitrary arrest and detention by the Member State machineries and also provides a right to claim compensation in the event of unlawful encroachment to liberty. Thus, the European Convention on Human Rights provides effective protection for right to life, liberty and freedom from unlawful arrest, illegal detention and torture.

The significant part of European Convention on Human Rights is the enforceability mechanism that is made available to a person whose human right has been violated and has not been satisfied by the decision of the national tribunal. In such cases the European Convention on Human Rights provides for the establishment of the European Court of Human Rights.[9] The European Court of Human Rights (ECtHR) has jurisdiction over Member States of the Council of Europe which has opted to accept the jurisdiction of the European Court of Human Rights.[10] Once a State has accepted the jurisdiction,

9. The original structure of mechanism for handling cases provided for a two-tier system of rights protection, which included the European Commission of Human Rights which was constituted in 1954 and the European Court of Human Rights which was constituted in 1959. The dichotomy between the two institutions initially worked well since the Court dealt with a relatively small caseload. However, the caseload facing the court grew from 16 cases between 1960 and 1975 to 119 cases in 1997 alone (See Steven Greer, European Convention on Human Rights: Achievements, problems and prospects, Cambridge University Press, (2006), pp. 17-18). On 1 November 1998, Protocol 11 of the European Convention on Human Rights came into force, eliminating the Commission of Human Rights and restructuring a new European Court of Human Rights and replacing the former system. Although the European Commission on Human Rights became obsolete, it held an important role in assisting the European Court of Human Rights from 1954 to 1998. Their role was to consider if a petition was admissible to the Court. If so, the Commission would examine the petition to determine the facts of the case and look for parties that could help settle the case in a friendly manner. If a friendly settlement could not take place, the Commission would issue a report on the established facts with an opinion on whether or not a violation had occurred to the Court. Thus the Commission acted independently and at the same time supported the Court before it has been abolished. After 1998, there exists only the European Court of Human Rights in settling the disputes that arise from within member States.
10. The European Court of Human Rights stands as a Super national Court among the Member Countries of the Council of Europe, some of which follow adversarial system such as England, Ireland and Scotland while some others follow inquisitorial system such as German, France, Italy, Belgium, Italy and so on. The European Court of Human Rights was not very active until 1980s due to the fact that the court existed in between the two known block of countries with ideologies of communism and capitalism and two known procedural systems viz., adversarial and

all the decisions of the Court in connection with the State are binding on it. Judges are elected to the Court by the Parliamentary Assembly of the Council of Europe. The Court accepts applications of instances of human rights violations from individuals as well as States. However, it is rare for a State to submit allegations against another State, unless the violation is severe. For an application to be accepted by the Court, all domestic legal remedies available to the applicant must have been exhausted.[11] Additionally petitioner must bring the case to the Court within six months of the final domestic ruling on it. The petitioner must not be an anonymous person. The issue must be a violation of a guarantee set forth in the European Convention on Human Rights. Article 25 provides that any person, non-governmental organization or group of individuals can claim to be the victim of a violation of human rights specified in the convention.

The Court then holds a public hearing to determine if there has been a violation to the provisions of Convention.[12] The Court normally sits as a Chamber of nine judges[13] including one from the country in question, but in rare instances it can sit as a Grand Chamber consisting of 21 judges.[14] If the application is declared admissible, the Court pursues for reaching a friendly settlement, which ranges from a change in the law(s) to compensation.[15] If not possible, Court proceeds with the hearing. Chamber judgments may be appealed to the Grand Chamber until they become final after

---

inquisitorial. After the disintegration of Soviet Russia many eastern and central European Countries joined (Hungary joined Council of Europe in 1990, Poland in 1991, Bulgaria in 1992; and Estonia, Lithuania, Slovenia, the Czech Republic, Slovakia, and Romania all joined in 1993. Latvia, Albania, Moldova, Ukraine, and the Former Yugoslav Republic of Macedonia became members in 1995, while Russia and Croatia joined the following year. The newest members of the Council of Europe are Georgia (1999), Armenia and Azerbaijan (2001), Bosnia and Herzegovina (2002), and Serbia and Montenegro (2003) the Council of Europe. The number of cases of human rights violations that were brought before the Court increased suddenly. During and after 90s the European Court of Human Rights became active and gave authoritative judgments that have far reaching effects in the protection and promotion of Human rights.

11. European Convention on Human Rights, Art. 26.
12. The Court normally sits as a Chamber of nine judges, including one from the country in question, but in rare instances can seat a Grand Chamber consisting of 21 judges.
13. Expanded from seven originally by Protocol 11.
14. Expanded from seventeen originally by Protocol 11.
15. Article 28 of the European Convention on Human Rights.

three months; Grand Chamber judgments are always final. Once the Court considers a case as a violation, States are obliged to prevent similar violations from occurring in the future. In appropriate cases the decision of the Court can afford "just satisfaction"[16] to the victims, including compensation paid by the State at fault.

The Committee of Ministers[17] of the Council of Europe monitors whether the Court's judgments are being complied with by the Member States.[18] The Committee of Ministers also observe that the requisite changes are made following a judgment, such as changes in the legislation, case law, rules, and practices, building prisons or the appointment of new domestic judges.[19] The mechanism for the effective protection of human rights through a supranational European Court of Human Rights and the monitoring by the Committee of Ministers of Council of Europe that the decision of the European Court of Human Rights are properly implemented in the respective national jurisdictions of Member States makes the European regional system a distinctive mechanism for the protection of the human rights.

1.2. European Convention for the Prevention of Torture

Besides the European Convention on Human Rights, there exists another Convention known as the European Convention for the Prevention of Torture and Inhuman or Degrading Treatment or Punishment, 1987.[20] The main purpose of the convention is to provide effective remedy from police action and state brutality within the Council of Europe. The Convention creates the European Committee for the Prevention of Torture to monitor the implementation of the Convention provisions in the Member States.[21] Any State whether member of Council of Europe or not can become a party to the Convention.[22] Once a State, whether Member of Council of Europe or otherwise, has become a party to the

16. European Convention on Human Rights, Art. 50.
17. The Committee of Ministers is the main decision-making body of the COE. It is composed of the Foreign Affairs Ministers of all member States.
18. See Supra n.16.
19. *Ibid.*
20. The European Convention for the Prevention of Torture was adopted in 1987 and came into force in 1989; hereinafter referred as "European Convention against Torture".
21. *See* Art. 1, ECPT.
22. *See* Art. 18, ECPT.

Convention, it shall be bound by the monitoring mechanism provided by the Convention.

1.2.1. Committee for the Prevention of Torture

The Convention provides for the constitution of a Committee for the Prevention of Torture for effective monitoring to determine that no acts of torture takes place within the domain of any Member State. The Committee shall consist of as many members as the number of the State Parties.[23] According to its mission statement "the Committee shall, by means of visits, examine the treatment of persons deprived of their liberty with a view to strengthening, if necessary, the protection of such persons from torture and from inhuman or degrading treatment or punishment."[24] The Committee visits places of detention, such as police stations, prisons, detention centers, etc., in any Member State.[25] Before the visit, the Committee shall give notice to the Government of the Party concerned of its intention to carry out a visit. After such notification, it may at any time visit any place of detention center.[26] The Member State shall provide the Committee with: (a) the free access to its territory and the right to travel without restriction; (b) full information on the places where persons deprived of their liberty are being held; (c) unlimited access to any place where persons are deprived of their liberty, including the right to move inside such places without restriction;(d) other information available to the Party which is necessary for the Committee to carry out its task.[27] The Committee may interview in private the persons deprived of their liberty and may communicate freely with any person whom it believes can supply relevant information.[28] If necessary, the Committee may immediately communicate observations to the competent authorities of the State Party concerned.[29]

After each visit, the Committee shall draw up a report on the facts found during the visit and shall transmit to the State Party concerned its report containing any recommendations.[30] The Committee may consult with the State Party with a view to suggest

23. *See* Art. 4, ECPT.
24. Article 28 of the European Convention on Human Rights.
25. *See* Art. 4, ECPT.
26. *See* Art. 8 (1), ECPT.
27. *See* Art. 8 (2), ECPT.
28. *See* Art. 8 (3) &(4), ECPT.
29. *See* Art. 8 (5), ECPT.
30. *See* Art. 10, ECPT.

improvements in the protection of persons deprived of their liberty.[31] The information gathered by the Committee in relation to a visit, its report and its consultations with the Party concerned shall be confidential.[32] However, the Committee shall annually submit a general report to the Committee of Ministers on its activities which shall be transmitted to the Consultative Assembly and to any non-Member State of the Council of Europe which is a party to the Convention and make a public statement, if necessary, on the report.[33] Thus, the committee has the authority to visit a Member State where it deems that a person's liberty has been violated. When such intention is expressed by the committee it becomes obligation on the State Party to provide facilities and access to visit such places. Although the Committee has no judicial authority, yet it can report to the Committee of Ministers regarding its visit to a country.

1.3. Charter of Fundamental Rights of the European Union 2000

The structure and composition of the European Union are different from that of Council of Europe and all the members of the Council of Europe are not members of the European Union. However, there is a close relationship between Council of Europe and European Union. The Parliament Assembly of Council of Europe adjoins the European Parliament of European Union at Strasbourg in France. The European Court of Human Rights situated at Strasbourg in France is part of the Council of Europe structure. A similar European Union Court is located in Luxemburg for the matters connected only with European Union. The former court abides to the European Convention on Human Rights adopted by the Council of Europe, while the later abides to the Charter of the Fundamental Rights of the European Union. The purpose for the creation of the separate Charter for the European Union is evident from the preamble of the Charter of the Fundamental Rights which provides "the peoples of Europe, in creating an ever closer union among them, are resolved to share a peaceful future based on common values" and to strengthen the protection of fundamental rights in the light of changes in society, social progress and scientific and technological developments.[34] Charter of the Fundamental

31. *Ibid.*
32. *See* Art. 11, ECPT.
33. *See* Art. 12, ECPT.
34. *See* Charter of Fundamental Rights of the European Union, 2000.

Rights consists of 54 Articles in 7 Chapters. First chapter deals with human dignity and it guarantees right to life,[35] prohibits torture and other cruel or inhuman treatment.[36] Chapter 2 deals with freedoms and it guarantees, *inter alia*, right to liberty and security of a person.[37] However, it does not provide for the procedural guarantee in the event of arrest or detention of a person as is provided in other Conventions. It also lacks provisions for the enforceability and monitoring mechanisms. Since it is a document created by the European Union, as and when there is a violation of rights guaranteed by the Charter, they can approach the Court in Luxemburg created under the treaty of the European Union. However, it confirms the authority of other European Treaties and Conventions including European Convention on Human Rights. The preamble of the Charter provides :

> This Charter reaffirms, with due regard for the powers and tasks of the Community and the Union and the principle of subsidiarity, the rights as they result, in particular, from the constitutional traditions and international obligations common to the Member States, the Treaty on European Union, the Community Treaties, the European Convention for the Protection of Human Rights and Fundamental Freedoms, the Social Charters adopted by the Community and by the Council of Europe and the case-law of the Court of Justice of the European Communities and of the European Court of Human Rights.

In fact, there is no restriction for an aggrieved party to approach the European Court of Human Rights from the Council of Europe or from the European Union as is evident from the preamble. However, only an aggrieved person from the European Union can approach the European Union Court in Luxemburg. It appears that the Charter is a corollary to the other international and regional instruments for the effective protection of the human rights within the European Union community.

2. THE INTER-AMERICAN REGIONAL SYSTEM

The Inter-American regional system operates among the

35. *See* Art. 2.
36. *See* Art. 4.
37. *See* Art. 6.

Member countries of American continent. It also stands for the protection and promotion of human rights. The system works based on: a) American Declaration of the Rights and Duties of Man 1948; b) American Convention on Human Rights 1969; c) Inter-American Convention to Prevent and Punish Torture 1985; and d) Inter-American Convention on the Forced Disappearance of Person 1994. The Organization of American States can be considered as the beginning for the establishment of the Inter-American regional system in relation to the protection and promotion of human rights.[38] The Organization of American States constituted the Inter-American Commission on Human rights in 1959. The Commission was behind making the Inter-American Convention on Human rights, 1969 and the Convention came into force in 1978.[39] There are 35 Organization of American Member States, 25 having ratified the convention and 20 having recognized the jurisdiction of the Court established under the Convention.[40]

2.1. American Convention on Human Rights, 1969

Though American Declaration of the Rights and Duties of Man 1948 pre-dates the Universal Declaration of Human Rights and European Convention on Human Rights, it did not in itself establish the American regional settings in relation to human rights protection nor did it provide a mechanism for supervision and enforcement. This led to the adoption of American Convention on Human Rights in 1969 (ACHR) and there were better mechanisms for the

38. The Organization of American States originated in the International Union of American Republics in 1890, but was established in its modern form at the 1948 Bogota conference. The 1948 charter entered into force in 1951, and was subsequently amended by the protocols of Buenos Aries 1967, Cartagena de India 1985, Washington 1992, and Managua 1993 (See Charter of the Organization of American States). It has a number of objectives, including; strengthening peace and security on the continent; promoting democracy; providing for common action against aggression; and seeking solution to political, juridical and economic problems (See Preamble of the Charter of the Organization of American States). It operates through general assembly annual meetings, consultation between foreign ministers, and has a General secretariat and permanent council 576 located in Washington DC.
39. See *Supra* Ch.1,Peter Halstead.
40. Lucio Martins Rodrigues, Sixty years after the Universal Declaration: navigating the contradictions, International Journal on Human Rights (2008), p. 7.

supervision and enforcement for the protection of human rights only after the adoption of the ACHR in 1969.

The American Convention on Human Rights is the treaty based on the Declaration of the Rights and Duties of Man 1948, sometimes referred to as the Pact of San Jose, Costa Rica. The American Convention contains specific rights to life,[41] liberty,[42] human treatment[43] and judicial protection by laws.[44] The Convention provides for the establishment of Inter-American Commission on Human Rights and the Inter-American Court of Human Rights. The Commission shall consist of as many members as the Member countries of the Organization of American States (OAS).[45] The Commission has power to make recommendations to the Governments of the Member States for the adoption of progressive measures in favor of human rights within the framework of their domestic law and constitutional provisions as well as appropriate measures to further the observance of those rights; to request the Governments of the Member States to supply it with information on the measures adopted by them in matters of human rights; to take action on petitions and other communications pursuant to its authority under the provisions of Articles 44 through 51 of the Convention; and to submit an annual report to the General Assembly of the Organization of American States.[46] Article 44 makes it clear that any person or group of persons, or any non-governmental entity legally recognized in one or more Member States of the Organization, may lodge petitions with the Commission containing complaints of violation of the rights covered under the Convention. Thus, a single individual can file a complaint against the State which has violated or not taken any appropriate action against the violation of human rights.

Article 52 provides for the constitution of a 7 Judge Inter-American Court of Human Rights. The Commission shall appear in all cases before the Court.[47] It is provided under Article 61 that only the States Parties and the Commission shall have the right to submit a case to the Court. Thus, an individual or a group cannot have direct

41. *See* Art. 4.
42. *See* Art. 7.
43. *See* Art. 5.
44. *See* Art. 25.
45. *See* Art. 35.
46. *See* Art. 41.
47. *See* Art. 57.

access with the Court. It is only through the Commission that their cases are filed before the Court. If the Court finds that there has been violation of a right or freedom protected by this Convention, the Court shall have authority to rule that the injured party be ensured the enjoyment of his right or freedom that was violated and if appropriate, it shall order that fair compensation be paid to the injured party.[48] Sub-article 2 of Article 63 further provides that in cases of extreme gravity and urgency, and when necessary to avoid irreparable damage to persons, the Court shall adopt such provisional measures as it deems pertinent in matters it has under consideration. Thus, the Court has ample discretionary powers to decide the issues that may arise in connection with human rights violations under the Convention. Unlike European Convention on Human Rights where individual person can approach the European Court of Human Rights directly, the individuals do not have direct access to the Court though they have access to Human Rights Commission which represent in the Court.

2.2. Inter-American Convention on the Forced Disappearance of Persons 1994

The Inter-American Convention on the Forced Disappearance of Persons 1994 was made due to the forced disappearances and abuse of human rights that were widespread in Latin and South America for much of the twentieth century. The police and other law enforcement officials within many National States played a vital role in the forced disappearance cases. The preamble of the Convention states that Organization of American States' Members were disturbed by the persistence of the forced disappearance of persons, which affronted the conscience of the hemisphere; and concerned at violations of numerous non-derogable and essential human rights in the American and U.N. Declarations, and in the American Convention on Human Right. Article I of the Convention provides that the Member State Parties undertake not to practice or tolerate forced disappearances. Article II defines forced disappearance as :

> ...the act of depriving a person or persons of his or their freedom, in whatever way, perpetrated by agents of the state or by persons or groups of persons acting with the authorization, support, or acquiescence of the state, followed by an absence of information or a refusal to

48. *See* Art. 63(1).

acknowledge that deprivation of freedom or to give information on the whereabouts of that person, thereby impeding his or her recourse to the applicable legal remedies and procedural guarantees.

Thus, forced disappearance includes four essential elements :

(a) depriving persons of their freedom in whatever way;
(b) perpetration by or with the support of the State;
(c) absence of information and refusal to acknowledge occurrences;
(d) impedance or negation of legal and procedural remedies.

The Convention makes it clear that forced disappearance could not be treated as political offences[49] and criminal prosecutions would not be subject to statutes of limitation,[50] i.e. they could be prosecuted at any time in the future, with no defense of 'superior orders'. Convention is categorical in stating that war, threats of political instability, or other public emergencies, would not justify the crime of disappearance of persons,[51] and detainees should be held in an officially recognized place of detention.[52] Convention casts a duty on the States Parties to establish and maintain official up-to-date registries of the detainees and to make them available to relatives, judges, attorneys, any other person having a legitimate interest, and other authorities.[53] Complaint regarding the alleged forced disappearance shall be made to the Inter-American Commission on Human Rights.

Article XIV provides that when the Inter-American Commission on Human Rights receives a petition or communication regarding an alleged forced disappearance, its Executive Secretariat shall urgently and confidentially address the respective Government, and shall request that Government to provide as soon as possible information as to the whereabouts of the allegedly disappeared person. Many cases of forced disappearances occur due to political rivalry and it occurs with the aid of police or other law enforcement machineries and hence, State Government may suppress such issues.

49. *See* Art. V.
50. *See* Art. VII.
51. *See* Art. X.
52. *See* Art. XI.
53. *See* Art. XI.

The Inter- American regional settings provides fairly good procedure in the event of forced disappearances to bring the matter before the Inter-American Commission on Human rights.

3. AFRICAN REGIONAL SYSTEM

The regional African human rights system is based on the African Charter on Human and Peoples' Rights (ACHPR), shortly known as the "African Charter" or "Banjul Charter", which entered into force on October 21, 1986 upon ratification by a simple majority of Member States of the Organization of African Unity.[54] The Organization of African Unity (OAU) was the regional body of the African States until 2002.[55] In 2002, the Organization of African Unity was disbanded and new African Union was launched in Durban, South Africa, to replace the Organization of African Unity. The new African Union (AU) is structured broadly modelling the European Union[56] and it, *inter alia*, provides the objective as to promote and protect human rights and human dignity among the African Countries effectively.

3.1. African Charter on Human and Peoples' Rights

The African Charter on Human and Peoples' Rights 1981 contains three parts. The first part of the Charter deals with rights and duties, second part deals with measures of safeguard and the third part with general provisions. Preamble of the Charter states that it has been created in pursuance of Charter of the Organization of African Unity, which stipulates that "freedom, equality, justice and dignity are essential objectives for the achievement of the legitimate aspirations of the African people and for the establishment of bodies to promote and protect human and peoples' rights." The preamble has reference to Universal Declaration of Human Rights and U.N. Charter. Article 4 of the African Charter states that human beings are

54. The African Charter was adopted in 1981 by the 18th Assembly of Heads of State and Government of the OAU, the official body of African states. It is also known as the Banjul Charter because a final draft of it was produced in Banjul, the capital of the Gambia
55. By the Charter of the Organization of African Unity since its adoption in 1963.
56. Daniella Sicurell, "The European Union as a Model for the African Union—Effectiveness and Limits of European Norm Promotion", Paper presented at the annual meeting of the International Studies Association's 50th Annual Convention "Exploring the Past, Anticipating the Future", New York, (Feb. 15-18, 2000), p. 5.

inviolable. It guarantees right to life and prohibit arbitrary deprivation of it. Article 5 provides for the respect of the inherent dignity of human beings and prohibits all forms of torture, cruel, inhuman or degrading punishment and treatment. Article 6 provides the right to liberty and the security of person and it further guarantees that no one may be deprived of his freedom except for reasons and conditions previously laid down by law. In particular, it provides no person may be arbitrarily arrested, detained or tortured. Article 7 guarantees a right to an appeal to competent national organs against acts of violation of fundamental rights, the right to defense and to be defended by counsel of one's choice. These are the important safeguards that the Charter provides from arbitrary arrest, illegal detention, torture, etc. These safeguards are similar with the Universal Declaration of Human Rights, International Covenant on Civil and Political Rights and European Convention on Human Rights. However, what matters is how the system works and how effectively the rights are enforced. In order to assess the effectiveness, it would be better to see the mechanisms that are provided by the Charter and the Protocols.

3.1.1. Enforceable Mechanism

The African Charter provides for the constitution of African Commission on Human and Peoples' Rights for the promotion and protection of human rights in Africa.[57] In 1998, the Protocol to the African Charter for the establishment of an African Court of Human and Peoples' Rights (ACtHPR) was adopted by the Organization of African Unity. However, the ACtHPR came into being only in January, 2004 with the ratification by fifteen Member States.[58] On July 1, 2008, at the African Union Summit of Heads of State and Government in *Sharm El Sheikh*, Egypt, the African Court of Human and Peoples' Rights was merged with the African Court of Justice.[59] The Court is now known as the African Court of Justice and Human Rights.[60] However, the African Court of Justice and Human Rights is

57. African Charter on Human and Peoples' Rights, Art. 30.
58. *Id.*, Art. 31.
59. African Court of Justice is the Court for African Union for all matters; See Gina Bekker, Recent Developments in the African Human Rights System 2008-09, Human Rights Law Review, 9 (4), (2009), pp. 674.
60. By the time the Constitutive Act of the African Union was adopted in 2000, the African Court on Human and Peoples' Rights was already legally established through the Protocol to the African Charter on Human and People's Rights which was adopted in 1998. The

not functional yet.[61] So the only enforceable mechanism available is through African Commission on Human and Peoples' Rights.

(a) African Commission on Human and Peoples' Rights

The African Charter provides for the constitution of eleven Member Human Rights Commission.[62] The main function of the Commission is to ensure protection of human and peoples' rights within the region.[63] There are two mechanisms provided under the charter for the enforceability of the rights, namely: (i) Inter-State communications, and (ii) Communication from other sources.

(i) Inter-State Communications

If a State Party has good reasons to believe that another State Party to the Charter has violated the provisions of the Charter, it may intimate by written communication to that State Party regarding the violation. Within three months of the receipt of the communication, the State to which the communication is addressed shall give a written explanation or statement elucidating the matter to the complained State Party.[64] If the issue is not settled within three months through bilateral negotiations or by any other peaceful procedure, either State shall have the right to submit the matter to the Commission.[65] The Commission may require the States concerned to provide it with all relevant information. The concerned

Constitutive Act created the Court of Justice of the African Union as one of the African Union organs. In July 2006, the African Union Assembly decided that the Court of Justice of the African Union and the African Court on Human and Peoples' Rights should be merged to form the African Court of Justice and Human Rights. By then, the Protocol of the African Charter on Human and People's Rights had entered into force in January 2004 and judges of the Court had been elected by the Assembly in January 2006. The Human Rights Court became operational on the understanding that, once the Protocol on the Statute of the African Charter on Human and People's Rights enters into force, the merged Court will commence full operations. However, the current situation in African regional settings is that although the African Court on Human and Peoples' Rights is established, it is not operational; See Gina Bekker, Recent Developments in the African Human Rights System 2008-09, Human Rights Law Review, 9 (4), (2009), p. 674.

61. George MukundiWachira, African Court on Human and Peoples' Rights: Ten years on and still no justice (2008), p. 2.
62. Art. 31.
63. Art. 45.
64. Art. 47.
65. Art. 48.

State may represent before the Commission and submit written or oral representation.[66] The Commission will try to reach an amicable solution based on the respect of human and peoples' rights. Thereafter, the Commission shall prepare, within a reasonable period of time, a report stating the facts and its findings. The report shall be sent to the States concerned and communicated to the Assembly of Heads of State and Government.[67] While transmitting its report, the Commission may make such recommendations as it deems necessary to the Assembly of Heads of State and Government.[68] It must be noted here that the authority available to the Commission is only amicable settlement. If there is no possibility of amicable settlement, the Commission has no power to enforce its decision. To this extent, it is a weak enforceable mechanism.

(ii) Communication from other sources

The Charter does not specifically provide that individual can make complaints to the Commission. However, the Charter provides that before each session of the Commission, its Secretary "shall make a list of the communications other than those from the State Parties ... and transmit them to the Members of the Commission, who shall indicate which communication should be considered by the Commission".[69] Further, the Charter provides for fulfilling certain criteria before submitting communications such as : (i) the communication must indicate the author (ii) it must be submitted only after all domestic remedies have been exhausted "unless it is obvious that this procedure is unduly prolonged"; (iii) it must be submitted "within a reasonable period from the time local remedies are exhausted", etc. These criteria points towards making individual communications to the Commission. Here again, the authority available to the Commission is only to resort to amicable settlement. Thus, the Commission is very weak in enforcing its decisions.

Thus, there exists a super-national mechanism for the protection of human rights for African countries. The model adopted by the African system is more or less similar to that of European system, but functionally it is far away from the European system. European arrangement is much more advanced from the enforceability point of view of human rights; whereas the African

66. Art. 51.
67. Art. 52.
68. Art. 53.
69. Art. 55(1).

system is not even up to the level. The African human rights protection mechanism requires much work and task to make the enforceability of human and peoples' rights more effective.

4. THE MINSK CONVENTION

The Commonwealth of Independent States Convention on Human Rights 1995, shortly the Minsk convention, is an association of those former Soviet Union States which cannot become members of the Council of Europe as they are outside the European territory. Since these States cannot become part of European Convention of Human Rights, they rightly decided to have a separate convention for the protection of human rights within their region and hence, formed the Minsk Convention. The Minsk Convention was opened for signature on 26th May 1995 at Minsk, the capital city of Republic of Belarus.[70] The Convention guarantees right to life,[71] liberty and security of person,[72] and prohibits torture and cruel, inhuman or degrading treatment[73]. It provides that anyone who is arrested shall be informed, at the time of his arrest, in a language which he understands, of the reasons for his arrest.[74] Everyone who is deprived of his liberty by arrest or detention, in accordance with national legislation, shall be entitled to have the lawfulness of his arrest or detention examined by a court.[75] It also provides that any person who is deprived of his liberty shall be entitled to humane treatment and to respect for his dignity as a human being.[76] Persons who have been subjected to unlawful arrest or detention shall be entitled to compensation in accordance with national legislation for the damage caused.[77]

Article 6 provides procedural guarantee in the event of deprivation of liberty of any person that are enshrined by the Convention. The Article 6 states:

---

70. *See* Commonwealth of Independent States Convention on Human Rights and Fundamental Freedoms; originally signed by Armenia, Belarus, Georgia, Kyrgyzstan, Moldova, Russia and Tajikistan and subsequently ratified by the Russian Federation, Tajikistan and Belarus.
71. Article 2 of Commonwealth of Independent States Convention on Human Rights and Fundamental Freedoms
72. Art. 4.
73. Art. 5.
74. Art. 5(2).
75. Art. 5(3).
76. Art. 5(4).
77. Art. 5.

1. Everyone shall have the right to liberty and security of person. No one shall be deprived of his liberty save in the following cases and in accordance with a procedure established by national legislation:
   (a) the lawful detention of a person after conviction by a competent court;
   (b) the lawful arrest or detention of a person;
   (c) the lawful detention of a minor for the purpose of referring his case for investigation, sentencing or trial.
2. Everyone who is arrested shall be informed, at the time of his arrest, in a language which he understands, of the reasons for his arrest.
3. Everyone who is deprived of his liberty by arrest or detention, in accordance with national legislation, shall be entitled to have the lawfulness of his arrest or detention examined by a court.
4. Everyone who is deprived of his liberty shall be entitled to humane treatment and to respect for his dignity as a human being.

   Persons who have been subjected to unlawful arrest or detention shall be entitled, in accordance with national legislation, to compensation for the damage caused."

In fact, the Convention is very elaborate in providing protection from arbitrary arrest, illegal detention, torture and other inhuman treatment, etc. It also elaborates the procedure while making arrest or detention of a person. Thus, the Convention takes care of unlawful arrest, illegal detention, torture, etc., and provides for measure for compensation in case of damage caused due to such unlawful arrest or detention.

The control mechanism comprises the Human Rights Commission of the Commonwealth of Independent States, which monitors practices of the States by issuing recommendations.[78] With a view to effectively monitoring the fulfillment of the human rights obligations entered into by the Member States a "Regulation on the Human Rights Commission of Commonwealth of Independent States" was adopted on 24th September 1993 in consonance with Article 34 of the Commonwealth of Independent States Convention. Article 10 of the Regulation provides that the decisions of the

78. Art. 34.

Commission shall take the form of understanding, conclusions and recommendations. The Commission shall submit annual activity report to the council of Heads of State of the Commonwealth of Independent States.[79] However, the operational aspect of Commission is at minimal level as the regional setting is not a full-fledged one.

5. ARAB REGIONAL SYSTEM

The Arab regional system works for the protection of human rights in Muslim countries in the Middle Eastern region. The protection system is mainly based on the Arab Charter on Human Rights 2004. However, before the Charter of 2004, there were attempts to have a protection system in the region. The first document in this regard was the Cairo Declaration on Human Rights 1990.

5.1. The Cairo Declaration on Human Rights 1990

The Cairo Declaration on Human Rights 1990, or shortly the Cairo Declaration, is considered to be the Arab world's pioneer Declaration in respect of human rights protection documents. It was adopted after the conference held in Cairo in 1990. The Declaration contains the preamble and 25 articles, and issued to serve as general guidance for Member States of League of Arab States[80] in the field of human rights. It is expressed in Islamic religious terms, referring to the human family descended from Adam, subordinate to Allah, with life being a God-given gift and it is thus guaranteed.[81] Article 20 declares that it is not permitted without legitimate reason to arrest an individual, or restrict his freedom, to exile or to punish him. It further prohibits from physical or psychological torture or to any form of maltreatment, cruelty or indignity. All rights and freedoms stipulated in the Declaration are subject to the *Shari'ah*, the only

79. Art. 11, regulations on the Human Rights Commission of commonwealth of Independent States
80. The Arab League was founded on 22 March 1945 by a group of Arab countries, namely Egypt, Lebanon, Iraq, Saudi Arabia, Syria, and Yemen. The Arab League currently has 22 members. The main goal of the league is to attain closer the relations among member States and co-ordinate collaboration between them, to safeguard their independence and sovereignty, and to consider in a general way the affairs and interests of the Arab countries.
81. *See* Art. 2, Cairo Declaration of the Human Rights.

source of reference for explanation or clarification of any of its Articles.[82] By a simple gaze at the provisions of the Declaration it can be seen that at one place the Declaration provides that physical or psychological torture or any form of maltreatment, cruelty or indignity is prohibited. At another place it provides that the declaration shall be subject to *Shari'ah* which provides for amputation in case of theft, a kind of cruel and inhuman punishment. Due to these inconsistencies, this Declaration has attracted much criticism due to the superfluous dominance of Islamic religious tenets in limiting the enjoyment of human rights.

5.2. Arab Charter on Human Rights 2004

Considering the widespread criticisms on the Cairo Declaration, League of Arab States considered the matter and decided to adopt a separate document for the effective protection of human rights within the region. As a result an Arab Charter on Human Rights was adopted by the Arab League in 1994.[83] It was also widely criticized by many human rights organisations both within the region and beyond as failing to meet international human rights standards.[84] This has resulted into the adoption of a new version of Arab Charter on Human Rights at the Arab summit in Tunis in 2004.[85] The 2004 Charter in its preamble refers the Arab world as the birthplace of civilization and cradle of religions, and rejects racism and Zionism. It acknowledges the eternal principles of brotherhood established by the *Shari'ah*[86] and other divinely revealed religions. The preamble further expresses belief in the rule of law and reaffirms the principles of the U.N. Charter with the international Bill of Human Rights, together with the Cairo Declaration. The 2004 Arab Charter on Human Rights is a binding treaty since it has entered into force on March 15, 2008 by virtue of the ratification of it by 7 Arab States.[87]

82. *See* Art. 24, Cairo Declaration of the Human Rights.
83. M. Rishmawi, The Revised Arab Charter on Human Rights: A Step Forward?, Human Rights Law Review, Vol.(5) (2005), 368.
84. *Ibid.*
85. Mervat Rishmawi, The Arab Charter on Human Rights and the League of Arab States: An Update, Human Rights Law Review, Oxford University Press (2010), p.170.
86. Islamic Personal Law.
87. The States that ratified the Charter are Algeria, Bahrain, United Arab Emirates, Jordan, Libya, Palestine, and Syria. The Yemen and Qatar ratified recently this Arab Charter. See Mohammed Amin Al-Midani,

Article 5 of the Charter guarantees the right to life. Article 8 prohibits torture or cruel, inhuman or degrading treatment or punishment. Article 14 guarantees right to liberty and security of person and prohibit any person to be arrested, searched or detained without a legal warrant. It states:

1. Every individual has the right to liberty and security of person and no one shall be arrested, searched or detained without a legal warrant.
2. No one shall be deprived of his liberty except on such grounds and in accordance with such procedures as are established by law.
3. Anyone who is arrested shall be informed at the time of arrest, in a language which he understands, of the reasons for his arrest, and shall be promptly informed of any charges against him. Anyone who is arrested has a right to contact his relatives.
4. Anyone who has been deprived of his liberty by arrest or detention is entitled to be subjected to a medical examination, and shall be informed of such right.
5. Anyone arrested or detained on a criminal charge shall be brought promptly before a Judge or other officer authorized by law to exercise judicial power, and shall be entitled to trial within a reasonable time, or to release. The release may be subject to guarantees to appear for trial. It shall not be a general rule that persons awaiting trial shall be held in custody.
6. Anyone who is deprived of his liberty by arrest or detention shall be entitled to proceedings before a court, in order that a court may decide without delay on the lawfulness of his arrest or detention, and order his release if the arrest or the detention is not lawful.
7. Anyone who is the victim of unlawful arrest or detention shall be entitled to compensation.

Thus, the Arab Charter provides safeguards and procedural guarantees in the event of deprivation of liberty such as the right to

---

The Enforcement Mechanisms of the Arab Charter on Human Rights and the Need for an Arab Court of Human Right, Regional Human Rights Mechanisms, The European Convention and the Arab Charter,' International Conference, Bologna (Italy), p. 3, December 2-3, 2008.

information about the grounds of arrest, right to know the charges, right to be medically examined and right to be produced before the ordinary court. It also guarantees a right to claim compensation, if anyone is aggrieved by unlawful arrest or detention. The Charter provides for the constitution of an Arab Committee on Human Rights for the effective protection of human rights. Unfortunately, it has not been constituted so far.

The Charter 2004, like Cairo Declaration, also suffers from superfluous religious tenets into the enjoyment of human rights. The Arab human rights documents appears to be more of cultural than of universal due to the religious subjugation of human rights. However, it provides for the protection of persons from arbitrary arrest, illegal detention, torture, etc. But the main criticism connected with the Charter is that it does not provide any effective mechanism for the enforcement of rights guaranteed in the Charter.[88] No serious measures have been taken to constitute Arab Committee on Human Rights for the effective protection of rights under the Charter.

6. ASIAN REGIONAL SYSTEM

Probably Asia is the only continent which does not have a regional human rights system like that of European, Inter- American or African systems for the redressal of grievances against violation of human rights. The reason for not having a unified system for Asia might be due to its geographical vastness and cultural, economic, religious and social diversities. However, there were attempts to create a separate system for Asia. As a result, "The Association of Asian Parliament for Peace" (AAPP) was established in September 1999 in Dhaka, Bangladesh due to the collective effort of a group of parliamentarians and members of civil society in Asia for promoting peace, democracy and human rights in the Asian region. The AAPP has been converted into Asian Parliamentary Assembly (APA) in 2006 broadening the areas of co-operation towards regional integration.The APA consisted of forty one Member nations and eighteen observers in 2007.[89] India is a member of APA.

In fact, there were attempts to have a Charter of Human Rights for Asia. Through the efforts of a Non-Governmental Agency named Asian Human Rights Commission along with other working groups

88. Art. 24, Cairo Declaration of the Human Rights.
89. Asian Parliamentary Assembly, available at : <http://www.asianparl.net/members.html> (Visited on March 17,2011)

drafted an Asian Charter of Human Rights in 1997.[90] The AAPP has also made a draft Charter but it attracted much criticism because AAPP itself has clothed with the authority to monitor and enforceability.[91] In sum, none of these attempts have been successful and the Charter of Human Rights for Asian region remains still a dream. It is not an easy task to formulate a unified regional Charter for Asia due to the vast diversities that exist in the continent and in many countries in Asia. However, the argument of geographical, cultural, religious, ideological or linguistic diversities cannot be a sound ground for not having a human rights institution for the protection of human rights.

7. CONCLUSION

There exist different regional systems for the protection of human rights, some of which are effective while some are not. Among the regional systems, European system can be considered as very successful one. It is successful due to the fact that it provides efficient mechanism for the redressal of the grievances and violations through a full-fledged super-national Court system. What is more significant is that individuals whose rights have been violated and is not satisfied by the remedy provided by the national tribunal can directly approach European Court of Human Rights. The decision of the Court is binding on all Member States. The successfulness of the system supplements to the fact that it provides an effective monitoring mechanism by the Committee of Ministers of the Council of Europe to see that the decision of the Court has been implemented by the Member State. Although the Europe has divergent ideologies and legal systems, yet the Court functions productively. The European Union system and the Charter of Fundamental Rights can be seen as a positive measure for providing further protection and effective remedy within European Union and Community.

The Inter-American regional system is more complex than the European regional system. The Inter-American system is based on the Declaration and the Convention. In this system, the Commission hears cases, makes visits and prepares country reports on the human rights position of Member States. Human rights violations in Europe

90. Fernand De Varennes, Asia-Pacific Human Rights Documents and Resources, Vol. 1, Martinus- Nijhoff Publishers (1998) p. 133.

91. *Ibid.*

tend to be individual rather than collective whereas in the American continent there have been repeated and large scale gross violations and hence, the inter-American system focuses collective violations too. Under European system, even an individual can directly approach the European Court of Human Rights to redress his grievance against the State action. However, this is not available in the Inter-American system. There is shabby enforcement procedure in the American system and decisions are not necessarily accepted as legally bindings, whereas in Europe the Committee of Ministers of Council of Europe guarantees that the decision of the European Court of Human Rights is implemented effectively. This shows that the European system is more acceptable in terms of effectiveness and enforceability.

The African system, though not fully functional, has been trying to follow the footsteps of the Council of Europe system. In the African regional system the only enforceable mechanism available is through African Commission on Human and Peoples' Rights. However, due to diverse political situations that exist among the Member Nations within the Union makes it more complex for the monitoring and remedial mechanisms in this system. Further, the Member Nations are not as transparent and responsible as the Member Nations of Council of Europe. This adversely influences people not to bring cases of violation before the Commission. Even when case is brought and decision is rendered, there is no efficient mechanism for monitoring that the decision is properly implemented or complied with by the Member Nations.

Though the Minsk Convention has been adopted and entered into force for the protection and promotion of human rights particularly for the former Soviet Union Nations which are not part of Council of Europe, it is not fully operational in the first place. Secondly, there is no effective Court mechanism to enforce it. The only mechanism provided is for the establishment of Human Rights Commission. However, that there are possibilities for effectively working of the system in future since there is no other effective system available for them in the region to remedy the human rights violations.

The Arab Charter elaborately provides provisions for the protection of human rights, dignity and freedoms. However, the major problem with it is that it provides human rights and freedoms within the four walls of Islam and *Shari'ah.* It is because of this reason there is wide criticism about the human rights protection under Arab

Charter. Though the Arab Charter is not functional, at least it is in existence, while the Asian Charter is not even in existence even after repeated attempts. Thus, scenario of regional countries systems is diverse in its scope, application and level of effectiveness and enforceability in the protection of human rights.

9

United Nation's Guidelines on the Exercise of Police Powers

The police and the law enforcement machinery is the most important weapon in the hands of the State administration to enforce law and order whenever necessary in the day-to-day affairs within a State domain. The constructive mission of the police in the society strengthens the rule of law within the territory. However, the unfettered powers that are entrusted with the police may be abused by the police to the prejudice of the individuals and the community. Any police activity or operation that achieves results through unlawful or inhumane action is a complete negation of the purposes and principles of policing.[1] Since there used to be large number of violations of human rights by the police globally, specifically in developing countries, the U.N. and other International Agencies have been attempting to provide a minimum level of standard of human rights protection that has to be guaranteed by the police within any Nation. The objective is that the minimum standard must be kept by all policemen under any circumstances. The most important areas where there require the police to be entrusted with wide powers are interrogation, arrest without warrant, pre-trial

1. *Ihsan and M. Bedri Eryilmaz, Police Professional Ethics* (2002),p.4; See also Ralph Crawshaw, Human Rights and Policing, The Journal of Turkish Weekly (2005).

detention and matters connected with search and seizure. Since unfettered powers are entrusted with the police, there is always a risk of misusing such powers by the police in any State domain. Taking into consideration of such circumstances and situations that is prevalent in different parts of the world, the U.N. has come up with a number of Declarations, Conventions, Covenants, Code of Conducts and Basic Principles for providing guidelines to control the exercise of the police powers during the course of investigation, interrogation, arrest and pre-trial detention.

I. INVESTIGATION

During investigation police officials may suspect one or more persons who may have roles in the crime. In order to guide and control the police and other law enforcement officials in the exercise of their powers the U.N. has adopted the Code of Conduct for Law Enforcement Officers in 1979. The resolution in which the Code of Conduct was adopted recognizes the importance and relationship of functions of law enforcement officials and the manner of exercising such functions by them with its direct impact on the quality of life for individuals, as well as for society as a whole.[2] While the General Assembly stressed the important task that the law enforcement officials were performing, it also pointed out the potential abuse of power in the discharge of their duties.[3] Article 2 specifies that law enforcement officials in the performance of their duty shall respect and protect human dignity and maintain and uphold the human rights of all persons.

The connotation of these provisions has broad spectrum for the fair criminal investigation process. Generally, as part of investigation the police require to make searches in order to discover materials that are subject of crime and to seize those materials. The searches, especially of persons, and their homes and other properties including vehicles and interceptions of correspondence, telephone messages or other communications must be strictly legal and necessary for the

2. United Nations Criminal Justice Information Network, Use and Application of the Code of Conduct for Law Enforcement Officials, Including the Basic Principles on the Use of Force and Firearms, Crime Prevention and Criminal Justice Division, United Nations Office at Vienna (1999), p. 6.
3. *Ibid.*

legitimate law enforcement purpose.[4] The protection of privacy is reinforced by Article 4 of the U.N. Code of Conduct which provides that matters which are of confidential nature shall be kept confidential by the law enforcement officials. Thus, the police officers are not supposed to conduct searches or seizure arbitrarily. They shall also not disclose the confidential information about a person's private affairs or matters that are injurious to his reputation or honour unless it is so essential for the crime investigation.

2. INTERROGATION

Interrogation by the police is one of the areas where there exist continuing controversies of arbitrariness or abuse of power. In many developing countries, police employs gruesome methods in order to extract facts and information about the crimes without taking into consideration the human dignity and human rights of accused, witnesses or detainees. The Declaration on the Protection of All Persons from Enforced Disappearance[5] provides that no pressure, physical or mental, shall be exerted on suspects, witnesses, or victims in attempting to obtain information.[6] It further provides that the

---

4. High Commissioner for Human Rights, Human Rights and Law Enforcement: Manual on Human Rights Training for the Police, Professional Training Series No.5 (1995), p. 62.
5. Hereinafter "the UN Declaration on the Enforced Disappearance".
6. Declaration on the Enforced Disappearance, Art. 13 (3); See for similar protection principle 15of thePrinciples on the Effective Prevention and Investigation of Extralegal, Arbitrary and Summary Executions [hereinafter "the UN Principles on Summary Executions"]; Art. 2 of the UN Code of Conduct on the basic duties of law enforcement officials with regard to all persons (including victims, witnesses and suspects) whether conducting investigations or otherwise; Art. 13 of the Convention against Torture and Other Cruel, Inhuman or Degrading Treatment or Punishment [hereinafter "the UN Torture Convention"] includes a special provision that in cases of allegation of torture witnesses be protected against ill-treatment or intimidation. For more specific information regarding the rights of victims to appropriate treatment and sensitivity, see Principles 4, 5 and 6(d) of the Declaration of Basic Principles of Justice for Victims of Crime and Abuse of Power [hereinafter "the UN Declaration for Victims"]; on the rights of suspects and other detained persons during investigation and interrogation, see Principles 1, 17, 18, 21, 23 and 36 of the Principles of Detention or Imprisonment. See cited United Nations High Commissioner or Human Rights, International Human Rights Standard for Law Enforcement: A pocket Book on the Human Rights for the police (1997), p. 18.

duration of the process of any interrogation, the intervals between the interrogations, the identity of the officials who conducted the interrogations, other persons present, etc., shall be recorded in the prescribed form[7] and a detained person or his counsel shall have access to such information.[8] It is prohibited to take undue advantage of the situation of a detained or imprisoned person for the purpose of compelling him to confess, to incriminate himself otherwise or to testify against any other person.[9] No detained person while being interrogated shall be subject to violence, threats or methods of interrogation which impair his capacity of decision or his judgment.[10] Thus, there are clear stipulations and guidelines that may be followed by the Police during investigation and interrogation under the U.N. scheme.

3. ARREST

Arrest is that quarter which is controversial in the pre-trial stage procedure in almost every country as the arresting process inevitably affects the deprivation of liberty of a person. In developing countries, most frequently, police abuses such powers of arrest thereby violating the human rights of people, and in many countries, the police arrests innocent people at the instance of State machineries. It is due to these reasons that the U.N. has set guidelines, basic principles, standard rules and code of conducts that must be kept by the police in the event of arrest.

The U.N. adopted the "Body of Principles for the Protection of All Persons under Any Form of Detention or Imprisonment 1988"[11] for providing effective safeguards for all persons under arrest or detention and to be treated in a humane manner with respect for the inherent dignity of the human person.[12] It provides that the authorities which arrest a person or investigate the case is required to exercise only those powers that are granted to them under the law and the exercise of these powers shall be subject to recourse to a

7. Body of Principles for the Protection of All Persons under Any Form of Detention or Imprisonment, Principle 23(1); hereinafter referred also as "the UN Principles of Detention or Imprisonment".
8. *Id.*, Principle 23(2).
9. *Id.*, Principle 21 (1).
10. *Id.*, Principle 21 (2).
11. The United Nations General Assembly in its 76th plenary meeting adopted by Resolution No: A/RES/43/173 on 9 December 1988.
12. The UN Principles of Detention or Imprisonment, Principle 1.

judicial authority.[13] "The Principles on the Effective Prevention and Investigation of Extra-legal, Arbitrary and Summary Executions" also provides for ensuring strict control over police officials making arrest and detention. The principle reads:

> In order to prevent extra-legal, arbitrary and summary executions, Governments shall ensure strict control, including a clear chain of command over all officials responsible for apprehension, arrest, detention, custody and imprisonment, as well as those officials authorized by law to use force and firearms.[14]

The arrested person shall be informed of the reasons for his arrest at the time of arrest and shall be promptly informed of any charges levelled against him.[15] It casts a duty to duly record: (a) the reasons for the arrest; (b) the time of the arrest, the taking of the arrested person to a place of custody and his first appearance before a judicial or other authority; (c) the identity of the arresting official/s concerned; and (d) a precise information concerning the place of custody.[16] Such records shall be communicated to the detained person, or his counsel, if any, in the form prescribed by law.[17] It is also the duty of the arresting official to provide with the information on and an explanation of his rights and how he can avail himself of such rights at the time of his arrest.[18] Promptly after the arrest, the arrested person shall be entitled to notify or to require the competent authority to notify members of his family or other appropriate persons of his choice of his arrest and of the place where he is kept in custody.[19] Where an arrested person does not adequately understand the language used by the authorities responsible for his arrest, the communication and information shall be provided in a language understandable by the arrested or detained person.[20] He shall be entitled to communicate with and consult his legal counsel[21] and shall

13. *Id.*, Principle 9.
14. The Principles on the Effective Prevention and Investigation of Extra-legal, Arbitrary and Summary Executions 1989, Principle 2.
15. The UN Principles of Detention or Imprisonment, Principle 10.
16. *Id.*, Principle 12 (1).
17. *Id.*, Principle 12 (2).
18. *Id.*, Principle 13.
19. *Id.*, Principle 16.
20. *Id.*, Principle 14.
21. *Id.*, Principle 18 (1).

be provided adequate time and facilities for consultation with his legal counsel.[22] The rights contained herein are similar with Constitutional and legal safeguards provided under the Constitution of India, the Indian Criminal legal framework and the principles laid down by the Hon'ble Supreme Court of India in *D.K. Basu*'s case. It is interesting to note that even 10 years before the Supreme Court has given the guidelines, the U.N. has laid down these fair procedures of arrest.

3.1. Use of Force

The police officials may encounter situations whereby the use of force becomes inevitable and, hence, they are entrusted with such powers to use force. However, the power at some police hands may be abused. The U.N. Code of Conduct for Law Enforcement Officials in Article 3 regulates and controls the use of force. It sets out that the use of force is not to be considered as a general rule rather it implies only an exception. It should be used only when strictly necessary and to the extent required for the performance of the duty.[23] It implies that police officials may be authorized to use force as is reasonably necessary under the circumstances for the prevention of crime or in effecting or assisting the lawful arrest of offenders or suspected offenders.[24] The U.N. Code of Conduct for Law Enforcement Officials envisions that the National law, in many countries, ordinarily restricts the use of force by the law enforcement officials in accordance with the principle of proportionality and it is to be understood that such national principles of proportionality are to be respected in the interpretation of this provision.[25]

3.2. Use of Firearms

Use of force sometimes requires use of firearms and the U.N. Code of Conduct for Law Enforcement Officials warns that the use

---

22. *Id.*, Principle 18 (2); however Principle 18 (3)provides that the right of such persons to be visited by and to consult and communicate, without delay or censorship and in full confidentiality, with his legal counsel may not be suspended or restricted except in exceptional circumstances to be specified by law when it is considered indispensable by a judicial or other authority in order to maintain security and good order.
23. The UN Code of Conduct, Art. 3.
24. The UN Code of Conduct for Law Enforcement Officials, commentary (a), Art. 3.
25. *Id.*, commentary (b), Art. 3.

of firearms should be considered only as an extreme measure.[26] Every effort should be made to exclude the use of firearms. The general principle should be not to use fire arms as far as possible. If circumstances are such that suspected offender offers armed resistance or otherwise jeopardizes the lives of others and less extreme measures are not sufficient to restrain or apprehend the suspected offender[27] use of fire arms becomes inevitable and can be used only to the extent of minimum level needed. In every instance in which a firearm is discharged, a report should be made promptly to the competent authorities.[28] Thus, the U.N. Code of Conduct for Law Enforcement Officials provides effective regulation and control in the use of fire arms by making the use only in exceptional circumstances inevitably warranted by the situation. When such fire arms are used, obligation is cast on the officials using the fire arms to report the matter promptly to higher and competent authorities.

In addition to the U.N. Code of Conduct for Law Enforcement Officials, there is another U.N. Basic Principles which specifically deal with the use of force and firearms by the law enforcement officials in any National State. The Basic Principles on the Use of Force and Firearms by Law Enforcement Officials, 1990[29] provides that the law enforcement officials in carrying out their duty should apply non-violent means as far as possible before resorting to the use of force and firearms.[30] Principle 5 stipulates the circumstances to use the fire arms wherein it is unavoidable. It provides:

> Whenever the lawful use of force and firearms is unavoidable, law enforcement officials shall:
>
> (a) Exercise restraint in such use and act in proportion to the seriousness of the offence and the legitimate objective to be achieved;
>
> (b) Minimize damage and injury, and respect and preserve human life;

26. *Id.*, commentary (c), Art. 3.
27. *Ibid.*
28. *Ibid.*
29. Hereinafter called as "the UN Principles on Force & Firearms" was adopted by the Eighth United Nations Congress on the Prevention of Crime and the Treatment of Offenders, in Havana in September 1990 and accepted by the General Assembly in its resolution 45/166 of 18 December 1990, were formulated in order to provide effective regulation on the use of force and firearms by law enforcement officials.
30. The UN Principles on Force and Firearms, Principle 4.

(c) Ensure that assistance and medical aid are rendered to any injured or affected persons at the earliest possible moment;

(d) Ensure that relatives or close friends of the injured or affected person are notified at the earliest possible moment.

Where injury or death is caused due to the use of force and firearms, the official should report the incident promptly to their superiors.[31] The U.N. Principles on Use of Force & Firearms casts a duty on the Government to ensure that arbitrary or abusive use of force and firearms by law enforcement officials is punished as a criminal offence under their National law.[32] It specifies the exceptional circumstances where the law enforcement officials may use firearms such as to arrest a person presenting a danger and resisting their authority, or to prevent his escape, and only when less extreme means are insufficient to achieve these objectives.[33]

The police may also use fire arms in self-defence or defence of others against the imminent threat of death or serious injury or to prevent the perpetration of a particularly serious crime involving grave threat to life, where there are no other alternatives available to prevent the criminal.[34] The U.N. Principles on Use of Force and Firearms also provides the procedure to be followed in the event of use of firearms such as (a) the police officials must identify themselves as such; (b) they must give a clear warning of their intent to use firearms if the criminals do not surrender; and (c) sufficient time shall be given for the warning to be observed. However, these principles are not needed to be observed when the circumstances are such that it would unduly place the police officials at risk or would create a risk of death or serious harm to other persons, or would be clearly inappropriate or pointless in the circumstances of the incident.[35] Principle 11 provides certain guidelines whenever the rules and regulations are made by National States on the use of firearms. It states :

> Rules and regulations on the use of firearms by law enforcement officials should include guidelines that:

---

31. *Id.*, Principle 6.
32. *Id.*, Principle 7.
33. *Id.*, Principle 9.
34. *Ibid.*
35. *Id.*, Principle 10.

(a) Specify the circumstances under which law enforcement officials are authorized to carry firearms and prescribe the types of firearms and ammunition permitted;
(b) Ensure that firearms are used only in appropriate circumstances and in a manner likely to decrease the risk of unnecessary harm;
(c) Prohibit the use of those firearms and ammunition that cause unwarranted injury or present an unwarranted risk;
(d) Regulate the control, storage and issuing of firearms, including procedures for ensuring that law enforcement officials are accountable for the firearms and ammunition issued to them;
(e) Provide for warnings to be given, if appropriate, when firearms are to be discharged;
(f) Provide for a system of reporting whenever law enforcement officials use of firearms in the performance of their duty.

Thus, the U.N. recognizes significance of the role of police in any society, on the one hand, but on the other hand it provides guidelines to take serious considerations and stringent control over the possible illegal arrests, unlawful use of force and firearms. The U.N. intends only that the minimum level of human rights and human dignity must be kept by all police in all countries.

4. DETENTION/CUSTODY

Detention/Custody of a person is inevitable in many cases for different reasons such as prevention of further crime, to produce before the judicial authority, to collect evidences, etc. What the U.N. envisages in such unavoidable circumstances is to keep the dignity of human beings and non-interference with the recognized fundamental human rights of detainees by the police and other law enforcement officials. The U.N. Principles of Detention or Imprisonment provides that all persons under any form of detention shall be treated in a humane manner and with respect for the inherent dignity of the human person.[36] Principle 2 of the U.N. Principles of Detention or Imprisonment provides that the detention shall only be carried out strictly in accordance with the provisions of the law and by

36. The UN Principles of Detention or Imprisonment, Principle 1.
37. *Id.*, Principle 2.

competent officials or persons authorized for that purpose.[37] Any form of detention and all measures affecting the human rights of person under any form of detention shall be ordered by, or be subject to the effective control of a judicial authority.[38] The authority which keeps a person under detention is required to exercise only the powers granted to them under the law and the exercise of these powers shall be subject to recourse to a judicial authority.[39] Any detained person should be provided with information on and an explanation of his rights and how he can avail himself of such rights.[40] No person shall be kept in detention without affording an opportunity of being heard by judicial or other authority.[41]

Interviews and communications between a detained person and his legal counsel may be within sight, but not within the hearing of police official.[42] It is prohibited to take undue advantage of the situation of a detained person for compelling him to confess.[43] Detainees shall be kept in humane facilities, designed to preserve health, and shall be provided with adequate food, water, shelter, clothing, medical services, exercise and items of personal hygiene.[44] Principle 24 affords for proper medical examination to be offered to a detained person as promptly as possible after his admission to the place of detention, and thereafter whenever necessary, that too free of charge.

The U.N. Principles on the Use of Force & Firearms provides that the Law enforcement officials are not permitted to use firearms against persons in custody or detention except in self-defence or in the defence of others against the immediate threat of death or serious

38. *Id.*, Principle 4.
39. *Id.*, Principle 9 .
40. *Id.*, Principle 13.
41. *Id.*, Principle 11.
42. *Id.*, Principle 18 (4).
43. *Id.*, Principle 21 (1).
44. International Covenant on Civil and Political Rights, Art. 10 (1); The UN Principles of Detention or Imprisonment, Principles 1, 22, 24, 25, and 26; Standard Minimum Rule for the Treatment of Prisoners, Rules 9-14, 15-16, 17-19, 20, 21, 22-26, 66, 82-83, 86-88, and 91; Article 6 of the U.N. Code of Conduct casts a duty on the Law enforcement officials to ensure the full protection of the health of persons in their custody and, in particular, to take immediate action to secure medical attention 673 whenever required. Commentary (b) to the article provides that law enforcement officials must take into account the judgment of medical personnel when they recommend providing the person in custody with appropriate treatment.

injury, or when strictly necessary to prevent the escape of a person in custody or detention presenting the danger referred to in principle 9.[45] Principle 34 of the UN Principles of Detention or Imprisonment provides that whenever the death or disappearance of a detained or imprisoned person occurs during his detention or imprisonment, an inquiry into the cause of death or disappearance shall be held by a judicial or other authority. This may be initiated either on its own motion or at the instance of a member of the family of such a person or any person who has knowledge of the case.[46] It stretches to the extent of circumstances which warrants that such an inquiry shall be held on the same procedural basis whenever the death or disappearance occurs shortly after the termination of the detention.[47] Principle 34 provides that the findings of such inquiry or a report should be made available upon request, unless doing so would jeopardize an ongoing criminal investigation. Principle 35 of the U.N. Principles of Detention or Imprisonment further provides that any damage incurred because of acts or omissions by a public official contrary to the rights contained in these principles shall be compensated according to the applicable rules on liability provided by domestic law. Thus, illegal detentions are controlled by making payment of compensation to the victim of illegal detention.

Thus, considering the helplessness of the persons under detention by the organized and mighty police in any country, the U.N. has made efforts to make guidelines, principles and rules that may be taken into consideration by the National States for controlling the police keeping a person under detention. The significance lies in the fact that a duty is cast on the detaining official to provide facilities for the detained person to consult with his legal counsel, and communicate with his family or friend.

5. TORTURE

In many countries, police employ torture or cruel and inhuman treatment against persons under arrest and custody. Many developed countries have absolutely prohibited torture by law. Article 5 of the U.N. Code of Conduct for Law Enforcement Officials prohibits any

45. The U.N. Principles on the use of Force & Firearms, Principle 16; Principle 17 states that Principle 15 and 16 are without prejudice to the rights, duties and responsibilities of prison officials, as set out in the U.N. SMR for Prisoners, particularly rules 33, 34 and 54.
46. *Id.*, Principle 34.
47. *Ibid.*

kind of torture not only of inflicting but instigating and tolerating it also.[48] It bars invoking superior orders or exceptional circumstances as a justification for torture or such other acts. Commentary to the Article 5 states that the prohibition is derived from the U.N. Declaration Against Torture. The U.N. Torture Convention[49] casts an obligation on the State Parties to take effective measures to prevent torture,[50] to criminalize all acts of torture,[51] and to investigate thoroughly the complaint or suspicious circumstances of torture.[52] The U.N. Torture Declaration and the U.N. Torture Convention later resulted into the adoption of the U.N. Principles of Detention or Imprisonment which also prohibits any person under detention to be subjected to torture or to cruel, inhuman or degrading treatment or punishment.[53] Thus, the U.N. totally bans any form of torture or employing any cruel or inhuman methods by the police. Significant fact that must be noted here is that no justification whatever might be cannot be raised by the police for employing torture or other cruel or inhuman methods against persons.[54] This has been expressly provided in both the U.N. Code of Conduct and the U.N. Principles of Detention or Imprisonment.

6. NON-CUSTODIAL MEASURES

The United Nations Standard Minimum Rules for Non-

48. The Art. 5 of the U.N. Code of Conduct for Law Enforcement Officials provides "No law enforcement official may inflict, instigate or tolerate any act of torture or other cruel, inhuman or degrading treatment or punishment, nor may any law enforcement official invoke superior orders or exceptional circumstances such as a state of war or a threat of war, a threat to national security, internal political instability or any other public emergency as a justification of torture or other cruel, inhuman or degrading treatment or punishment".
49. The U.N. Convention against Torture
50. The U.N. Torture Declaration, Art. 4; the U.N. Torture Convention, Art. 2.
51. *Id.*, Art. 7; the U.N. Torture Convention, Art. 4.
52. *Id.*, Art. 9; the U.N. Torture Convention, Art. 13.
53. The Principle 6 appendix provides that the term "cruel, inhuman or degrading treatment or punishment "should be interpreted so as to extend the widest possible protection against abuses, whether physical or mental, including the holding of a detained or imprisoned person in conditions which deprive him, temporarily or permanently, of the use of any of his natural senses, such as sight or hearing or of his awareness of place and the passing of time.
54. The U.N. Principles of Detention or Imprisonment, Principle 6.

custodial Measures 1990, shortly known as "The Tokyo Rules",[55] is adopted, *inter alia*, to promote the use of non-custodial measures and to provide minimum safeguards for such persons. The Tokyo Rules provides that the Member States should develop non-custodial measures within their legal systems to provide other options for detentions, thus reducing the use of detention.[56] It also provides that when implementing the Rules, Member States should ensure a proper balance between the rights of individual offenders, the rights of victims, and the concern of society for public safety and crime prevention.[57] The selection of a non-custodial measure should be based on an assessment of established criteria after due consideration of the nature and gravity of the offence, the personality and background of the offender, the purposes of sentencing and the rights of victims.[58] Decisions on the imposition of non-custodial measures should also be subject to review by a judicial or other competent independent authority, upon application by the offender.[59] The offender should be entitled to make a request or complaint to a judicial or other competent independent authority on matters affecting his individual rights in the implementation of non-custodial measures.[60] The dignity of the offender subject to non-custodial measures should also be protected at all times.

6.1. Pre-trial Disposing of Offenders

Pre-trial disposing of the offenders is one of the effective non-custodial measures. Rule 5 of the Tokyo Rules provides regarding the pre-trial dispositions of offenders. It provides, *inter alia*, that where appropriate and compatible with the legal system in any domestic jurisdiction of a State, the police should be empowered to discharge the offender if they consider that it is not necessary to proceed with the case.[61] For the purpose of deciding upon the appropriateness of discharge the Standard Minimum Rules requires the Member States to develop a set of established criteria within each legal system.[62] Rule

55. The United Nations Standard Minimum Rules for Non-custodial Measures [hereinafter "the Tokyo Rules"], G.A. Res. 45/110 of 14 December 1990.
56. The Tokyo Rules, Rule 1.5.
57. *Id.*, Rule 1.4.
58. *Id.*, Rule 3.2.
59. *Id.*, Rule 3.5.
60. *Id.*, Rule 3.6.
61. *Id.*, Rule 5.1.
62. *Ibid.*

6 provides that the pre-trial detention shall be used as a last resort with due regards to investigation of the alleged offence and for the protection of society and the victim.[63] In other words, as far as possible detention shall not be employed. Rule 6 provides:

"(1) Pre-trial detention shall be used as a means of last resort in criminal proceedings, with due regard for the investigation of the alleged offence and for the protection of society and the victim.

(2) Alternatives to pre-trial detention shall be employed at as early a stage as possible. Pre-trial detention shall last no longer than necessary to achieve the objectives stated under rule 5.1 and shall be administered humanely and with respect for the inherent dignity of human beings.

(3) The offender shall have the right to appeal to a judicial or other competent independent authority in cases where pre-trial detention is employed."

Thus, if alternatives to detention are possible such methods should be resorted to first rather than arrest and detention. The person under custody shall have the right to judicial recourse about the justifiability of pre-trial detention.

7. WOMEN AND SPECIAL PROCEDURES

Women as vulnerable category in any society require special attention, status and protection. Realizing the situation, the U.N. has made different Principles, Declarations and Conventions which deal with the women such as Declaration on Elimination of All forms of Discrimination Against Women (DEADA), Convention on Elimination of All forms of Discrimination Against Women (CEADA), etc., as guidelines to be adopted by any National States. These instruments, *inter alia*, provides guidelines for the police in dealing with women. Arrested or detained women should not be discriminated, and should be protected from all forms of violence or exploitation.[64] Women detainees must be supervised and searched by

63. *Id.*, Rule 6.1.

64. Universal Declaration of Human Rights (UDHR), Art. 2; International Covenant on Civil and Political Rights (International Covenant on Civil and Political Rights), articles 2 and 3; Code of Conduct, articles 1 and 2; Convention for Elimination of all forms of Discrimination Against Women (CEDAW), Art.15; Declaration on Discrimination against Women, articles 1 and 6; Principles on Detention or Imprisonment, Principle 5.

female officers and staff only.[65] Women should be detained separately from male detainees.[66] Pregnant women and nursing mothers should be provided with special facilities in detention.[67] Thus, the international instruments set for the women primarily focuses the non-discrimination of women by police officials; secondly, special status of women must be kept by all police at all times; and thirdly, as vulnerable members of the society special protection and support shall be provided to them always.

8. JUVENILE OFFENDERS AND SPECIAL PROCEDURES

Juvenile offenders require special kind of treatment and procedure due to their vulnerable character, lower mental strength and easily susceptible nature to undesirable situations. The 1959 U.N. Declaration on the Rights of the Child declares that "humankind owes the child the best it has to give"[68] and sets out ten principles which provided a framework for children's rights. The Convention on the Rights of the Child 1989 (CRC), defines a child as a person who has not attained the age of 18 years.[69] Article 3 of the Convention on the Rights of the Child provides that in all actions concerning children, "the best interests of the child" shall be the primary consideration. Article 37 casts obligation on the State Parties to ensure on juvenile offenders that torture is not employed nor arbitrarily or unlawfully deprived of his liberty.[70] Every child

65. The U.N. Standard Minimum Rules for Prisoners, Rule 53.
66. *Ibid.*
67. *Id.*, Rule 23.
68. The U.N. Declaration on the Rights of Child, Preamble, paragraph 5.
69. Convention on the Rights of Child, Art. 1.
70. Art.37 of the Convention on the Rights of the Child provides "The States Parties shall ensure that (a) No child shall be subjected to torture or other cruel, inhuman or degrading treatment or punishment. Neither capital punishment nor life imprisonment without possibility of release shall be imposed for offences committed by persons below eighteen years of age;(b) No child shall be deprived of his or her liberty unlawfully or arbitrarily. The arrest, detention or imprisonment of a child shall be in conformity with the law and shall be used only as a measure of last resort and for the shortest appropriate period of time;(c) Every child deprived of liberty shall be treated with humanity and respect for the inherent dignity of the human person, and in a manner which takes into account the needs of persons of his or her age. In particular, every child deprived of liberty shall be separated from adults unless it is considered in the child's best interest not to do so and shall have the right to maintain contact with his or her family through correspondence and visits, save in

deprived of liberty should be treated with humanity and respect for the inherent dignity of the human person, and in a manner which takes into account the needs of persons of his or her age. It should be noted that all the procedural safeguards that are available to adults shall equally be applicable in the case of juvenile persons such as presumption of innocence,[71] right to be informed promptly about the charge with which he is indicted,[72] right to have the matter determined without delay by a competent judicial authority,[73] etc. The Convention on the Rights of the Child is enforceable and works only as a guideline within the Member Nations. The U.N. Rules for the Protection of Juveniles Deprived of Their Liberty[74] provides that it is only when there is absolute necessity that child's liberty is deprived of and put in an institution.

The United Nations Standard Minimum Rules for the Administration of Juvenile Justice 1985,[75] popularly known as "The Beijing Rules" elaborately deals with minimum requirement that has to be complied with under all circumstances in the event of dealing with juvenile offenders. It defines 'juvenile offender' as a child or young person who is alleged to have committed or who has been found to have committed an offence.[76]

---

exceptional circumstances;(d) Every child deprived of his or her liberty shall have the right to prompt access to legal and other appropriate assistance, as well as the right to challenge the legality of the deprivation of his or her liberty before a court or other competent, independent and impartial authority, and to a prompt decision on any such action.

71. Convention on the Rights of Child, Art.40 2(b) (i).
72. *Id.*, Art.40 2(b) (ii).
73. *Id.*, Art. 40 2(b) (iii).
74. Adopted by the General Assembly resolution 45/113 of 14 December 1990.
75. Adopted by General Assembly by Resolution 40/33 of 29 November 1985; Adopted by General Assembly by Resolution 40/33 of 29 November 1985; The Beijing Rules are deliberately formulated so as to be applicable within different legal systems and, at the same time, to set some minimum standards for the handling of juvenile offenders under any definition of a juvenile and under any system of dealing with juvenile offenders.
76. However, Beijing Rules does not specifically say who is a child. Different legal systems follow different age limit to determine the criminal responsibility and hence, the Beijing Rules leaves it to the national legal system to determine the same:; the age limit of 12 years for Canada, Greece, Netherlands; 13 years—France, Israel, New Zealand (except for murder/manslaughter where the age limit of 10 applies); 14 years—Austria, Germany, Italy and many Eastern European countries; 15

In the case of arrest or apprehension of a juvenile, the parents or guardian shall be immediately notified of such apprehension, and, where such immediate notification is not possible, the parents or guardian shall be notified within the shortest possible time thereafter.[77] A judge or other competent official should consider the issue of release without delay.[78] The police, dealing with juvenile cases should be empowered to dispose of such cases, at their discretion, without recourse to formal hearings. In order to best fulfill their functions, police officers who frequently or exclusively deal with juveniles or who are primarily engaged in the prevention of juvenile crime should be specially instructed and trained.[79] The U.N. Guidelines for the Prevention of Juvenile Delinquency 1990[80] shortly known as "the Riyadh Guidelines", also stresses the aspect of providing training for the law enforcement officials dealing with juvenile delinquents. It provides that the Law enforcement and other relevant personnel, of both sexes, should be trained to be familiar with and use programmes and referral possibilities for the diversion of young persons from the justice system.[81]

If a detained or imprisoned person is a juvenile or is incapable of understanding his entitlement, the competent authority should, on its own initiative, undertake the notification referred to in this principle. Juveniles under pre-trial detention shall be entitled to all

years—Denmark, Finland, Iceland, Norway, Sweden; 16 years—Japan, Portugal, Spain; 18 years—Belgium, Luxembourg and 7 years—India, Myanmar, Pakistan, Nigeria, South Africa;

77. The Beijing Rules, Rule 10.1.
78. *Id.*, Rule10.2.
79. Commentary Rule 12 draws attention to the need for specialized training for all law enforcement officials who are involved in the administration of juvenile justice. As police are the first point of contact with the juvenile justice system, it is most important that they act in an informed and appropriate manner. While the relationship between urbanization and crime is clearly complex, an increase in juvenile crime has been associated with the growth of large cities, particularly with rapid and unplanned growth. Specialized police units would therefore be indispensable, not only in the interest of implementing specific principles contained in the present instrument (such as rule 1.6) but more generally for improving the prevention and control of juvenile crime and the handling of juvenile offenders.
80. Adopted and proclaimed by General Assembly resolution 45/112 of 14 December 1990.
81. The United Nations Guidelines for the Prevention of Juvenile Delinquency (The Riyadh Guidelines), Guideline 58.

rights and guarantees of the U.N. Standard Minimum Rules for Prisoners adopted by the United Nations.[82] Thus, the U.N. provides a number of guidelines in the case of protection of juveniles from arrest, detention and interrogation.

9. VICTIMS OF CRIME AND ABUSE OF POWER

The protection of victims of crime due to abuse of power had been a critical area for the U.N. and on 29th November, 1985 the U.N. has adopted the Declaration of Basic Principles of Justice for Victims of Crime and Abuse of Power.[83] The Declaration defines 'victims' of abuse of power as persons who, individually or collectively, have suffered harm, including physical or mental injury, emotional suffering, economic loss or substantial impairment of their fundamental rights, through acts or omissions that do not yet constitute violations of national criminal laws but of internationally recognized norms relating to human rights.[84] Principle 19 persuades the States to incorporate into the national legal systems norms forbidding abuse of power and prescribing remedies to victims of such abuses. In particular, the remedies should include restitution and/or compensation, and necessary material, medical, psychological and social assistance and support.[85] It further provides that States should periodically review existing legislation and practices to ensure their responsiveness to changing circumstances, should enact and enforce, if necessary, legislation proscribing acts that constitute serious abuses of political or economic power, as well as promoting policies and mechanisms for the prevention of such acts, and should develop and make readily available appropriate rights and remedies for victims of such acts.[86] It provides that victims and witnesses are to be treated with compassion and consideration.[87] No person shall be compelled to confess or to testify against themselves.[88] Investigatory activities shall be conducted only lawfully and with due cause.[89]

82. The U.N. Standard Minimum Rules for Prisoners, Rule 13.3.
83. Hereinafter "the U.N. Declaration for Victims of Crime".
84. The U.N. Victims Declaration, Principle 18.
85. *Id.*, Principle 19.
86. *Id.*, Principle 21.
87. *Id.*, Principle 4.
88. Universal Declaration of Human Rights, Art.11 (1); International Covenant on Civil and Political Rights, Art.14 (3) (g); The U.N. Principles of Detention or Imprisonment, Principle 21(1).
89. The U.N. Code of Conduct, Art.4; The U.N. Principles of Detention or Imprisonment, principles 21, 23, 36; The U.N. Principles on Summary Executions, principles 9, 10 and 11.

Commentary (b) to Article 6 of the U.N. Code of Conduct for Law Enforcement Officers also provides that the law enforcement officials shall also secure medical attention for victims of violations of law or of accidents occurring in the course of violations of law. Thus, the U.N. makes guideline, stipulations and remedies that are essential for the victims of crime and abuse of power.

10. COMPLAINTS, REPORTING AND REVIEWING PROCEDURES

The police enjoy immense powers in any State jurisdiction and, at times, they tend to abuse those powers. The mechanism for complaint, reporting or review procedure is predominantly warranted in the cases of police actions against people. The system can work well only when there is effective complaint procedure or efficient reporting and reviewing course of action on the police actions. The U.N. Principles of Detention or Imprisonment provides that in order to supervise the strict observance of relevant laws and regulations, places of detention shall be visited regularly by qualified and experienced persons appointed by, and responsible to, a competent authority distinct from the authority directly in charge of the administration of the place of detention.[90] A detained person shall have the right to communicate freely and in full confidentiality with the persons who visit the places of detention subject to reasonable conditions to ensure security and good order in such places.[91]

Principle 32 of the U.N. Body of Principles for the Protection of Persons provides that a detained person or his counsel should be entitled to take proceedings at any time according to domestic law before a judicial authority to challenge the lawfulness of his detention. The proceedings shall be simple and expeditious and at no cost for detained persons having inadequate means.[92] The detaining authority shall produce without unreasonable delay the detained person before the reviewing authority.[93] Principle 33 provides that a detained person or his counsel shall have the right to make a request or complaint regarding his treatment, in particular, in case of torture or other cruel, inhuman or degrading treatment, to the authorities responsible for the administration of the place of detention and to

90. The U.N. Principles of Detention or Imprisonment, Principle 29 (1).
91. *Id.*, Principle 29 (2).
92. *Id.*, Principle 32 (2).
93. *Ibid.*

higher authorities and, when necessary, to appropriate authorities vested with reviewing or remedial powers. The Article further provides in cases where neither the detained person nor his counsel has opportunity to exercise his rights, a member of the family of the detained person or any other person who has knowledge of the case may exercise such rights.[94] Confidentiality of the request or complaint shall be maintained if so requested by the complainant.[95] Every request or complaint shall be promptly dealt with and replied to without undue delay. If the request or complaint is rejected or in case of inordinate delay the complainant shall be entitled to bring it before a judicial or other authority.[96] Principle 33 (4) further guarantees that neither the detained person nor any person on his behalf complaining shall suffer prejudice for making a request or complain.

10.1. Review and Reporting in the Use of Firearms

The U.N. Principles on Force & Firearms also provides provisions for effective reporting and review procedures. It provides that the Governments and law enforcement agencies shall establish effective reporting and review procedures for all incidents where injury or death is caused by the use of force and firearms.[97] It further provides that rules and regulations for the use of firearms made by officials should contain a guideline for a system of reporting to superior officials.[98] For incidents reported pursuant to these principles, Governments and law enforcement agencies shall ensure that an effective review process is available and that independent administrative or prosecutorial authorities are in a position to exercise jurisdiction in appropriate circumstances.[99] In cases of death and serious injury or other grave consequences, a detailed report shall be sent promptly to the competent authorities responsible for administrative review and judicial control.[100] Persons affected by the use of force and firearms or their legal representatives shall have access to an independent process, including a judicial process.[101] In the

94. *Id.*, Principle 33 (2).
95. *Id.*, Principle 33 (3).
96. *Id.*, Principle 33 (4).
97. The U.N. Principles on Force & Firearms, Principle 6.
98. *Id.*, Principle 11(f).
99. *Id.*, Principle 22.
100. *Ibid.*
101. *Id.*, Principle 23.

event of the death of such persons, their dependents can invoke the provision accordingly.[102] Governments and law enforcement agencies shall ensure that superior officers are held responsible if they know, or should have known, that law enforcement officials under their command are resorting, or have resorted, to the unlawful use of force and firearms, and they did not take all measures in their power to prevent, suppress or report such use.[103]

Article 25 provides a guarantee to the official who, in compliance with the U.N. Code of Conduct and the provisions of the U.N. Principles on Force & Firearms, refuse to carry out an order to use force and firearms, or who report such use by other officials and casts a duty on Governments and law enforcement agencies to ensure that no criminal or disciplinary sanction is imposed on such law enforcement officials. It further makes clear that defense of obedience to superior orders should not be a defense if law enforcement officials knew that an order to use force and firearms resulting in the death or serious injury of a person was manifestly unlawful and had a reasonable opportunity to refuse to follow it. In any case, the responsibility also rests on the superior officers who gave the unlawful order for using the firearms in a particular situation.[104] Thus, the U.N. Principles on Force & Firearms provides an effective review and reporting mechanism in the use of fire arms by law enforcement officials. It also provides that these basic principles as provided by the U.N. should be adopted by the Government of States to ensure that use of force and firearms are regulated properly within their jurisdiction so that the law enforcement officials can be controlled in the use of force or firearms.

10.2. Acts Contrary to U.N. Principles of Detention or Imprisonment

The U.N. Principles of Detention or Imprisonment provides three important measures in the event of occurrence of any act contrary to these principles: (i) It provides that States should prohibit by law any act contrary to the rights and duties contained in these principles, make any such act subject to appropriate sanctions and conduct impartial investigations upon complaints; (ii) Officials who have reason to believe that a violation of this Body of Principles has

102. *Ibid.*
103. *Id.*, Principle 24.
104. *Id.*, Principle 26.

occurred or is about to occur shall report the matter to their superior authorities and, where necessary, to other appropriate authorities or organs vested with reviewing or remedial powers; (iii) Any other person who has grounds to believe that a violation of this Body of Principles has occurred or is about to occur shall have the right to report the matter to the superiors of the officials involved as well as to other appropriate authorities or organs vested with reviewing or remedial powers.[105]

10.3. Acts Contrary to the U.N. Code of Conduct

The U.N. Code of Conduct for Law Enforcement officials also provides that Law enforcement officials who have reason to believe that a violation of the provisions of the U.N. Code of Conduct has occurred or is about to occur shall report the matter to their superior authorities and, where necessary, to other appropriate authorities or organs vested with reviewing or remedial power.[106] Law enforcement officials shall report violations within the chain of command and take other lawful action outside the chain of command only when no other remedies are available or effective.[107] It also guarantees that the law enforcement officials shall not suffer administrative or other penalties because they have reported that a violation of the Code has occurred or is about to occur.[108] Commentary (c) to Article 8 provides that the term "appropriate authorities or organs vested with reviewing or remedial power" refers to any authority or organ existing under national law, whether internal to the law enforcement agency or independent thereof, with statutory, customary or other power to review grievances and complaints arising out of violations within the purview of this Code. In some countries, the mass media may be regarded as performing complaint review functions similar to those described in commentary (c).[109] Law enforcement officials may be justified if, as a last resort, bring violations to the attention of public opinion through the mass media.[110] It is to be noted that the U.N., considering the role of mass media, gives footing for reporting the violations by the police. The U.N. has also provided reporting by the police officers about violation of human rights committed by

105. The U.N. Principles of Detention or Imprisonment, Principle 7.
106. The U.N. Code of Conduct, Art. 8.
107. *Id.*, Commentary (b) to Art. 8.
108. *Ibid.*
109. *Id.*, Commentary (d) to Art. 8.
110. *Ibid.*

other police officers. However, if his reporting is not fruitful he may be justified in bringing the matter to the notice of the media.

11. CONCLUSION

As James Madison said in Federalist Papers "If men were angels, no government would be necessary. If angels were to govern men, neither external nor internal controls on government would be necessary."[111] But we are not angels. This may be absolutely true with the police. The U.N., therefore, puts the efforts to provide guidelines to keep minimum standards to the law enforcement officials in dealing with investigation, interrogation, arrest and detention of people. The Standard Minimum Rules for Non-custodial Measures sets out a number of rules that the National State may make use of in order to avoid the pre-trial detention. It provides that the pre-trial detention may be used as a last resort. The U.N. Code of Conduct for Law Enforcement Officers sets out a number of conduct rules that the National States may adopt into their legal system. It also prohibits any kind of torture by law enforcement agencies not only of inflicting but instigating and tolerating it also. The U.N. Principles of Detention or Imprisonment further provides a number of principles that National State may make rules in the cases of detention and imprisonment. It provides that if any damage incurred because of acts or omissions by a public official contrary to these principles must be compensated according to the applicable rules on liability provided by domestic law.

The Basic Principles on the Use of Force and Firearms by Law Enforcement Officials sets out guidelines for the use of firearms against persons. However, police officials are not permitted to use fire arms against a person in custody or detention except in self-defense or in the defense of others against the immediate threat of death or serious injury. The Declaration on the Protection of All Persons from Enforced Disappearance provides that National States must ensure that no pressure, physical or mental, is exerted on suspects, witnesses, or victims in attempting to obtain information. It further provides that the duration of interrogation, the intervals between the interrogations, the identity of the officials who conducted the interrogations, other persons present, etc., should be

111. James Madison, The Structure of the Government Must Furnish the Proper Checks and Balances between the Different Departments; The Federalist papers No. 51, Independent Journal, (1978).

recorded in the prescribed form. The United Nations Standard Minimum Rules for the Administration of Juvenile Justice, 1985 directs a number of safeguards and special treatments that are to be taken by the National States in the cases of arrest and detention of juveniles. Similarly, U.N. Standard Minimum Rules for Prisoners provides a number of safeguards for women in custody also. Thus, the U.N. has made elaborate guidelines in order to control the exercise of police powers and avoid abuse of such powers within any National State. However, the point is not that there is the U.N. Body of Principle or the Standard Minimum Rules or Code of Conduct, but the point is to what extent the National States are incorporating into their legal systems and how effectively they are implemented. This determines the success of these rules and principles.

10

Conclusion

The human rights are inherent in every person by virtue of the fact that he is born as human being. In this context, human rights are considered as in existence with the existence of human beings on the earth. The concept of human rights developed during the eighteenth and nineteenth centuries in Europe, though the terminology used was "natural rights"—the rights belonging to a person by nature by virtue of being born as human being. And these rights were referred to as natural rights until Second World War. Due to the horrific and barbaric acts committed on human beings by the Nazi Germany prior to and during Second World War, there arose a divergent thought to protect the human beings from being inhumanly attacked by the authorities who were entrusted to protect them. Hence, the notion of "human rights" emerged as a solemn premise among the international community after the Second World War. However, the concept of human rights can be traced from western philosophy and the Stoic natural law doctrines. The ideas that originated with Zeno of *Citium* and the Stoics teachings that there were pervasive laws of nature and hence, the Man's conduct should be measured in accordance with those laws have roots in the development of the concept of human rights.

The real concept of protection of human rights started emerging from England with the signing of the *Magna Carta* in 1215. The *Magna Carta* provided that the King would follow the legal procedure before His officials arrest, detain or punish a person. The procedural safeguards provided in the *Magna Carta* was further broadened in the Petition of Rights 1628 which provided protection against arbitrary arrest and detention by affirming that no person may be imprisoned without showing a cause for the arrest and detention. The Virginia Declaration of Rights 1776, though not provided provisions against arbitrary arrest and detention, but asserted that all people have certain inherent rights such as right to life and liberty which they enjoy as human beings and such rights cannot be "compacted, deprived or divested from their posterity". The American Declaration of Independence 1776 elaborated the rights guaranteed by the Virginia Declaration of Rights and it declared that (i) man possess certain inalienable rights of life, liberty and pursuit of human happiness, and (ii) the purpose of the Government is to secure those inalienable rights. Following the American Declaration of Independence, the French Declaration also provided that men are born free, equal with the rights to liberty, property and security; but the French declaration specifically granted freedom from unlawful arrest or imprisonment. Overwhelmed by the genocide and atrocious acts committed by the Nazi Germany during the Second World War when the United Nations' Charter was drafted, it incorporated the spirit of these declarations in its preamble to uphold and protect human rights, human dignity and worth of the human personality.

Torture, unlawful arrest, illegal detention, false implication, etc., are the chief areas of human rights violations committed by the police. Among these, torture is the most aggravated form of violation of human rights committed by the police. It varies from simple beating to causing death in custody. Police in India are generally blamed of employing the methods of torture for different reasons. They employ "third degree methods" to collect evidences from the accused. However, the evidence collected by torturing human beings is not justified in law, and often violates norms of human rights protection. Some police officers are rough and rude by nature and find pleasure in torturing his fellow beings who are caught in their net. Pre-set offensive attitudinal behavioural pattern developed through training or years of experience by the police also results into the violations. Some Police officials have the false notion that they can keep their dignity and obtain respect from people only when they horrify the people by showing rude behavior or undignified attitudes towards accused or witnesses or even to general public. Corruption, political nexus or personal bias in particular cases under investigation may also cause violations of human rights by the police. They also employ torture on individuals who stand against the police officer's abuse of power. The extreme form of torture in custody is causing death of a person by the police. Asian Centre for Human Rights in its report "Torture in India 2011" states that from April 2001 to March 2010 it is estimated that 14,231 persons were killed in police custody in India. Most of the victims were killed as a result of torture within the first 48 hours of being taken into custody. This depicts the picture of violation of human rights by the police taking place in the country.

At international level, there were many attempts to protect the human rights. The major documents that deal with protection of persons from the violation of human rights by the police are the Universal Declaration of Human Rights, the International Covenant on Civil and Political Rights and Convention Against Torture. These documents provide protection from torture, arbitrary arrest, illegal detention, illegal search and seizure, etc. However, the Universal Declaration of Human Rights does not provide any mechanism to enforce the human rights in the event of any violation. The International Covenant on Civil and Political Rights and the Convention Against Torture contain provisions for the enforcement of violation of human rights. The mechanisms provided under these documents are 'State Reporting', 'Inter-State Communications' and 'Individual Complaint' mechanisms. In fact, State Reporting and Inter-State communications cannot be considered as an effective enforcement mechanism as these mechanisms provide only the mode of decision making by conciliations and negotiations. They are more of a compromise than a mechanism of enforcement. Individual communication mechanism again is very weak, since the decision making Committee can only give an opinion, on the basis of its findings, to the State and the aggrieved individual. If the State is not complying with the opinion expressed, the Committee has no authority to compel the State to act in accordance with the opinion.

India follows dualist system for the implementation of International treaties, declarations, conventions, etc., into its *corpus juris* and hence, an Act of Parliament is essential to incorporate it. However, the Supreme Court of India held that the International treaties, declarations and conventions can be applied by the Courts in India, even in the absence of an Act of Parliament, if the provisions of such instruments are not inconsistent with the municipal law of India. Thus, even in the absence of Act of

Parliament, such covenants and declarations are enforceable in India if there is no inconsistency with the Constitution and the laws of India.

The Constitution of India provides protection from the violation of human rights by the police. Clause (3) of Article 20 which provides prohibition against self-incrimination, Article 21 which guarantees right to life and personal liberty, and Article 22 which provides safeguards against arbitrary arrest and detention are the significant constitutional provisions in this regard. The right to remain silent is not expressly provided under the Indian Constitution. The Supreme Court held that the right to remain silent is implied under Article 20 (3). The dynamic interpretation that has been given to Article 21 in *Maneka Gandhi*'s case has widened the horizons of human rights jurisprudence in India and the Supreme Court held that Article 21 takes within its sweep the right to live with human dignity, the right against inhuman treatment, the right against torture, the right to compensation in case of death in police custody, the right against hand cuffing, etc. Article 22 provides safeguards against arbitrary arrest and detention. Article 22 (1) and (2) provide that the arrested person has a right to know the grounds of arrest, to consult and to be defended by a lawyer, to be produced before a Magistrate within twenty-four hours. In *Joginder Kumar* and *D.K. Basu*'s cases, the Supreme Court has laid down detailed procedures to be complied with in making the arrest such as to inform about the arrest to a friend, relative or other person who is known to him, where he is being detained, etc. Further, it has been made obligatory to the arresting officer to inform the arrested person about this right. In the event of preventive detention, Article 22 (4) provides that no preventive law shall authorize a person to be detained for more than three months, and in exceptional situations the period of detention can be extended for more than three months after obtaining an opinion from the advisory body constituted for this purpose. The Article 22(5) of the Constitution provides two categories of protection in the event of preventive detention, namely, (i) the grounds on which the detention order is passed must be communicated to the detenue as soon as possible; and (ii) an earliest opportunity of making representation against the detention order shall be provided.

There are many statutes in India which provide protection from torture, arbitrary arrest, unlawful detention, interrogation, false implication and vexatious searches and seizures by the police. The

Code of Criminal Procedure provides provisions that are to be followed in making arrest, detention, search and seizure. The new Amendment to the Code of Criminal Procedure in 2008 and 2010 made significant changes in the arrest and detention matters such as police to compulsorily record the reasons both for making as well as for not making an arrest in respect of offences carrying punishment up to 7 years and, in general cases, the officer has to issue a 'notice of appearance' first before making arrest in these cases, prepare a memorandum of arrest which shall be attested by at least one witness and counter signed by the person arrested,etc. The Indian Penal Code does not provide an exclusive definition of "torture" nor does it prescribe punishment as such for torture committed by the police officers. The Indian Penal Code provides very few specific provisions such as Sections 330 and 331 which provide punishment for causing hurt or grievous hurt to extort confession or to compel restoration of property respectively and Section 376(2)(a) which provides punishment for committing rape in police custody. Since the police commit torture and other atrocities in the custody where there are no witnesses other than the police personnel, the general provisions of the Indian Penal Code have proved to be inadequate in order to bring the erring police officers to justice. The Indian Evidence Act bans the admissibility of confessions made to police or confession made to any person while in the custody of police altogether.

The Indian Police Act which was enacted in 1861 during the period of British rule to coerce and suppress people who stood against the rule is still followed in India. Many Commissions and Committees such as Dharma Veera Commission (National Police Commission), Reibero Committee, Soli Sorbjee committee, Mallimath Committee, etc., recommended for the reform of law relating to the police. However, the recommendation of these Commissions and Committees were not implemented by the Government of India. Hence, the Supreme Court in *Prakash Singh's* case gave directions with specific guidelines to the Government to reform police Acts both at the Centre and the States. Consequent to the directives of the Supreme Court, the Kerala Government has passed new Kerala Police Act in 2011 totally replacing the Kerala Police Act, 1960. The New Act contains provisions for taking care of human rights and human dignity of individuals. The Act provides for the establishment of a Police Establishment Board for posting, promotion and transfer of employment of police, State Security Commission for effectively improving the police department, Police

Complaint Authorities at State and the District level to redress the grievances against police actions.

National Human Rights Commission in India and State Human Rights Commissions in many States have established in accordance with the provisions of Protection of Human Rights Act, 1993. These institutions work as recommendatory bodies for the greater protection and promotion of human rights. The National Human Rights Commission has dealt with many death and torture cases in police custody which would not have come to lime light but for the involvement of the Commission. There are no procedural hurdles of formal court procedure and lawyerings in the case of these institutions to redress a grievance against the police. The major problem that these institutions suffer is that they cannot execute their decisions.

The comparative analysis on the protection of human rights in different regional systems of the world such as Europe, inter-American, African, etc., reveals that these systems guarantee the protection from torture, arbitrary arrest, illegal detention, etc. However, the enforceability mechanism in some regional systems is very effective while in some it is not. Among the regional systems, European system is very successful one due to the efficient mechanism for the redressal of the individual grievances of violations through a full-fledged super-national European Court of Human Rights system. Under the European system, even an individual can directly approach the European Court of Human Rights to redress his grievance against the State action. However, this is not available in the Inter-American system. There is no effective enforcement procedure in the American system and the decisions are not necessarily accepted as legally binding in this system. In the African regional system the only enforceable mechanism available is through the African Commission on Human and Peoples' Rights. However, due to diverse political situations that exist among the Member Nations within the Union makes it more complex for the monitoring and remedial mechanisms in this system. Though the Minsk convention or the Commonwealth of Independent States Convention on Human Rights 1995 provides elaborate safeguards against violations of human rights by the police, the system is not fully operational in the first place. Secondly, there is no effective Court mechanism to enforce it. The only mechanism provided is for the establishment of Human Rights Commission. Though the Arab Charter is not operational, at least, it is in existence, while the Asian

Charter is not even in existence even after repeated attempts. Thus, the scenario of regional systems for the protection of human rights is diverse in its scope, application, level of effectiveness and enforceability in the protection of human rights.

The U.N. has made Code of Conduct for Law Enforcement Officers, the Basic Principles on the Use of Force and Firearms by Law Enforcement Officials, Body of Principles for the Protection of All Persons under Any Form of Detention or Imprisonment,The Standard Minimum Rules for Non-custodial Measures, *etc,* which work as guidelines for National States for making laws in their respective Nations. The Standard Minimum Rules for Non-custodial Measures sets out a number of rules that the National State may make use of in order to avoid the pre-trial detention. It provides that the pre-trial detention shall be used as a last resort. The U.N. Code of Conduct for Law Enforcement Officers sets out a number of conduct rules that the National States must adopt into their States. It also prohibits any kind of torture by law enforcement agencies not only of inflicting but instigating and tolerating it also. The U.N. Principles of Detention or Imprisonment further provides a number of principles that National State may make rules in the cases of detention and imprisonment. It provides that if any damage incurred because of acts or omissions by a public official contrary to the rights contained in these principles must be compensated according to the applicable rules on the liability provided by the domestic law. The Basic Principles on the Use of Force and Firearms by Law Enforcement Officials sets out guidelines for the use of firearms against persons. However, they are not permitted to use firearms against a person in custody or detention except in self-defense or in the defense of others against the immediate threat of death or serious injury. The Declaration on the Protection of All Persons from Enforced Disappearance provides that National States must ensure that no pressure, physical or mental, is exerted on suspects, witnesses, or victims in attempting to obtain information. It further provides that the duration of the process of any interrogation of a detained person and of the intervals between the interrogations as well as the identity of the officials who conducted the interrogations and other persons present shall be recorded in the prescribed form. The United Nations Standard Minimum Rules for the Administration of Juvenile Justice, 1985 directs a number of safeguards and special treatments to be taken by the National States in the cases of arrest and detention of juveniles. Similarly, U.N. Standard Minimum Rules for Prisoners provides a number of safeguards for women in custody. Thus, the U.N. has made elaborate guidelines in order to control exercise of police powers and to avoid abuse of such powers within any National State.

SUGGESTIONS AND RECOMMENDATIONS

In the interest of effective protection of human rights from being violated by the police, the author makes the following suggestions and recommendations:

1. A separate Act should be made consolidating the protection of human rights from being violated by the Police officials. The Act should define 'torture' and other offences in the custody and outside custody, prescribe special and speedy procedures for redressal, shift burden of proof from victims to the accused officials, specify the authorities competent to investigate and decide, provide severe punishments for the violations, etc. The Act should be in tune with the "U.N. Convention Against Torture" and the "U.N. Code of Conduct for Law Enforcement Officers". The Law should also be made to punish instigators of torture. It should also punish those who do not reasonably take any steps to prevent the torture that takes place in their presence.
2. The 'burden of proving' custodial torture should be shifted to the police officer who is accused in a crime of torture in custody. There is always lack of independent witnesses in custodial torture. Even if someone is present, the police by coercion or otherwise influence such witnesses to favour their side and hence, the victims of torture are always in a disadvantageous position to prove their side. Consequently, the accused police officer escapes from justice.
3. The Indian Penal Code should be amended to incorporate provisions to punish a police officer who refuses or fails to record, without reasonable cause, a First Information Report or who does not conduct investigation properly in a case of human rights violations by the police. The Law Commission's 84th Report recommended that any police officer who refused or without reasonable cause failed to

record a First Information Report be subject to imprisonment for a term of one year or fine or both.

4. Currently, Sections 197 and 132 of the Code Criminal Procedure require the prior sanction of the government before prosecuting public servants for any offence alleged to have been done in discharge of their official duty. The immunity given as per these provisions to the police officers as public servant should be withdrawn in the cases of violation of human rights committed by the police. The National Police Commission's 8th Report also recommended for the withdrawal of the immunity given to police officers under Sections 197 and 132 of the Code Criminal Procedure.
5. Indian Penal Code should be amended to provide severe punishments for perjury for witnesses turning hostile during trial in the cases where the police officer is the accused. The Law should also provide procedure for Magistrate/ Judges to order separate investigations into the suspicious circumstances such as influence, coercion, promise, etc., which led to the turning hostile.
6. Delay in the disposal of cases also affords greater opportunity for the accused to win over the witnesses by threats or inducements. So the law with special procedure should be made to provide time bound investigation and trial in all cases of human rights violation by the police.
7. National Human Rights Commission and State Human Rights Commissions should be given tribunal like power to implement its findings and decisions particularly in the matters of violations of human rights by the police. Currently, the National Human Rights Commission and State Human Rights Commissions operate only as recommendatory bodies.
8. Protection of Human Rights Act should be amended to provide clear demarcations of jurisdictions of the National Human Rights Commission and the State Human Rights Commissions to inquire into cases.
9. The National Human Rights Commission should be given appellate power from the cases arising from the State Human Rights Commissions. Currently, the National Human Rights Commission does not have appellate power.

10. Domestic enquiries related with human rights violations by the police should be made more transparent and be completed within three months from the date of occurrence, and the result of the enquiry should be made known to public through the media. Currently, the domestic enquiry conducted by a superior police officer on a complaint against his subordinates impedes the propriety due to the departmental brethren solidarity among officers.
11. A presumption of complicity should be incorporated in the Evidence Act in all cases where the superior officer, even after the incident came to his knowledge, does not institute disciplinary action against a subordinate police officer who had committed violation of human rights.
12. The Prevention of Terrorism Act should be amended to create a separate and independent body consisting of Judges of High Court/ District Court to monitor each and every case where the police make arrest and detention of persons invoking such laws.
13. Currently, it is the discretion of the Government to give sanction if the victim of police excesses requests that he may engage a lawyer of his choice at his own expense. The Government has authority even to refuse to give permission for it. Rules should be amended to make it mandatory for the Government to give sanction if such a request is made by a victim.
14. India should initiate that South Asian Association for Regional Cooperation (SAARC) countries should have a regional system for the protection of human rights within the region like that of European Union or Inter-American or African system which provide protection through a supra- national body .
15. India should make laws in tune with the "U.N. Declaration of Victims of Crime and Abuse of Power" to prevent abuse of power by the police. Such laws should also prescribe remedies such as restitution and/or compensation, and necessary material, medical, psychological and social assistance and support to the victims of such abuses.
16. India should make laws in tune with the "U.N.Body of Principles for the Protection of All Persons under Any

Form of Detention or Imprisonment" laying down clear procedure for recording the process of any interrogation of a detained person, the duration of interrogation, the intervals between the interrogations, the identity of the officials who conducted the interrogations and other persons present at the interrogation.

17. The Government and the Police Department should take appropriate steps to implement the laws and the Supreme Court guidelines on arrest, detention, search and seizure effectively. The Government and the Police Department should, for achieving this purpose, create an efficient monitoring mechanism within the Department at State and District level.
18. Victims of violations of human rights by the police shall be given free legal services at the expenses of the State to engage a lawyer of his own choice in all cases of human rights violation by the police.
21. A team of expert psychologists should periodically give training to police officers so that the traditional colonial attitudinal behaviour towards common man can be transformed gradually.
22. Periodic in-service training, seminar, workshop, etc., on human rights should be imparted to all police officers. This will sensitize and inculcate respect for human rights in them and also improve police-public relations.
23. The capacity building of the investigating officers should be improved through proper training including the strengthening of the crime-investigation curriculum at police academies, training low-ranking officers to assist in crime investigations, and providing basic forensic equipment to every police officer. Torturing accused person in order to elicit facts in a crime is a cruel and barbarous practice and should not be used as a short cut method in crime investigation. If crime investigators are intelligent and efficient, the valuable information can be gathered through proper and scientific investigations without violating the human rights and human dignity of persons.

APPENDIX I

Universal Declaration of Human Rights 1948

PREAMBLE

Whereas recognition of the inherent dignity and of the equal and inalienable rights of all members of the human family is the foundation of freedom, justice and peace in the world,

Whereas disregard and contempt for human rights have resulted in barbarous acts which have outraged the conscience of mankind, and the advent of a world in which human beings shall enjoy freedom of speech and belief and freedom from fear and want has been proclaimed as the highest aspiration of the common people,

Whereas it is essential, if man is not to be compelled to have recourse, as a last resort, to rebellion against tyranny and oppression, that human rights should be protected by the rule of law,

Whereas it is essential to promote the development of friendly relations between nations,

Whereas the peoples of the United Nations have in the Charter reaffirmed their faith in fundamental human rights, in the dignity and worth of the human person and in the equal rights of men and women and have determined to promote social progress and better standards of life in larger freedom,

Whereas Member States have pledged themselves to achieve, in cooperation with the United Nations, the promotion of universal respect for and observance of human rights and fundamental freedoms,

Whereas a common understanding of these rights and freedoms is of the greatest importance for the full realization of this pledge,

Now, therefore,

THE GENERAL ASSEMBLY

proclaims

THIS UNIVERSAL DECLARATION OF HUMAN RIGHTS

as a common standard of achievement for all peoples and all nations, to the end that every individual and every organ of society, keeping this Declaration constantly in mind, shall strive by teaching and education to promote respect for these rights and freedoms and by progressive measures, national and international, to secure their universal and effective recognition and observance, both among the peoples of Member States themselves and among the peoples of territories under their jurisdiction.

Article 1

All human beings are born free and equal in dignity and rights. They are endowed with reason and conscience and should act towards one another in a spirit of brotherhood.

Article 2

Everyone is entitled to all the rights and freedoms set forth in this Declaration, without distinction of any kind, such as race, colour, sex, language, religion, political or other opinion, national or social origin, property, birth or other status.

Furthermore, no distinction shall be made on the basis of the political, jurisdictional or international status of the country or territory to which a person belongs,whether it be independent, trust, non-self-governing or under any other limitation of sovereignty.

Article 3

Everyone has the right to life, liberty and security of person.

Article 4

No one shall be held in slavery or servitude; slavery and the slave trade shall be prohibited in all their forms.

Article 5

No one shall be subjected to torture or to cruel, inhuman or degrading treatment or punishment.

Article 6

Everyone has the right to recognition everywhere as a person before the law.

Article 7

All are equal before the law and are entitled without any discrimination to equal protection of the law. All are entitled to equal protection against any discrimination in violation of this Declaration and against any incitement to such discrimination.

Article 8

Everyone has the right to an effective remedy by the competent national tribunals for acts violating the fundamental rights granted him by the constitution or by law.

Article 9

No one shall be subjected to arbitrary arrest, detention or exile.

Article 10

Everyone is entitled in full equality to a fair and public hearing by an independent and impartial tribunal, in the determination of his rights and obligations and of any criminal charge against him.

Article 11

(1) Everyone charged with a penal offence has the right to be presumed innocent until proved guilty according to law in a public trial at which he has had all the guarantees necessary for his defence.

(2) No one shall be held guilty of any penal offence on account of any act or omission which did not constitute a penal offence, under national or international law, at the time when it was committed. Nor shall a heavier penalty be imposed than the one that was applicable at the time the penal offence was committed.

Article 12

No one shall be subjected to arbitrary interference with his privacy, family, home or correspondence, nor to attacks upon his honour and reputation. Everyone has the right to the protection of the law against such interference or attacks.

Article 13

(1) Everyone has the right to freedom of movement and residence within the borders of each State.

(2) Everyone has the right to leave any country, including his own, and to return to his country.

Article 14

(1) Everyone has the right to seek and to enjoy in other countries asylum from persecution.

(2) This right may not be invoked in the case of prosecutions genuinely arising from non-political crimes or from acts contrary to the purposes and principles of the United Nations.

Article 15

(1) Everyone has the right to a nationality.

(2) No one shall be arbitrarily deprived of his nationality nor denied the right to change his nationality.

Article 16

(1) Men and women of full age, without any limitation due to race, nationality or religion, have the right to marry and to found a family. They are entitled to equal rights as to marriage, during marriage and at its dissolution.

(2) Marriage shall be entered into only with the free and full consent of the intending spouses.

(3) The family is the natural and fundamental group unit of society and is entitled to protection by society and the State.

Article 17

(1) Everyone has the right to own property alone as well as in association with others.

(2) No one shall be arbitrarily deprived of his property.

Article 18

Everyone has the right to freedom of thought, conscience and religion; this right includes freedom to change his religion or belief, and freedom, either alone or in community with others and in public or private, to manifest his religion or belief in teaching, practice, worship and observance.

Article 19

Everyone has the right to freedom of opinion and expression; this right includes freedom to hold opinions without interference and to seek, receive and impart information and ideas through any media and regardless of frontiers.

Article 20

(1) Everyone has the right to freedom of peaceful assembly and association.

(2) No one may be compelled to belong to an association.

Article 21

(1) Everyone has the right to take part in the government of his country, directly or through freely chosen representatives.
(2) Everyone has the right to equal access to public service in his country.
(3) The will of the people shall be the basis of the authority of government; this will shall be expressed in periodic and genuine elections which shall be by universal and equal suffrage and shall be held by secret vote or by equivalent free voting procedures.

Article 22

Everyone, as a member of society, has the right to social security and is entitled to realization, through national effort and international co-operation and in accordance with the organization and resources of each State, of the economic, social and cultural rights indispensable for his dignity and the free development of his personality.

Article 23

(1) Everyone has the right to work, to free choice of employment, to just and favourable conditions of work and to protection against unemployment.
(2) Everyone, without any discrimination, has the right to equal pay for equal work.
(3) Everyone who works has the right to just and favourable remuneration ensuring for himself and his family an existence worthy of human dignity, and supplemented, if necessary, by other means of social protection.
(4) Everyone has the right to form and to join trade unions for the protection of his interests.

Article 24

Everyone has the right to rest and leisure, including reasonable limitation of working hours and periodic holidays with pay.

Article 25

(1) Everyone has the right to a standard of living adequate for the health and well-being of himself and of his family, including food, clothing, housing and medical care and necessary social services, and the right to security in the event of

unemployment, sickness, disability, widowhood, old age or other lack of livelihood in circumstances beyond his control.

(2) Motherhood and childhood are entitled to special care and assistance. All children, whether born in or out of wedlock, shall enjoy the same social protection.

Article 26

(1) Everyone has the right to education. Education shall be free, at least in the elementary and fundamental stages. Elementary education shall be compulsory. Technical and professional education shall be made generally available and higher education shall be equally accessible to all on the basis of merit.

(2) Education shall be directed to the full development of the human personality and to the strengthening of respect for human rights and fundamental freedoms. It shall promote understanding, tolerance and friendship among all nations, racial or religious groups, and shall further the activities of the United Nations for the maintenance of peace.

(3) Parents have a prior right to choose the kind of education that shall be given to their children.

Article 27

(1) Everyone has the right freely to participate in the cultural life of the community, to enjoy the arts and to share in scientific advancement and its benefits.

(2) Everyone has the right to the protection of the moral and material interests resulting from any scientific, literary or artistic production of which he is the author.

Article 28

Everyone is entitled to a social and international order in which the rights and freedoms set forth in this Declaration can be fully realized.

Article 29

(1) Everyone has duties to the community in which alone the free and full development of his personality is possible.

(2) In the exercise of his rights and freedoms, everyone shall be subject only to such limitations as are determined by law solely for the purpose of securing due recognition and respect for the rights and

freedoms of others and of meeting the just requirements of morality, public order and the general welfare in a democratic society.

(3) These rights and freedoms may in no case be exercised contrary to the purposes and principles of the United Nations.

Article 30

Nothing in this Declaration may be interpreted as implying for any State, group or person any right to engage in any activity or to perform any act aimed at the destruction of any of the rights and freedoms set forth herein.

G.A. res. 217A (III), U.N. Doc A/810 at 71 (1948)

Adopted on December 10, 1948 by the General Assembly of the United Nations (without dissent).

Appendix II

International Covenant on Civil and Political Rights

Adopted and opened for signature, ratification and accession by General Assembly resolution 2200A (XXI) of 16 December 1966; entry into force on 23 March 1976, in accordance with Article 49.

PREAMBLE

The States Parties to the present Covenant,

Considering that, in accordance with the principles proclaimed in the Charter of the United Nations, recognition of the inherent dignity and of the equal and inalienable rights of all members of the human family is the foundation of freedom, justice and peace in the world,

Recognizing that these rights derive from the inherent dignity of the human person,

Recognizing that, in accordance with the Universal Declaration of Human Rights, the ideal of free human beings enjoying civil and political freedom and freedom from fear and want can only be achieved if conditions are created whereby everyone may enjoy his civil and political rights, as well as his economic, social and cultural rights,

Considering the obligation of States under the Charter of the United Nations to promote universal respect for, and observance of, human rights and freedoms,

Realizing that the individual, having duties to other individuals and to the community to which he belongs, is under a responsibility to strive for the promotion and observance of the rights recognized in the present Covenant,

Agree upon the following articles:

PART I

Article 1

1. All peoples have the right of self-determination. By virtue of that right they freely determine their political status and freely pursue their economic, social and cultural development.
2. All peoples may, for their own ends, freely dispose of their natural wealth and resources without prejudice to any obligations arising out of international economic co-operation, based upon the principle of mutual benefit, and international law. In no case may a people be deprived of its own means of subsistence.
3. The States Parties to the present Covenant, including those having responsibility for the administration of Non-Self-Governing and Trust Territories, shall promote the realization of the right of self-determination, and shall respect that right, in conformity with the provisions of the Charter of the United Nations.

PART II

Article 2

1. Each State Party to the present Covenant undertakes to respect and to ensure to all individuals within its territory and subject to its jurisdiction the rights recognized in the present Covenant, without distinction of any kind, such as race, colour, sex, language, religion, political or other opinion, national or social origin, property, birth or other status.
2. Where not already provided for by existing legislative or other measures, each State Party to the present Covenant undertakes to take the necessary steps, in accordance with its constitutional processes and with the provisions of the present Covenant, to adopt such laws or other measures as may be necessary to give effect to the rights recognized in the present Covenant.
3. Each State Party to the present Covenant undertakes:
   (a) To ensure that any person whose rights or freedoms as

herein recognized are violated shall have an effective remedy, notwithstanding that the violation has been committed by persons acting in an official capacity;

(b) To ensure that any person claiming such a remedy shall have his right thereto determined by competent judicial, administrative or legislative authorities, or by any other competent authority provided for by the legal system of the State, and to develop the possibilities of judicial remedy;

(c) To ensure that the competent authorities shall enforce such remedies when granted.

Article 3

The States Parties to the present Covenant undertake to ensure the equal right of men and women to the enjoyment of all civil and political rights set forth in the present Covenant.

Article 4

1. In time of public emergency which threatens the life of the nation and the existence of which is officially proclaimed, the States Parties to the present Covenant may take measures derogating from their obligations under the present Covenant to the extent strictly required by the exigencies of the situation, provided that such measures are not inconsistent with their other obligations under international law and do not involve discrimination solely on the ground of race, colour, sex, language, religion or social origin.
2. No derogation from articles 6, 7, 8 (paragraphs I and 2), 11, 15, 16 and 18 may be made under this provision.
3. Any State Party to the present Covenant availing itself of the right of derogation shall immediately inform the other States Parties to the present Covenant, through the intermediary of the Secretary-General of the United Nations, of the provisions from which it has derogated and of the reasons by which it was actuated. A further communication shall be made, through the same intermediary, on the date on which it terminates such derogation.

Article 5

1. Nothing in the present Covenant may be interpreted as implying for any State, group or person any right to engage in any activity or perform any act aimed at the destruction of any

of the rights and freedoms recognized herein or at their limitation to a greater extent than is provided for in the present Covenant.

2. There shall be no restriction upon or derogation from any of the fundamental human rights recognized or existing in any State Party to the present Covenant pursuant to law, conventions, regulations or custom on the pretext that the present Covenant does not recognize such rights or that it recognizes them to a lesser extent.

PART III

Article 6

1. Every human being has the inherent right to life. This right shall be protected by law. No one shall be arbitrarily deprived of his life.
2. In countries which have not abolished the death penalty, sentence of death may be imposed only for the most serious crimes in accordance with the law in force at the time of the commission of the crime and not contrary to the provisions of the present Covenant and to the Convention on the Prevention and Punishment of the Crime of Genocide. This penalty can only be carried out pursuant to a final judgment rendered by a competent court.
3. When deprivation of life constitutes the crime of genocide, it is understood that nothing in this article shall authorize any State Party to the present Covenant to derogate in any way from any obligation assumed under the provisions of the Convention on the Prevention and Punishment of the Crime of Genocide.
4. Anyone sentenced to death shall have the right to seek pardon or commutation of the sentence. Amnesty, pardon or commutation of the sentence of death may be granted in all cases.
5. Sentence of death shall not be imposed for crimes committed by persons below eighteen years of age and shall not be carried out on pregnant women.
6. Nothing in this Article shall be invoked to delay or to prevent the abolition of capital punishment by any State Party to the present Covenant.

Article 7

No one shall be subjected to torture or to cruel, inhuman or degrading treatment or punishment. In particular, no one shall be subjected without his free consent to medical or scientific experimentation.

Article 8

1. No one shall be held in slavery; slavery and the slave-trade in all their forms shall be prohibited.
2. No one shall be held in servitude.
3. (a) No one shall be required to perform forced or compulsory labour;
   (b) Paragraph 3 (a) shall not be held to preclude, in countries where imprisonment with hard labour may be imposed as a punishment for a crime, the performance of hard labour in pursuance of a sentence to such punishment by a competent court;
   (c) For the purpose of this paragraph the term "forced or compulsory labour" shall not include:
      (i) Any work or service, not referred to in subparagraph (b), normally required of a person who is under detention in consequence of a lawful order of a court, or of a person during conditional release from such detention;
      (ii) Any service of a military character and, in countries where conscientious objection is recognized, any national service required by law of conscientious objectors;
      (iii) Any service exacted in cases of emergency or calamity threatening the life or well-being of the community;
      (iv) Any work or service which forms part of normal civil obligations.

Article 9

1. Everyone has the right to liberty and security of person. No one shall be subjected to arbitrary arrest or detention. No one shall be deprived of his liberty except on such grounds and in accordance with such procedure as are established by law.
2. Anyone who is arrested shall be informed, at the time of arrest, of the reasons for his arrest and shall be promptly informed of any charges against him.
3. Anyone arrested or detained on a criminal charge shall be

brought promptly before a judge or other officer authorized by law to exercise judicial power and shall be entitled to trial within a reasonable time or to release. It shall not be the general rule that persons awaiting trial shall be detained in custody, but release may be subject to guarantees to appear for trial, at any other stage of the judicial proceedings, and, should occasion arise, for execution of the judgment.

4. Anyone who is deprived of his liberty by arrest or detention shall be entitled to take proceedings before a court, in order that that court may decide without delay on the lawfulness of his detention and order his release if the detention is not lawful.
5. Anyone who has been the victim of unlawful arrest or detention shall have an enforceable right to compensation.

Article 10

1. All persons deprived of their liberty shall be treated with humanity and with respect for the inherent dignity of the human person.
2. (a) Accused persons shall, save in exceptional circumstances, be segregated from convicted persons and shall be subject to separate treatment appropriate to their status as unconvicted persons;
   (b) Accused juvenile persons shall be separated from adults and brought as speedily as possible for adjudication.
3. The penitentiary system shall comprise treatment of prisoners the essential aim of which shall be their reformation and social rehabilitation. Juvenile offenders shall be segregated from adults and be accorded treatment appropriate to their age and legal status.

Article 11

No one shall be imprisoned merely on the ground of inability to fulfil a contractual obligation.

Article 12

1. Everyone lawfully within the territory of a State shall, within that territory, have the right to liberty of movement and freedom to choose his residence.
2. Everyone shall be free to leave any country, including his own.
3. The above-mentioned rights shall not be subject to any restrictions except those which are provided by law, are necessary to protect national security, public order (*ordre*

public), public health or morals or the rights and freedoms of others, and are consistent with the other rights recognized in the present Covenant.

4. No one shall be arbitrarily deprived of the right to enter his own country.

Article 13

An alien lawfully in the territory of a State Party to the present Covenant may be expelled therefrom only in pursuance of a decision reached in accordance with law and shall, except where compelling reasons of national security otherwise require, be allowed to submit the reasons against his expulsion and to have his case reviewed by, and be represented for the purpose before, the competent authority or a person or persons especially designated by the competent authority.

Article 14

1. All persons shall be equal before the courts and tribunals. In the determination of any criminal charge against him, or of his rights and obligations in a suit at law, everyone shall be entitled to a fair and public hearing by a competent, independent and impartial tribunal established by law. The press and the public may be excluded from all or part of a trial for reasons of morals, public order (*ordre* public) or national security in a democratic society, or when the interest of the private lives of the parties so requires, or to the extent strictly necessary in the opinion of the court in special circumstances where publicity would prejudice the interests of justice; but any judgment rendered in a criminal case or in a suit at law shall be made public except where the interest of juvenile persons otherwise requires or the proceedings concern matrimonial disputes or the guardianship of children.
2. Everyone charged with a criminal offence shall have the right to be presumed innocent until proved guilty according to law.
3. In the determination of any criminal charge against him, everyone shall be entitled to the following minimum guarantees, in full equality:
   (a) To be informed promptly and in detail in a language which he understands of the nature and cause of the charge against him;
   (b) To have adequate time and facilities for the preparation of his defence and to communicate with counsel of his own choosing;

(c) To be tried without undue delay;
(d) To be tried in his presence, and to defend himself in person or through legal assistance of his own choosing; to be informed, if he does not have legal assistance, of this right; and to have legal assistance assigned to him, in any case where the interests of justice so require, and without payment by him in any such case if he does not have sufficient means to pay for it;
(e) To examine, or have examined, the witnesses against him and to obtain the attendance and examination of witnesses on his behalf under the same conditions as witnesses against him;
(f) To have the free assistance of an interpreter if he cannot understand or speak the language used in court;
(g) Not to be compelled to testify against himself or to confess guilt.

4. In the case of juvenile persons, the procedure shall be, such as will take account of their age and the desirability of promoting their rehabilitation.
5. Everyone convicted of a crime shall have the right to his conviction and sentence being reviewed by a higher tribunal according to law.
6. When a person has by a final decision been convicted of a criminal offence and when subsequently his conviction has been reversed or he has been pardoned on the ground that a new or newly discovered fact shows conclusively that there has been a miscarriage of justice, the person who has suffered punishment as a result of such conviction shall be compensated according to law, unless it is proved that the non-disclosure of the unknown fact in time is wholly or partly attributable to him.
7. No one shall be liable to be tried or punished again for an offence for which he has already been finally convicted or acquitted in accordance with the law and penal procedure of each country.

Article 15

1. No one shall be held guilty of any criminal offence on account of any act or omission which did not constitute a criminal offence, under national or international law, at the time when it was committed. Nor shall a heavier penalty be imposed than

the one that was applicable at the time when the criminal offence was committed. If, subsequent to the commission of the offence, provision is made by law for the imposition of the lighter penalty, the offender shall benefit thereby.

2. Nothing in this article shall prejudice the trial and punishment of any person for any act or omission which, at the time when it was committed, was criminal according to the general principles of law recognized by the community of nations.

Article 16

Everyone shall have the right to recognition everywhere as a person before the law.

Article 17

1. No one shall be subjected to arbitrary or unlawful interference with his privacy, family, home or correspondence, nor to unlawful attacks on his honour and reputation.
2. Everyone has the right to the protection of the law against such interference or attacks.

Article 18

1. Everyone shall have the right to freedom of thought, conscience and religion. This right shall include freedom to have or to adopt a religion or belief of his choice, and freedom, either individually or in community with others and in public or private, to manifest his religion or belief in worship, observance, practice and teaching.
2. No one shall be subject to coercion which would impair his freedom to have or to adopt a religion or belief of his choice.
3. Freedom to manifest one's religion or beliefs may be subject only to such limitations as are prescribed by law and are necessary to protect public safety, order, health, or morals or the fundamental rights and freedoms of others.
4. The States Parties to the present Covenant undertake to have respect for the liberty of parents and, when applicable, legal guardians to ensure the religious and moral education of their children in conformity with their own convictions.

Article 19

1. Everyone shall have the right to hold opinions without interference.
2. Everyone shall have the right to freedom of expression; this

right shall include freedom to seek, receive and impart information and ideas of all kinds, regardless of frontiers, either orally, in writing or in print, in the form of art, or through any other media of his choice.

3. The exercise of the rights provided for in paragraph 2 of this article carries with it special duties and responsibilities. It may therefore be subject to certain restrictions, but these shall only be such as are provided by law and are necessary:
   (a) For respect of the rights or reputations of others;
   (b) For the protection of national security or of public order (*ordre* public), or of public health or morals.

Article 20

1. Any propaganda for war shall be prohibited by law.
2. Any advocacy of national, racial or religious hatred that constitutes incitement to discrimination, hostility or violence shall be prohibited by law.

Article 21

The right of peaceful assembly shall be recognized. No restrictions may be placed on the exercise of this right other than those imposed in conformity with the law and which are necessary in a democratic society in the interests of national security or public safety, public order (*ordre* public), the protection of public health or morals or the protection of the rights and freedoms of others.

Article 22

1. Everyone shall have the right to freedom of association with others, including the right to form and join trade unions for the protection of his interests.
2. No restrictions may be placed on the exercise of this right other than those which are prescribed by law and which are necessary in a democratic society in the interests of national security or public safety, public order (*ordre* public), the protection of public health or morals or the protection of the rights and freedoms of others. This article shall not prevent the imposition of lawful restrictions on members of the armed forces and of the police in their exercise of this right.
3. Nothing in this article shall authorize States Parties to the International Labour Organisation Convention of 1948 concerning Freedom of Association and Protection of the Right to Organize to take legislative measures which would

prejudice, or to apply the law in such a manner as to prejudice, the guarantees provided for in that Convention.

Article 23

1. The family is the natural and fundamental group unit of society and is entitled to protection by society and the State.
2. The right of men and women of marriageable age to marry and to found a family shall be recognized.
3. No marriage shall be entered into without the free and full consent of the intending spouses.
4. States Parties to the present Covenant shall take appropriate steps to ensure equality of rights and responsibilities of spouses as to marriage, during marriage and at its dissolution. In the case of dissolution, provision shall be made for the necessary protection of any children.

Article 24

1. Every child shall have, without any discrimination as to race, colour, sex, language, religion, national or social origin, property or birth, the right to such measures of protection as are required by his status as a minor, on the part of his family, society and the State.
2. Every child shall be registered immediately after birth and shall have a name.
3. Every child has the right to acquire a nationality.

Article 25

Every citizen shall have the right and the opportunity, without any of the distinctions mentioned in article 2 and without unreasonable restrictions :

(a) To take part in the conduct of public affairs, directly or through freely chosen representatives;

(b) To vote and to be elected at genuine periodic elections which shall be by universal and equal suffrage and shall be held by secret ballot, guaranteeing the free expression of the will of the electors;

(c) To have access, on general terms of equality, to public service in his country.

Article 26

All persons are equal before the law and are entitled without any discrimination to the equal protection of the law. In this respect, the law shall prohibit any discrimination and guarantee to all persons equal and effective protection against discrimination on any ground such as race, colour, sex, language, religion, political or other opinion, national or social origin, property, birth or other status.

Article 27

In those States in which ethnic, religious or linguistic minorities exist, persons belonging to such minorities shall not be denied the right, in community with the other members of their group, to enjoy their own culture, to profess and practise their own religion, or to use their own language.

PART IV

Article 28

1. There shall be established a Human Rights Committee (hereafter referred to in the present Covenant as the Committee). It shall consist of eighteen members and shall carry out the functions hereinafter provided.
2. The Committee shall be composed of nationals of the States Parties to the present Covenant who shall be persons of high moral character and recognized competence in the field of human rights, consideration being given to the usefulness of the participation of some persons having legal experience.
3. The members of the Committee shall be elected and shall serve in their personal capacity.

Article 29

1. The members of the Committee shall be elected by secret ballot from a list of persons possessing the qualifications prescribed in article 28 and nominated for the purpose by the States Parties to the present Covenant.
2. Each State Party to the present Covenant may nominate not more than two persons. These persons shall be nationals of the nominating State.
3. A person shall be eligible for re-nomination.

Article 30

1. The initial election shall be held no later than six months after the date of the entry into force of the present Covenant.
2. At least four months before the date of each election to the

Committee, other than an election to fill a vacancy declared in accordance with article 34, the Secretary-General of the United Nations shall address a written invitation to the States Parties to the present Covenant to submit their nominations for membership of the Committee within three months.

3. The Secretary-General of the United Nations shall prepare a list in alphabetical order of all the persons thus nominated, with an indication of the States Parties which have nominated them, and shall submit it to the States Parties to the present Covenant no later than one month before the date of each election.

4. Elections of the members of the Committee shall be held at a meeting of the States Parties to the present Covenant convened by the Secretary General of the United Nations at the Headquarters of the United Nations. At that meeting, for which two thirds of the States Parties to the present Covenant shall constitute a quorum, the persons elected to the Committee shall be those nominees who obtain the largest number of votes and an absolute majority of the votes of the representatives of States Parties present and voting.

Article 31

1. The Committee may not include more than one national of the same State.
2. In the election of the Committee, consideration shall be given to equitable geographical distribution of membership and to the representation of the different forms of civilization and of the principal legal systems.

Article 32

1. The members of the Committee shall be elected for a term of four years. They shall be eligible for re-election if re-nominated. However, the terms of nine of the members elected at the first election shall expire at the end of two years; immediately after the first election, the names of these nine members shall be chosen by lot by the Chairman of the meeting referred to in article 30, paragraph 4.
2. Elections at the expiry of office shall be held in accordance with the preceding articles of this part of the present Covenant.

Article 33

1. If, in the unanimous opinion of the other members, a member

of the Committee has ceased to carry out his functions for any cause other than absence of a temporary character, the Chairman of the Committee shall notify the Secretary-General of the United Nations, who shall then declare the seat of that member to be vacant.

2. In the event of the death or the resignation of a member of the Committee, the Chairman shall immediately notify the Secretary-General of the United Nations, who shall declare the seat vacant from the date of death or the date on which the resignation takes effect.

Article 34

1. When a vacancy is declared in accordance with article 33 and if the term of office of the member to be replaced does not expire within six months of the declaration of the vacancy, the Secretary-General of the United Nations shall notify each of the States Parties to the present Covenant, which may within two months submit nominations in accordance with article 29 for the purpose of filling the vacancy.
2. The Secretary-General of the United Nations shall prepare a list in alphabetical order of the persons thus nominated and shall submit it to the States Parties to the present Covenant. The election to fill the vacancy shall then take place in accordance with the relevant provisions of this part of the present Covenant.
3. A member of the Committee elected to fill a vacancy declared in accordance with article 33 shall hold office for the remainder of the term of the member who vacated the seat on the Committee under the provisions of that article.

Article 35

The members of the Committee shall, with the approval of the General Assembly of the United Nations, receive emoluments from United Nations resources on such terms and conditions as the General Assembly may decide, having regard to the importance of the Committee's responsibilities.

Article 36

The Secretary-General of the United Nations shall provide the necessary staff and facilities for the effective performance of the functions of the Committee under the present Covenant.

Article 37

1. The Secretary-General of the United Nations shall convene the initial meeting of the Committee at the Headquarters of the United Nations.
2. After its initial meeting, the Committee shall meet at such times as shall be provided in its rules of procedure.
3. The Committee shall normally meet at the Headquarters of the United Nations or at the United Nations Office at Geneva.

Article 38

Every member of the Committee shall, before taking up his duties, make a solemn declaration in open committee that he will perform his functions impartially and conscientiously.

Article 39

1. The Committee shall elect its officers for a term of two years. They may be re-elected.
2. The Committee shall establish its own rules of procedure, but these rules shall provide, inter alia, that:
   (a) Twelve members shall constitute a quorum;
   (b) Decisions of the Committee shall be made by a majority vote of the members present.

Article 40

1. The States Parties to the present Covenant undertake to submit reports on the measures they have adopted which give effect to the rights recognized herein and on the progress made in the enjoyment of those rights:
   (a) Within one year of the entry into force of the present Covenant for the States Parties concerned;
   (b) Thereafter whenever the Committee so requests.
2. All reports shall be submitted to the Secretary-General of the United Nations, who shall transmit them to the Committee for consideration. Reports shall indicate the factors and difficulties, if any, affecting the implementation of the present Covenant.
3. The Secretary-General of the United Nations may, after consultation with the Committee, transmit to the specialized agencies concerned copies of such parts of the reports as may fall within their field of competence.
4. The Committee shall study the reports submitted by the States Parties to the present Covenant. It shall transmit its reports,

and such general comments as it may consider appropriate, to the States Parties. The Committee may also transmit to the Economic and Social Council these comments along with the copies of the reports it has received from States Parties to the present Covenant.

5. The States Parties to the present Covenant may submit to the Committee observations on any comments that may be made in accordance with paragraph 4 of this article.

Article 41

1. A State Party to the present Covenant may at any time declare under this article that it recognizes the competence of the Committee to receive and consider communications to the effect that a State Party claims that another State Party is not fulfilling its obligations under the present Covenant. Communications under this article may be received and considered only if submitted by a State Party which has made a declaration recognizing in regard to itself the competence of the Committee. No communication shall be received by the Committee if it concerns a State Party which has not made such a declaration. Communications received under this article shall be dealt with in accordance with the following procedure:
   (a) If a State Party to the present Covenant considers that another State Party is not giving effect to the provisions of the present Covenant, it may, by written communication, bring the matter to the attention of that State Party. Within three months after the receipt of the communication the receiving State shall afford the State which sent the communication an explanation, or any other statement in writing clarifying the matter which should include, to the extent possible and pertinent, reference to domestic procedures and remedies taken, pending, or available in the matter;
   (b) If the matter is not adjusted to the satisfaction of both States Parties concerned within six months after the receipt by the receiving State of the initial communication, either State shall have the right to refer the matter to the Committee, by notice given to the Committee and to the other State;
   (c) The Committee shall deal with a matter referred to it only after it has ascertained that all available domestic

remedies have been invoked and exhausted in the matter, in conformity with the generally recognized principles of international law. This shall not be the rule where the application of the remedies is unreasonably prolonged;

(d) The Committee shall hold closed meetings when examining communications under this article;

(e) Subject to the provisions of subparagraph (c), the Committee shall make available its good offices to the States Parties concerned with a view to a friendly solution of the matter on the basis of respect for human rights and fundamental freedoms as recognized in the present Covenant;

(f) In any matter referred to it, the Committee may call upon the States Parties concerned, referred to in subparagraph (b), to supply any relevant information;

(g) The States Parties concerned, referred to in subparagraph (b), shall have the right to be represented when the matter is being considered in the Committee and to make submissions orally and/or in writing;

(h) The Committee shall, within twelve months after the date of receipt of notice under subparagraph (b), submit a report:

(i) If a solution within the terms of subparagraph (e) is reached, the Committee shall confine its report to a brief statement of the facts and of the solution reached;

(ii) If a solution within the terms of subparagraph (e) is not reached, the Committee shall confine its report to a brief statement of the facts; the written submissions and record of the oral submissions made by the States Parties concerned shall be attached to the report. In every matter, the report shall be communicated to the States Parties concerned.

2. The provisions of this article shall come into force when ten States Parties to the present Covenant have made declarations under paragraph I of this article. Such declarations shall be deposited by the States Parties with the Secretary-General of the United Nations, who shall transmit copies thereof to the other States Parties. A declaration may be withdrawn at any time by notification to the Secretary-General. Such a

withdrawal shall not prejudice the consideration of any matter which is the subject of a communication already transmitted under this article; no further communication by any State Party shall be received after the notification of withdrawal of the declaration has been received by the Secretary-General, unless the State Party concerned has made a new declaration.

Article 42

1. (a) If a matter referred to the Committee in accordance with article 41 is not resolved to the satisfaction of the States Parties concerned, the Committee may, with the prior consent of the States Parties concerned, appoint an ad hoc Conciliation Commission (hereinafter referred to as the Commission). The good offices of the Commission shall be made available to the States Parties concerned with a view to an amicable solution of the matter on the basis of respect for the present Covenant;

   (b) The Commission shall consist of five persons acceptable to the States Parties concerned. If the States Parties concerned fail to reach agreement within three months on all or part of the composition of the Commission, the members of the Commission concerning whom no agreement has been reached shall be elected by secret ballot by a two-thirds majority vote of the Committee from among its members.

2. The members of the Commission shall serve in their personal capacity. They shall not be nationals of the States Parties concerned, or of a State not Party to the present Covenant, or of a State Party which has not made a declaration under article 41.

3. The Commission shall elect its own Chairman and adopt its own rules of procedure.

4. The meetings of the Commission shall normally be held at the Headquarters of the United Nations or at the United Nations Office at Geneva. However, they may be held at such other convenient places as the Commission may determine in consultation with the Secretary-General of the United Nations and the States Parties concerned.

5. The secretariat provided in accordance with article 36 shall also service the commissions appointed under this article.

6. The information received and collated by the Committee shall be made available to the Commission and the Commission may call upon the States Parties concerned to supply any other relevant information.
7. When the Commission has fully considered the matter, but in any event not later than twelve months after having been seized of the matter, it shall submit to the Chairman of the Committee a report for communication to the States Parties concerned:
   (a) If the Commission is unable to complete its consideration of the matter within twelve months, it shall confine its report to a brief statement of the status of its consideration of the matter;
   (b) If an amicable solution to the matter on tie basis of respect for human rights as recognized in the present Covenant is reached, the Commission shall confine its report to a brief statement of the facts and of the solution reached;
   (c) If a solution within the terms of subparagraph (b) is not reached, the Commission's report shall embody its findings on all questions of fact relevant to the issues between the States Parties concerned, and its views on the possibilities of an amicable solution of the matter. This report shall also contain the written submissions and a record of the oral submissions made by the States Parties concerned;
   (d) If the Commission's report is submitted under subparagraph (c), the States Parties concerned shall, within three months of the receipt of the report, notify the Chairman of the Committee whether or not they accept the contents of the report of the Commission.
8. The provisions of this article are without prejudice to the responsibilities of the Committee under article 41.
9. The States Parties concerned shall share equally all the expenses of the members of the Commission in accordance with estimates to be provided by the Secretary-General of the United Nations.
10. The Secretary-General of the United Nations shall be empowered to pay the expenses of the members of the Commission, if necessary, before reimbursement by the States

Parties concerned, in accordance with paragraph 9 of this article.

Article 43

The members of the Committee, and of the ad hoc conciliation commissions which may be appointed under article 42, shall be entitled to the facilities, privileges and immunities of experts on mission for the United Nations as laid down in the relevant sections of the Convention on the Privileges and Immunities of the United Nations.

Article 44

The provisions for the implementation of the present Covenant shall apply without prejudice to the procedures prescribed in the field of human rights by or under the constituent instruments and the conventions of the United Nations and of the specialized agencies and shall not prevent the States Parties to the present Covenant from having recourse to other procedures for settling a dispute in accordance with general or special international agreements in force between them.

Article 45

The Committee shall submit to the General Assembly of the United Nations, through the Economic and Social Council, an annual report on its activities.

PART V

Article 46

Nothing in the present Covenant shall be interpreted as impairing the provisions of the Charter of the United Nations and of the constitutions of the specialized agencies which define the respective responsibilities of the various organs of the United Nations and of the specialized agencies in regard to the matters dealt with in the present Covenant.

Article 47

Nothing in the present Covenant shall be interpreted as impairing the inherent right of all peoples to enjoy and utilize fully and freely their natural wealth and resources.

PART VI

Article 48

1. The present Covenant is open for signature by any State Member of the United Nations or member of any of its specialized agencies, by any State Party to the Statute of the International Court of Justice, and by any other State which has been invited by the General Assembly of the United Nations to become a Party to the present Covenant.
2. The present Covenant is subject to ratification. Instruments of ratification shall be deposited with the Secretary-General of the United Nations.
3. The present Covenant shall be open to accession by any State referred to in paragraph 1 of this article.
4. Accession shall be effected by the deposit of an instrument of accession with the Secretary-General of the United Nations.
5. The Secretary-General of the United Nations shall inform all States which have signed this Covenant or acceded to it of the deposit of each instrument of ratification or accession.

Article 49

1. The present Covenant shall enter into force three months after the date of the deposit with the Secretary-General of the United Nations of the thirty-fifth instrument of ratification or instrument of accession.
2. For each State ratifying the present Covenant or acceding to it after the deposit of the thirty-fifth instrument of ratification or instrument of accession, the present Covenant shall enter into force three months after the date of the deposit of its own instrument of ratification or instrument of accession.

Article 50

The provisions of the present Covenant shall extend to all parts of federal States without any limitations or exceptions.

Article 51

1. Any State Party to the present Covenant may propose an amendment and file it with the Secretary-General of the United Nations. The Secretary-General of the United Nations shall thereupon communicate any proposed amendments to the States Parties to the present Covenant with a request that they notify him whether they favour a conference of States Parties

for the purpose of considering and voting upon the proposals. In the event that at least one third of the States Parties favours such a conference, the Secretary-General shall convene the conference under the auspices of the United Nations. Any amendment adopted by a majority of the States Parties present and voting at the conference shall be submitted to the General Assembly of the United Nations for approval.

2. Amendments shall come into force when they have been approved by the General Assembly of the United Nations and accepted by a two-thirds majority of the States Parties to the present Covenant in accordance with their respective constitutional processes.
3. When amendments come into force, they shall be binding on those States Parties which have accepted them, other States Parties still being bound by the provisions of the present Covenant and any earlier amendment which they have accepted.

Article 52

1. Irrespective of the notifications made under article 48, paragraph 5, the Secretary-General of the United Nations shall inform all States referred to in paragraph I of the same article of the following particulars:
   (a) Signatures, ratifications and accessions under article 48;
   (b) The date of the entry into force of the present Covenant under article 49 and the date of the entry into force of any amendments under article 51.

Article 53

1. The present Covenant, of which the Chinese, English, French, Russian and Spanish texts are equally authentic, shall be deposited in the archives of the United Nations.
2. The Secretary-General of the United Nations shall transmit certified copies of the present Covenant to all States referred to in article 48.

APPENDIX III

Convention against Torture and Other Cruel, Inhuman or Degrading Treatment or Punishment

Adopted and opened for signature, ratification and accession by General Assembly resolution 39/46 of 10 December 1984; Entry into force 26 June 1987, in accordance with article 27 (1) The States Parties to this Convention,

Considering that, in accordance with the principles proclaimed in the Charter of the United Nations, recognition of the equal and inalienable rights of all members of the human family is the foundation of freedom, justice and peace in the world,

Recognizing that those rights derive from the inherent dignity of the human person,

Considering the obligation of States under the Charter, in particular Article 55, to promote universal respect for, and observance of, human rights and fundamental freedoms,

Having regard to article 5 of the Universal Declaration of Human Rights and article 7 of the International Covenant on Civil and Political Rights, both of which provide that no one shall be subjected to torture or to cruel, inhuman or degrading treatment or punishment,

Having regard also to the Declaration on the Protection of All Persons from Being Subjected to Torture and Other Cruel, Inhuman or Degrading Treatment or Punishment, adopted by the General Assembly on 9 December 1975,

Desiring to make more effective the struggle against torture and other cruel, inhuman or degrading treatment or punishment throughout the world,

Have agreed as follows :

PART II

Article 1

1. For the purposes of this Convention, the term "torture" means any act by which severe pain or suffering, whether physical or mental, is intentionally inflicted on a person for such purposes as obtaining from him or a third person information or a confession, punishing him for an act he or a third person has committed or is suspected of having committed, or intimidating or coercing him or a third person, or for any reason based on discrimination of any kind, when such pain or suffering is inflicted by or at the instigation of or with the consent or acquiescence of a public official or other person acting in an official capacity. It does not include pain or suffering arising only from, inherent in or incidental to lawful sanctions.
2. This article is without prejudice to any international instrument or national legislation which does or may contain provisions of wider application.

Article 2

1. Each State Party shall take effective legislative, administrative, judicial or other measures to prevent acts of torture in any territory under its jurisdiction.
2. No exceptional circumstances whatsoever, whether a state of war or a threat of war, internal political instability or any other public emergency, may be invoked as a justification of torture.
3. An order from a superior officer or a public authority may not be invoked as a justification of torture.

Article 3

1. No State Party shall expel, return ("refouler") or extradite a person to another State where there are substantial grounds for believing that he would be in danger of being subjected to torture.
2. For the purpose of determining whether there are such grounds, the competent authorities shall take into account all

relevant considerations including, where applicable, the existence in the State concerned of a consistent pattern of gross, flagrant or mass violations of human rights.

Article 4

1. Each State Party shall ensure that all acts of torture are offences under its criminal law. The same shall apply to an attempt to commit torture and to an act by any person which constitutes complicity or participation in torture.
2. Each State Party shall make these offences punishable by appropriate penalties which take into account their grave nature.

Article 5

1. Each State Party shall take such measures as may be necessary to establish its jurisdiction over the offences referred to in article 4 in the following cases:
   (a) When the offences are committed in any territory under its jurisdiction or on board a ship or aircraft registered in that State;
   (b) When the alleged offender is a national of that State;
   (c) When the victim is a national of that State if that State considers it appropriate.
2. Each State Party shall likewise take such measures as may be necessary to establish its jurisdiction over such offences in cases where the alleged offender is present in any territory under its jurisdiction and it does not extradite him pursuant to article 8 to any of the States mentioned in paragraph I of this article.
3. This Convention does not exclude any criminal jurisdiction exercised in accordance with internal law.

Article 6

1. Upon being satisfied, after an examination of information available to it, that the circumstances so warrant, any State Party in whose territory a person alleged to have committed any offence referred to in article 4 is present shall take him into custody or take other legal measures to ensure his presence. The custody and other legal measures shall be as provided in the law of that State but may be continued only for such time as is necessary to enable any criminal or extradition proceedings to be instituted.
2. Such State shall immediately make a preliminary inquiry into the facts.

3. Any person in custody pursuant to paragraph I of this article shall be assisted in communicating immediately with the nearest appropriate representative of the State of which he is a national, or, if he is a stateless person, with the representative of the State where he usually resides.
4. When a State, pursuant to this article, has taken a person into custody, it shall immediately notify the States referred to in article 5, paragraph 1, of the fact that such person is in custody and of the circumstances which warrant his detention. The State which makes the preliminary inquiry contemplated in paragraph 2 of this article shall promptly report its findings to the said States and shall indicate whether it intends to exercise jurisdiction.

Article 7

1. The State Party in the territory under whose jurisdiction a person alleged to have committed any offence referred to in article 4 is found shall in the cases contemplated in article 5, if it does not extradite him, submit the case to its competent authorities for the purpose of prosecution.
2. These authorities shall take their decision in the same manner as in the case of any ordinary offence of a serious nature under the law of that State. In the cases referred to in article 5, paragraph 2, the standards of evidence required for prosecution and conviction shall in no way be less stringent than those which apply in the cases referred to in article 5, paragraph 1.
3. Any person regarding whom proceedings are brought in connection with any of the offences referred to in article 4 shall be guaranteed fair treatment at all stages of the proceedings.

Article 8

1. The offences referred to in article 4 shall be deemed to be included as extraditable offences in any extradition treaty existing between States Parties. States Parties undertake to include such offences as extraditable offences in every extradition treaty to be concluded between them.
2. If a State Party which makes extradition conditional on the existence of a treaty receives a request for extradition from another State Party with which it has no extradition treaty, it may consider this Convention as the legal basis for extradition in respect of such offences. Extradition shall be subject to the

other conditions provided by the law of the requested State.

3. States Parties which do not make extradition conditional on the existence of a treaty shall recognize such offences as extraditable offences between themselves subject to the conditions provided by the law of the requested State.

4. Such offences shall be treated, for the purpose of extradition between States Parties, as if they had been committed not only in the place in which they occurred but also in the territories of the States required to establish their jurisdiction in accordance with article 5, paragraph 1.

Article 9

1. States Parties shall afford one another the greatest measure of assistance in connection with criminal proceedings brought in respect of any of the offences referred to in article 4, including the supply of all evidence at their disposal necessary for the proceedings.

2. States Parties shall carry out their obligations under paragraph I of this article in conformity with any treaties on mutual judicial assistance that may exist between them.

Article 10

1. Each State Party shall ensure that education and information regarding the prohibition against torture are fully included in the training of law enforcement personnel, civil or military, medical personnel, public officials and other persons who may be involved in the custody, interrogation or treatment of any individual subjected to any form of arrest, detention or imprisonment.

2. Each State Party shall include this prohibition in the rules or instructions issued in regard to the duties and functions of any such person.

Article 11

Each State Party shall keep under systematic review interrogation rules, instructions, methods and practices as well as arrangements for the custody and treatment of persons subjected to any form of arrest, detention or imprisonment in any territory under its jurisdiction, with a view to preventing any cases of torture.

Article 12

Each State Party shall ensure that its competent authorities proceed to a prompt and impartial investigation, wherever there is reasonable ground to believe that an act of torture has been committed in any territory under its jurisdiction.

Article 13

Each State Party shall ensure that any individual who alleges he has been subjected to torture in any territory under its jurisdiction has the right to complain to, and to have his case promptly and impartially examined by, its competent authorities. Steps shall be taken to ensure that the complainant and witnesses are protected against all ill-treatment or intimidation as a consequence of his complaint or any evidence given.

Article 14

1. Each State Party shall ensure in its legal system that the victim of an act of torture obtains redress and has an enforceable right to fair and adequate compensation, including the means for as full rehabilitation as possible. In the event of the death of the victim as a result of an act of torture, his dependants shall be entitled to compensation.
2. Nothing in this article shall affect any right of the victim or other persons to compensation which may exist under national law.

Article 15

Each State Party shall ensure that any statement which is established to have been made as a result of torture shall not be invoked as evidence in any proceedings, except against a person accused of torture as evidence that the statement was made.

Article 16

1. Each State Party shall undertake to prevent in any territory under its jurisdiction other acts of cruel, inhuman or degrading treatment or punishment which do not amount to torture as defined in article I, when such acts are committed by or at the instigation of or with the consent or acquiescence of a public official or other person acting in an official capacity. In particular, the obligations contained in articles 10, 11, 12 and 13 shall apply with the substitution for references to torture of references to other forms of cruel, inhuman or degrading treatment or punishment.
2. The provisions of this Convention are without prejudice to the

provisions of any other international instrument or national law which prohibits cruel, inhuman or degrading treatment or punishment or which relates to extradition or expulsion.

PART II

Article 17

1. There shall be established a Committee against Torture (hereinafter referred to as the Committee) which shall carry out the functions hereinafter provided. The Committee shall consist of ten experts of high moral standing and recognized competence in the field of human rights, who shall serve in their personal capacity. The experts shall be elected by the States Parties, consideration being given to equitable geographical distribution and to the usefulness of the participation of some persons having legal experience.
2. The members of the Committee shall be elected by secret ballot from a list of persons nominated by States Parties. Each State Party may nominate one person from among its own nationals. States Parties shall bear in mind the usefulness of nominating persons who are also members of the Human Rights Committee established under the International Covenant on Civil and Political Rights and who are willing to serve on the Committee against Torture.
3. Elections of the members of the Committee shall be held at biennial meetings of States Parties convened by the Secretary-General of the United Nations. At those meetings, for which two thirds of the States Parties shall constitute a quorum, the persons elected to the Committee shall be those who obtain the largest number of votes and an absolute majority of the votes of the representatives of States Parties present and voting.
4. The initial election shall be held no later than six months after the date of the entry into force of this Convention. At least four months before the date of each election, the Secretary-General of the United Nations shall address a letter to the States Parties inviting them to submit their nominations within three months. The Secretary-General shall prepare a list in alphabetical order of all persons thus nominated, indicating the States Parties which have nominated them, and shall submit it to the States Parties.
5. The members of the Committee shall be elected for a term of

four years. They shall be eligible for re-election if re-nominated. However, the term of five of the members elected at the first election shall expire at the end of two years; immediately after the first election the names of these five members shall be chosen by lot by the chairman of the meeting referred to in paragraph 3 of this article.

6. If a member of the Committee dies or resigns or for any other cause can no longer perform his Committee duties, the State Party which nominated him shall appoint another expert from among its nationals to serve for the remainder of his term, subject to the approval of the majority of the States Parties. The approval shall be considered given unless half or more of the States Parties respond negatively within six weeks after having been informed by the Secretary-General of the United Nations of the proposed appointment.
7. States Parties shall be responsible for the expenses of the members of the Committee while they are in performance of Committee duties.

Article 18

1. The Committee shall elect its officers for a term of two years. They may be re-elected.
2. The Committee shall establish its own rules of procedure, but these rules shall provide, inter alia, that:
   (a) Six members shall constitute a quorum;
   (b) Decisions of the Committee shall be made by a majority vote of the members present.
3. The Secretary-General of the United Nations shall provide the necessary staff and facilities for the effective performance of the functions of the Committee under this Convention.
4. The Secretary-General of the United Nations shall convene the initial meeting of the Committee. After its initial meeting, the Committee shall meet at such times as shall be provided in its rules of procedure.
5. The States Parties shall be responsible for expenses incurred in connection with the holding of meetings of the States Parties and of the Committee, including reimbursement to the United Nations for any expenses, such as the cost of staff and facilities, incurred by the United Nations pursuant to paragraph 3 of this article.

Article 19

1. The States Parties shall submit to the Committee, through the Secretary-General of the United Nations, reports on the measures they have taken to give effect to their undertakings under this Convention, within one year after the entry into force of the Convention for the State Party concerned. Thereafter the States Parties shall submit supplementary reports every four years on any new measures taken and such other reports as the Committee may request.
2. The Secretary-General of the United Nations shall transmit the reports to all States Parties.
3. Each report shall be considered by the Committee which may make such general comments on the report as it may consider appropriate and shall forward these to the State Party concerned. That State Party may respond with any observations it chooses to the Committee.
4. The Committee may, at its discretion, decide to include any comments made by it in accordance with paragraph 3 of this article, together with the observations thereon received from the State Party concerned, in its annual report made in accordance with article 24. If so requested by the State Party concerned, the Committee may also include a copy of the report submitted under paragraph I of this article.

Article 20

1. If the Committee receives reliable information which appears to it to contain well-founded indications that torture is being systematically practised in the territory of a State Party, the Committee shall invite that State Party to co-operate in the examination of the information and to this end to submit observations with regard to the information concerned.
2. Taking into account any observations which may have been submitted by the State Party concerned, as well as any other relevant information available to it, the Committee may, if it decides that this is warranted, designate one or more of its members to make a confidential inquiry and to report to the Committee urgently.
3. If an inquiry is made in accordance with paragraph 2 of this article, the Committee shall seek the co-operation of the State Party concerned. In agreement with that State Party, such an inquiry may include a visit to its territory.

4. After examining the findings of its member or members submitted in accordance with paragraph 2 of this article, the Commission shall transmit these findings to the State Party concerned together with any comments or suggestions which seem appropriate in view of the situation.
5. All the proceedings of the Committee referred to in paragraphs I to 4 of th is article s hall be con fidential , and at all stages of the proceedings the co-operation of the State Party shall be sought. After such proceedings have been completed with regard to an inquiry made in accordance with paragraph 2, the Committee may, after consultations with the State Party concerned, decide to include a summary account of the results of the proceedings in its annual report made in accordance with article 24.

Article 21

1. A State Party to this Convention may at any time declare under this article that it recognizes the competence of the Committee to receive and consider communications to the effect that a State Party claims that another State Party is not fulfilling its obligations under this Convention. Such communications may be received and considered according to the procedures laid down in this article only if submitted by a State Party which has made a declaration recognizing in regard to itself the competence of the Committee. No communication shall be dealt with by the Committee under this article if it concerns a State Party which has not made such a declaration. Communications received under this article shall be dealt with in accordance with the following procedure;
   (a) If a State Party considers that another State Party is not giving effect to the provisions ofthis Convention, it may, by written communication, bring the matter to the attention of that State Party. Within three months after the receipt of the communication the receiving State shall afford the State which sent the communication an explanation or any other statement in writing clarifying the matter, which should include, to the extent possible and pertinent, reference to domestic procedures and remedies taken, pending or available in the matter;
   (b) If the matter is not adjusted to the satisfaction of both States Parties concerned within six months after the

receipt by the receiving State of the initial communication, either State shall have the right to refer the matter to the Committee, by notice given to the Committee and to the other State;

(c) The Committee shall deal with a matter referred to it under this article only after it has ascertained that all domestic remedies have been invoked and exhausted in the matter, in conformity with the generally recognized principles of international law. This shall not be the rule where the application of the remedies is unreasonably prolonged or is unlikely to bring effective relief to the person who is the victim of the violation of this Convention;

(d) The Committee shall hold closed meetings when examining communications under this article; (e) Subject to the provisions of subparagraph

(e) The Committee shall make available its good offices to the States Parties concerned with a view to a friendly solution of the matter on the basis of respect for the obligations provided for in this Convention. For this purpose, the Committee may, when appropriate, set up an ad hoc conciliation commission;

(f) In any matter referred to it under this article, the Committee may call upon the States Parties concerned, referred to in subparagraph (b), to supply any relevant information;

(g) The States Parties concerned, referred to in subparagraph (b), shall have the right to be represented when the matter is being considered by the Committee and to make submissions orally and/or in writing;

(h) The Committee shall, within twelve months after the date of receipt of notice under subparagraph (b), submit a report:

  (i) If a solution within the terms of subparagraph (e) is reached, the Committee shall confine its report to a brief statement of the facts and of the solution reached;

  (ii) If a solution within the terms of subparagraph (e) is not reached, the Committee shall confine its report to a brief statement of the facts; the written submissions and record of the oral submissions made by the States Parties concerned shall be attached to the report.

In every matter, the report shall be communicated to the States Parties concerned.

2. The provisions of this article shall come into force when five States Parties to this Convention have made declarations under paragraph 1 of this article. Such declarations shall be deposited by the States Parties with the Secretary-General of the United Nations, who shall transmit copies thereof to the other States Parties. A declaration may be withdrawn at any time by notification to the Secretary-General. Such a withdrawal shall not prejudice the consideration of any matter which is the subject of a communication already transmitted under this article; no further communication by any State Party shall be received under this article after the notification of withdrawal of the declaration has been received by the Secretary-General, unless the State Party concerned has made a new declaration.

Article 22

1. A State Party to this Convention may at any time declare under this article that it recognizes the competence of the Committee to receive and consider communications from or on behalf of individuals subject to its jurisdiction who claim to be victims of a violation by a State Party of the provisions of the Convention. No communication shall be received by the Committee if it concerns a State Party which has not made such a declaration.
2. The Committee shall consider inadmissible any communication under this article which is anonymous or which it considers to be an abuse of the right of submission of such communications or to be incompatible with the provisions of this Convention.
3. Subject to the provisions of paragraph 2, the Committee shall bring any communications submitted to it under this article to the attention of the State Party to this Convention which has made a declaration under paragraph I and is alleged to be violating any provisions of the Convention. Within six months, the receiving State shall submit to the Committee written explanations or statements clarifying the matter and the remedy, if any, that may have been taken by that State.
4. The Committee shall consider communications received under this article in the light of all information made available to it by

or on behalf of the individual and by the State Party concerned.

5. The Committee shall not consider any communications from an individual under this article unless it has ascertained that:
   (a) The same matter has not been, and is not being, examined under another procedure of international investigation or settlement;
   (b) The individual has exhausted all available domestic remedies; this shall not be the rule where the application of the remedies is unreasonably prolonged or is unlikely to bring effective reliefto the person who is the victim of the violation of this Convention.
6. The Committee shall hold closed meetings when examining communications under this article.
7. The Committee shall forward its views to the State Party concerned and to the individual.
8. The provisions of this article shall come into force when five States Parties to this Convention have made declarations under paragraph 1 of this article. Such declarations shall be deposited by the States Parties with the Secretary-General of the United Nations, who shall transmit copies thereof to the other States Parties. A declaration may be withdrawn at any time by notification to the Secretary-General. Such a withdrawal shall not prejudice the consideration of any matter which is the subject of a communication already transmitted under this article; no further communication by or on behalf of an individual shall be received under this article after the notification of withdrawal of the declaration has been received by the SecretaryGeneral, unless the State Party has made a new declaration.

Article 23

The members of the Committee and of the ad hoc conciliation commissions which may be appointed under article 21, paragraph I (e), shall be entitled to the facilities, privileges and immunities of experts on mission for the United Nations as laid down in the relevant sections of the Convention on the Privileges and Immunities of the United Nations.

Article 24

The Committee shall submit an annual report on its activities under this Convention to the States Parties and to the General Assembly of the United Nations.

PART III

Article 25

1. This Convention is open for signature by all States.
2. This Convention is subject to ratification. Instruments of ratification shall be deposited with the Secretary-General of the United Nations.

Article 26

This Convention is open to accession by all States. Accession shall be effected by the deposit of an instrument of accession with the SecretaryGeneral of the United Nations.

Article 27

1. This Convention shall enter into force on the thirtieth day after the date of the deposit with the Secretary-General of the United Nations of the twentieth instrument of ratification or accession.
2. For each State ratifying this Convention or acceding to it after the deposit of the twentieth instrument of ratification or accession, the Convention shall enter into force onthe thirtieth day after the date of the deposit of its own instrument of ratification or accession.

Article 28

1. Each State may, at the time of signature or ratification of this Convention or accession thereto, declare that it does not recognize the competence of the Committee provided for in article 20.
2. Any State Party having made a reservation in accordance with paragraph I of this article may, at any time, withdraw this reservation by notification to the Secretary-General of the United Nations.

Article 29

1. Any State Party to this Convention may propose an amendment and file it with the Secretary-General of the United Nations. The Secretary General shall thereupon communicate the proposed amendment to the States Parties with a request that they notify him whether they favour a conference of States Parties for the purpose of considering an d voting upon the proposal. In the event that within four months from the date of such communication at least one third of the States Parties

favours such a conference, the Secretary General shall convene the conference under the auspices of the United Nations. Any amendment adopted by a majority of the States Parties present and voting at the conference shall be submitted by the Secretary-General to all the States Parties for acceptance.

2. An amendment adopted in accordance with paragraph I of this article shall enter into force when two thirds of the States Parties to this Convention have notified the Secretary-General of the United Nations that they have accepted it in accordance with their respective constitutional processes.

3. When amendments enter into force, they shall be binding on those States Parties which have accepted them, other States Parties still being bound by the provisions of this Convention and any earlier amendments which they have accepted.

Article 30

1. Any dispute between two or more States Parties concerning the interpretation or application of this Convention which cannot be settled through negotiation shall, at the request of one of them, be submitted to arbitration. If within six months from thc date of the request for arbitration the Parties are unable to agree on the organization of the arbitration, any one of those Parties may refer the dispute to the International Court of Justice by request in conformity with the Statute of the Court.

2. Each State may, at the time of signature or ratification of this Convention or accession thereto, declare that it does not consider itself bound by paragraph I of this article. The other States Parties shall not be bound by paragraph I of this article with respect to any State Party having made such a reservation.

3. Any State Party having made a reservation in accordance with paragraph 2 of this article may at any time withdraw this reservation by notification to the Secretary-General of the United Nations.

Article 31

1. A State Party may denounce this Convention by written notification to the Secretary-General of the United Nations. Denunciation becomes effective one year after the date of receipt of- the notification by the SecretaryGeneral .

2. Such a denunciation shall not have the effect of releasing the State Party from its obligations under this Convention in regard to any act or omission which occurs prior to the date at which the denunciation becomes effective, nor shall denunciation prejudice in any way the continued consideration of any matter which is already under consideration by the Committee prior to the date at which the denunciation becomes effective.
3. Following the date at which the denunciation of a State Party becomes effective, the Committee shall not commence consideration of any new matter regarding that State.

Article 32

The Secretary-General of the United Nations shall inform all States Members of the United Nations and all States which have signed this Convention or acceded to it of the following:

(a) Signatures, ratifications and accessions under articles 25 and 26;

(b) The date of entry into force of this Convention under article 27 and the date of the entry into force of any amendments under article 29;

(c) Denunciations under article 31.

Article 33

1. This Convention, of which the Arabic, Chinese, English, French, Russian and Spanish texts are equally authentic, shall be deposited with the Secretary-General of the United Nations.
2. The Secretary-General of the United Nations shall transmit certified copies of this Convention to all States.

Appendix IV

The European Convention on Human Rights and Fundamental Freedoms

(Adopted in Rome on 4th November 1950)

The Governments signatory hereto, being Members of the Council of Europe,

Considering the Universal Declaration of Human Rights proclaimed by the General Assembly of the United Nations on 10 December 1948;

Considering that this Declaration aims at securing the universal and effective recognition and observance of the Rights therein declared;

Considering that the aim of the Council of Europe is the achievement of greater unity between its Members and that one of the methods by which the aim is to be pursued is the maintenance and further realization of Human Rights and Fundamental Freedoms;

Reaffirming their profound belief in those Fundamental Freedoms which are the foundation of justice and peace in the world and are best maintained on the one hand by an effective political democracy and on the other by a common understanding and observance of the Human Rights upon which they depend;

Being resolved, as the Governments of European countries which are like-minded and have a common heritage of political traditions, ideals, freedom and the rule of law to take the first steps for the collective enforcement of certain of the Rights stated in the Universal Declaration;

Have agreed as follows:

Article 1

The High Contracting Parties shall secure to everyone within their jurisdiction the rights and freedoms defined in Section I of this Convention.

SECTION I

Article 2

1. Everyone's right to life shall be protected by law. No one shall be deprived of his life intentionally save in the execution of a sentence of a court following his conviction of a crime for which this penalty is provided by law.
2. Deprivation of life shall not be regarded as inflicted in contravention of this article when it results from the use of force which is no more than absolutely necessary:
   (a) in defence of any person from unlawful violence;
   (b) in order to effect a lawful arrest or to prevent escape of a person lawfully detained;
   (c) in action lawfully taken for the purpose of quelling a riot or insurrection.

Article 3

No one shall be subjected to torture or to inhuman or degrading treatment or punishment.

Article 4

1. No one shall be held in slavery or servitude.
2. No one shall be required to perform forced or compulsory labour.
3. For the purpose of this article the term forced or compulsory labour' shall not include:
   (a) any work required to be done in the ordinary course of detention imposed according to the provisions of Article 5 of this Convention or during conditional release from such detention;
   (b) any service of a military character or, in case of conscientious objectors in countries where they are recognized, service exacted instead of compulsory military service;

(c) any service exacted in case of an emergency or calamity threatening the life or well-being of the community;

(d) any work or service which forms part of normal civic obligations.

Article 5

1. Everyone has the right to liberty and security of person. No one shall be deprived of his liberty save in the following cases and in accordance with a procedure prescribed by law:

   (a) the lawful detention of a person after conviction by a competent court;

   (b) the lawful arrest or detention of a person for non-compliance with the lawful order of a court or in order to secure the fulfilment of any obligation prescribed by law;

   (c) the lawful arrest or detention of a person effected for the purpose of bringing him before the competent legal authority of reasonable suspicion of having committed and offence or when it is reasonably considered necessary to prevent his committing an offence or fleeing after having done so;

   (d) the detention of a minor by lawful order for the purpose of educational supervision or his lawful detention for the purpose of bringing him before the competent legal authority;

   (e) the lawful detention of persons for the prevention of the spreading of infectious diseases, of persons of unsound mind, alcoholics or drug addicts, or vagrants;

   (f) the lawful arrest or detention of a person to prevent his effecting an unauthorized entry into the country or of a person against whom action is being taken with a view to deportation or extradition.

2. Everyone who is arrested shall be informed promptly, in a language which he understands, of the reasons for his arrest and the charge against him.

3. Everyone arrested or detained in accordance with the provisions of paragraph 1(c) of this article shall be brought promptly before a judge or other officer authorized by law to exercise judicial power and shall be entitled to trial within a reasonable time or to release pending trial. Release may be conditioned by guarantees to appear for trial.

4. Everyone who is deprived of his liberty by arrest or detention

shall be entitled to take proceedings by which the lawfulness of his detention shall be decided speedily by a court and his release ordered if the detention is not lawful.

5. Everyone who has been the victim of arrest or detention in contravention of the provisions of this article shall have an enforceable right to compensation.

Article 6

1. In the determination of his civil rights and obligations or of any criminal charge against him, everyone is entitled to a fair and public hearing within a reasonable time by an independent and impartial tribunal established by law. Judgement shall be pronounced publicly by the press and public may be excluded from all or part of the trial in the interest of morals, public order or national security in a democratic society, where the interests of juveniles or the protection of the private life of the parties so require, or the extent strictly necessary in the opinion of the court in special circumstances where publicity would prejudice the interests of justice.
2. Everyone charged with a criminal offence shall be presumed innocent until proved guilty according to law.
3. Everyone charged with a criminal offence has the following minimum rights:
   (a) to be informed promptly, in a language which he understands and in detail, of the nature and cause of the accusation against him;
   (b) to have adequate time and the facilities for the preparation of his defence;
   (c) to defend himself in person or through legal assistance of his own choosing or, if he has not sufficient means to pay for legal assistance, to be given it free when the interests of justice so require;
   (d) to examine or have examined witnesses against him and to obtain the attendance and examination of witnesses on his behalf under the same conditions as witnesses against him;
   (e) to have the free assistance of an interpreter if he cannot understand or speak the language used in court.

Article 7

1. No one shall be held guilty of any criminal offence on account of any act or omission which did not constitute a criminal

offence under national or international law at the time when it was committed. Nor shall a heavier penalty be imposed than the one that was applicable at the time the criminal offence was committed.

2. This article shall not prejudice the trial and punishment of any person for any act or omission which, at the time when it was committed, was criminal according the general principles of law recognized by civilized nations.

Article 8

1. Everyone has the right to respect for his private and family life, his home and his correspondence.
2. There shall be no interference by a public authority with the exercise of this right except such as is in accordance with the law and is necessary in a democratic society in the interests of national security, public safety or the economic well-being of the country, for the prevention of disorder or crime, for the protection of health or morals, or for the protection of the rights and freedoms of others.

Article 9

1. Everyone has the right to freedom of thought, conscience and religion; this right includes freedom to change his religion or belief, and freedom, either alone or in community with others and in public or private, to manifest his religion or belief, in worship, teaching, practice and observance.
2. Freedom to manifest one's religion or beliefs shall be subject only to such limitations as are prescribed by law and are necessary in a democratic society in the interests of public safety, for the protection of public order, health or morals, or the protection of the rights and freedoms of others.

Article 10

1. Everyone has the right to freedom of expression. this right shall include freedom to hold opinions and to receive and impart information and ideas without interference by public authority and regardless of frontiers. This article shall not prevent States from requiring the licensing of broadcasting, television or cinema enterprises.
2. The exercise of these freedoms, since it carries with it duties and responsibilities, may be subject to such formalities, conditions, restrictions or penalties as are prescribed by law

and are necessary in a democratic society, in the interests of national security, territorial integrity or public safety, for the prevention of disorder or crime, for the protection of health or morals, for the protection of the reputation or the rights of others, for preventing the disclosure of information received in confidence, or for maintaining the authority and impartiality of the judiciary.

Article 11

1. Everyone has the right to freedom of peaceful assembly and to freedom of association with others, including the right to form and to join trade unions for the protection of his interests.
2. No restrictions shall be placed on the exercise of these rights other than such as are prescribed by law and are necessary in a democratic society in the interests of national security or public safety, for the prevention of disorder or crime, for the protection of health or morals or for the protection of the rights and freedoms of others. this article shall not prevent the imposition of lawful restrictions on the exercise of these rights by members of the armed forces, of the police or of the administration of the State.

Article 12

Men and women of marriageable age have the right to marry and to found a family, according to the national laws governing the exercise of this right.

Article 13

Everyone whose rights and freedoms as set forth in this Convention are violated shall have an effective remedy before a national authority notwithstanding that the violation has been committed by persons acting in an official capacity.

Article 14

The enjoyment of the rights and freedoms set forth in this Convention shall be secured without discrimination on any ground such as sex, race, colour, language, religion, political or other opinion, national or social origin, association with a national minority, property, birth or other status.

Article 15

1. In time of war or other public emergency threatening the life of the nation any High Contracting Party may take measures

derogating from its obligations under this Convention to the extent strictly required by the exigencies of the situation, provided that such measures are not inconsistent with its other obligations under international law.

2. No derogation from Article 2, except in respect of deaths resulting from lawful acts of war, or from Articles 3, 4 (paragraph 1) and 7 shall be made under this provision.
3. Any High Contracting Party availing itself of this right of derogation shall keep the Secretary-General of the Council of Europe fully informed of the measures which it has taken and the reasons therefor. It shall also inform the Secretary-General of the Council of Europe when such measures have ceased to operate and the provisions of the Convention are again being fully executed.

Article 16

Nothing in Articles 10, 11, and 14 shall be regarded as preventing the High Contracting Parties from imposing restrictions on the political activity of aliens.

Article 17

Nothing in this Convention may be interpreted as implying for any State, group or person any right to engage in any activity or perform any act aimed at the destruction on any of the rights and freedoms set forth herein or at their limitation to a greater extent than is provided for in the Convention.

Article 18

The restrictions permitted under this Convention to the said rights and freedoms shall not be applied for any purpose other than those for which they have been prescribed.

SECTION II

Article 19

To ensure the observance of the engagements undertaken by the High Contracting Parties in the present Convention, there shall be set up:

1. A European Commission of Human Rights hereinafter referred to as 'the Commission';
2. A European Court of Human Rights, hereinafter referred to as 'the Court'.

SECTION III

Article 20

The Commission shall consist of a number of members equal to that of the High Contracting Parties. No two members of the Commission may be nationals of the same state.

Article 21

1. The members of the Commission shall be elected by the Committee of Ministers by an absolute majority of votes, from a list of names drawn up by the Bureau of the Consultative Assembly; each group of the Representatives of the High Contracting Parties in the Consultative Assembly shall put forward three candidates, of whom two at least shall be its nationals.
2. As far as applicable, the same procedure shall be followed to complete the Commission in the event of other States subsequently becoming Parties to this Convention, and in filing casual vacancies.

Article 22

1. The members of the Commission shall be elected for a period of six years. They may be re-elected. However, of the members elected at the first election, the terms of seven members shall expire at the end of three years.
2. The members whose terms are to expire at the end of the initial period of three years shall be chosen by lot by the Secretary-General of the Council of Europe immediately after the first election has been completed.
3. A member of the Commission elected to replace a member whose term of office has not expired shall hold office for the remainder of his predecessor's term.
4. The members of the Commission shall hold office until replaced. After having been replaced, they shall continue to deal with such cases as they already have under consideration.

Article 23

The members of the Commission shall sit on the Commission in their individual capacity.

Article 24

Any High Contracting Party may refer to the Commission, through the Secretary-General of the Council of Europe, any alleged breach of the provisions of the Convention by another High Contracting Party.

Article 25

1. The Commission may receive petitions addressed to the Secretary-General of the Council of Europe from any person, non- governmental organization or group of individuals claiming to the victim of a violation by one of the High Contracting Parties of the rights set forth in this Convention, provided that the High Contracting Party against which the complaint has been lodged has declared that it recognizes the competence of the Commission to receive such petitions. Those of the High Contracting Parties who have made such a declaration undertake not to hinder in any way the effective exercise of this right.
2. Such declarations may be made for a specific period.
3. The declarations shall be deposited with the Secretary-General of the Council of Europe who shall transmit copies thereof to the High Contracting Parties and publish them.
4. The Commission shall only exercise the powers provided for in this article when at least six High Contracting Parties are bound by declarations made in accordance with the preceding paragraphs.

Article 26

The Commission may only deal with the matter after all domestic remedies have been exhausted, according to the generally recognized rules of international law, and within a period of six months from the date on which the final decision was taken.

Article 27

1. the Commission shall not deal with any petition submitted under Article 25 which
   (a) is anonymous, or
   (b) is substantially the same as a matter which has already been examined by the Commission or has already been submitted to another procedure or international investigation or settlement and if it contains no relevant new information.
2. The Commission shall consider inadmissible any petition submitted under Article 25 which it considers incompatible with the provisions of the present Convention, manifestly ill-founded, or an abuse of the right of petition.

3. The Commission shall reject any petition referred to it which it considers inadmissible under Article 26.

Article 28

In the event of the Commission accepting a petition referred to it:

(a) it shall, with a view to ascertaining the facts undertake together with the representatives of the parties and examination of the petition and, if need be, an investigation, for the effective conduct of which the States concerned shall furnish all necessary facilities, after an exchange of views with the Commission;

(b) it shall place itself at the disposal of the parties concerned with a view to securing a friendly settlement of the matter on the basis of respect for Human Rights as defined in this Convention.

Article 29

1. The Commission shall perform the functions set out in Article 28 by means of a Sub-Commission consisting of seven members of the Commission.
2. Each of the parties concerned may appoint as members of this Sub-Commission a person of its choice.
3. The remaining members shall be chosen by lot in accordance with arrangements prescribed in the Rules of Procedure of the Commission.

Article 30

1. If the Sub-Commission succeeds in effecting a friendly settlement in accordance with Article 28, it shall draw up a Report which shall be sent to the States concerned, to the Committee of Ministers and to the Secretary-General of the Council of Europe for publication. This Report shall be confined to a brief statement of the facts and of the solution reached.

Article 31

1. If a solution is not reached, the Commission shall draw up a Report on the facts and state its opinion as to whether the facts found disclose a breach by the State concerned of its obligations under the Convention. The opinions of all the members of the Commission on this point may be stated in the Report.

2. The Report shall be transmitted to the Committee of Ministers. It shall also be transmitted to the States concerned, who shall not be at liberty to publish it.
3. In transmitting the Report to the Committee of Ministers the Commission may make such proposals as it thinks fit.

Article 32

1. If the question is not referred to the Court in accordance with Article 48 of this Convention within a period of three months from the date of the transmission of the Report to the Committee of Ministers, the Committee of Ministers shall decide by a majority of two-thirds of the members entitled to sit on the Committee whether there has been a violation of the Convention.
2. In the affirmative case the Committee of Ministers shall prescribe a period during which the Contracting Party concerned must take the measures required by the decision of the Committee of Ministers.
3. If the High Contracting Party concerned has not taken satisfactory measures within the prescribed period, the Committee of Ministers shall decide by the majority provided for in paragraph 1 above what effect shall be given to its original decision and shall publish the Report.
4. The High Contracting Parties undertake to regard as binding on them any decision which the Committee of Ministers may take in application of the preceding paragraphs.

Article 33

The Commission shall meet 'in camera'.

Article 34

The Commission shall take its decision by a majority of the Members present and voting; the Sub-Commission shall take its decisions by a majority of its members.

Article 35

The Commission shall meet as the circumstances require. The meetings shall be convened by the Secretary-General of the Council of Europe.

Article 36

The Commission shall draw up its own rules of procedure.

Article 37

The secretariat of The Commission shall be provided by the Secretary-General of the Council of Europe.

SECTION IV

Article 38

The European Court of Human Rights shall consist of a number of judges equal to that of the Members of the Council of Europe. No two judges may be nationals of the State.

Article 39

1. The members of the Court shall be elected by the Consultative Assembly by a majority of the votes cast from a list of persons nominated by Members of the Council of Europe; each Member shall nominate three candidates, of whom two at least shall be its nationals.
2. As far as applicable, the same procedure shall be followed to complete the Court in the event of the admission of new members of the Council of Europe, and in filling casual vacancies.
3. The candidates shall be of high moral character and must either possess the qualifications required for appointment to high judicial office or be *juris* consults of recognized competence.

Article 40

1. The members of the Court shall be elected for a period of nine years. They may be re-elected. However, of the members elected at the first election the terms of four members shall expire at the end of three years, and the terms of four more members shall expire at the end of six years.
2. The members whose terms are to expire at the end of the initial periods of three and six years shall be chosen by lot by the Secretary-General immediately after the first election has been completed.

A member of the Court elected to replace a member whose term of office has not expired shall hold office for the remainder of his predecessor's term.

The members of the Court shall hold office until replaced. After having been replaced, they shall continue to deal with such cases as they already have under consideration.

Article 41

The Court shall elect the President and Vice-President for a period of three years. They may be re-elected.

Article 42

The members of the Court shall receive for each day of duty a compensation to be determined by the Committee of Ministers.

Article 43

For the consideration of each case brought before it the Court shall consist of a Chamber composed of seven judges. There shall sit as an 'ex officio' member of the Chamber the judge who is a national of any State party concerned, or, if there is none, a person of its choice who shall sit in the capacity of judge; the names of the other judges shall be chosen by lot by the President before the opening of the case.

Article 44

Only the High Contracting Parties and the Commission shall have the right to bring a case before the Court.

Article 45

The jurisdiction of the Court shall extend to all cases concerning the interpretation and application of the present Convention which the High Contracting Parties or the Commission shall refer to it in accordance with Article 48.

Article 46

Any of the High Contracting Parties may at any time declare that it recognizes as compulsory 'ipso facto' and without special agreement the jurisdiction of the Court in all matters concerning the interpretation and application of the present Convention.

The declarations referred to above may be made unconditionally or on condition of reciprocity on the part of several or certain other High Contracting Parties or for a specified period.

These declarations shall be deposited with the Secretary-General of the Council of Europe who shall transmit copies thereof to the High Contracting Parties.

Article 47

The Court may only deal with a case after the Commission has acknowledged the failure of efforts for a friendly settlement and within the period of three months provided for in Article 32.

Article 48

The following may bring a case before the Court, provided that the High Contracting Party concerned, if there is only one, or the High Contracting Parties concerned, if there is more than one, are subject to the compulsory jurisdiction of the Court, or failing that, with the consent of the High Contracting Party concerned, if there is only one, or of the High Contracting Parties concerned if there is more than one:

(a) the Commission;
(b) a High Contracting Party whose national is alleged to be a victim;
(c) a High Contracting Party which referred the case to the Commission;
(d) a High Contracting Party against which the complaint has been lodged.

Article 49

In the event of dispute as to whether the Court has the jurisdiction, the matter shall be settled by the decision of the Court.

Article 50

If the Court finds that a decision or a measure taken by a legal authority or any other authority of a High Contracting Party, is completely or partially in conflict with the obligations arising from the present convention, and if the internal law of the said Party allows only partial reparation to be made for the consequences of this decision or measure, the decision of the Court shall, if necessary, afford just satisfaction to the injured party.

Article 51

Reasons shall be given for the judgment of the Court.

If the judgment does not represent in whole or in part the unanimous opinion of the judges, any judges shall be entitled to deliver a separate opinion.

Article 52

The judgment of the Court shall be final.

Article 53

The High Contracting Parties undertake to abide by the decision of the Court in any case to which they are parties.

Article 54

The judgment of the Court shall be transmitted to the Committee of Ministers which shall supervise its execution.

Article 55

The Court shall draw up its own rules and shall determine its own procedure.

Article 56

The first election of the members of the Court shall take place after the declarations by the High Contracting Parties mentioned in Article 46 have reached a total of eight.

No case can be brought before the Court before this election.

SECTION V

Article 57

On receipt of a request from the Secretary-General of the Council of Europe any High Contracting Party shall furnish an explanation of the manner in which its internal law ensures the effective implementation of any of the provisions of this Convention.

Article 58

The expenses of the Commission and the Court shall be borne by the Council of Europe.

Article 59

The members of the Commission and of the Court shall be entitled, during the discharge of their functions, to the privileges and immunities provided for in Article 40 of the Statute of the Council of Europe and in the agreements made thereunder.

Article 60

Nothing in this Convention shall be construed as limiting or derogating from any of the human rights and fundamental freedoms which may be ensured under the laws of any High Contracting Party or under any other agreement to which it is a Party.

Article 61

Nothing in this Convention shall prejudice the powers conferred on the Committee of Ministers by the Statute of the Council of Europe.

Article 62

The High Contracting Parties agree that, except by special agreement, they will not avail themselves of treaties, conventions or declarations in force between them for the purpose of submitting, by way of petition, a dispute arising out of the interpretation or application of this Convention to a means of settlement other than those provided for in this Convention.

Article 63

Any State may at the time of its ratification or at any time thereafter declare by notification addressed to the Secretary- General of the Council of Europe that the present Convention shall extend to all or any of the territories for whose international relations it is responsible.

The Convention shall extend to the territory or territories named in the notification as from the thirtieth day after the receipt of this notification by the Secretary-General of the Council of Europe.

The provisions of this Convention shall be applied in such territories with due

Any State which has made a declaration in accordance with paragraph 1 of this article may at any time thereafter declare on behalf of one or more of the territories to which the declaration relates that it accepts the competence of the Commission to receive petitions from individuals, non-governmental organizations or groups of individuals in accordance with Article 25 of the present Convention.

Article 64

Any State may, when signing this Convention or when depositing its instrument of ratification, make a reservation in respect of any particular provision of the Convention to the extent that any law then in force in its territory is not in conformity with the provision. Reservations of a general character shall not be permitted under this article.

Any reservation made under this article shall contain a brief statement of the law concerned.

Article 65

A High Contracting Party may denounce the present Convention only after the expiry of five years from the date of which it became a Party to it and after six months' notice contained in a notification addressed to the Secretary-General of the Council of Europe, who shall inform the other High Contracting Parties.

Such a denunciation shall not have the effect of releasing the High Contracting Party concerned from its obligations under this Convention in respect of any act which, being capable of constituting a violation of such obligations, may have been performed by it before the date at which the denunciation became effective.

Any High Contracting Party which shall cease to be a Member of the Council of Europe shall cease to be a Party to this Convention under the same conditions.

The Convention may be denounced in accordance with the provisions of the preceding paragraphs in respect of any territory to which it has been declared to extend under the terms Article 63.

Article 66

This Convention shall be open to the signature of the Members of the Council of Europe. It shall be ratified. Ratifications shall be deposited with the Secretary-General of the Council of Europe.

The present Convention shall come into force after the deposit of ten instruments of ratification.

As regards any signatory ratifying subsequently, the Convention shall come into force at the date of the deposit of its instrument of ratification.

The Secretary-General of the Council of Europe shall notify all the Members of the Council of Europe of the entry into force of the Convention, the names of the High Contracting Parties who have ratified it, and the deposit of all instruments of ratification which may be effected subsequently.

Done at Rome this 4th day of November, 1950, in English and French, both text being equally authentic, in a single copy which shall remain deposited in the archives of the Council of Europe. The Secretary-General shall transmit certified copies to each of the signatories.

PROTOCOLS TO THE EUROPEAN CONVENTION ON HUMAN RIGHTS AND FUNDAMENTAL FREEDOMS

Protocol 1. Enforcement of certain Rights and Freedoms not included in Section I of the Convention

The Governments signatory hereto, being Members of the Council of Europe,

Being resolved to take steps to ensure the collective enforcement of certain rights and freedoms other than those already included in Section I of the Convention for the Protection of Human

Rights and Fundamental Freedoms signed at Rome on 4th November, 1950 (hereinafter referred to as 'the Convention'),

Have agreed as follows :

Article 1

Every natural or legal person is entitled to the peaceful enjoyment of his possessions. No one shall be deprived of his possessions except in the public interest and subject to the conditions provided for by law and by the general principles of international law.

The preceding provisions shall not, however, in any way impair the right of a State to enforce such laws as it deems necessary to control the use of property in accordance with the general interest or to secure the payment of taxes or other contributions or penalties.

Article 2

No person shall be denied the right to education. In the exercise of any functions which it assumes in relation to education and to teaching, the State shall respect the right of parents to ensure such education and teaching in conformity with their own religions and philosophical convictions.

Article 3

The High Contracting Parties undertake to hold free elections at reasonable intervals by secret ballot, under conditions which will ensure the free expression of the opinion of the people in the choice of the legislature.

Article 4

Any High Contracting Party may at the time of signature or ratification or at any time thereafter communicate to the Secretary-General of the Council of Europe a declaration stating the extent to which it undertakes that the provisions of the present Protocol shall apply to such of the territories for the international relations of which it is responsible as are named therein.

Any High Contracting Party which has communicated a declaration in virtue of the preceding paragraph may from time to time communicate a further declaration modifying the terms of any former declaration or terminating the application of the provisions of this Protocol in respect of any territory.

A declaration made in accordance with this article shall be deemed to have been made in accordance with paragraph 1 of Article 63 of the Convention.

Article 5

As between the High Contracting Parties the provisions of Articles 1, 2, 3 and 4 of this Protocol shall be regarded as additional articles to the convention and all the provisions of the Convention shall apply accordingly.

Article 6

This Protocol shall be open for signature by the Members of the Council of Europe, who are the signatories of the Convention; it shall be ratified at the same time as or after the ratification of the Convention. It shall enter into force after the deposit of ten instruments of ratification. As regards any signatory ratifying subsequently, the Protocol shall enter into force at the date of the deposit of its instrument of ratification.

The instruments of ratification shall be deposited with the Secretary-General of the Council of Europe, who will notify all the Members of the names of those who have ratified.

Done at Paris on the 20th day of March 1952, In English and French, both text being equally authntic, in a single copy which shall remain deposited in the archives of the Council of Europe. The Secretary-General shall transmit certified copies to each of the signatory Governments

Protocol 2. Conferring upon the European Court of Human Rights Competence to Give Advisory Opinions

The Member States of the Council of Europe signatory hereto:

Having regard to the provisions of the Convention for the Protection of Human Rights and Fundamental Freedoms signed at Rome on 4 November 1950 (hereinafter referred to as 'the Convention'), and in particular Article 19 instituting, among other bodies, a European Court of Human Rights (hereinafter referred to as 'the Court');

Considering that it is expedient to confer upon the Court competence to give advisory opinions subject to certain conditions;

Have agreed as follows:

Article 1

The Court may, at the request of the Committee of Ministers, give advisory opinions on legal questions concerning the interpretation of the Convention and the Protocols thereto.

Such opinions shall not deal with any question relating to the content or scope of the rights or freedoms defined in Section I of the convention and in the Protocols thereto, or with any other question which the Commission, the Court, or the committee of Ministers might have to consider in consequence of any such proceedings as could be instituted in accordance with the Convention.

Decisions of the Committee of Ministers to request an advisory opinion of the Court shall require a two-thirds majority vote of the representatives entitled to sit on the Committee.

Article 2

The Court shall decide whether a request for an advisory opinion submitted by the Committee of Ministers is within its consultative competence as defined in Article 1 of this Protocol.

Article 3

For the consideration of requests for an advisory opinion, the Court shall sit in plenary session.

Reasons shall be given for advisory opinions of the Court.

If the advisory opinion does not represent in whole or in part the unanimous opinion of the judges, any judge shall be entitled to deliver a separate opinion.

Advisory opinions of the Court shall be communicated to the Committee of Ministers.

Article 4

The powers of the Court under Article 55 of the Convention shall extend to the drawing up of such rules and the determination of such procedure as the Court may think necessary for the purposes of this Protocol.

Article 5

This Protocol shall be open to signature by member States of the Council of Europe, signatories to the Convention, who may become Parties to it by:

(a) signature without reservation in respect of ratification or acceptance;

(b) signature with reservation in respect of ratification or acceptance, followed by ratification or acceptance. Instruments of ratification or acceptance shall be deposited with the Secretary-General of the Council of Europe.

This Protocol shall enter into force as soon as all the States Parties to the Convention shall have become Parties to the Protocol in accordance with the Provisions of paragraph 1 of this Article.

From the date of the entry into force of this Protocol, Articles 1 to 4 shall be considered an integral part of the Convention.

The Secretary-General of the Council of Europe shall notify the Member States of the Council of:

(a) any signature without reservation in respect of ratification or acceptance;
(b) any signature with reservation in respect of ratification or acceptance;
(c) the deposit of any instrument of ratification or acceptance;
(d) the date of entry into force of this Protocol in accordance with paragraph 2 of this article.

In witness whereof the undersigned, being duly authorized thereto, have signed this Protocol.

Done at Strasbourg, this 6th day of May 1963, in English and French, both text being equally authentic, in a single copy which shall remain deposited in the archives of the Council of Europe. The Secretary-General shall transmit certified copies to each of the signatory States.

Protocol 3. Amending Articles 29, 30, and 94 of the Convention

The member States of the Council, signatories to this Protocol,

Considering that it is advisable to amend certain provisions of the Convention for the Protection of Human Rights and Fundamental Freedoms signed at rome on 4 November 1950 (hereinafter referred to as 'the Convention') concerning the procedure of the European Commission of Human Rights,

Have agreed as follows :

Article 1

Article 29 of the Convention is deleted.

The following provision shall be inserted in the Convention:

"ARTICLE 29

After it has accepted a petition submitted under Article 25, the Commission may nevertheless decide unanimously to reject the petition if, in the course of its examination, it finds that the existence of one of the grounds for non-acceptance provided for in Article 27 has been established.

In such a case, the decision shall be communicated to the parties."

Article 2

At the beginning of Article 34 of the Convention, the following shall be inserted: "Subject to the provisions of Article 29..."

At the end of the same article, the sentence "the Sub-commission shall take its decisions by a majority of its members" shall be deleted.

Article 3

The Protocol shall be open to signature by the member States of the Council of Europe, who may become Parties to it either by:

(a) signature without reservation in respect of ratification or acceptance, or

(b) signature with reservation in respect of ratification or acceptance, followed by ratification or acceptance. Instruments of ratification shall be deposited with the Secretary-General of the Council of Europe.

This Protocol shall enter force as soon as all States Parties to the Convention shall have become Parties to the Protocol, in accordance with paragraph 1 of this article.

The Secretary-General of the Council of Europe shall notify the Member States of the Council of:

(a) any signature without reservation in respect of ratification or acceptance;

(b) any signature with reservation in respect of ratification or acceptance;

(c) the deposit of any instrument of ratification or acceptance;

(d) the date of entry into force of this Protocol in accordance with paragraph 2 of this article.

In witness whereof the undersigned, being duly authorized thereto, have signed this Protocol.

Done at Strasbourg, this 6th day of May 1963, in English and French, both text being equally authentic, in a single copy which shall remain deposited in the archives of the Council of Europe. The Secretary-General shall transmit certified copies to each of the signatory States.

Protocol 4. Protecting certain Additional Rights

The Governments signatory hereto, being Members of the Council of Europe,

Being resolved to take steps to ensure the collective enforcement of certain rights and freedoms other than those already included in Section 1 of the Convention for the Protection of Human Rights and Fundamental Freedoms signed at Rome on 4 November 1950 (hereinafter referred to as 'the Convention') and in Articles 1 to 3 of the First Protocol to the Convention, signed at Paris on 20 March 1952,

Have agreed as follows:

Article 1

No one shall be deprived of his liberty merely on the ground of inability to fulfil a contractual obligation.

Article 2

Everyone lawfully within the territory of a State shall, within that territory, have the right to liberty of movement and freedom to choose his residence.

Everyone shall be free to leave any country, including his own.

No restrictions shall be placed on the exercise of these rights other than such as are in accordance with law and are necessary in a democratic society in the interests of national security or public safety for the maintenance of 'ordre public', for the prevention of crime, for the protection of rights and freedoms of others.

The rights set forth in paragraph 1 may also be subject, in particular areas, to restrictions imposes in accordance with law and justified by the public interest in a democratic society.

Article 3

No one shall be expelled, by means either of an individual or of a collective measure, from the territory of the State of which he is a national.

No one shall be deprived of the right to enter the territory of the State of which he is a national.

Article 4

Collective expulsion of aliens is prohibited.

Article 5

Any High Contracting Party may, at the time of signature or ratification of this Protocol, or at any time thereafter, communicate to the Secretary-General of the Council of Europe a declaration stating the extent to which it undertakes that the provisions of this Protocol shall apply to such of the territories for the international relations of which it is responsible as are named therein.

Any High Contracting Party which has communicated a declaration in virtue of the preceding paragraph may, from time to time, communicate a further declaration modifying the terms of any former declaration or terminating the application of the provisions of this Protocol in respect of territory.

A declaration made in accordance with this article shall be deemed to have been made in accordance with paragraph 1 of Article 63 of the Convention.

The territory of any State to which this Protocol applies by virtue of the ratification or acceptance by that State, and each territory to which this Protocol is applied by virtue of a declaration by that State under this article, shall be treated as separate territories for the purpose of the references in Articles 2 and 3 to the territory of a State.

Article 6

As between the High Contracting Parties the provisions of Articles 1 to 5 of this Protocol shall be regarded as additional articles to the convention, and all the provisions of the Convention shall apply accordingly.

Nevertheless, the right of individual recourse recognized by a declaration made under Article 25 of the convention, or the acceptance of the compulsory jurisdiction of the court by a declaration made under Article 46 of the convention, shall not be effective in relation to this Protocol unless the High Contracting Party concerned has made a statement recognizing such a right, or accepting such jurisdiction, in respect of all or any of Articles 1 to 4 of the Protocol.

Article 7

This Protocol shall be open for signature by the members of the Council of Europe who are the signatories of the Convention; it shall be ratified at the same time as or after the ratification of the Convention. It shall enter into force after the deposit of five instruments of ratification. As regards any signatory ratifying subsequently, the Protocol shall enter into force at the date of the deposit of its instrument of ratification.

The instruments of ratification shall be deposited with the Secretary-General of the Council of Europe, who will notify all members of the names of those who have ratified.

In witness thereof, the undersigned, being duly authorized thereto, have signed this Protocol.

Done at Strasbourg, this 16th day of September 1963, in English and French, both texts being equally authentic, in a single copy which shall remain deposited in the archives of the Council of Europe. The Secretary-General shall transmit certified copies to each of the signatory States.

Protocol 5. Amending Articles 22 and 40 of the Convention

The Governments signatory hereto, being Members of the Council of Europe,

Considering that certain inconveniences have arisen in the application of the provisions of Articles 22 and 40 of the Convention for the Protection of Human Rights and fundamental Freedoms signed at Rome of 4th November 1950 (hereinafter referred to as 'the Convention') relating to the length of the terms of office of the members of the European Commission of Human Rights (hereinafter referred to as 'the Commission') and of the European Court of Human Rights (hereinafter referred to as 'the Court');

Considering that it is desirable to ensure as far as possible an election every three years of one half of the members of the Commission and of one third of the members of the Court;

Considering therefore that it is desirable to amend certain provisions of the Convention,

Have agreed as follows:

Article 1

In Article 22 of the Convention, the following two paragraphs shall be inserted after paragraph (2):

"(3) In order to ensure that, as far as possible, one half of the membership of the Commission shall be renewed every three years, the Committee of Ministers may decide, before proceeding to any subsequent election, that the term or terms of office of one or more members to be elected shall be for a period other than six years but not more than nine and not less than three years.

(4) In cases where more than one term of office is involved and the Committee of Ministers applies the preceding paragraph, the

allocation of the terms of office shall be effected by the drawing of lots by the Secretary-General, immediately after the election."

Article 2

In Article 22 of the Convention, the former paragraphs (3) and (4) shall become respectively paragraphs (5) and (6).

Article 3

In Article 40 of the Convention, the following two paragraphs shall be inserted after paragraph (2):

"(3) In order to ensure that, as far as possible, one half of the membership of the Court shall be renewed every three years, the Consultative Assembly may decide, before proceeding to any subsequent election, that the term or terms of office of one or more members to be elected shall be for a period other than nine years but not more than twelve and not less than six years.

(4) In cases where more than one term of office is involved and the Consultative Assembly applies the preceding paragraph, the allocation of the terms of office shall be effected by the drawing of lots by the Secretary-General, immediately after the election."

Article 4

In Article 40 of the Convention, the former paragraphs (3) and (4) shall become respectively paragraphs (5) and (6).

Article 5

This Protocol shall be open to signature by Members of the Council of Europe, signatories to the Convention, who may become Parties to it by;

(a) signature without reservation in respect of ratification or acceptance;

(b) signature with reservation in respect of ratification or acceptance, followed by ratification or acceptance.

Instruments of ratification or acceptance shall be deposited with the Secretary-General of the Council of Europe.

This Protocol shall enter into force as soon as all Contracting Parties to the Convention shall have become Parties to the Protocol, in accordance with the provisions of paragraph 1 of this article.

The Secretary-General of the Council of Europe shall notify the Members of the Council of:

(a) any signature without reservation in respect of ratification or acceptance;

(b) any signature with reservation in respect of ratification or acceptance;

(c) the deposit of any instrument of ratification or acceptance;

(d) the date of entry into force of this Protocol in accordance with paragraph 2 of this article.

In witness whereof the undersigned, being duly authorized thereto, have signed this Protocol.

Done at Strasbourg, this 20th day of January 1966, in English and French, both texts being equally authentic, in a single copy which shall remain deposited in the archives of the Council of Europe. The Secretary-General shall transmit certified copies to each of the signatory Governments.

APPENDIX V

European Convention for the Prevention of Torture and Inhuman or Degrading Treatment or Punishment

The member States of the Council of Europe, signatory hereto,

Having regard to the provisions of the Convention for the Protection of Human Rights and Fundamental Freedoms,

Recall-ing that, under Article 3 of the same Conven-tion, "no one shall be subjected to torture or to inhuman or degrading treatment or punishment";

Noting that the machinery provided for in that Convention operates in relation to persons who allege that they are victims of viola-tions of Article 3;

Convinced that the protection of persons deprived of their liberty against torture and inhuman or degrading treatment or punishment could be streng-thened by non judicial means of a preven-tive character based on visits,

Have agreed as follows:

CHAPTER I

Article 1

There shall be established a European Committee for the Prevention of Torture and Inhuman or Degrading Treatment or Punishment (herein-after referred to as "the Committee"). The Committee shall, by means of visits, examine the treatment of persons deprived of their liberty with a view to strengthening, if necessary, the protection of such persons from torture and from inhuman or degrading treatment or punishment.

Article 2

Each Party shall permit visits, in accordance with this Convention, to any place within its jurisdic-tion where persons are deprived of their liberty by a public authority.

Article 3

In the application of this Convention, the Committee and the competent national authori-ties of the Party concerned shall co ope-rate with each other.

CHAPTER II

Article 4

1. The Committee shall consist of a number of members equal to that of the Parties.
2. The members of the Committee shall be chosen from among persons of high moral character, known for their competence in the field of human rights or having pro-fessional experience in the areas covered by this Convention.
3. No two members of the Committee may be nationals of the same State.
4. The members shall serve in their individual capacity, shall be indepen-dent and impartial, and shall be available to serve the Committee effectively.

Article 5*

1. The members of the Committee shall be elected by the Committee of Ministers of the Council of Europe by an absolute majority of votes, from a list of names drawn up by the Bureau of the Consultative Assembly of the Council of Europe; each national delegation of the Parties in the Consultative Assembly shall put forward three candidates, of whom two at least shall be its nationals.
2. Where a member is to be elected to the Committee in respect of a non-member State of the Council of Europe, the Bureau of the Consultative Assembly shall invite the Parliament of that State to put forward three candidates, of whom two at least

* The text amended according to the provisions of Protocols No. 1 (ETS No. 151) and No. 2 (ETS No. 152).

shall be its nationals. The election by the Committee of Ministers shall take place after consultation with the Party concerned.

The same procedure shall be followed in filling casual vacancies.

3. The members of the Committee shall be elected for a period of four years. They may be re-elected twice. However, among the members elected at the first election, the terms of three members shall expire at the end of two years. The members whose terms are to expire at the end of the initial period of two years shall be chosen by lot by the Secretary General of the Council of Europe immediately after the first election has been completed.
4. In order to ensure that, as far as possible, one half of the membership of the Committee shall be renewed every two years, the Committee of Ministers may decide, before proceeding to any subsequent election, that the term or terms of office of one or more members to be elected shall be for a period other than four years but not more than six and not less than two years.
5. In cases where more than one term of office is involved and the Committee of Ministers applies the preceding paragraph, the allocation of the terms of office shall be effected by the drawing of lots by the Secretary General, immediately after the election.

Article 6

The Committee shall meet in camera. A quorum shall be equal to the majority of its members. The decisions of the Committee shall be taken by a majority of the members present, subject to the provisions of Article 10, paragraph 2.

* *Text amended according to the provisions of Protocols No. 1 (ETS No.151) and No. 2 (ETS No.151).*

The Committee shall draw up its own rules of procedure.

The Secretariat of the Committee shall be provided by the Secretary General of the Council of Europe.

CHAPTER III

Article 7

The Committee shall organise visits to places referred to in Article 2. Apart from periodic visits, the Committee may organise such other visits as appear to it to be required in the circumstances.

As a general rule, the visits shall be carried out by at least two members of the Committee. The Committee may, if it considers it necessary, be assisted by experts and interpreters.

Article 8

1. The Committee shall notify the Government of the Party concerned of its intention to carry out a visit. After such notification, it may at any time visit any place referred to in Article 2.
2. A Party shall provide the Committee with the following facilities to carry out its task:
   (a) access to its territory and the right to travel without restriction;
   (b) full information on the places where persons deprived of their liberty are being held;
   (c) unlimited access to any place where persons are deprived of their liberty, including the right to move inside such places without restriction;
   (d) other information available to the Party which is necessary for the Committee to carry out its task. In seeking such information, the Committee shall have regard to applicable rules of national law and professional ethics.
3. The Committee may interview in private persons deprived of their liberty.
4. The Committee may communicate freely with any person whom it believes can supply relevant information.
5. If necessary, the Committee may immedi-ately communicate observa-tions to the competent authorities of the Party concerned.

Article 9

In exceptional circumstances, the competent authorities of the Party concerned may make representations to the Committee against a visit at the time or to the particular place proposed by the Committee. Such representations may only be made on grounds of national defence, public safety, serious disorder in places where persons are deprived of their liberty, the medical condition of a person or that an urgent interrogation relating to a serious crime is in progress. Following such representations, the Committee and the Party shall immediately enter into consultations in order to clarify the situation and seek agreement on arrangements to enable the

Committee to exercise its functions expeditiously. Such arrangements may include the transfer to another place of any person whom the Committee proposed to visit. Until the visit takes place, the Party shall provide information to the Committee about any person concerned.

Article 10

1. After each visit, the Committee shall draw up a report on the facts found during the visit, taking account of any observations which may have been submitted by the Party concerned. It shall transmit to the latter its report containing any recommendations it considers necessary. The Committee may consult with the Party with a view to suggesting, if necessary, improvements in the protection of persons deprived of their liberty.
2. If the Party fails to co-operate or refuses to improve the situation in the light of the Committee's recommendations, the Committee may decide, after the Party has had an opportunity to make known its views, by a majority of two-thirds of its members to make a public statement on the matter.

Article 11

1. The information gathered by the Committee in relation to a visit, its report and its consultations with the Party concerned shall be confidential.
2. The Committee shall publish its report, together with any comments of the Party concerned, whenever requested to do so by that Party.
3. However, no personal data shall be published without the express consent of the person concerned.

Article 12*

Subject to the rules of confidentiality in Article 11, the Committee shall every year submit to the Committee of Ministers a general report on its activities which shall be transmitted to the Consultative Assembly and to any non-member State of the Council of Europe which is a party to the Convention, and made public.

Article 13

The members of the Committee, experts and other persons assisting the Committee are required, during and after their terms of office, to maintain the confidentiality of the facts or information of

* The text amended according to the provisions of Protocols No. 1 (ETS Bi, 151).

which they have become aware during the discharge of their functions.

Article 14

1. The names of persons assisting the Committee shall be specified in the notification under Article 8, paragraph (1).
2. Experts shall act on the instructions and under the authority of the Committee. They shall have particular knowledge and experience in the areas covered by this Convention and shall be bound by the same duties of independence, impartiality and availability as the members of the Committee.
3. A Party may exceptionally declare that an expert or other person assisting the Committee may not be allowed to take part in a visit to a place within its jurisdiction.

CHAPTER IV

Article 15

Each Party shall inform the Committee of the name and address of the authority competent to receive notifications to its Government, and of any liaison officer it may appoint.

Article 16

The Committee, its members and experts referred to in Article 7, paragraph 2 shall enjoy the privileges and immunities set out in the annex to this Convention.

Article 17

1. This Convention shall not prejudice the provisions of domestic law or any international agreement which provide greater protection for persons deprived of their liberty.
2. Nothing in this Convention shall be construed as limiting or derogating from the competence of the organs of the European Convention on Human Rights or from the obligations assumed by the Parties under that Convention.
3. The Committee shall not visit places which representatives or delegates of Protecting Powers or the International Committee of the Red Cross effectively visit on a regular basis by virtue of the Geneva Conventions of 12 August 1949 and the Additional Protocols of 8 June 1977 thereto.

CHAPTER V

Article 18

1. This Convention shall be open for signature by the member

States of the Council of Europe. It is subject to ratification, acceptance or approval. Instruments of ratification, acceptance or approval shall be deposited with the Secretary General of the Council of Europe.

2. The Committee of Ministers of the Council of Europe may invite any non-member State of the Council of Europe to accede to the Convention.

Article 19

1. This Convention shall enter into force on the first day of the month following the expiration of a period of three months after the date on which seven member States of the Council of Europe have expressed their consent to be bound by the Convention in accordance with the provisions of Article 18.
2. In respect of any State which subsequently expresses its consent to be bound by it, the Convention shall enter into force on the first day of the month following the expiration of a period of three months after the date of the deposit of the instrument of ratification, acceptance, approval or accession.

Article 20*

1. Any State may at the time of signature or when depositing its instrument of ratification, acceptance, approval or accession, specify the territory or territories to which this Convention shall apply.
2. Any State may at any later date, by a declaration addressed to the Secretary General of the Council of Europe, extend the application of this Convention to any other territory specified in the declaration. In respect of such territory the Convention shall enter into force on the first day of the month following the expiration of a period of three months after the date of receipt of such declaration by the Secretary General.
3. Any declaration made under the two preceding paragraphs may, in respect of any territory specified in such declaration, be withdrawn by a notification addressed to the Secretary General. The withdrawal shall become effective on the first day of the month following the expiration of a period of three months after the date of receipt of such notification by the Secretary General.

---

* Text amended according to the provisions of Protocol No. 1 (ETS No. 151).

Article 21

No reservation may be made in respect of the provisions of this Convention.

Article 22

1. Any Party may, at any time, denounce this Convention by means of a notification addressed to the Secretary General of the Council of Europe.
2. Such denunciation shall become effective on the first day of the month following the expiration of a period of twelve months after the date of receipt of the notification by the Secretary General.

Article 23

The Secretary General of the Council of Europe shall notify the member States and any non-member State of the Council of Europe party to the Convention of:
any signature;
the deposit of any instrument of ratification, acceptance, approval or accession;
any date of entry into force of this Convention in accordance with Articles 19 and 20;
any other act, notification or communication relating to this Convention, except for action taken in pursuance of Articles 8 and 10.

In witness whereof, the undersigned, being duly authorised thereto, have signed this Convention.

Done at Strasbourg, the 26 November 1987, in English and in French, both texts being equally authentic, in a single copy which shall be deposited in the archives of the Council of Europe. The Secretary General of the Council of Europe shall transmit certified copies to each member State of the Council of Europe.

Annex

Privileges and immunities

(Article 16)

1. For the purpose of this annex, references to members of the Committee shall be deemed to include references to experts mentioned in Article 7, paragraph 2.
2. The members of the Committee shall, while exercising their functions and during journeys made in the exercise of their functions, enjoy the following privileges and immunities:

a. immunity from personal arrest or detention and from seizure of their personal baggage and, in respect of words spoken or written and all acts done by them in their official capacity, immunity from legal process of every kind;

b. exemption from any restrictions on their freedom of movement on exit from and return to their country of residence, and entry into and exit from the country in which they exercise their functions, and from alien registration in the country which they are visiting or through which they are passing in the exercise of their functions.

3. In the course of journeys undertaken in the exercise of their functions, the members of the Committee shall, in the matter of customs and exchange control, be accorded:

a. by their own Government, the same facilities as those accorded to senior officials travelling abroad on temporary official duty;

b. by the Governments of other Parties, the same facilities as those accorded to representatives of foreign Governments on temporary official duty.

4. Documents and papers of the Committee, in so far as they relate to the business of the Committee, shall be inviolable. The official correspondence and other official communications of the Committee may not be held up or subjected to censorship.

5. In order to secure for the members of the Committee complete freedom of speech and complete independence in the discharge of their duties, the immunity from legal process in respect of words spoken or written and all acts done by them in discharging their duties shall continue to be accorded, notwithstanding that the persons concerned are no longer engaged in the discharge of such duties.

6. Privileges and immunities are accorded to the members of the Committee, not for the personal benefit of the individuals themselves but in order to safeguard the independent exercise of their functions. The Committee alone shall be competent to waive the immunity of its members; it has not only the right, but is under a duty, to waive the immunity of one of its members in any case where, in its opinion, the immunity would impede the course of justice, and where it can be waived without prejudice to the purpose for which the immunity is accorded.

APPENDIX VI

African (Banjul) Charter on Human and Peoples' Rights

(Adopted 27 June 1981, OAU Doc. CAB/LEG/67/3 rev. 5, 21 I.L.M. 58 (1982), entered into force 21 October 1986)

PREAMBLE

The African States members of the Organization of African Unity, parties to the present convention entitled "African Charter on Human and Peoples' Rights",

Recalling Decision 115 (XVI) of the Assembly of Heads of State and Government at its Sixteenth Ordinary Session held in Monrovia, Liberia, from 17 to 20 July 1979 on the preparation of a "preliminary draft on an African Charter on Human and Peoples' Rights providing inter alia for the establishment ofbodies to promote and protect human and peoples' rights";

Considering the Charter of the Organization of African Unity, which stipulates that "freedom, equality, justice and dignity are essential objectives for the achievement of the legitimate aspirations of the African peoples";

Reaffirming the pledge they solemnly made in Article 2 of the said Charter to eradicate all forms of colonialism from Africa, to coordinate and intensify their cooperation and efforts to achieve a better life for the peoples of Africa and to promote international cooperation having due regard to the Charter of the United Nations. and the Universal Declaration of Human Rights;

Taking into consideration the virtues of their historical tradition and the values of African civilization which should inspire and characterize their reflection on the concept of human and peoples' rights;

Recognizing on the one hand, that fundamental human rights stem from the attributes of human beings which justifies their national and international protection and on the other hand that the reality and respect of people's rights should necessarily guarantee human rights;

Considering that the enjoyment of rights and freedoms also implies the performance of duties on the part of everyone; Convinced that it is henceforth essential to pay a particular attention to the right to development and that civil and political rights cannot be dissociated from economic, social and cultural rights in their conception as well as universality and that the satisfaction of economic, social and cultural rights ia a guarantee for the enjoyment of civil and political rights;

Conscious of their duty to achieve the total liberation of Africa, the peoples of which are still struggling for their dignity and genuine independence, and undertaking to eliminate colonialism, neo colonialism, apartheid, *zionism* and to dismantle aggressive foreign military bases and all forms of discrimination, particularly those based on race, ethnic group, colour, sex, language, religion or political opinions;

Reaffirming their adherence to the principles of human and peoples' rights and freedoms contained in the declarations, conventions and other instrument adopted by the Organization of African Unity, the Movement of Non Aligned Countries and the United Nations;

Firmly convinced of their duty to promote and protect human and people' rights and freedoms taking into account the importance traditionally attached to these rights and freedoms in Africa;

Have agreed as follows:

PART I
RIGHTS AND DUTIES

CHAPTER I
HUMAN AND PEOPLES' RIGHTS

Article 1

The Member States of the Organization of African Unity

parties to the present Charter shall recognize the rights, duties and freedoms enshrined in this Chapter and shall undertake to adopt legislative or other measures to give effect to them.

Article 2

Every individual shall be entitled to the enjoyment of the rights and freedoms recognized and guaranteed in the present Charter without distinction of any kind such as race, ethnic group, color, sex, language, religion, political or any other opinion, national and social origin, fortune, birth or other status.

Article 3

1. Every individual shall be equal before the law.
2. Every individual shall be entitled to equal protection of the law.

Article 4

Human beings are inviolable. Every human being shall be entitled to respect for his life and the integrity of his person. No one may be arbitrarily deprived of this right.

Article 5

Every individual shall have the right to the respect of the dignity inherent in a human being and to the recognition of his legal status. All forms of exploitation and degradation of man particularly slavery, slave trade, torture, cruel, inhuman or degrading punishment and treatment shall be prohibited.

Article 6

Every individual shall have the right to liberty and to the security of his person. No one may be deprived of his freedom except for reasons and conditions previously laid down by law. In particular, no one may be arbitrarily arrested or detained.

Article 7

1. Every individual shall have the right to have his cause heard. This comprises: (a) the right to an appeal to competent national organs against acts of violating his fundamental rights as recognized and guaranteed by conventions, laws, regulations and customs in force; (b) the right to be presumed innocent until proved guilty by a competent court or tribunal; (c) the right to defence, including the right to be defended by counsel of his choice; (d) the right to be tried within a reasonable time by an impartial court or tribunal.

2. No one may be condemned for an act or omission which did not constitute a legally punishable offence at the time it was committed. No penalty may be inflicted for an offence for which no provision was made at the time it was committed. Punishment is personal and can be imposed only on the offender.

Article 8

Freedom of conscience, the profession and free practice of religion shall be guaranteed. No one may, subject to law and order, be submitted to measures restricting the exercise of these freedoms.

Article 9

1. Every individual shall have the right to receive information.
2. Every individual shall have the right to express and disseminate his opinions within the law.

Article 10

1. Every individual shall have the right to free association provided that he abides by the law.
2. Subject to the obligation of solidarity provided for in 29 no one may be compelled to join an association.

Article 11

Every individual shall have the right to assemble freely with others. The exercise of this right shall be subject only to necessary restrictions provided for by law in particular those enacted in the interest of national security, the safety, health, ethics and rights and freedoms of others.

Article 12

1. Every individual shall have the right to freedom of movement and residence within the borders of a State provided he abides by the law.
2. Every individual shall have the right to leave any country including his own, and to return to his country. This right may only be subject to restrictions, provided for by law for the protection of national security, law and order, public health or morality.
3. Every individual shall have the right, when persecuted, to seek and obtain asylum in other countries in accordance with laws of those countries and international conventions.

4. A non national legally admitted in a territory of a State Party to the present Charter, may only be expelled from it by virtue of a decision taken in accordance with the law.
5. The mass expulsion of non nationals shall be prohibited. Mass expulsion shall be that which is aimed at national, racial, ethnic or religious groups.

Article 13

1. Every citizen shall have the right to participate freely in the government of his country, either directly or through freely chosen representatives in accordance with the provisions of the law.
2. Every citizen shall have the right of equal access to the public service of his country.
3. Every individual shall have the right of access to public property and services in strict equality of all persons before the law.

Article 14

The right to property shall be guaranteed. It may only be encroached upon in the interest of public need or in the general interest of the community and in accordance with the provisions of appropriate laws.

Article 15

Every individual shall have the right to work under equitable and satisfactory conditions, and shall receive equal pay for equal work.

Article 16

1. Every individual shall have the right to enjoy the best attainable state of physical and mental health.
2. States parties to the present Charter shall take the necessary measures to protect the health of their people and to ensure that they receive medical attention when they are sick.

Article 17

1. Every individual shall have the right to education.
2. Every individual may freely, take part in the cultural life of his community.
3. The promotion and protection of morals and traditional values recognized by the community shall be the duty of the State.

Article 18

1. The family shall be the natural unit and basis of society. It shall be protected by the State which shall take care of its physical health and moral.
2. The State shall have the duty to assist the family which is the custodian or morals andtraditional values recognized by the community.
3. The State shall ensure the elimination of every discrimination against women and also ensure the protection of the rights of the woman and the child as stipulated in international declarations and conventions.
4. The aged and the disabled shall also have the right to special measures of protection in keeping with their physical or moral needs.

Article 19

All peoples shall be equal; they shall enjoy the same respect and shall have the same rights. Nothing shall justify the domination of a people by another.

Article 20

1. All peoples shall have the right to existence. They shall have the unquestionable and inalienable right to self determination. They shall freely determine their political status and shall pursue their economic and social development according to the policy they have freely chosen.
2. Colonized or oppressed peoples shall have the right to free themselves from the bonds of domination by resorting to any means recognized by the international community.
3. All peoples shall have the right to the assistance of the States parties to the present Charter in their liberation struggle against foreign domination, be it political, economic or cultural.

Article 21

1. All people shall freely dispose of their wealth and natural resources. This right shall be exercised in the exclusive interest of the people. In no case shall a people be deprived of it.
2. In case of spoliation the dispossessed people shall have the right to the lawful recovery of its property as well as to an adequate compensation.
3. The free disposal of wealth and natural resources shall be

exercised without prejudice to the obligation of promoting international economic cooperation based on mutual respect, equitable exchange and the principles of international law.

4. States parties to the present Charter shall individually and collectively exercise the right to free disposal of their wealth and natural resources with a view to strengthening African unity and solidarity.
5. States parties to the present Charter shall undertake to eliminate all forms of foreign economic exploitation particularly that practiced by international monopolies so as to enable their peoples to fully benefit from the advantages derived from their national resources.

Article 22

1. All peoples shall have the right to their economic, social and cult ural development with due regard to their freedom and identity and in the equal enjoyment of the common heritage of mankind.
2. States shall have the duty, individually or collectively, to ensure the exercise of the right to development.

Article 23

1. All peoples shall have the right to national and international peace and security. The principles of solidarity and friendly relations implicitly affirmed by the Charter of the United Nations and reaffirmed by that of the Organization of African Unity shall govern relations between States.
2. For the purpose of strengthening peace, solidarity and friendly relations, States parties to the present Charter shall ensure that:
   (a) any individual enjoying the right of asylum under 12 of the present Charter shall not engage in subversive activities against his country of origin or any other State party to the present Charter;
   (b) their territories shall not be used as bases for subversive or terrorist activities against the people of any other State party to the present Charter.

Article 24

All peoples shall have the right to a general satisfactory environment favourable to their development.

Article 25

States parties to the present Charter shall have the duty to promote and ensure through teaching, education and publication, the respect of the rights and freedoms contained in the present Charter and to see to it that these freedoms and rights as well as corresponding obligations and duties are understood.

Article 26

States parties to the present Charter shall have the duty to guarantee the independence of the Courts and shall allow the establishment and improvement of appropriate national institutions entrusted with the promotion and protection of the rights and freedoms guaranteed by the present Charter.

CHAPTER II
DUTIES

Article 27

1. Every individual shall have duties towards his family and society, the State and other legally recognized communities and the international community.
2. The rights and freedoms of each individual shall be exercised with due regard to the rights of others, collective security, morality and common interest.

Article 28

Every individual shall have the duty to respect and consider his fellow beings without discrimination, and to maintain relations aimed at promoting, safeguarding and reinforcing mutual respect and tolerance.

Article 29

The individual shall also have the duty :

1. To preserve the harmonious development of the family and to work for the cohesion and respect of the family; to respect his parents at all times, to maintain them in case of need;
2. To serve his national community by placing his physical and intellectual abilities at its service;
3. Not to compromise the security of the State whose national or resident he is;
4. To preserve and strengthen social and national solidarity, particularly when the latter is threatened;
5. To preserve and strengthen the national independence and the

territorial integrity of his country and to contribute to its defence in accordance with the law;

6. To work to the best of his abilities and competence, and to pay taxes imposed by law in the interest of the society;
7. To preserve and strengthen positive African cultural values in his relations with other members of the society, in the spirit of tolerance, dialogue and consultation and, in general, to contribute to the promotion of the moral wellbeing of society;
8. To contribute to the best of his abilities, at all times and at all levels, to the promotion and achievement of African unity.

PART II
MEASURES OF SAFEGUARD

CHAPTER I
ESTABLISHMENT AND ORGANIZATION OF THE AFRICAN COMMISSION ON HUMAN AND PEOPLES' RIGHTS

Article 30

An African Commission on Human and Peoples' Rights, hereinafter called "the Commission", shall be established within the Organization of African Unity to promote human and peoples' rights and ensure their protection in Africa.

Article 31

1. The Commission shall consist of eleven members chosen from amongst African personalities of the highest reputation, known for their high morality, integrity, impartiality and competence in matters of human and peoples' rights; particular consideration being given to persons having legal experience.
2. The members of the Commission shall serve in their personal capacity.

Article32

The Commission shall not include more than one national of the same state.

Article 33

The members of the Commission shall be elected by secret ballot by the Assembly of Heads of State andGovernment, from a list of persons nominated by the States parties to thepresent Charter.

Article 34

Each State party to the present Charter may not nominate more than two candidates. The candidates must have the nationality of one of the States party to the present Charter.When two candidates are nominated by a State, one of them may not be a national of thatState.

Article 35

1. The Secretary General of the Organization of African Unity shall invite States parties to the present Charter at least four months before the elections to nominate candidates;
2. The Secretary General of the Organization of African Unity shall make analphabetical list of the persons thus nominated and communicate it to the Heads of State and Government at least one month before the elections.

Article 36

The members of the Commission shall be elected for a six year period and shall be eligible for re-election. However, the term of office of four of the members elected at the first election shall terminate after two years and the term of office of three others, at the end of four years.

Article 37

Immediately after the first election, the Chairman of the Assembly of Heads of State and Government of the Organization of African Unity shall draw lots to decide the names of those members referred to in Article 36.

Article 38

After their election, the members of the Commission shall make a solemn declaration to discharge their duties impartially and faithfully.

Article 39

1. In case of death or resignation of a member of the Commission the Chairman of the Commission shall immediately inform the Secretary General of the Organization of African Unity, who shall declare the seat vacant from the date of death or from thedate on which the resignation takes effect.
2. If, in the unanimous opinion of other members of the Commission, a member has stopped discharging his duties for any reason other than a temporary absence, the Chairman of the Commission shall inform the Secretary General of the Organization of African Unity, who shall then declare the seat vacant.

3. In each of the cases anticipated above, the Assembly of Heads of State and Government shall replace the member whose seat became vacant for the remaining period of his term unless the period is less than six months.

Article 40

Every member of the Commission shall be in office until the date his successor assumes office.

Article 41

The Secretary General of the Organization of African Unity shall appoint the Secretary of the Commission. He shall also provide the staff and services necessary for the effective discharge of the duties of the Commission. The Organization of African Unity shall bear the costs of the staff and services.

Article 42

1. The Commission shall elect its Chairman and Vice Chairman for a two-year period.They shall be eligible for re-election.
2. The Commission shall lay down its rules of procedure.
3. Seven members shall form the quorum.
4. In case of an equality of votes, the Chairman shall have a casting vote.
5. The Secretary General may attend the meetings of the Commission. He shall not participate in deliberations nor shall he be entitled to vote. The Chairman of the Commission may, however, invite him to speak.

Article 43

In discharging their duties, members of the Commission shall enjoy diplomatic privileges and immunities provided for in the General Convention on the Privileges and Immunities of the Organization of African Unity.

Article 44

Provision shall be made for the emoluments and allowances of the members of the Commission in the Regular Budget of the Organization of African Unity.

CHAPTER II
MANDATE OF THE COMMISSION

Article 45

The functions of the Commission shall be:

1. To promote Human and Peoples' Rights and in particular:
   (a) to collect documents, undertake studies and researches on African problems in the field of human and peoples' rights, organize seminars, symposia and conferences, disseminate information, encourage national and local institutions concerned with human and peoples' rights, and should the case arise, give its views or make recommendations to Governments.
   (b) to formulate and lay down, principles and rules aimed at solving legal problems relating to human and peoples' rights and fundamental freedoms upon which African Governments may base their legislations.
   (c) co-operate with other African and international institutions concerned with the promotion and protection of human and peoples' rights.
2. Ensure the protection of human and peoples' rights under conditions laid down by the present Charter.
3. Interpret all the provisions of the present Charter at the request of a State party, an institution of the OAU or an African Organization recognized by the OAU.
4. Perform any other tasks which may be entrusted to it by the Assembly of Heads of State and Government.

CHAPTER III
PROCEDURE OF THE COMMISSION

Article 46

The Commission may resort to any appropriate method of investigation; it may hear from the Secretary General of the Organization of African Unity or any other person capable of enlightening it.

Communication from States

Article 47

If a State party to the present Charter has good reasons to believe that another State party to this Charter has violated the provisions of the Charter, it may draw, by written communication, the attention of that State to the matter. This communication shall also be addressed to the Secretary General of the OAU and to the Chairman of the Commission. Within three months of the receipt of the communication, the State to which the communication is addressed shall give the enquiring State, written explanation or statement elucidating the matter. This should include as much as possible relevant information relating to the laws and rules of procedure applied and applicable, and the redress already given or course of action available.

Article 48

If within three months from the date on which the original communication is received by the State to which it is addressed, the issue is not settled to the satisfaction of the two States involved through bilateral negotiation or by any other peaceful procedure, either State shall have the right to submit the matter to the Commission through the Chairman and shall notify the other States involved.

Article 49

Not withstanding the provisions of 47, if a State party to the present Charter considers that another State party has violated the provisions of the Charter, it may refer the matter directly to the Commission by addressing a communication to the Chairman, to the Secretary General of the Organization of African Unity and the State concerned.

Article 50

The Commission can only deal with a matter submitted to it after making sure that all local remedies, if they exist, have been exhausted, unless it is obvious to the Commission that the procedure of achieving these remedies would be unduly prolonged.

Article 51

1. The Commission may ask the States concerned to provide it with all relevant information.
2. When the Commission is considering the matter, States concerned may be represented before it and submit written or oral representation.

Article 52

After having obtained from the States concerned and from other sources all the information it deems necessary and after having tried all appropriate means to reach an amicable solution based on the respect of Human and Peoples' Rights, the Commission shall prepare, within a reasonable period of time from the notification referred to in 48, a report stating the facts and its findings. This report shall be sent to the States and communicated to the Assembly of Heads of State and Government.

Article 53

While transmitting its report, the Commission may make to the Assembly of Heads of State and Government such recommendations as it deems useful.

Article 54

The Commission shall submit to each ordinary Session of the Assembly of Heads of State and Government a reporton its activities.

Other Communications

Article 55

1. Before each Session, the Secretary of the Commission shall make a list of the communications other than those of States parties to the present Charter and transmit them to the members of the Commission, who shall indicate which communications should be considered by the Commission.
2. A communication shall be considered by the Commission if a simple majority of its members so decide.

Article 56

Communications relating to human and peoples' rights referred to in 55 received by the Commission, shall be considered if they:

1. Indicate their authors even if the latter request anonymity,
2. Are compatible with the Charter of the Organization of African Unity or with the present Charter,
3. Are not written in disparaging or insulting language directed against the State concerned and its institutions or to the Organization of African Unity,
4. Are not based exclusively on news discriminated through the mass media,
5. Are sent after exhausting local remedies, if any, unless it is obvious that this procedure is unduly prolonged,
6. Are submitted within a reasonable period from the time local remedies are exhausted or from the date the Commission is seized of the matter, and
7. Do not deal with cases which have been settled by these States involved in accordance with the principles of the Charter of the

United Nations, or the Charter of the Organization of African Unity or the provisions of the present Charter.

Article 57

Prior to any substantive consideration, all communications shall be brought to the knowledge of the State concerned by the Chairman of the Commission.

Article 58

1. When it appears after deliberations of the Commission that one or more communications apparently relate to special cases which reveal the existence of a series of serious or massive violations of human and peoples' rights, the Commission shall draw the attention of the Assembly of Heads of State and Government to these special cases.
2. The Assembly of Heads of State and Government may then request the Commission to undertake an in depth study of these cases and make a factual report, accompanied by its findings and recommendations.
3. A case of emergency duly noticed by the Commission shall be submitted by the latter to the Chairman of the Assembly of Heads of State and Government who may request an in depth study.

Article 59

1. All measures taken within the provisions of the present Chapter shall remain confidential until such a time as the Assembly of Heads of State and Government shall otherwise decide. . . . 3. The report on the activities of the Commission shall be published by its Chairman after it has been considered by the Assembly of Heads of State and Government.
2. However, the report shall be published by the Chairman of the Commission upon the decision of the Assembly of Heads of State and Government.
3. The report on the activities of the Commission shall be published by its Chairman after it has been considered by the Assembly of Heads of State and Government.

CHAPTER IV
APPLICABLE PRINCIPLES

Article 60

The Commission shall draw inspiration from international law on human and peoples' rights, particularly from the provisions of various African instruments on human and peoples' rights, the Charter of the United Nations, the Charter of the Organization of African Unity, the Universal Declaration of Human Rights, other instruments adopted by the United Nations and by African countries in the field of human and peoples' rights as well as from the provisions of various instruments adopted within the Specialized Agencies of the United Nations of which the parties to the present Charter are members.

Article 61

The Commission shall also take into consideration, as subsidiary measures to determine the principles of law, other general or special international conventions, laying down rules expressly recognized by member states of the Organization of African Unity, African practices consistent with international norms on human and people's rights, customs generally accepted as law, general principles of law recognized by African states as well as legal precedents and doctrine.

Article 62

Each state party shall undertake to submit every two years, from the date the present Charter comes into force, a report on the legislative or other measures taken with a view to giving effect to the rights and freedoms recognized and guaranteed by the present Charter.

Article 63

1. The present Charter shall be open to signature, ratification or adherence of thememberstates of the Organization of African Unity.
2. The instruments of ratification or adherence to the present Charter shall be depositedwith the Secretary General of the Organization of African Unity.
3. The present Charter shall come into force three months after the reception by the Secretary General of the instruments of ratification or adherence of a simple majorityof the member states of the Organization of African Unity.

PART III
GENERAL PROVISIONS

Article 64

1. After the coming into force of the present Charter, members of

the Commission shall be elected in accordance with the relevant Articles of the present Charter.

2. The Secretary General of the Organization of African Unity shall convene the first meeting of the Commission at the Headquarters of the Organization within three months of the constitution of the Commission. Thereafter, the Commission shall be convened by its Chairman whenever necessary but at least once a year.

Article 65

For each of the States that will ratify or adhere to the present Charter after its coming intoforce, the Charter shall take effect three months after the date of the deposit by that Stateof its instrument of ratification or adherence.

Article 66

Special protocols or agreements may, if necessary, supplement the provisions of the presentCharter.

Article 67

The Secretary General of the Organization of African Unity shall inform member states ofthe Organization of the deposit of each instrument of ratification or adherence.

Article 68

The present Charter may be amended if a State party makes a written request to that effect to the Secretary General of the Organization of African Unity. The Assembly of Heads of State and Government may only consider the draft amendment after all the States parties have been duly informed of it and the Commission has given its opinion on it at the request of the sponsoring State. The amendment shall be approved by a simple majority of the States parties. It shall come into force for each State which has accepted it in accordance with its constitutional procedure three months after the Secretary General has received notice of the acceptance.

APPENDIX VII

Arab Charter on Human Rights 2004

Given the Arab nation's belief in human dignity since God honoured it by making the Arab World the cradle of religions and the birthplace of civilizations which confirms its right to a life of dignity, based on freedom, justice and equality,

Pursuant to the eternal principles of brotherhood, equality and tolerance among all human beings which were firmly established by the Islamic *Shari'a* and other divinely-revealed religions,

Being proud of the humanitarian principles which it firmly established in the course of its long history and which played a major role in disseminating centres of learning between the East and the West, thereby making it an international focal point forseekers of knowledge, culture and wisdom,

Conscious of the fact that the entire Arab World has always worked together to preserve its faith, believed in its unity, struggled to protect its freedom, defended the right of nations to self-determination, to safeguard their resources and to development, believed in the rule of law and its contribution to the protection of universal and interrelated human rights, and believed that every individual's enjoyment of freedom, justice, and equality of opportunity is the yardstick by which the merits of any society are gauged,

Rejecting racism and *zionism* which constitute a violation of human rights and pose a threat to international peace and security, acknowledging the close interrelationship between human rights and world peace, reaffirming the principles of the Charter of the United

Nations and the Universal Declaration of Human Rights, as well as the provisions of theUnited Nations International Covenant on Civil and Political Rights and International Covenant on Economic, Social and Cultural Rights and the Cairo Declaration of Human Rights in Islam.

The State Parties to this Charter have agreed as follows:

Article 1

The present Charter shall undertake, in the context of the national identity of the Arab States, their sense of belonging to a common civilization,to achieve the following goals:

1. To place human rights at the centre of national preoccupation in the Arab States, to create great (fundamental) ideals for guiding the individual's will in these Arab States, and to help him improve his situation (life) in accordance with the noblest human values.
2. To instill (teach) in the human being in the Arab States pride in his identity, to (be) be faithful to his nation and to have a bond with his land, his history and common interests with all human beings in the Arab States. To encourage humane brotherhood, tolerance and open-mindedness in accordance with universal principles and the principles set out in human rights international instruments.
3. To prepare future generations in the Arab States to live free and responsible lives in a civil society united by a balance between consciousness of rights and respect for obligations, and governed by principles of equality, tolerance and moderation.
4. To establish the principle that all human rights are universal, indivisible, interdependent and indissoluble.

Article 2

1. All peoples have the right of self-determination and control over their natural wealth and resources and, accordingly, have the right to freely determine the form of their political structure and to freely pursue their economic, social and cultural development.
2. All peoples have the right to live under national sovereignty and territorial unity.
3. All forms of racism, *zionism*, occupation and foreign domination pose a challenge to human dignity and constitute a fundamental obstacle to the realization of the basic rights of

peoples. There is a need to condemn and endeavour to eliminate all such practices.

4. All peoples have the right to resist foreign occupation.

Article 3

1. Each State Party to the present Charter undertakes to ensure to all individuals within its territory and subject to its jurisdiction the right to enjoy all the rights and freedoms recognized herein, without any distinction on grounds of race, colour, sex, language, religion, opinion, thought, national or social origin, property, birth or physical or mental disability.
2. The States Party to the present Charter shall undertake necessary measures to guarantee effective equality in the enjoyment of all rights and liberties established in the present Charter, so as to protect against all forms of discrimination based on any reason mentioned in the previous paragraph.
3. Men and women are equal in human dignity, in rights and in duties, within the framework of the positive discrimination established in favour of women by Islamic *Shari'a* and other divine laws, legislation and international instruments. Consequently, each State Party to the present Charter shall undertake all necessary measures to guarantee the effective equality between men and women.

Article 4

1. In time of public emergency which threatens the life of the nation and which shall be officially proclaimed as such, the State Parties may take measures derogating from their obligations under the present Charter to the extent strictly required by the exigencies of the situation, provided that such measures are not inconsistent with their other obligations under international law and do not involve discrimination solely on the ground of race, colour, sex, language, religion or social origin.
2. No derogation from Articles 5, 8, 9, 10, 13, 14, 15, 18, 19, 20, 22, 27, 28, and 29 shall be made under this provision. The legal guarantees for the protection of those rights may not be suspended.
3. Any State Party to the present Charter availing itself of the right of derogation shall immediately inform the other States Parties, through the intermediary of the Secretary General of

the League of Arab States, of the provisions from which it has derogated and of the reason for which the derogation was declared. A further communication shall be made, through the same intermediary, on the date on which it shall terminate such derogation.

Article 5

1. Every human being has an inherent right to life.
2. This right shall be protected by law. No one shall be arbitrarily deprived of his life.

Article 6

The death penalty shall be inflicted only for the most serious crimes in accordance with the law in force at the time of the commission of the crime. Such a penalty can only be carried out pursuant to a final judgment rendered by a competent court. Anyone sentenced to death shall have the right to seek pardon or commutation of the sentence.

Article 7

1. The death penalty shall not be inflicted on a person under 18 years of age, unless otherwise provided by the law in force at the time of the commission of the crime.
2. The death penalty shall not be carried out on a pregnant woman prior to her delivery or on a nursing mother within two years from the date on which she gave birth. In any case, the interests of the infant shall prevail.

Article 8

1. No one shall be subjected to physical or mental torture or to cruel, inhuman or degrading treatment or punishment.
2. The State Parties shall protect every person in their territory from being subjected to such practices and take effective measures to prevent such acts. The practice thereof, or participation therein, shall be regarded as a punishable offense. Each victim of an act of torture is entitled to a right to compensation and rehabilitation.

Article 9

No medical or scientific experimentation, or use of organs shall be carried out on any person without his free and informed consent about the consequences resulting from it. Ethical, humanitarian and professional rules shall be complied with. Medical procedures in conformity with the relevant laws of each State Party aiming to ensure the concerned person's security shall be respected. The market of human organs is prohibited under all circumstances.

Article 10

1. Slavery and slave trade in all their forms shall be prohibited and punishable by law. No one shall, under any circumstances, be held in slavery or in servitude.
2. Forced labor, human trafficking for prostitution or sexual exploitation, the exploitation of others for prostitution and any other form of exploitation, as well as exploiting children during armed conflicts, are prohibited.

Article 11

All persons are equal before the law and have a right to enjoy its protection without discrimination.

Article 12

All persons are equal before the courts. The State Parties ensure the independence of the courts and the protection of judges against interference, pressure or threat. All persons within the territory of the State Parties are ensured a right to legal remedy.

Article 13

1. Everybody has the right to a fair trial in which sufficient guarantees are ensured, conducted by a competent, independent and impartial tribunal established by law, in judging the grounds of criminal charges brought against him or in determining his rights and obligations. State Parties shall ensure financial aid to those without the necessary means to pay for legal assistance to enable them to defend their rights.
2. The hearing shall be public other than (except) in exceptional cases where the interests of justice so require in a democratic society which respects freedom and human rights.

Article 14

1. Every individual has the right to liberty and security of person and no one shall be arrested, searched or detained without a legal warrant.
2. No one shall be deprived of his liberty except on such grounds and in accordance with such procedures as are established by law.
3. Anyone who is arrested shall be informed at the time of arrest,

in a language which he understands, of the reasons for his arrest, and shall be promptly informed of any charges against him. Anyone who is arrested has a right to contact his relatives.

4. Anyone who has been deprived of his liberty by arrest or detention is entitled to be subjected to a medical examination, and shall be informed of such right.
5. Anyone arrested or detained on a criminal charge shall be brought promptly before a Judge or other officer authorized by law to exercise judicial power, and shall be entitled to trial within a reasonable time, or to release. The release may be subject to guarantees to appear for trial. It shall not be a general rule that persons awaiting trial shall be held in custody.
6. Anyone who is deprived of his liberty by arrest or detention shall be entitled to proceedings before a court, in order that a court may decide without delay on the lawfulness of his arrest or detention, and order his release if the arrest or the detention is not lawful.
7. Anyone who is the victim of unlawful arrest or detention shall be entitled to compensation.

Article 15

There shall be no crime or punishment except as provided by a previously promulgated law. The accused shall benefit from subsequent legislation if it is in his favour.

Article 16

The accused shall be presumed innocent until proven guilty at a lawful trial. During the investigation and the trial, the accused shall be entitled to the following minimum guarantees:

1. To be informed promptly and in detail, in a language which he understands, of the nature and cause of the charge against him.
2. To have adequate time and facilities for the preparation of his defense and to contact his relatives.
3. To be tried in his presence in front of a judge, and to defend himself or through legal assistance of his own choosing or with the assistance of his lawyer, with whom he can freely and confidentially communicate.
4. To have free legal assistance of a lawyer to defend himself if he does not have sufficient means to pay for his defense, and if the interests of justice so require. To have the free assistance of an interpreter if he cannot understand or speak the language of the court.

5. To examine, or have examined, the witnesses against him, and to obtain the attendance and examination of witnesses on his behalf under the same conditions as witnesses against him.
6. Not to be compelled to testify against himself or to confess to guilt.
7. If convicted of a crime, to have his conviction and sentence reviewed by a higher tribunal according to law.
8. To have the security of his person and his private life respected in all circumstances

Article 17

Each State Party shall ensure to all children deemed "at risk" and juvenile persons accused of an infraction the right to a special legal regime for minors during the length of the hearing, the trial, and application of judgment. Such special treatment shall be appropriate for their age, protect their dignity and promote their rehabilitation, and allow them to play a constructive role in society.

Article 18

No one shall be imprisoned on the ground of his proven inability to meet a debt or fulfil any civil obligation.

Article 19

1. No one shall be tried twice for the same offense. Anyone against whom such proceedings are brought shall have the right to challenge their legality and to demand his release.
2. Anyone whose innocence has been established by a final judgment shall be entitled to compensation for damages suffered.

Article 20

1. Persons sentenced to a penalty of deprivation of liberty shall be treated with humanity and with respect for the inherent dignity of the human person.
2. Accused persons shall be separated from convicted persons and shall be subject to treatment appropriate to their status as unconvicted persons.
3. The essential aim of the penitentiary system is the reformation and social rehabilitation of prisoners.

Article 21

1. No one shall be subjected to arbitrary or unlawful interference with his privacy, family, home or correspondence, or to unlawful attacks on his honor and reputation.

2. Everyone has a right to the protection of the law against such interference or attacks.

Article 22

Everyone shall have the inherent right to recognition as a person before the law.

Article 23

Each State Party to the present Charter shall ensure that any person whose rights or freedoms recognized in the present Charter are violated shall have an effective remedy, not withstanding that the violation has been committed by persons acting in an official capacity.

Article 24

Every citizen has the right to:

1. Freedom of political activity.
2. Take part in the conduct of public affairs, directly or through freely chosen representatives.
3. Stand for election and to choose his representative in free and fair elections under conditions guaranteeing equality between all citizens and ensuring the free expression of the will of the electorate.
4. The opportunity to gain access, on general terms of equality, to public service in his country under equal conditions of opportunity.
5. Form associations with others and to join associations.
6. Freedom of peaceful assembly and association.
7. No restrictions may be placed on the exercise of these rights other than those imposed in conformity with the law and which are necessary in a society that respects freedom and human rights, in the interests of national security or public safety, public order, the protection of public health or morals or the protection of the rights and freedoms of others.

Article 25

Persons belonging to minorities shall not be denied the right to enjoy their own culture, to use their own language or to profess and practise their own religion. The law shall regulate the exercise of such rights.

Article 26

1. Every person lawfully within the territory of a State Party shall, within that territory, have the right to liberty of

movement and freedom to choose his residence in accordance with applicable regulations.

2. An alien lawfully in the territory of a State Party may be expelled only in pursuance of a decision reached according to the law and shall, except where compelling reasons of national security otherwise require, be given the possibility of having his case reviewed by a competent authority. Collective expulsions are prohibited in all cases.

Article 27

1. No one shall be arbitrarily or unlawfully prevented from leaving any country, including his own, nor prohibited from residing, or compelled to reside, in any part of his country.
2. No one shall be expelled from his country or prevented from returning thereto.

Article 28

Everyone shall have the right to seek political asylum in other countries to escape persecution. This right shall not be enjoyed by persons facing prosecution for an offense under ordinary criminal law. Political refugees shall not be extraditable.

Article 29

1. Every person has the right to a nationality, and no citizen shall be deprived of his nationality without a legally valid reason.
2. The State Parties shall undertake, in accordance with their legislation, all appropriate measures to allow a child to acquire the nationality of his mother with regard to the interest of the child.
3. No one shall be denied the right to acquire another nationality in accordance with the applicable legal procedures of his country.

Article 30

1. Every person shall have the right to freedom of thought, belief and religion, which may be subject only to such limitations as are prescribed by law.
2. Freedom to manifest or practice one's religion or beliefs or to perform rituals, either individually or in community with others, shall be subject only to such limitations as are prescribed by law and are necessary in a tolerant society that respects freedoms and human rights, to protect public safety,

public order, health or morals or the fundamental rights and freedoms of others.

3. Parents and legal guardians are guaranteed the freedom to ensure the religious and moral education of their children.

Article 31

Everyone has a guaranteed right to own private property. No person shall under any circumstances be divested of all or any part of his property in an arbitrary or unlawful manner.

Article 32

1. The present Charter shall ensure the right to information, freedom of opinion and freedom of expression, freedom to seek, receive and impart information by all means, regardless of frontiers.
2. Such rights and freedoms are exercised in the framework of society's fundamental principles and shall only be subjected to restrictions necessary for the respect of the rights or reputation of others and for the protection of national security or of public order, health or morals.

Article 33

1. The family is the natural and fundamental unit of society, founded by the marriage of a man and a woman. The right of men and women of marriageable age to marry and to found a family shall be recognized. No marriage shall be entered without the full consent of the intending spouses. The law in force shall regulate the rights and responsibilities of spouses as to marriage, during marriage and at its dissolution.
2. The State and society provide for the protection of the family and its members, for the strengthening of its bonds. All forms of violence and abusive treatment in the relations between family members, especially towards women and children, shall be prohibited. The State and society undertake to provide outstanding care and special protection for mothers, children and the elderly. Young persons have the right to be ensured maximum opportunities for physical and mental development.
3. The State Parties shall take all appropriate legislative, administrative and judicial provisions to ensure the protection, survival and well-being of children in an atmosphere of freedom and dignity. The best interest of the child, in all circumstances, serves as the basis for all measures taken, whether the child is a juvenile delinquent or a child "at risk".

4. The State Parties shall take all appropriate measures to ensure to young persons the right to engage in sports activities.

Article 34

1. Every citizen shall have the right to work. The State undertakes to ensure employment for as many employment seekers as possible, while ensuring maximum state production, and the freedom to work and equality of opportunity without discrimination of any kind as to race, colour, sex, language, religion, political opinion, affiliation to a trade union, national or social origin, handicap or other status.
2. Every worker shall have the right to the enjoyment of just and favourable conditions of work which provide for: a fair wage allowing workers to sustain a decent living for themselves and their families, limitation of working hours, rest and periodic holidays with pay, safe and healthy working conditions, the protection of women, children and handicapped persons in the workplace.
3. State Parties recognize the right of the child to be protected from economic exploitation and from performing any work that is likely to be hazardous or to interfere with the child's education, or to be harmful to the child's health or physical, mental, spiritual, moral or social development. To this end, and having regard to the relevant provisions of other international instruments, State Parties shall in particular:
   (a) Provide for a minimum age of employment.
   (b) Provide for appropriate regulation of the hours and conditions of employment.
   (c) Provide for appropriate penalties or other sanctions to ensure the effective enforcement of the present article.
4. No distinction between men and women shall be made in the exercise of the right to benefit effectively from training, employment, protection of work, and equal pay for work of equal value and quality.
5. Every State Party shall ensure protection to workers migrating to its territory in accordance with its laws.

Article 35

1. Every individual shall have the right to form trade unions, become a member of a trade union and to freely exercise trade union activity to defend his interests.

2. No restrictions shall be placed on the exercise of this right other than those imposed in conformity with law and which are necessary in the interests of national security, public safety, public order, the protection of public health, morals or the rights and freedoms of others.
3. Each State Party shall ensure the right to strike provided that it is exercised in conformity with its laws.

Article 36

The State Parties shall ensure the right of everyone to social security, including social insurance.

Article 37

The right to development is a fundamental human right. All State Parties shall establish development policies and take measures to ensure this right. They must give effect to the values of solidarity and cooperation among them and, at the international level, to eliminate poverty and achieve economic, social, cultural and political development. In accordance with this right, every citizen shall have the right to participate in the development, and contribute to and enjoy the benefits, of their goods and fruits of their labor.

Article 38

Everyone shall have the right to an adequate standard of living for himself and his family, ensuring well-being and a decent life, including adequate food, clothing, housing, services and a right to a safe environment. The State Parties shall take appropriate measures within their available resources to ensure the realization of this right.

Article 39

1. The State Parties shall recognize the right of everyone to the enjoyment of the highest attainable standard of physical and mental health and the right of every citizen to enjoy free and non-discriminatory access to health services and health care centres.
2. The steps to be taken by the State Parties shall include those necessary to:
   (a) Develop basic healthcare and ensure the free and non-discriminatory access to the services of health care centres.
   (b) Make every effort to fight disease by means of prevention and cure in order to reduce mortality.

(c) Take action to increase awareness and promote health education.
(d) Fight against traditional practices which are harmful to an individual's health.
(e) Ensure basic nutrition and clean water for everybody.
(f) Fight environmental pollution and supply sanitation systems.
(g) Fight against tobacco, drugs, and psychotropic substances.

Article 40

1. The State Parties undertake to ensure that mentally or physically disabled persons should enjoy a decent life, in conditions which ensure dignity, promote self-reliance and facilitate their active participation in society.
2. The State Parties shall provide social services free of charge to all disabled persons, including material support for those in need, directly or through their family to enable the family to provide for them and do all necessary to keep them out of an institution. In all cases, the disabled person's best interest will be taken into account.
3. The State Parties shall take all necessary measures to fight disability by all possible means, including preventive health programmes, awareness-raising efforts and education.
4. The State Parties shall provide all educational services suitable for disabled persons, taking into account the importance of integrating these persons in the educational system, the importance of professional training and preparation for pursuit of a professional activity, and the creation of suitable job opportunities in public or private sectors.
5. The State Parties shall provide all health services for disabled persons, including rehabilitation services, to integrate them into society.
6. The State Parties shall ensure to disabled persons access to all public and private collective services.

Article 41

1. The eradication of illiteracy is a binding obligation and every citizen has a right to education.
2. The State Parties ensure free primary and fundamental education to their citizens. Primary education, at the very least, shall be compulsory and shall be made easily accessible to all.

3. The State Parties shall, in every domain, take the appropriate measures to ensure partnership between men and women to reach the goals of development.
4. The State Parties shall ensure an education aimed at the total fulfilment of the human being and the strengthening of respect of human rights and fundamental liberties.
5. The State Parties shall work to promote the principles of human rights and fundamental liberties through educational programs and activities, educational methods and training programs, both official and non-official.
6. The State Parties shall ensure the establishment of mechanisms necessary to ensure primary education to all citizens, and shall establish national plans for the education of adults.

Article 42

1. Every person shall have the right to take part in cultural life, and to enjoy the benefits of scientific progress and their applications.
2. The State Parties shall respect freedom of scientific research and creativity, and shall ensure the protection of moral and material principles linked to scientific, literary or artistic production.
3. The State Parties shall work together and reinforce cooperation between them at all levels, with full participation of intellectuals and inventors and their organizations, in order to expand and implement recreational, cultural, artistic and scientific programs.

Article 43

Nothing in the present Charter shall be interpreted as impairing the rights and freedoms protected by the State Parties' own laws, or as set out in international or regional instruments of human rights that the State Parties have signed or ratified, including women's rights, children's rights and minorities' rights.

Article 44

Where not already provided for by existing legislative or other measures, the State Parties undertake to adopt, in accordance with their constitutional processes and with the provisions of the present Charter, the necessary laws or other measures in order to give effect to the rights recognized by the present Charter

Article 45

1. There shall be established, pursuant to the present Charter, an Arab Human Rights Committee, hereafter referred to as "the Committee". The Committee shall be composed of seven members elected by secret ballot by the State Parties to the present Charter.2.The Committee shall consist of nationals of the State Parties to the present Charter, who shall be highly experienced persons competent in the Committee's field of work. The members of the Committee shall serve in their personal capacity with full impartiality and integrity.
3. The Committee shall not include more than one person from the same State Party. Such member shall be eligible for re-election only once. The principle of rotation shall be strictly observed.
4. The members of the Committee shall be elected for a four-year term. However, the terms of three of the members elected at the first election shall expire at the end of two years, with the names of these three members chosen by lot.
5. Six months before the date of the election, the Secretary General of the League of Arab States shall invite the State Parties to submit their candidates over a three-month period. He shall give them the list of candidates two months before the date of the election. The candidates who obtain the most votes will be the elected members of the Committee. If, because two or more candidates have an equal number of votes, the number of candidates with the largest number of votes exceeds the number required, a second ballot will be held between the persons with equal numbers of votes. If the votes are again equal, the member or members shall be chosen by lot. The first election of the Committee's members shall take place no later than six months after the Charter comes into force.
6. The Secretary General shall convene the State Parties to a meeting dedicated to the election of the members of the Committee at the Headquarters of the League of Arab States. The majority of the State Parties shall constitute a quorum. If the quorum is not reached, the Secretary General shall convene a new meeting where a third of the State Parties shall constitute a quorum. If the quorum is still not reached, the Secretary General shall convene a third meeting which will take place without regard to the number of State Parties present.

7. The Committee's first meeting shall be convened by the Secretary General. During this meeting, the Committee shall elect its chairman from its members, for a two-year term renewable for one further term of two years. The Committee shall establish its own statute and rules of procedure and shall determine how often it shall meet. The Committee shall hold its meetings at the headquarters of the League of Arab States. It may also meet in any other State party to the present Charter at that party's invitation.

Article 46

1. The Secretary-General shall declare a seat vacant after being notified by the Chairman of the Committee in case of :
   (a) Death.
   (b) Resignation.
   (c) If, in the unanimous opinion of the other members, a member of the Committee has ceased to carry out his functions for any acceptable cause or for any reason other than a temporary absence.
2. When a vacancy is declared in accordance with subparagraph (1), and if the term of office of the member to be replaced does not expire within six months of the vacancy, the Secretary-General of the League of Arab States shall notify each of the State Parties to the present Charter, which may within two months submit nominations in accordance with article 45 for the purpose of filling the vacancy.
3. The Secretary-General of the League of Arab States shall prepare a list in alphabetical order of the persons thus nominated and shall submit it to the States Parties to the present Charter. The election to fill the vacancy shall then take place in accordance with the relevant provisions.
4. A member of the Committee elected to fill a vacancy declared in accordance with subparagraphs (1) shall hold office for the remainder of the term of the member who vacated the seat under the provisions of those subparagraphs.
5. The Secretary-General shall award on the budget of the League of Arab States the necessary financial resources, staff and facilities for the effective performance of the functions of the Committee. The members of the Committee shall be considered, regarding remuneration and reimbursement of expenses, as experts of the Secretariat.

Article 47

The States Parties undertake to ensure that members of the Committee shall enjoy the immunities necessary for their protection against any form of harassment, moral or material pressure or prosecution on account of the positions they take or statements they make while carrying out their functions as members of the Committee.

Article 48

1. The State Parties shall submit reports to the Secretary-General of the League of Arab States on the measures they have taken to give effect to the rights and freedoms recognized in this Charter and on the progress made towards the enjoyment thereof. The Secretary- General shall transmit these reports to the Committee for its consideration.
2. The State Parties shall submit an initial report to the Committee within one year from the date on which the Charter enters into force, and a periodic report every three years thereafter. The Committee may request the States Parties to supply it with additional information relating to the implementation of the Charter.
3. The Committee shall study in public the reports submitted by the States Parties under paragraph b) of this article in the presence and with the collaboration of the representative of the State Parties whose report is being considered.
4. The Committee shall examine the report, comment thereon and make the necessary recommendations in accordance with the aims of the Charter.
5. The Committee shall submit an annual report containing its comments and recommendations to the Council of the League, through the intermediary of the Secretary-General.
6. The Committee's reports, concluding observations and recommendations shall be public documents which the Committee shall disseminate widely.

Article 49

1. The Secretary General of the League of Arab States shall submit the present Charter to the State Parties once approved by the League for signature, ratification or accession.
2. The present Charter shall enter into force two months after the date of the deposit of the seventh instrument of ratification with the Secretariat of the League of Arab States.

3. After its entry into force, the present Charter shall become effective for each State two months after the State in question has deposited its instrument of ratification or accession with the secretariat.
4. The Secretary General shall inform the State Parties of the deposit of each instrument of ratification or accession.

Article 50

Any State Party may propose an amendment to the present Charter and file it in writing with the Secretary General. Upon notification of the amendments to the other State Parties, the Secretary General shall convene the State Parties to examine the amendments for approval prior to the submission to the Council of the League for adoption.

Article 51

Amendments shall come into force and be binding on those State Parties which have accepted them when they have been approved by two thirds of the State Parties to the Charter.

Article 52

Any State Party may propose supplementary protocols to the present Charter, which shall be adopted according to the same process as followed for the adoption of amendments to the Charter.

Article 53

1. Any State Party, when signing this Charter, depositing the instruments of ratification or accession, may make a reservation to any article of the Charter, provided that such reservation does not conflict with the aims and fundamental purposes of the Charter.
2. Any State Party that has made a reservation pursuant to paragraph a) of this article may withdraw it at any time by addressing a notification to the Secretary-General of the League of Arab States.
3. The Secretary General shall notify the State Parties of reservations made and petitions for withdrawal

This is the first English translation of the 2004 Arab Charter on Human Rights made by Dr. Mohammed Amin Al-Midani, President of Arab Center for International Humanitarian Law and Human Rights Education and Mathilde Cabanettes (Boston University School of Law).

APPENDIX VIII

American Convention on Human Rights "Pact of San Jose, Costa Rica"

PREAMBLE

The American states signatory to the present Convention,

Reaffirming their intention to consolidate in this hemisphere, within the framework of democratic institutions, a system of personal liberty and social justice based on respect for the essential rights of man;

Recognizing that the essential rights of man are not derived from one's being a national of a certain state, but are based upon attributes of the human personality, and that they therefore justify international protection in the form of a convention reinforcing or complementing the protection provided by the domestic law of the American states;

Considering that these principles have been set forth in the Charter of the Organization of American States, in the American Declaration of the Rights and Duties of Man, and in the Universal Declaration of Human Rights, and that they have been reaffirmed and refined in other international instruments, worldwide as well as regional in scope;

Reiterating that, in accordance with the Universal Declaration of Human Rights, the ideal of free men enjoying freedom from fear and want can be achieved only if conditions are created whereby everyone may enjoy his economic, social, and cultural rights, as well as his civil and political rights; and

Considering that the Third Special Inter-American Conference (Buenos Aires, 1967) approved the incorporation into the Charter of the Organization itself of broader standards with respect to economic, social, and educational rights and resolved that an inter-American convention on human rights should determine the structure, competence, and procedure of the organs responsible for these matters,

Have agreed upon the following:

PART I
STATE OBLIGATIONS AND RIGHTS PROTECTED

CHAPTER I
GENERAL OBLIGATIONS

Article 1. Obligation to Respect Rights

1. The States Parties to this Convention undertake to respect the rights and freedoms recognized herein and to ensure to all persons subject to their jurisdiction the free and full exercise of those rights and freedoms, without any discrimination for reasons of race, color, sex, language, religion, political or other opinion, national or social origin, economic status, birth, or any other social condition.
2. For the purposes of this Convention, "person" means every human being.

Article 2. Domestic Legal Effects

Where the exercise of any of the rights or freedoms referred to in Article 1 is not already ensured by legislative or other provisions, the States Parties undertake to adopt, in accordance with their constitutional processes and the provisions of this Convention, such legislative or other measures as may be necessary to give effect to those rights or freedoms.

CHAPTER II
CIVIL AND POLITICAL RIGHT

Article 3. Right to Juridical Personality

Every person has the right to recognition as a person before the law.

Article 4. Right to Life

1. Every person has the right to have his life respected. This right shall be protected by law and, in general, from the moment of conception. No one shall be arbitrarily deprived of his life.
2. In countries that have not abolished the death penalty, it may be imposed only for the most serious crimes and pursuant to a final judgment rendered by a competent court and in accordance with a law establishing such punishment, enacted prior to the commission of the crime. The application of such punishment shall not be extended to crimes to which it does not presently apply.
3. The death penalty shall not be reestablished in states that have abolished it.
4. In no case shall capital punishment be inflicted for political offenses or related common crimes.
5. Capital punishment shall not be imposed upon persons who, at the time the crime was committed, were under 18 years of age or over 70 years of age; nor shall it be applied to pregnant women.
6. Every person condemned to death shall have the right to apply for amnesty, pardon, or commutation of sentence, which may be granted in all cases. Capital punishment shall not be imposed while such a petition is pending decision by the competent authority.

Article 5. Right to Humane Treatment

1. Every person has the right to have his physical, mental, and moral integrity respected.
2. No one shall be subjected to torture or to cruel, inhuman, or degrading punishment or treatment. All persons deprived of their liberty shall be treated with respect for the inherent dignity of the human person.
3. Punishment shall not be extended to any person other than the criminal.
4. Accused persons shall, save in exceptional circumstances, be segregated from convicted persons, and shall be subject to separate treatment appropriate to their status as unconvicted persons.
5. Minors while subject to criminal proceedings shall be separated from adults and brought before specialized tribunals, as speedily as possible, so that they may be treated in accordance with their status as minors.

6. Punishments consisting of deprivation of liberty shall have as an essential aim the reform and social readaptation of the prisoners.

Article 6. Freedom from Slavery

1. No one shall be subject to slavery or to involuntary servitude, which are prohibited in all their forms, as are the slave trade and traffic in women.
2. No one shall be required to perform forced or compulsory labor. This provision shall not be interpreted to mean that, in those countries in which the penalty established for certain crimes is deprivation of liberty at forced labor, the carrying out of such a sentence imposed by a competent court is prohibited. Forced labor shall not adversely affect the dignity or the physical or intellectual capacity of the prisoner.
3. For the purposes of this article, the following do not constitute forced or compulsory labour:
   a. work or service normally required of a person imprisoned in execution of a sentence or formal decision passed by the competent judicial authority. Such work or service shall be carried out under the supervision and control of public authorities, and any persons performing such work or service shall not be placed at the disposal of any private party, company, or juridical person;
   b. military service and, in countries in which conscientious objectors are recognized, national service that the law may provide for in lieu of military service;
   c. service exacted in time of danger or calamity that threatens the existence or the well-being of the community; or
   d. work or service that forms part of normal civic obligations.

Article 7. Right to Personal Liberty

1. Every person has the right to personal liberty and security.
2. No one shall be deprived of his physical liberty except for the reasons and under the conditions established beforehand by the constitution of the State Party concerned or by a law established pursuant thereto.
3. No one shall be subject to arbitrary arrest or imprisonment.
4. Anyone who is detained shall be informed of the reasons for

his detention and shall be promptly notified of the charge or charges against him.

5. Any person detained shall be brought promptly before a judge or other officer authorized by law to exercise judicial power and shall be entitled to trial within a reasonable time or to be released without prejudice to the continuation of the proceedings. His release may be subject to guarantees to assure his appearance for trial.

6. Anyone who is deprived of his liberty shall be entitled to recourse to a competent court, in order that the court may decide without delay on the lawfulness of his arrest or detention and order his release if the arrest or detention is unlawful. In States Parties whose laws provide that anyone who believes himself to be threatened with deprivation of his liberty is entitled to recourse to a competent court in order that it may decide on the lawfulness of such threat, this remedy may not be restricted or abolished. The interested party or another person in his behalf is entitled to seek these remedies.

7. No one shall be detained for debt. This principle shall not limit the orders of a competent judicial authority issued for nonfulfillment of duties of support.

Article 8. Right to a Fair Trial

1. Every person has the right to a hearing, with due guarantees and within a reasonable time, by a competent, independent, and impartial tribunal, previously established by law, in the substantiation of any accusation of a criminal nature made against him or for the determination of his rights and obligations of a civil, labor, fiscal, or any other nature.

2. Every person accused of a criminal offense has the right to be presumed innocent so long as his guilt has not been proven according to law. During the proceedings, every person is entitled, with full equality, to the following minimum guarantees:

   a. the right of the accused to be assisted without charge by a translator or interpreter, if he does not understand or does not speak the language of the tribunal or court;

   b. prior notification in detail to the accused of the charges against him;

   c. adequate time and means for the preparation of his defense;

d. the right of the accused to defend himself personally or to be assisted by legal counsel of his own choosing, and to communicate freely and privately with his counsel;

e. the inalienable right to be assisted by counsel provided by the state, paid or not as the domestic law provides, if the accused does not defend himself personally or engage his own counsel within the time period established by law;

f. the right of the defense to examine witnesses present in the court and to obtain the appearance, as witnesses, of experts or other persons who may throw light on the facts;

g. the right not to be compelled to be a witness against himself or to plead guilty; and

h. the right to appeal the judgment to a higher court.

3. A confession of guilt by the accused shall be valid only if it is made without coercion of any kind.

4. An accused person acquitted by a non-appealable judgment shall not be subjected to a new trial for the same cause.

5. Criminal proceedings shall be public, except insofar as may be necessary to protect the interests of justice.

Article 9. Freedom from Ex Post Facto Laws

No one shall be convicted of any act or omission that did not constitute a criminal offense, under the applicable law, at the time it was committed. A heavier penalty shall not be imposed than the one that was applicable at the time the criminal offense was committed. If subsequent to the commission of the offense the law provides for the imposition of a lighter punishment, the guilty person shall benefit therefrom.

Article 10. Right to Compensation

Every person has the right to be compensated in accordance with the law in the event he has been sentenced by a final judgment through a miscarriage of justice.

Article 11. Right to Privacy

1. Everyone has the right to have his honour respected and his dignity recognized.
2. No one may be the object of arbitrary or abusive interference with his private life, his family, his home, or his correspondence, or of unlawful attacks on his honour or reputation.

3. Everyone has the right to the protection of the law against such interference or attacks.

Article 12. Freedom of Conscience and Religion

1. Everyone has the right to freedom of conscience and of religion. This right includes freedom to maintain or to change one's religion or beliefs, and freedom to profess or disseminate one's religion or beliefs, either individually or together with others, in public or in private.
2. No one shall be subject to restrictions that might impair his freedom to maintain or to change his religion or beliefs.
3. Freedom to manifest one's religion and beliefs may be subject only to the limitations prescribed by law that are necessary to protect public safety, order, health, or morals, or the rights or freedoms of others.
4. Parents or guardians, as the case may be, have the right to provide for the religious and moral education of their children or wards that is in accord with their own convictions.

Article 13. Freedom of Thought and Expression

1. Everyone has the right to freedom of thought and expression. This right includes freedom to seek, receive, and impart information and ideas of all kinds, regardless of frontiers, either orally, in writing, in print, in the form of art, or through any other medium of one's choice.
2. The exercise of the right provided for in the foregoing paragraph shall not be subject to prior censorship but shall be subject to subsequent imposition of liability, which shall be expressly established by law to the extent necessary to ensure:
   a. respect for the rights or reputations of others; or
   b. the protection of national security, public order, or public health or morals.
3. The right of expression may not be restricted by indirect methods or means, such as the abuse of government or private controls over newsprint, radio broadcasting frequencies, or equipment used in the dissemination of information, or by any other means tending to impede the communication and circulation of ideas and opinions.
4. Notwithstanding the provisions of paragraph 2 above, public entertainments may be subject by law to prior censorship for the sole purpose of regulating access to them for the moral protection of childhood and adolescence.

5. Any propaganda for war and any advocacy of national, racial, or religious hatred that constitute incitements to lawless violence or to any other similar action against any person or group of persons on any grounds including those of race, color, religion, language, or national origin shall be considered as offenses punishable by law.

Article 14. Right of Reply

1. Anyone injured by inaccurate or offensive statements or ideas disseminated to the public in general by a legally regulated medium of communication has the right to reply or to make a correction using the same communications outlet, under such conditions as the law may establish.
2. The correction or reply shall not in any case remit other legal liabilities that may have been incurred.
3. For the effective protection of honor and reputation, every publisher, and every newspaper, motion picture, radio, and television company, shall have a person responsible who is not protected by immunities or special privileges.

Article 15. Right of Assembly

The right of peaceful assembly, without arms, is recognized. No restrictions may be placed on the exercise of this right other than those imposed in conformity with the law and necessary in a democratic society in the interest of national security, public safety or public order, or to protect public health or morals or the rights or freedom of others.

Article 16. Freedom of Association

1. Everyone has the right to associate freely for ideological, religious, political, economic, labor, social, cultural, sports, or other purposes.
2. The exercise of this right shall be subject only to such restrictions established by law as may be necessary in a democratic society, in the interest of national security, public safety or public order, or to protect public health or morals or the rights and freedoms of others.
3. The provisions of this article do not bar the imposition of legal restrictions, including even deprivation of the exercise of the right of association, on members of the armed forces and the police.

Article 17. Rights of the Family

1. The family is the natural and fundamental group unit of society and is entitled to protection by society and the state.
2. The right of men and women of marriageable age to marry and to raise a family shall be recognized, if they meet the conditions required by domestic laws, insofar as such conditions do not affect the principle of non-discrimination established in this Convention.
3. No marriage shall be entered into without the free and full consent of the intending spouses.
4. The States Parties shall take appropriate steps to ensure the equality of rights and the adequate balancing of responsibilities of the spouses as to marriage, during marriage, and in the event of its dissolution. In case of dissolution, provision shall be made for the necessary protection of any children solely on the basis of their own best interests.
5. The law shall recognize equal rights for children born out of wedlock and those born in wedlock.

Article 18. Right to a Name

Every person has the right to a given name and to the surnames of his parents or that of one of them. The law shall regulate the manner in which this right shall be ensured for all, by the use of assumed names if necessary.

Article 19. Rights of the Child

Every minor child has the right to the measures of protection required by his condition as a minor on the part of his family, society, and the state.

Article 20. Right to Nationality

1. Every person has the right to a nationality.
2. Every person has the right to the nationality of the state in whose territory he was born if he does not have the right to any other nationality.
3. No one shall be arbitrarily deprived of his nationality or of the right to change it.

Article 21. Right to Property

1. Everyone has the right to the use and enjoyment of his property. The law may subordinate such use and enjoyment to the interest of society.

2. No one shall be deprived of his property except upon payment of just compensation, for reasons of public utility or social interest, and in the cases and according to the forms established by law.
3. Usury and any other form of exploitation of man by man shall be prohibited by

Article 22. Freedom of Movement and Residence

1. Every person lawfully in the territory of a State Party has the right to move about in it, and to reside in it subject to the provisions of the law.
2. Every person has the right lo leave any country freely, including his own.
3. The exercise of the foregoing rights may be restricted only pursuant to a law to the extent necessary in a democratic society to prevent crime or to protect national security, public safety, public order, public morals, public health, or the rights or freedoms of others.
4. The exercise of the rights recognized in paragraph 1 may also be restricted by law in designated zones for reasons of public interest.
5. No one can be expelled from the territory of the state of which he is a national or be deprived of the right to enter it.
6. An alien lawfully in the territory of a State Party to this Convention may be expelled from it only pursuant to a decision reached in accordance with law.
7. Every person has the right to seek and be granted asylum in a foreign territory, in accordance with the legislation of the state and international conventions, in the event he is being pursued for political offenses or related common crimes.
8. In no case may an alien be deported or returned to a country, regardless of whether or not it is his country of origin, if in that country his right to life or personal freedom is in danger of being violated because of his race, nationality, religion, social status, or political opinions.
9. The collective expulsion of aliens is prohibited.

Article 23. Right to Participate in Government

1. Every citizen shall enjoy the following rights and opportunities:
   a. to take part in the conduct of public affairs, directly or through freely chosen representatives;

b. to vote and to be elected in genuine periodic elections, which shall be by universal and equal suffrage and by secret ballot that guarantees the free expression of the will of the voters; and
c. to have access, under general conditions of equality, to the public service of his country.

2. The law may regulate the exercise of the rights and opportunities referred to in the preceding paragraph only on the basis of age, nationality, residence, language, education, civil and mental capacity, or sentencing by a competent court in criminal proceedings.

Article 24. Right to Equal Protection

All persons are equal before the law. Consequently, they are entitled, without discrimination, to equal protection of the law.

Article 25. Right to Judicial Protection

1. Everyone has the right to simple and prompt recourse, or any other effective recourse, to a competent court or tribunal for protection against acts that violate his fundamental rights recognized by the constitution or laws of the state concerned or by this Convention, even though such violation may have been committed by persons acting in the course of their official duties.
2. The States Parties undertake:
   a. to ensure that any person claiming such remedy shall have his rights determined by the competent authority provided for by the legal system of the state;
   b. to develop the possibilities of judicial remedy; and
   c. to ensure that the competent authorities shall enforce such remedies when granted.

CHAPTER III
ECONOMIC, SOCIAL AND CULTURAL RIGHT

Article 26. Progressive Development

The States Parties undertake to adopt measures, both internally and through international cooperation, especially those of an economic and technical nature, with a view to achieving progressively, by legislation or other appropriate means, the full realization of the rights implicit in the economic, social, educational, scientific, and cultural standards set forth in the Charter of the

Organization of American States as amended by the Protocol of Buenos Aires.

CHAPTER IV
SUSPENSION OF GUARANTEES, INTERPRETATION AND APPLICATION

Article 27. Suspension of Guarantees

1. In time of war, public danger, or other emergency that threatens the independence or security of a State Party, it may take measures derogating from its obligations under the present Convention to the extent and for the period of time strictly required by the exigencies of the situation, provided that such measures are not inconsistent with its other obligations under international law and do not involve discrimination on the ground of race, colour, sex, language, religion, or social origin.
2. The foregoing provision does not authorize any suspension of the following articles: Article 3 (Right to Juridical Personality), Article 4 (Right to Life), Article 5 (Right to Humane Treatment), Article 6 (Freedom from Slavery), Article 9 (Freedom from *Ex Post Facto* Laws), Article 12 (Freedom of Conscience and Religion), Article 17 (Rights of the Family), Article 18 (Right to a Name), Article 19 (Rights of the Child), Article 20 (Right to Nationality), and Article 23 (Right to Participate in Government), or of the judicial guarantees essential for the protection of such rights.
3. Any State Party availing itself of the right of suspension shall immediately inform the other States Parties, through the Secretary General of the Organization of American States, of the provisions the application of which it has suspended, the reasons that gave rise to the suspension, and the date set for the termination of such suspension.

Article 28. Federal Clause

1. Where a State Party is constituted as a federal state, the national government of such State Party shall implement all the provisions of the Convention over whose subject matter it exercises legislative and judicial jurisdiction.
2. With respect to the provisions over whose subject matter the constituent units of the federal state have jurisdiction, the national government shall immediately take suitable measures, in accordance with its constitution and its laws, to the end that

the competent authorities of the constituent units may adopt appropriate provisions for the fulfilment of this Convention.

3. Whenever two or more States Parties agree to form a federation or other type of association, they shall take care that the resulting federal or other compact contains the provisions necessary for continuing and rendering effective the standards of this Convention in the new state that is organized.

Article 29. Restrictions Regarding Interpretation

No provision of this Convention shall be interpreted as:

a. permitting any State Party, group, or person to suppress the enjoyment or exercise of the rights and freedoms recognized in this Convention or to restrict them to a greater extent than is provided for herein;
b. restricting the enjoyment or exercise of any right or freedom recognized by virtue of the laws of any State Party or by virtue of another convention to which one of the said states is a party;
c. precluding other rights or guarantees that are inherent in the human personality or derived from representative democracy as a form of government; or
d. excluding or limiting the effect that the American Declaration of the Rights and Duties of Man and other international acts of the same nature may have.

Article 30. Scope of Restrictions

The restrictions that, pursuant to this Convention, may be placed on the enjoyment or exercise of the rights or freedoms recognized herein may not be applied except in accordance with laws enacted for reasons of general interest and in accordance with the purpose for which such restrictions have been established.

Article 31. Recognition of Other Rights

Other rights and freedoms recognized in accordance with the procedures established in Articles 76 and 77 may be included in the system of protection of this Convention.

Chapter V
Personal Responsibilities

Article 32. Relationship between Duties and Rights

1. Every person has responsibilities to his family, his community, and mankind.

2. The rights of each person are limited by the rights of others, by the security of all, and by the just demands of the general welfare, in a democratic society.

PART II
MEANS OF PROTECTION

CHAPTER VI
COMPETENT ORGANS

Article 33

The following organs shall have competence with respect to matters relating to the fulfillment of the commitments made by the States Parties to this Convention:

a. the Inter-American Commission on Human Rights, referred to as "The Commission;" and
b. the Inter-American Court of Human Rights, referred to as "The Court."

CHAPTER VII
INTER-AMERCAN COMMISSION ON HUMAN RIGHTS

Section 1. Organization

Article 34

The Inter-American Commission on Human Rights shall be composed of seven members, who shall be persons of high moral character and recognized competence in the field of human rights.

Article 35

The Commission shall represent all the member countries of the Organization of American States.

Article 36

1. The members of the Commission shall be elected in a personal capacity by the General Assembly of the Organization from a list of candidates proposed by the governments of the member states.
2. Each of those governments may propose up to three candidates, who may be nationals of the states proposing them or of any other member state of the Organization of American States. When a slate of three is proposed, at least one of the candidates shall be a national of a state other than the one proposing the slate.

Article 37

1. The members of the Commission shall be elected for a term of four years and may be reelected only once, but the terms of three of the members chosen in the first election shall expire at the end of two years. Immediately following that election the General Assembly shall determine the names of those three members by lot.
2. No two nationals of the same state may be members of the Commission.

Article 38

Vacancies that may occur on the Commission for reasons other than the normal expiration of a term shall be filled by the Permanent Council of the Organization in accordance with the provisions of the Statute of the Commission.

Article 39

The Commission shall prepare its Statute, which it shall submit to the General Assembly for approval. It shall establish its own Regulations.

Article 40

Secretariat services for the Commission shall be furnished by the appropriate specialized unit of the General Secretariat of the Organization. This unit shall be provided with the resources required to accomplish the tasks assigned to it by the Commission.

Section 2. Functions

Article 41

The main function of the Commission shall be to promote respect for and defense of human rights. In the exercise of its mandate, it shall have the following functions and powers:

a. to develop an awareness of human rights among the peoples of America;
b. to make recommendations to the governments of the member states, when it considers such action advisable, for the adoption of progressive measures in favor of human rights within the framework of their domestic law and constitutional provisions as well as appropriate measures to further the observance of those rights;
c. to prepare such studies or reports as it considers advisable in the performance of its duties;

d. to request the governments of the member states to supply it with information on the measures adopted by them in matters of human rights;

e. to respond, through the General Secretariat of the Organization of American States, to inquiries made by the member states on matters related to human rights and, within the limits of its possibilities, to provide those states with the advisory services they request;

f. to take action on petitions and other communications pursuant to its authority under the provisions of Articles 44 through 51 of this Convention; and

g. to submit an annual report to the General Assembly of the Organization of American States.

Article 42

The States Parties shall transmit to the Commission a copy of each of the reports and studies that they submit annually to the Executive Committees of the Inter-American Economic and Social Council and the Inter-American Council for Education, Science, and Culture, in their respective fields, so that the Commission may watch over the promotion of the rights implicit in the economic, social, educational, scientific, and cultural standards set forth in the Charter of the Organization of American States as amended by the Protocol of Buenos Aires.

Article 43

The States Parties undertake to provide the Commission with such information as it may request of them as to the manner in which their domestic law ensures the effective application of any provisions of this Convention.

Section 3. Competence

Article 44

Any person or group of persons, or any nongovernmental entity legally recognized in one or more member states of the Organization, may lodge petitions with the Commission containing denunciations or complaints of violation of this Convention by a State Party.

Article 45

1. Any State Party may, when it deposits its instrument of ratification of or adherence to this Convention, or at any later

time, declare that it recognizes the competence of the Commission to receive and examine communications in which a State Party alleges that another State Party has committed a violation of a human right set forth in this Convention.

2. Communications presented by virtue of this article may be admitted and examined only if they are presented by a State Party that has made a declaration recognizing the aforementioned competence of the Commission. The Commission shall not admit any communication against a State Party that has not made such a declaration.
3. A declaration concerning recognition of competence may be made to be valid for an indefinite time, for a specified period, or for a specific case.
4. Declarations shall be deposited with the General Secretariat of the Organization of American States, which shall transmit copies thereof to the member states of that Organization.

Article 46

1. Admission by the Commission of a petition or communication lodged in accordance with Articles 44 or 45 shall be subject to the following requirements:
   a. that the remedies under domestic law have been pursued and exhausted in accordance with generally recognized principles of international law;
   b. that the petition or communication is lodged within a period of six months from the date on which the party alleging violation of his rights was notified of the final judgment;
   c. that the subject of the petition or communication is not pending in another international proceeding for settlement; and
   d. that, in the case of Article 44, the petition contains the name, nationality, profession, domicile, and signature of the person or persons or of the legal representative of the entity lodging the petition.
2. The provisions of paragraphs 1.a and 1.b of this article shall not be applicable when:
   a. the domestic legislation of the state concerned does not afford due process of law for the protection of the right or rights that have allegedly been violated;
   b. the party alleging violation of his rights has been denied

access to the remedies under domestic law or has been prevented from exhausting them; or

c. there has been unwarranted delay in rendering a final judgment under the aforementioned remedies.

Article 47

The Commission shall consider inadmissible any petition or communication submitted under Articles 44 or 45 if:

a. any of the requirements indicated in Article 46 has not been met;

b. the petition or communication does not state facts that tend to establish a violation of the rights guaranteed by this Convention;

c. the statements of the petitioner or of the state indicate that the petition or communication is manifestly groundless or obviously out of order; or

d. the petition or communication is substantially the same as one previously studied by the Commission or by another international organization.

Section 4. Procedure

Article 48

1. When the Commission receives a petition or communication alleging violation of any of the rights protected by this Convention, it shall proceed as follows:

a. If it considers the petition or communication admissible, it shall request information from the government of the state indicated as being responsible for the alleged violations and shall furnish that government a transcript of the pertinent portions of the petition or communication. This information shall be submitted within a reasonable period to be determined by the Commission in accordance with the circumstances of each case.

b. After the information has been received, or after the period established has elapsed and the information has not been received, the Commission shall ascertain whether the grounds for the petition or communication still exist. If they do not, the Commission shall order the record to be closed.

c. The Commission may also declare the petition or

communication inadmissible or out of order on the basis of information or evidence subsequently received.

d. If the record has not been closed, the Commission shall, with the knowledge of the parties, examine the matter set forth in the petition or communication in order to verify the facts. If necessary and advisable, the Commission shall carry out an investigation, for the effective conduct of which it shall request, and the states concerned shall furnish to it, all necessary facilities.

e. The Commission may request the states concerned to furnish any pertinent information and, if so requested, shall hear oral statements or receive written statements from the parties concerned.

f. The Commission shall place itself at the disposal of the parties concerned with a view to reaching a friendly settlement of the matter on the basis of respect for the human rights recognized in this Convention.

2. However, in serious and urgent cases, only the presentation of a petition or communication that fulfills all the formal requirements of admissibility shall be necessary in order for the Commission to conduct an investigation with the prior consent of the state in whose territory a violation has allegedly been committed.

Article 49

If a friendly settlement has been reached in accordance with paragraph 1.f of Article 48, the Commission shall draw up a report, which shall be transmitted to the petitioner and to the States Parties to this Convention, and shall then be communicated to the Secretary General of the Organization of American States for publication. This report shall contain a brief statement of the facts and of the solution reached. If any party in the case so requests, the fullest possible information shall be provided to it.

Article 50

1. If a settlement is not reached, the Commission shall, within the time limit established by its Statute, draw up a report setting forth the facts and stating its conclusions. If the report, in whole or in part, does not represent the unanimous agreement of the members of the Commission, any member may attach to it a separate opinion. The written and oral statements made by

the parties in accordance with paragraph 1.e of Article 48 shall also be attached to the report.

2. The report shall be transmitted to the states concerned, which shall not be at liberty to publish it.
3. In transmitting the report, the Commission may make such proposals and recommendations as it sees fit.

Article 51

1. If, within a period of three months from the date of the transmittal of the report of the Commission to the states concerned, the matter has not either been settled or submitted by the Commission or by the state concerned to the Court and its jurisdiction accepted, the Commission may, by the vote of an absolute majority of its members, set forth its opinion and conclusions concerning the question submitted for its consideration.
2. Where appropriate, the Commission shall make pertinent recommendations and shall prescribe a period within which the state is to take the measures that are incumbent upon it to remedy the situation examined.
3. When the prescribed period has expired, the Commission shall decide by the vote of an absolute majority of its members whether the state has taken adequate measures and whether to publish its report.

CHAPTER VIII
INTER-AMERICAN COURT OF HUMAN RIGHTS

Section 1. Organization

Article 52

1. The Court shall consist of seven judges, nationals of the member states of the Organization, elected in an individual capacity from among jurists of the highest moral authority and of recognized competence in the field of human rights, who possess the qualifications required for the exercise of the highest judicial functions in conformity with the law of the state of which they are nationals or of the state that proposes them as candidates.
2. No two judges may be nationals of the same state.

Article 53

1. The judges of the Court shall be elected by secret ballot by an

absolute majority vote of the States Parties to the Convention, in the General Assembly of the Organization, from a panel of candidates proposed by those states.

2. Each of the States Parties may propose up to three candidates, nationals of the state that proposes them or of any other member state of the Organization of American States. When a slate of three is proposed, at least one of the candidates shall be national of a State other than the one proposing the slate.

Article 54

1. The judges of the Court shall be elected for a term of six years and may be re-elected only once. The term of three of the judges chosen in the first election shall expire at the end of three years. Immediately after the election, the names of the three judges shall be determined by lot in the General Assembly.
2. A judge elected to replace a judge whose term has not expired shall complete the term of the latter.
3. The judges shall continue in office until the expiration of their term. However, they shall continue to serve with regard to cases that they have begun to hear and that are still pending, for which purposes they shall not be replaced by the newly elected judges.

Article 55

1. If a judge is a national of any of the States Parties to a case submitted to the Court, he shall retain his right to hear that case.
2. If one of the judges called upon to hear a case should be a national of one of the States Parties to the case, any other State Party in the case may appoint a person of its choice to serve on the Court as an *ad hoc* judge.
3. If among the judges called upon to hear a case none is a national of any of the States Parties to the case, each of the latter may appoint an *ad hoc* judge.
4. An *ad hoc* judge shall possess the qualifications indicated in Article 52.
5. If several States Parties to the Convention should have the same interest in a case, they shall be considered as a single party for purposes of the above provisions. In case of doubt, the Court shall decide.

Article 56

Five judges shall constitute a quorum for the transaction of business by the Court.

Article 57

The Commission shall appear in all cases before the Court.

Article 58

1. The Court shall have its seat at the place determined by the States Parties to the Convention in the General Assembly of the Organization; however, it may convene in the territory of any member state of the Organization of American States when a majority of the Court considers it desirable, and with the prior consent of the state concerned. The seat of the Court may be changed by the States Parties to the Convention in the General Assembly by a two-thirds vote.
2. The Court shall appoint its own Secretary.
3. The Secretary shall have his office at the place where the Court has its seat and shall attend the meetings that the Court may hold away from its seat.

Article 59

The Court shall establish its Secretariat, which shall function under the direction of the Secretary of the Court, in accordance with the administrative standards of the General Secretariat of the Organization in all respects not incompatible with the independence of the Court. The staff of the Court's Secretariat shall be appointed by the Secretary General of the Organization, in consultation with the Secretary of the Court.

Article 60

The Court shall draw up its Statute which it shall submit to the General Assembly for approval. It shall adopt its own Rules of Procedure.

Section 2. Jurisdiction and Functions

Article 61

1. Only the States Parties and the Commission shall have the right to submit a case to the Court.
2. In order for the Court to hear a case, it is necessary that the procedures set forth in Articles 48 and 50 shall have been completed.

Article 62

1. A State Party may, upon depositing its instrument of ratification or adherence to this Convention, or at any subsequent time, declare that it recognizes as binding, ipsofacto, and not requiring special agreement, the jurisdiction of the Court on all matters relating to the interpretation or application of this Convention.
2. Such declaration may be made unconditionally, on the condition of reciprocity, for a specified period, or for specific cases. It shall be presented to the Secretary General of the Organization, who shall transmit copies thereof to the other member states of the Organization and to the Secretary of the Court.
3. The jurisdiction of the Court shall comprise all cases concerning the interpretation and application of the provisions of this Convention that are submitted to it, provided that the States Parties to the case recognize or have recognized such jurisdiction, whether by special declaration pursuant to the preceding paragraphs, or by a special agreement.

Article 63

1. If the Court finds that there has been a violation of a right or freedom protected by this Convention, the Court shall rule that the injured party be ensured the enjoyment of his right or freedom that was violated. It shall also rule, if appropriate, that the consequences of the measure or situation that constituted the breach of such right or freedom be remedied and that fair compensation be paid to the injured party.
2. In cases of extreme gravity and urgency, and when necessary to avoid irreparable damage to persons, the Court shall adopt such provisional measures as it deems pertinent in matters it has under consideration. With respect to a case not yet submitted to the Court, it may act at the request of the Commission.

Article 64

1. The member states of the Organization may consult the Court regarding the interpretation of this Convention or of other treaties concerning the protection of human rights in the American states. Within their spheres of competence, the organs listed in Chapter X of the Charter of the Organization

of American States, as amended by the Protocol of Buenos Aires, may in like manner consult the Court.

2. The Court, at the request of a member state of the Organization, may provide that state with opinions regarding the compatibility of any of its domestic laws with the aforesaid international instruments.

Article 65

To each regular session of the General Assembly of the Organization of American States the Court shall submit, for the Assembly's consideration, a report on its work during the previous year. It shall specify, in particular, the cases in which a state has not complied with its judgments, making any pertinent recommendations.

Section 3. Procedure

Article 66

1. Reasons shall be given for the judgment of the Court.
2. If the judgment does not represent in whole or in part the unanimous opinion of the judges, any judge shall be entitled to have his dissenting or separate opinion attached to the judgment.

Article 67

The judgment of the Court shall be final and not subject to appeal. In case of disagreement as to the meaning or scope of the judgment, the Court shall interpret it at the request of any of the parties, provided the request is made within ninety days from the date of notification of the judgment.

Article 68

1. The States Parties to the Convention undertake to comply with the judgment of the Court in any case to which they are parties.
2. That part of a judgment that stipulates compensatory damages may be executed in the country concerned in accordance with domestic procedure governing the execution of judgments against the state.

Article 69

The parties to the case shall be notified of the judgment of the Court and it shall be transmitted to the States Parties to the Convention.

CHAPTER IX : COMMON PROVISIONS

Article 70

1. The judges of the Court and the members of the Commission shall enjoy, from the moment of their election and throughout their term of office, the immunities extended to diplomatic agents in accordance with international law. During the exercise of their official function they shall, in addition, enjoy the diplomatic privileges necessary for the performance of their duties.
2. At no time shall the judges of the Court or the members of the Commission be held liable for any decisions or opinions issued in the exercise of their functions.

Article 71

The position of judge of the Court or member of the Commission is incompatible with any other activity that might affect the independence or impartiality of such judge or member, as determined in the respective statutes.

Article 72

The judges of the Court and the members of the Commission shall receive emoluments and travel allowances in the form and under the conditions set forth in their statutes, with due regard for the importance and independence of their office. Such emoluments and travel allowances shall be determined in the budget of the Organization of American States, which shall also include the expenses of the Court and its Secretariat. To this end, the Court shall draw up its own budget and submit it for approval to the General Assembly through the General Secretariat. The latter may not introduce any changes in it.

Article 73

The General Assembly may, only at the request of the Commission or the Court, as the case may be, determine sanctions to be applied against members of the Commission or judges of the Court when there are justifiable grounds for such action as set forth in the respective statutes. A vote of a two-thirds majority of the member states of the Organization shall be required for a decision in the case of members of the Commission and, in the case of judges of the Court, a two-thirds majority vote of the States Parties to the Convention shall also be required.

PART III
GENERAL AND TRANSITORY PROVISIONS

CHAPTER X
SIGNATURE, RATIFICATION, RESERVATIONS, AMENDMENTS, PROTOCOLS AND DENUNCIATION

Article 74

1. This Convention shall be open for signature and ratification by or adherence of any member state of the Organization of American States.
2. Ratification of or adherence to this Convention shall be made by the deposit of an instrument of ratification or adherence with the General Secretariat of the Organization of American States. As soon as eleven states have deposited their instruments of ratification or adherence, the Convention shall enter into force. With respect to any state that ratifies or adheres thereafter, the Convention shall enter into force on the date of the deposit of its instrument of ratification or adherence.
3. The Secretary General shall inform all member states of the Organization of the entry into force of the Convention.

Article 75

This Convention shall be subject to reservations only in conformity with the provisions of the Vienna Convention on the Law of Treaties signed on May 23, 1969.

Article 76

1. Proposals to amend this Convention may be submitted to the General Assembly for the action it deems appropriate by any State Party directly, and by the Commission or the Court through the Secretary General.
2. Amendments shall enter into force for the States ratifying them on the date when two-thirds of the States Parties to this Convention have deposited their respective instruments of ratification. With respect to the other States Parties, the amendments shall enter into force on the dates on which they deposit their respective instruments of ratification.

Article 77

1. In accordance with Article 31, any State Party and the Commission may submit proposed protocols to this

Convention for consideration by the States Parties at the General Assembly with a view to gradually including other rights and freedoms within its system of protection.

2. Each protocol shall determine the manner of its entry into force and shall be applied only among the States Parties to it.

Article 78

1. The States Parties may denounce this Convention at the expiration of a five-year period from the date of its entry into force and by means of notice given one year in advance. Notice of the denunciation shall be addressed to the Secretary General of the Organization, who shall inform the other States Parties.
2. Such a denunciation shall not have the effect of releasing the State Party concerned from the obligations contained in this Convention with respect to any act that may constitute a violation of those obligations and that has been taken by that state prior to the effective date of denunciation.

CHAPTER XI
TRANSITORY PROVISIONS

Section 1. Inter-American Commission on Human Rights

Article 79

Upon the entry into force of this Convention, the Secretary General shall, in writing, request each member state of the Organization to present, within ninety days, its candidates for membership on the Inter-American Commission on Human Rights. The Secretary General shall prepare a list in alphabetical order of the candidates presented, and transmit it to the member states of the Organization at least thirty days prior to the next session of the General Assembly.

Article 80

The members of the Commission shall be elected by secret ballot of the General Assembly from the list of candidates referred to in Article 79. The candidates who obtain the largest number of votes and an absolute majority of the votes of the representatives of the member states shall be declared elected. Should it become necessary to have several ballots in order to elect all the members of the Commission, the candidates who receive the smallest number of votes shall be eliminated successively, in the manner determined by the General Assembly.

Section 2. Inter-American Court of Human Rights

Article 81

Upon the entry into force of this Convention, the Secretary General shall, in writing, request each State Party to present, within ninety days, its candidates for membership on the Inter-American Court of Human Rights. The Secretary General shall prepare a list in alphabetical order of the candidates presented and transmit it to the States Parties at least thirty days prior to the next session of the General Assembly.

Article 82

The judges of the Court shall be elected from the list of candidates referred to in Article 81, by secret ballot of the States Parties to the Convention in the General Assembly. The candidates who obtain the largest number of votes and an absolute majority of the votes of the representatives of the States Parties shall be declared elected. Should it become necessary to have several ballots in order to elect all the judges of the Court, the candidates who receive the smallest number of votes shall be eliminated successively, in the manner determined by the States Parties.

Appendix IX

Commonwealth of Independent States Convention on Human Rights and Fundamental Freedoms (1995)

The Participant States of the Commonwealth of Independent States, hereinafter referred to as the Contracting Parties,

Having regard to the Universal Declaration of Human Rights, the International Covenanton Economic, Social and Cultural Rights, the International Covenant on Civil and Political Rights and the Optional Protocol thereto, as well as to the international obligations concerning human rights entered into within the framework of the OSCE (CSCE);

Considering that the above-mentioned instruments are aimed at securing theuniversal and effective recognition and observance of the rights enshrined therein;

Having regard to the Declaration of the Heads of Participating States of the Commonwealth of Independent States on international obligations in the field ofhuman rights and fundamental freedoms;

Considering that the observance of international standards in the field of human rights by all Member States of the Commonwealth of Independent States, and the development and fostering of respect for human rights and fundamental freedoms forall, irrespective of race, sex, language, political beliefs, religion and social origin,contribute to the deepening of democratic reforms, economic and social growth andthe strengthening of law and order;

Striving for the effective fulfillment of their obligations to protect human rights and fundamental freedoms, in the spirit of the concerting of the efforts of the Contracting Parties for the purpose of asserting the ideals of freedom and the rule of law, preventing violations of human rights and fundamental freedoms, upholding the traditions of tolerance and friendship between peoples, and reinforcing civil peace and accord;

Assuming that such efforts will foster universal respect for and observance of human rights and fundamental freedoms in accordance with the basic instruments of international law in the field of human rights; Have agreed as follows:

Article 1

The Contracting Parties shall secure to everyone within their jurisdiction the rights and freedoms set out in the present Convention.

Article 2

1. Everyone's right to life shall be protected by law. No one shall be deprived ofhis life intentionally. Until abolished, the death penalty may be applied only inpursuance of a judicial sentence for particularly grave offences.
2. As a rule, women may not be sentenced to the death penalty. The death penalty may not be imposed on women who are pregnant at the time of sentencing, nor may it be executed in the case of women who are pregnant when the sentence is to be carried out.
3. The death penalty may not be imposed on persons for crimes committed by them before they attained the age of eighteen years.
4. Deprivation of life shall not be regarded as inflicted in contravention of the provisions of this Article when it results from the use of force solely in such cases of extreme necessity and necessary defense as are provided for in national legislation.

Article 3

No one shall be subjected to torture or to cruel, inhuman or degrading treatment or punishment. No one shall be subjected to medical or scientific experiments without his free consent.

Article 4

1. No one shall be held in slavery or servitude.
2. No one shall be constrained to perform forced or compulsory labour.

3. The term 'forced or compulsory labour' as used in the present Article shall not include:
   (a) any work required to be done in the ordinary course of detention imposed in accordance with the provisions of Article 5 of this Convention or during conditional release from such detention;
   (b) any service of a military character or, in the case of Contracting Parties recognising the right of conscientious objection on political or religious/ethical grounds, service exacted instead of compulsory military service;
   (c) any service exacted in the case of an emergency or calamity threatening the life or well-being of the community;
   (d) any work or service which forms part of normal civic obligations;
   (e) the fulfilment by parents of their duty to create the necessary conditions for their children, and by children who have reached the age of majority of their duty to support parents unable to work and requiring assistance.

Article 5

1. Everyone shall have the right to liberty and security of person. No one shall be deprived of his liberty save in the following cases and in accordance with a procedure established by national legislation:
   (a) the lawful detention of a person after conviction by a competent court;
   (b) the lawful arrest or detention of a person;
   (c) the lawful detention of a minor for the purpose of referring his case for investigation, sentencing or trial.
2. Everyone who is arrested shall be informed, at the time of his arrest, in a language which he understands, of the reasons for his arrest.
3. Everyone who is deprived of his liberty by arrest or detention, in accordance with national legislation, shall be entitled to have the lawfulness of his arrest or detention examined by a court.
4. Everyone who is deprived of his liberty shall be entitled to humane treatment and to respect for his dignity as a human being.Persons who have been subjected to unlawful arrest or detention shall be entitled, in accordance with national legislation, to compensation for the damage caused.

Article 6

1. All persons shall be equal before the judicial system. In the determination of any charge against him, everyone shall be entitled to a fair and public hearing within a reasonable time by an independent and impartial court.The decisions of the court or the sentence shall be pronounced publicly, but all or part of the trial may take place *in camera* for reasons of public order or state secrecy or where the interests of juveniles or the protection of the private life of the parties so require.
2. Everyone charged with a criminal offence shall be presumed innocent until proved guilty according to law.
3. Everyone charged with a criminal offence shall have the following minimum rights:
   (a) to be informed promptly and in detail, in a language which he understands, of the nature and cause of the accusation against him;
   (b) to have adequate time and facilities for the preparation of his defence;
   (c) to defend himself in person or through legal assistance of his own choosing or to have legal assistance assigned to him whenever the interests of justice so require, as well as to be provided with legal assistance free of charge in cases specified innational legislation;
   (d) to make applications to the court concerning the examination of witnesses, the carrying out of investigations, the obtaining of documents, the commissioning of expert appraisals and other procedural acts;
   (e) to have the free assistance of an interpreter if he cannot understand or speak the language used in court;
   (f) not to be forced to testify against himself or plead guilty.

Article 7

1. No one shall be held liable for an act which did not constitute an offence undernational legislation or international law at the time when it was committed. Nor shalla heavier penalty be imposed than the one that was applicable at the time the offencewas committed. If, after an offence is committed, a law establishes a lesser punishment for it or eliminates liability for it, the new law shall be applicable.
2. No one shall be convicted or punished a second time for an

offence for which he has already been convicted or punished in accordance with national legislation.Every convicted person shall be entitled, in accordance with the law, to have the judgment of the court reviewed by a higher judicial body as well as apply for a pardon or request a lighter sentence.

Article 8

No one shall be deprived of his liberty merely on the ground of his inability to fulfilla contractual obligation of any kind.

Article 9

1. Everyone shall have the right to respect for his private and family life, his home and his correspondence.
2. There shall be no interference by a public authority with the exercise of this right except such as is in accordance with the law.and is necessary in a democratic society in the interests of national security, public safety, public order, public health and morals or for the protection of the rights and freedoms of others.

Article 10

1. Everyone shall have the right to freedom of thought, conscience and faith. Thisright shall include freedom to choose one's religion or belief and freedom, either aloneor in community with others, to engage in religious worship, attend and performreligious and ritual ceremonies and act in accordance with them.
2. Freedom to manifest one's religion or beliefs shall be subject only to suchlimitations as are prescribed by law and are necessary in a democratic society in theinterests of national security, public safety, public order, public health or morals orfor the protection of the rights and freedoms of others.

Article 11

1. Everyone shall have the right to freedom of expression. This right shall include freedom to hold opinions and to receive and impart information and ideas by any legalmeans without interference by a public authority and regardless of frontiers.
2. The exercise of these freedoms, since it carries with it duties and responsibilities, may be subject to such formalities, conditions and restrictions as are prescribedby law and are necessary in a democratic society, in the interests of national

security, public safety or public order or for the protection of the rights and freedoms of others.

Article 12

1. Everyone shall have the right to freedom of peaceful assembly and to freedom of association with others, including the right to form and to join trade unions for the protection of his interests.
2. **No restrictions shall be placed on the exercise of these rights other than such as are prescribed by law and are necessary in a democratic society in the interests ofnational security or public safety, public order, public health or morals or for theprotection of the rights and freedoms of others. This Article shall not precludethe imposition of lawful restrictions on the exercise of these rights by members of the armed forces or by members of the law-enforcement or administrative organs of the State.**

Article 13

1. Men and women of marriageable age shall have the right to marry and to founda family, according to the national legislation governing the exercise of that right.
2. No marriage shall be entered into without the free and full consent of the intending spouses.
3. For the purpose of creating the necessary conditions for the full development of the family, which is the fundamental unit of society, the Contracting Parties shall contribute to the economic, legal and social protection of family life by such meansas social and family allowances, tax relief, the provision of accommodation for families, grants for newly-married couples and other appropriate measures.

Article 14

1. Everyone shall have the right to work and to protection from unemployment, as well as to equal remuneration for equal work, including work-related benefits, to identical conditions in respect of work of equal value and to equal treatment in the assessment of the quality of his work.
2. For the purpose of ensuring that working women may effectively exercise their rights, the Contracting Parties shall:
   (a) grant leave with pay, adequate social security benefits, or allowances frompublic funds for women taking leave

before and after childbirth within the period oftime prescribed by national legislation;

(b) regard as unlawful any notice of dismissal served by an employer on awoman during her absence on maternity leave or at such time that the period of notice would expire during her absence;

(c) ensure that mothers who nurse their children have sufficient free time for that purpose;

(d) regulate the employment of women for work on night shifts in industry;

(e) regulate the employment of women for underground mining activities as well as for other types of work that are unsuitable for women because of their dangerousness, harmfulness to health or arduousness.

Article 15

For the purpose of ensuring that the right to health protection may be effectively exercised, the Contracting Parties shall, either directly or in conjunction with publicor private bodies, take the appropriate measures, aimed *inter alia* at:

(a) eliminating the causes of health deterioration as far as possible;

(b) providing advisory services and an instructional scheme for the fortification of health and the encouragement of personal responsibility in health matters;

(c) creating sanitary and hygienic conditions calculated to prevent, as far as possible, outbreaks of epidemic, endemic and other diseases.

Article 16

1. Everyone shall have the right to social security, including social insurance, according to his age, in cases of illness, invalidity, loss of bread-winner and upbringing of children as well as in other cases provided for in national legislation.
2. For the purpose of ensuring that the right to social and medical assistance maybe effectively exercised, the Contracting Parties shall ensure that any person lacking sufficient means and unable to obtain such means through his own efforts or from other sources, particularly in the form of benefits under a social security system, receives the necessary assistance and in the case of illness, such care as is required by his condition.

3. For the purpose of ensuring that the right of mothers and children to social andeconomic protection may be effectively exercised, the Contracting Parties shall takeall appropriate and necessary measures to that end, including the establishment and maintenance of suitable institutions or services.

Article 17

Every minor child shall have the right to such special protective measures as his particular situation requires on the part of the family, society and the State.

Article 18

For the purpose of ensuring that persons who are physically or mentally unfit for work may effectively exercise their right to occupational rehabilitation, vocational training and social reintegration facilities, the Contracting Parties shall :

(a) take appropriate measures to provide educational establishments, including, where necessary, public or private specialized institutions;

(b) take appropriate measures for the occupational rehabilitation of persons unfit for work, including the setting up of specialized occupational rehabilitation services and establishments with special working conditions, as well as measures toencourage employers to engage disabled persons.

Article 19

Everyone whose rights and freedoms are violated shall be entitled to be effectively restored to his rights and freedoms in accordance with national legislation.

Article 20

1. All shall be equal before the law and shall be entitled, without any discrimination, to equal protection of the law.
2. The enjoyment of the rights and freedoms set forth in this Convention shall be guaranteed without discrimination on any ground such as sex, race, colour, language, religion, political or other opinion, national or social origin, association with a national minority, property or official capacity, place of birth or other status.

Article 21

Persons belonging to national minorities shall not be denied the right, either individually or collectively, to express, preserve and develop, without hindrance, their ethnic, linguistic, cultural or religious identity.

Article 22

1. Everyone who is lawfully within the territory of any Contracting Party shall, within that territory, have the right to liberty of movement and freedom to choose his residence.
2. Everyone shall be free to leave any country, including his own.
3. No restrictions shall be placed on the exercise of the rights set out in paragraphs1 and 2 of this Article other than such as are prescribed by the law in the interests ofnational security or public safety, public order, public health or morals or for the protection of the rights and freedoms of others.
4. The rights set forth in paragraph 1 of this Article may also be subject, in particularareas, to restrictions imposed in accordance with law and justified by the public interest.

Article 23

Everyone, regardless of where he may be, shall have the right to recognition of his legal capacity.

Article 24

1. Everyone shall have the right to citizenship.
2. No one shall be arbitrarily deprived of his citizenship or of the right to change it.

Article 25

1. No one shall he expelled, under an individual procedure or as a result of a collective measure, from the territory of the State of which he is a citizen.
2. No one shall be deprived of the right to enter the territory of the State of which he is a citizen.
3. Aliens who are lawfully in the territory of any Contracting Party may be expelled only in application of a lawful decision, and they shall have the opportunity of appealing against their expulsion.
4. Collective expulsion of aliens shall be prohibited.

Article 26

1. Every natural and legal person shall have the right to own property. No one shall be deprived of his property except in the public interest, under a judicial procedure and in

accordance with the conditions laid down in national legislation and the generally recognized principles of international law.

2. However, the foregoing provisions shall in no way affect the right of the Contracting Parties to adopt such laws as they deem necessary to control the use of items withdrawn from general circulation in the national or public interest.

Article 27

1. No person shall be denied the right to education. In the exercise of any functions which the Contracting Parties assume in relation to education and to teaching, they shall respect the right of parents to ensure for their children such education and teaching as corresponds with their own convictions and national traditions.
2. Elementary and fundamental education of a general kind shall be compulsory and free of charge.
3. Each Contracting Party shall set a minimum age up to which secondary education shall be compulsory and which may not be lower than the minimum age for employment established by law in accordance with internationally recognized standards.

Article 28

For the purpose of ensuring that the right to vocational training may be effectively exercised, the Contracting Parties shall:

1. provide or encourage, as far as necessary, technical or vocational training for all, including disabled persons, in agreement with trade union organisations, as wellas offer the opportunity to receive higher education exclusively on the basis of personal abilities;
2. establish or help to establish, as far as necessary:
   (a) an appropriate, widely available training system for workers;
   (b) special centres for such vocational retraining of workers as is called for by technical progress or by new trends in the occupational field;
3. foster the full exercise of such advantages as are available under the relevantmeasures, including those aimed at:
   (a) reducing or abolishing dues and extra charges;
   (b) providing material help where appropriate;

(c) incorporating into the normal working day, at the request of employers, thetime spent on the further training of workers during work;

(d) guaranteeing, with appropriate supervision and in agreement with trade union organisations, the effectiveness of apprenticeships and other training measures for young workers, as well as the proper protection of young workers' interests as a whole.

Article 29

In accordance with national legislation, everyone shall have the right and opportunityand in the State of which he is a citizen:

(a) to take part in the management and conduct of public affairs, either directlyor through freely chosen representatives;

(b) to vote and to be elected at elections held on the basis of universal and equal suffrage by secret ballot, that guarantees the free expression of the will of voters;

(c) to have access, on general conditions of equality, to the public service of his country.

Article 30

Nothing in Articles 11, 21 and 20 shall be regarded as preventing the Contracting Parties from imposing restrictions on the political activity of alien citizens and stateless persons.

Article 31

Nothing in this present Convention may be interpreted as implying for any Contracting Party, group or individual any right to engage in any activity or perform any actaimed at the destruction of any of the rights and freedoms set forth in the Convention.

Article 32

The restrictions permitted under this Convention to the said rights and freedoms shall not be applied for any purpose other than those for which they have been prescribed.

Article 33

Nothing in this Convention may be interpreted as limiting or detracting from any of the human rights and fundamental freedoms recognised and guaranteed under the legislation of the Contracting Party concerned or under a fundamental international instrument in the human rights field to which it has acceded.

Article 34

Monitoring of the execution of this Convention shall be effected by the Human Rights Commission of the Commonwealth of Independent States (HRC CIS), whose Regulations form a separate section of the Convention.

Article 35

1. In time of war or other emergency situation threatening the higher interests of any Contracting Party, that Party may take measures derogating from its obligations under this Convention to the extent strictly required by the gravity of the situation, provided that such measures are not inconsistent with other obligations under international lawand do not entail discrimination on the grounds set out in Article 20 of the Convention.
2. No derogation from Article 2 of this Convention, except in respect of deaths resulting from lawful military action, or from Articles 3, 4 (paragraph 1) and 7 shall be made under paragraph 1 of the present Article.
3. Any Contracting Party availing itself of this right of derogation shall keep the depositary of this Convention informed of the measures it has taken and of the reasons there for. It shall also inform the depositary when such measures have ceased to operate and the provisions of the Convention are again being fully executed.

Article 36

1. Any Contracting Party may, when signing this Convention or when depositing its instrument of ratification, make a reservation in respect of any particular provisionof the Convention concerning the fact that any law then in force in its territory is not in conformity with that provision. Reservations of a general character shall not be permitted under this Article.
2. Any reservation made under this Article shall contain a brief statement of the law concerned.

Article 37

1. Any Contracting Party may denounce this Convention after six months' notice contained in a notification addressed to the depositary, who shall inform the other Contracting Parties.
2. Such denunciation shall not have the effect of releasing the Contracting Partyconcerned from its obligations under this

Convention in respect of any act which, being capable of constituting a violation of such obligations, may have been performed by it before the date on which the denunciation became effective.

Article 38

1. This Convention, including the Regulations of the Human Rights Commission of the Commonwealth of Independent States, shall enter into force from the date of deposit of the third notification confirming that a Contracting Party has implemented the internal procedures necessary for its entry into force.
2. For the other Contracting Parties, this Convention shall enter into force fromthe date of receipt by the depositary of a notification confirming that they have implemented the internal procedures referred to in paragraph 1 of the present Article.

Article 39

After this Convention has entered into force, it shall be open to accession by other States sharing its aims and principles, by means of a notification delivered to the depositary confirming that they have implemented the internal procedures referred to in Article 38, paragraph 1, of the Convention. The date of receipt by the depositary of such notification shall be the date of entry into force of the Convention for the State concerned.

Done in Minsk on 26 May 1995 in Russian in a single authentic copy, to be kept in the Executive Secretariat of the Commonwealth of Independent States, which shall transmit certified copies there of to each of the States signatories to the Convention.

APPENDIX X

UN Code of Conduct for Law Enforcement Officials

G.A. res. 34/169, annex, 34 U.N. GAOR Supp. (No. 46) at 186, U.N. Doc. A/34/46 (1979).

Article 1

Law enforcement officials shall at all times fulfil the duty imposed upon them by law, by serving the community and by protecting all persons against illegal acts, consistent with the high degree of responsibility required by their profession.

Commentary:

(a) The term "law enforcement officials', includes all officers of the law, whether appointed or elected, who exercise police powers, especially the powers of arrest or detention.

(b) In countries where police powers are exercised by military authorities, whether uniformed or not, or by State security forces, the definition of law enforcement officials shall be regarded as including officers of such services.

(c) Service to the community is intended to include particularly the rendition of services of assistance to those members of the community who by reason of personal, economic, social or other emergencies are in need of immediate aid.

(d) This provision is intended to cover not only all violent, predatory and harmful acts, but extends to the full range of prohibitions under penal statutes. It extends to conduct by persons not capable of incurring criminal liability.

Article 2

In the performance of their duty, law enforcement officials shall respect and protect human dignity and maintain and uphold the human rights of all persons.

Commentary:

(a) The human rights in question are identified and protected by national and international law. Among the relevant international instruments are the Universal Declaration of Human Rights, the International Covenant on Civil and Political Rights, the Declaration on the Protection of All Persons from Being Subjected to Torture and Other Cruel, Inhuman or Degrading Treatment or Punishment, the United Nations Declaration on the Elimination of All Forms of Racial Discrimination, the International Convention on the Elimination of All Forms of Racial Discrimination, the International Convention on the Suppression and Punishment of the Crime of Apartheid, the Convention on the Prevention and Punishment of the Crime of Genocide, the Standard Minimum Rules for the Treatment of Prisoners and the Vienna Convention on Consular Relations.

(b) National commentaries to this provision should indicate regional or national provisions identifying and protecting these rights.

Article 3

Law enforcement officials may use force only when strictly necessary and to the extent required for the performance of their duty.

Commentary:

(a) This provision emphasizes that the use of force by law enforcement officials should be exceptional; while it implies that law enforcement officials may be authorized to use force as is reasonably necessary under the circumstances for the prevention of crime or in effecting or assisting in the lawful arrest of offenders or suspected offenders, no force going beyond that may be used.

(b) National law ordinarily restricts the use of force by law enforcement officials in accordance with a principle of proportionality. It is to be understood that such national principles of proportionality are to be respected in the interpretation of this provision. In no case should this provision be interpreted to authorize the use of force which is disproportionate to the legitimate objective to be achieved.

(c) The use of firearms is considered an extreme measure. Every effort should be made to exclude the use of firearms, especially against children. In general, firearms should not be used except when a suspected offender offers armed resistance or otherwise jeopardizes the lives of others and less extreme measures are not sufficient to restrain or apprehend the suspected offender. In every instance in which a firearm is discharged, a report should be made promptly to the competent authorities.

Article 4

Matters of a confidential nature in the possession of law enforcement officials shall be kept confidential, unless the performance of duty or the needs of justice strictly require otherwise.

Commentary :

By the nature of their duties, law enforcement officials obtain information which may relate to private lives or be potentially harmful to the interests, and especially the reputation, of others. Great care should be exercised in safeguarding and using such information, which should be disclosed only in the performance of duty or to serve the needs of justice. Any disclosure of such information for other purposes is wholly improper.

Article 5

No law enforcement official may inflict, instigate or tolerate any act of torture or other cruel, inhuman or degrading treatment or punishment, nor may any law enforcement official invoke superior orders or exceptional circumstances such as a state of war or a threat of war, a threat to national security, internal political instability or any other public emergency as a justification of torture or other cruel, inhuman or degrading treatment or punishment .

Commentary:

(a) This prohibition derives from the Declaration on the Protection of All Persons from Being Subjected to Torture and Other Cruel, Inhuman or Degrading Treatment or Punishment, adopted by the General Assembly, according to which: "[Such an act is] an offence to human dignity and shall be condemned as a denial of the purposes of the Charter of the United Nations and as a violation of the human rights and fundamental freedoms proclaimed in the Universal Declaration of Human Rights [and other international human rights instruments]."

(b) The Declaration defines torture as follows:
"... torture means any act by which severe pain or suffering, whether physical or mental, is intentionally inflicted by or at the instigation of a public official on a person for such purposes as obtaining from him or a third person information or confession, punishing him for an act he has committed or is suspected of having committed, or intimidating him or other persons. It does not include pain or suffering arising only from, inherent in or incidental to, lawful sanctions to the extent consistent with the Standard Minimum Rules for the Treatment of Prisoners."

(c) The term "cruel, inhuman or degrading treatment or punishment" has not been defined by the General Assembly but should be interpreted so as to extend the widest possible protection against abuses, whether physical or mental.

Article 6

Law enforcement officials shall ensure the full protection of the health of persons in their custody and, in particular, shall take immediate action to secure medical attention whenever required.

Commentary :

(a) "Medical attention", which refers to services rendered by any medical personnel, including certified medical practitioners and paramedics, shall be secured when needed or requested.

(b) While the medical personnel are likely to be attached to the law enforcement operation, law enforcement officials must take into account the judgement of such personnel when they recommend providing the person in custody with appropriate treatment through, or in consultation with, medical personnel from outside the law enforcement operation.

(c) It is understood that law enforcement officials shall also secure medical attention for victims of violations of law or of accidents occurring in the course of violations of law.

Article 7

Law enforcement officials shall not commit any act of corruption. They shall also rigorously oppose and combat all such acts.

Commentary :

(a) Any act of corruption, in the same way as any other abuse of authority, is incompatible with the profession of law enforcement officials. The law must be enforced fully with respect to any law enforcement official who commits an act of corruption, as Governments cannot expect to enforce the law among their citizens if they cannot, or will not, enforce the law against their own agents and within their agencies.

(b) While the definition of corruption must be subject to national law, it should be understood to encompass the commission or omission of an act in the performance of or in connection with one's duties, in response to gifts, promises or incentives demanded or accepted, or the wrongful receipt of these once the act has been committed or omitted.

(c) The expression "act of corruption" referred to above should be understood to encompass attempted corruption.

Article 8

Law enforcement officials shall respect the law and the present Code. They shall also, to the best of their capability, prevent and rigorously oppose any violations of them.

Law enforcement officials who have reason to believe that a violation of the present Code has occurred or is about to occur shall report the matter to their superior authorities and, where necessary, to other appropriate authorities or organs vested with reviewing or remedial power.

Commentary :

(a) This Code shall be observed whenever it has been incorporated into national legislation or practice. If legislation or practice contains stricter provisions than those of the present Code, those stricter provisions shall be observed.

(b) The article seeks to preserve the balance between the need for internal discipline of the agency on which public safety is largely dependent, on the one hand, and the need for dealing with violations of basic human rights, on the other. Law enforcement officials shall report violations within the chain of command and take other lawful action outside the chain of command only when no other remedies are available or effective. It is understood that law enforcement officials shall not suffer administrative or other penalties because they have reported that a violation of this Code has occurred or is about to occur.

(c) The term "appropriate authorities or organs vested with reviewing or remedial power" refers to any authority or organ existing under national law, whether internal to the law enforcement agency or independent thereof, with statutory, customary or other power to review grievances and complaints arising out of violations within the purview of this Code.

(d) In some countries, the mass media may be regarded as performing complaint review functions similar to those described in subparagraph (c) above. Law enforcement officials may, therefore, be justified if, as a last resort and in accordance with the laws and customs of their own countries and with the provisions of article 4 of the present Code, they bring violations to the attention of public opinion through the mass media.

(e) Law enforcement officials who comply with the provisions of this Code deserve the respect, the full support and the co-operation of the community and of the law enforcement agency in which they serve, as well as the law enforcement profession.

APPENDIX XI

Body of Principles for the Protection of All Persons under Any Form of Detention or Imprisonment

The General Assembly,

Recalling its resolution 35/177 of 15 December 1980, in which it referred the task of elaborating the draft Body of Principles for the Protection of All Persons under Any Form of Detention or Imprisonment to the Sixth Committee and decided to establish an open-ended working group for that purpose,

Taking note of the report of the Working Group on the Draft Body of Principles for the Protection of All Persons under Any Form of Detention or Imprisonment, which met during the forty-third session of the General Assembly and completed the elaboration of the draft Body of Principles,

Considering that the Working Group decided to submit the text of the draft Body of Principles to the Sixth Committee for its consideration and adoption,

Convinced that the adoption of the draft Body of Principles would make an important contribution to the protection of human rights,

Considering the need to ensure the wide dissemination of the text of the Body of Principles,

1. Approves the Body of Principles for the Protection of All Persons under Any Form of Detention or Imprisonment, the text of which is annexed to the present resolution;

2. Expresses its appreciation to the Working Group on the Draft Body of Principles for the Protection of All Persons under Any Form of Detention or Imprisonment for its important contribution to the elaboration of the Body of Principles;
3. Requests the Secretary-General to inform the States Members of the United Nations or members of specialized agencies of the adoption of the Body of Principles;
4. Urges that every effort be made so that the Body of Principles becomes generally known and respected.

ANNEX

Body of Principles for the Protection of All Persons under Any Form of Detention or Imprisonment Scope of the Body of Principles

These principles apply for the protection of all persons under any form of detention or imprisonment.

Use of terms

For the purposes of the Body of Principles:

(a) "Arrest" means the act of apprehending a person for the alleged commission of an offence or by the action of an authority;
(b) "Detained person" means any person deprived of personal liberty except as a result of conviction for an offence;
(c) "Imprisoned person" means any person deprived of personal liberty as a result of conviction for an offence;
(d) "Detention" means the condition of detained persons as defined above;
(e) "Imprisonment" means the condition of imprisoned persons as defined above;
(f) The words "a judicial or other authority" mean a judicial or other authority under the law whose status and tenure should afford the strongest possible guarantees of competence, impartiality and independence.

Principle 1

All persons under any form of detention or imprisonment shall be treated in a humane manner and with respect for the inherent dignity of the human person.

Principle 2

Arrest, detention or imprisonment shall only be carried out

strictly in accordance with the provisions of the law and by competent officials or persons authorized for that purpose.

Principle 3

There shall be no restriction upon or derogation from any of the human rights of persons under any form of detention or imprisonment recognized or existing in any State pursuant to law, conventions, regulations or custom on the pretext that this Body of Principles does not recognize such rights or that it recognizes them to a lesser extent.

Principle 4

Any form of detention or imprisonment and all measures affecting the human rights of a person under any form of detention or imprisonment shall be ordered by, or be subject to the effective control of, a judicial or other authority.

Principle 5

1. These principles shall be applied to all persons within the territory of any given State, without distinction of any kind, such as race, colour, sex, language, religion or religious belief, political or other opinion, national, ethnic or social origin, property, birth or other status.
2. Measures applied under the law and designed solely to protect the rights and special status of women, especially pregnant women and nursing mothers, children and juveniles, aged, sick or handicapped persons shall not be deemed to be discriminatory. The need for, and the application of, such measures shall always be subject to review by a judicial or other authority.

Principle 6

No person under any form of detention or imprisonment shall be subjected to torture or to cruel, inhuman or degrading treatment or punishment.* No circumstance whatever may be invoked as a justification for torture or other cruel, inhuman or degrading treatment or punishment.

Principle 7

1. States should prohibit by law any act contrary to the rights and duties contained in these principles, make any such act subject to appropriate sanctions and conduct impartial investigations upon complaints.

2. Officials who have reason to believe that a violation of this Body of Principles has occurred or is about to occur shall report the matter to their superior authorities and, where necessary, to other appropriate authorities or organs vested with reviewing or remedial powers.
3. Any other person who has ground to believe that a violation of this Body of Principles has occurred or is about to occur shall have the right to report the matter to the superiors of the officials involved as well as to other appropriate authorities or organs vested with reviewing or remedial powers.

Principle 8

Persons in detention shall be subject to treatment appropriate to theirunconvicted status. Accordingly, they shall, whenever possible, be kept separate from imprisoned persons.

Principle 9

The authorities which arrest a person, keep him under detention or investigate the case shall exercise only the powers granted to them under the law and the exercise of these powers shall be subject to recourse to a judicial or other authority.

Principle 10

Anyone who is arrested shall be informed at the time of his arrest of the reason for his arrest and shall be promptly informed of any charges against him.

Principle 11

1. A person shall not be kept in detention without being given an effective opportunity to be heard promptly by a judicial or other authority. A detained person shall have the right to defend himself or to be assisted by counsel as prescribed by law.
2. A detained person and his counsel, if any, shall receive prompt and full communication of any order of detention, together with the reasons therefore.
3. A judicial or other authority shall be empowered to review as appropriate the continuance of detention.

Principle 12

1. There shall be duly recorded:
   (a) The reasons for the arrest;
   (b) The time of the arrest and the taking of the arrested

person to a place of custody as well as that of his first appearance before a judicial or other authority;

(c) The identity of the law enforcement officials concerned;

(d) Precise information concerning the place of custody.

2. Such records shall be communicated to the detained person, or his counsel, if any, in the form prescribed by law.

Principle 13

Any person shall, at the moment of arrest and at the commencement of detention or imprisonment, or promptly thereafter, be provided by the authority responsible for his arrest, detention or imprisonment, respectively, with information on and an explanation of his rights and how to avail himself of such rights.

Principle 14

A person who does not adequately understand or speak the language used by the authorities responsible for his arrest, detention or imprisonment is entitled to receive promptly in a language which he understands the information referred to in principle 10, principle 11, paragraph 2, principle 12, paragraph 1, and principle 13 and to have the assistance, free of charge, if necessary, of an interpreter in connection with legal proceedings subsequent to his arrest.

Principle 15

Not withstanding the exceptions contained in principle 16, paragraph 4, and principle 18, paragraph 3, communication of the detained or imprisoned person with the outside world, and in particular his family or counsel, shall not be denied for more than a matter of days.

Principle 16

1. Promptly after arrest and after each transfer from one place of detention or imprisonment to another, a detained or imprisoned person shall be entitled to notify or to require the competent authority to notify members of his family or other appropriate persons of his choice of his arrest, detention or imprisonment or of the transfer and of the place where he is kept in custody.

2. If a detained or imprisoned person is a foreigner, he shall also be promptly informed of his right to communicate by appropriate means with a consular post or the diplomatic mission of the State of which he is a national or which is

otherwise entitled to receive such communication in accordance with international law or with the representative of the competent international organization, if he is a refugee or is otherwise under the protection of an intergovernmental organization.

3. If a detained or imprisoned person is a juvenile or is incapable of understanding his entitlement, the competent authority shall on its own initiative undertake the notification referred to in the present principle. Special attention shall be given to notifying parents or guardians.
4. Any notification referred to in the present principle shall be made or permitted to be made without delay. The competent authority may however delay a notification for a reasonable period where exceptional needs of the investigation so require.

Principle 17

1. A detained person shall be entitled to have the assistance of a legal counsel. He shall be informed of his right by the competent authority promptly after arrest and shall be provided with reasonable facilities for exercising it.
2. If a detained person does not have a legal counsel of his own choice, he shall be entitled to have a legal counsel assigned to him by a judicial or other authority in all cases where the interests of justice so require and without payment by him if he does not have sufficient means to pay.

Principle 18

1. A detained or imprisoned person shall be entitled to communicate and consult with his legal counsel.
2. A detained or imprisoned person shall be allowed adequate time and facilities for consultations with his legal counsel.
3. The right of a detained or imprisoned person to be visited by and to consult and communicate, without delay or censorship and in full confidentiality, with his legal counsel may not be suspended or restricted save in exceptional circumstances, to be specified by law or lawful regulations, when it is considered indispensable by a judicial or other authority in order to maintain security and good order.
4. Interviews between a detained or imprisoned person and his legal counsel may be within sight, but not within the hearing, of a law enforcement official.

5. Communications between a detained or imprisoned person and his legal counsel mentioned in the present principle shall be inadmissible as evidence against the detained or imprisoned person unless they are connected with a continuing or contemplated crime.

Principle 19

A detained or imprisoned person shall have the right to be visited by and to correspond with, in particular, members of his family and shall be given adequate opportunity to communicate with the outside world, subject to reasonable conditions and restrictions as specified by law or lawful regulations.

Principle 20

If a detained or imprisoned person so requests, he shall if possible be kept in a place of detention or imprisonment reasonably near his usual place of residence.

Principle 21

1. It shall be prohibited to take undue advantage of the situation of a detained or imprisoned person for the purpose of compelling him to confess, to incriminate himself otherwise or to testify against any other person.
2. No detained person while being interrogated shall be subject to violence, threats or methods of interrogation which impair his capacity of decision or his judgment.

Principle 22

No detained or imprisoned person shall, even with his consent, be subjected to any medical or scientific experimentation which may be detrimental to his health.

Principle 23

1. The duration of any interrogation of a detained or imprisoned person and of the intervals between interrogations as well as the identity of the officials who conducted the interrogations and other persons present shall be recorded and certified in such form as may be prescribed by law.
2. A detained or imprisoned person, or his counsel when provided by law, shall have access to the information described in paragraph 1 of the present principle.

Principle 24

A proper medical examination shall be offered to a detained or imprisoned person as promptly as possible after his admission to the place of detention or imprisonment, and thereafter medical care and treatment shall be provided whenever necessary. This care and treatment shall be provided free of charge.

Principle 25

A detained or imprisoned person or his counsel shall, subject only to reasonable conditions to ensure security and good order in the place of detention or imprisonment, have the right to request or petition a judicial or other authority for a second medical examination or opinion.

Principle 26

The fact that a detained or imprisoned person underwent a medical examination, the name of the physician and the results of such an examination shall be duly recorded. Access to such records shall be ensured. Modalities therefore shall be in accordance with relevant rules of domestic law.

Principle 27

Non-compliance with these principles in obtaining evidence shall be taken into account in determining the admissibility of such evidence against a detained or imprisoned person.

Principle 28

A detained or imprisoned person shall have the right to obtain within the limits of available resources, if from public sources, reasonable quantities of educational, cultural and informational material, subject to reasonable conditions to ensure security and good order in the place of detention orimprisonment.

Principle 29

1. In order to supervise the strict observance of relevant laws and regulations, places of detention shall be visited regularly by qualified and experienced persons appointed by, and responsible to, a competent authority distinct from the authority directly in charge of the administration of theplace of detention or imprisonment.
2. A detained or imprisoned person shall have the right to communicate freely and in full confidentiality with the persons who visit the places of detention or imprisonment in

accordance with paragraph l of the present principle, subject to reasonable conditions to ensure security and good orderin such places.

Principle 30

1. The types of conduct of the detained or imprisoned person that constitute disciplinary offences during detention or imprisonment, the description and duration of disciplinary punishment that may be inflicted and the authorities competent to impose such punishment shall be specified by law or lawfulregulations and duly published.
2. A detained or imprisoned person shall have the right to be heard before disciplinary action is taken. He shall have the right to bring such action to higher authorities for review.

Principle 31

The appropriate authorities shall endeavour to ensure, according to domestic law, assistance when needed to dependent and, in particular, minor members of the families of detained or imprisoned persons and shall devote a particular measure of care to the appropriate custody of children left without supervision.

Principle 32

1. A detained person or his counsel shall be entitled at any time to take proceedings according to domestic law before a judicial or other authority to challenge the lawfulness of his detention in order to obtain his release without delay, if it is unlawful.
2. The proceedings referred to in paragraph l of the present principle shall be simple and expeditious and at no cost for detained persons without adequate means. The detaining authority shall produce without unreasonable delay the detained person before the reviewing authority.

Princip' 33

1. A detained or imprisoned person or his counsel shall have the right to make a request or complaint regarding his treatment, in particular in case of torture or other cruel, inhuman or degrading treatment, to the authorities responsible for the administration of the place of detention and to higher authorities and, when necessary, to appropriate authorities vested with reviewing or remedial powers.
2. In those cases where neither the detained or imprisoned person

nor his counsel has the possibility to exercise his rights under paragraph 1 of the present principle, a member of the family of the detained or imprisoned person or any other person who has knowledge of the case may exercise such rights.

3. Confidentiality concerning the request or complaint shall be maintained if so requested by the complainant.
4. Every request or complaint shall be promptly dealt with and replied to without undue delay. If the request or complaint is rejected or, in case of inordinate delay, the complainant shall be entitled to bring it before a judicial or other authority. Neither the detained or imprisoned person nor any complainant under paragraph 1 of the present principle shall suffer prejudice for making a request or complaint.

Principle 34

Whenever the death or disappearance of a detained or imprisoned person occurs during his detention or imprisonment, an inquiry into the cause of death or disappearance shall be held by a judicial or other authority, either on its own motion or at the instance of a member of the family of such a person or any person who has knowledge of the case. When circumstances so warrant, such an inquiry shall be held on the same procedural basis whenever the death or disappearance occurs shortly after the termination of the detention or imprisonment. The findings of such inquiry or a report thereon shall be made available upon request, unless doing so would jeopardize an ongoing criminal investigation.

Principle 35

1. Damage incurred because of acts or omissions by a public official contrary to the rights contained in these principles shall be compensated according to the applicable rules on liability provided by domestic law.
2. Information required to be recorded under these principles shall be available in accordance with procedures provided by domestic law for use in claiming compensation under the present principle.

Principle 36

1. A detained person suspected of or charged with a criminal offence shall be presumed innocent and shall be treated as such until proved guilty according to law in a public trial at which he has had all the guarantees necessary for his defence.

2. The arrest or detention of such a person pending investigation and trial shall be carried out only for the purposes of the administration of justice on grounds and under conditions and procedures specified by law. The imposition of restrictions upon such a person which are not strictly required for the purpose of the detention or to prevent hindrance to the process of investigation or the administration of justice, or for the maintenance of security and good order in the place of detention shall be forbidden.

Principle 37

A person detained on a criminal charge shall be brought before a judicial or other authority provided by law promptly after his arrest. Such authority shall decide without delay upon the lawfulness and necessity of detention. No person may be kept under detention pending investigation or trial except upon the written order of such an authority. A detained person shall, when brought before such an authority, have the right to make a statement on the treatment received by him while in custody.

Principle 38

A person detained on a criminal charge shall be entitled to trial within a reasonable time or to release pending trial.

Principle 39

Except in special cases provided for by law, a person detained on a criminal charge shall be entitled, unless a judicial or other authority decides otherwise in the interest of the administration of justice, to release pending trial subject to the conditions that may be imposed in accordance with the law. Such authority shall keep the necessity of detention under review.

General clause

Nothing in this Body of Principles shall be construed as restricting or derogating from any right defined in the International Covenant on Civil and Political Rights.

APPENDIX XII

Basic Principles on the Use of Force and Firearms by Law Enforcement Officials

Eighth United Nations Congress on the Prevention of Crime and the Treatment of Offenders, Havana, 27 August to 7 September 1990, U.N. Doc. A/CONF.144/28/Rev.1 at 112 (1990).

Whereas the work of law enforcement officials* is a social service of great importance and there is, therefore, a need to maintain and, whenever necessary, to improve the working conditions and status of these officials,

Whereas a threat to the life and safety of law enforcement officials must be seen as a threat to the stability of society as a whole,

Whereas law enforcement officials have a vital role in the protection of the right to life, liberty and security of the person, as guaranteed in the Universal Declaration of Human Rights and reaffirmed in the International Covenant on Civil and Political Rights,

---

* In accordance with the commentary to article 1 of the Code of Conduct for Law Enforcement Officials, the term "law enforcement officials" includes all officers of the law, whether appointed or elected, who exercise police powers, especially the powers of arrest or detention. In countries where police powers are exercised by military authorities, whether uniformed or not, or by State security forces, the definition of law enforcement officials shall be regarded as including officers of such services.

Whereas the Standard Minimum Rules for the Treatment of Prisoners provide for the circumstances in which prison officials may use force in the course of their duties,

Whereas article 3 of the Code of Conduct for Law Enforcement Officials provides that law enforcement officials may use force only when strictly necessary and to the extent required for the performance of their duty,

Whereas the preparatory meeting for the Seventh United Nations Congress on the Prevention of Crime and the Treatment of Offenders, held at Varenna, Italy, agreed on elements to be considered in the course of further work on restraints on the use of force and firearms by law enforcement officials,

Whereas the Seventh Congress, in its resolution 14, inter alia, emphasizes that the use of force and firearms by law enforcement officials should be commensurate with due respect for human rights,

Whereas the Economic and Social Council, in its resolution 1986/10, section IX, of 21 May 1986, invited Member States to pay particular attention in the implementation of the Code to the use of force and firearms by law enforcement officials, and the General Assembly, in its resolution 41/149 of 4 December 1986, inter alia, welcomed this recommendation made by the Council,

Whereas it is appropriate that, with due regard to their personal safety, consideration be given to the role of law enforcement officials in relation to the administration of justice, to the protection of the right to life, liberty and security of the person, to their responsibility to maintain public safety and social peace and to the importance of their qualifications, training and conduct,

The basic principles set forth below, which have been formulated to assist Member States in their task of ensuring and promoting the proper role of law enforcement officials, should be taken into account and respected by Governments within the framework of their national legislation and practice, and be brought to the attention of law enforcement officials as well as other persons, such as judges, prosecutors, lawyers, members of the executive branch and the legislature, and the public.

General Provisions

1. Governments and law enforcement agencies shall adopt and implement rules and regulations on the use of force and firearms against persons by law enforcement officials. In developing such rules and regulations, Governments and law

enforcement agencies shall keep the ethical issues associated with the use of force and firearms constantly under review.

2. Governments and law enforcement agencies should develop a range of means as broad as possible and equip law enforcement officials with various types of weapons and ammunition that would allow for a differentiated use of force and firearms. These should include the development of non-lethal incapacitating weapons for use in appropriate situations, with a view to increasingly restraining the application of means capable of causing death or injury to persons. For the same purpose, it should also be possible for law enforcement officials to be equipped with self-defensive equipment such as shields, helmets, bullet-proof vests and bullet-proof means of transportation, in order to decrease the need to use weapons of any kind.
3. The development and deployment of non-lethal incapacitating weapons should be carefully evaluated in order to minimize the risk of endangering uninvolved persons, and the use of such weapons should be carefully controlled.
4. Law enforcement officials, in carrying out their duty, shall, as far as possible, apply non-violent means before resorting to the use of force and firearms. They may use force and firearms only if other means remain ineffective or without any promise of achieving the intended result.
5. Whenever the lawful use of force and firearms is unavoidable, law enforcement officials shall:
   (a) Exercise restraint in such use and act in proportion to the seriousness of the offence and the legitimate objective to be achieved;
   (b) Minimize damage and injury, and respect and preserve human life;
   (c) Ensure that assistance and medical aid are rendered to any injured or affected persons at the earliest possible moment;
   (d) Ensure that relatives or close friends of the injured or affected person are notified at the earliest possible moment.
6. Where injury or death is caused by the use of force and firearms by law enforcement officials, they shall report the incident promptly to their superiors, in accordance with principle 22.
7. Governments shall ensure that arbitrary or abusive use of force

and firearms by law enforcement officials is punished as a criminal offence under their law.

8. Exceptional circumstances such as internal political instability or any other public emergency may not be invoked to justify any departure from these basic principles.

Special Provisions

9. Law enforcement officials shall not use firearms against persons except in self-defence or defence of others against the imminent threat of death or serious injury, to prevent the perpetration of a particularly serious crime involving grave threat to life, to arrest a person presenting such a danger and resisting their authority, or to prevent his or her escape, and only when less extreme means are insufficient to achieve these objectives. In any event, intentional lethal use of firearms may only be made when strictly unavoidable in order to protect life.

10. In the circumstances provided for under principle 9, law enforcement officials shall identify themselves as such and give a clear warning of their intent to use firearms, with sufficient time for the warning to be observed, unless to do so would unduly place the law enforcement officials at risk or would create a risk of death or serious harm to other persons, or would be clearly inappropriate or pointless in the circumstances of the incident.

11. Rules and regulations on the use of firearms by law enforcement officials should include guidelines that:
   (a) Specify the circumstances under which law enforcement officials are authorized to carry firearms and prescribe the types of firearms and ammunition permitted;
   (b) Ensure that firearms are used only in appropriate circumstances and in a manner likely to decrease the risk of unnecessary harm;
   (c) Prohibit the use of those firearms and ammunition that cause unwarranted injury or present an unwarranted risk;
   (d) Regulate the control, storage and issuing of firearms, including procedures for ensuring that law enforcement officials are accountable for the firearms and ammunition issued to them;
   (e) Provide for warnings to be given, if appropriate, when firearms are to be discharged;
   (f) Provide for a system of reporting whenever law

enforcement officials use firearms in the performance of their duty.

Policing unlawful assemblies

12. As everyone is allowed to participate in lawful and peaceful assemblies, in accordance with the principles embodied in the Universal Declaration of Human Rights and the International Covenant on Civil and Political Rights, Governments and law enforcement agencies and officials shall recognize that force and firearms may be used only in accordance with principles 13 and 14.
13. In the dispersal of assemblies that are unlawful but non-violent, law enforcement officials shall avoid the use of force or, where that is not practicable, shall restrict such force to the minimum extent necessary.
14. In the dispersal of violent assemblies, law enforcement officials may use firearms only when less dangerous means are not practicable and only to the minimum extent necessary. Law enforcement officials shall not use firearms in such cases, except under the conditions stipulated in principle 9.

Policing persons in custody or detention

15. Law enforcement officials, in their relations with persons in custody or detention, shall not use force, except when strictly necessary for the maintenance of security and order within the institution, or when personal safety is threatened.
16. Law enforcement officials, in their relations with persons in custody or detention, shall not use firearms, except in self-defence or in the defence of others against the immediate threat of death or serious injury, or when strictly necessary to prevent the escape of a person in custody or detention presenting the danger referred to in principle 9.
17. The preceding principles are without prejudice to the rights, duties and responsibilities of prison officials, as set out in the Standard Minimum Rules for the Treatment of Prisoners, particularly rules 33, 34 and 54.

Qualifications, training and counselling

18. Governments and law enforcement agencies shall ensure that all law enforcement officials are selected by proper screening procedures, have appropriate moral, psychological and physical qualities for the effective exercise of their functions

and receive continuous and thorough professional training. Their continued fitness to perform these functions should be subject to periodic review.

19. Governments and law enforcement agencies shall ensure that all law enforcement officials are provided with training and are tested in accordance with appropriate proficiency standards in the use of force. Those law enforcement officials who are required to carry firearms should be authorized to do so only upon completion of special training in their use.

20. In the training of law enforcement officials, Governments and law enforcement agencies shall give special attention to issues of police ethics and human rights, especially in the investigative process, to alternatives to the use of force and firearms, including the peaceful settlement of conflicts, the understanding of crowd behaviour, and the methods of persuasion, negotiation and mediation, as well as to technical means, with a view to limiting the use of force and firearms. Law enforcement agencies should review their training programmes and operational procedures in the light of particular incidents.

21. Governments and law enforcement agencies shall make stress counselling available to law enforcement officials who are involved in situations where force and firearms are used.

Reporting and review procedures

22. Governments and law enforcement agencies shall establish effective reporting and review procedures for all incidents referred to in principles 6 and 11 (f). For incidents reported pursuant to these principles, Governments and law enforcement agencies shall ensure that an effective review process is available and that independent administrative or prosecutorial authorities are in a position to exercise jurisdiction in appropriate circumstances. In cases of death and serious injury or other grave consequences, a detailed report shall be sent promptly to the competent authorities responsible for administrative review and judicial control.

23. Persons affected by the use of force and firearms or their legal representatives shall have access to an independent process, including a judicial process. In the event of the death of such persons, this provision shall apply to their dependants accordingly.

24. Governments and law enforcement agencies shall ensure that superior officers are held responsible if they know, or should have known, that law enforcement officials under their command are resorting, or have resorted, to the unlawful use of force and firearms, and they did not take all measures in their power to prevent, suppress or report such use.
25. Governments and law enforcement agencies shall ensure that no criminal or disciplinary sanction is imposed on law enforcement officials who, in compliance with the Code of Conduct for Law Enforcement Officials and these basic principles, refuse to carry out an order to use force and firearms, or who report such use by other officials.
26. Obedience to superior orders shall be no defence if law enforcement officials knew that an order to use force and firearms resulting in the death or serious injury of a person was manifestly unlawful and had a reasonable opportunity to refuse to follow it. In any case, responsibility also rests on the superiors who gave the unlawful orders.

Appendix XIII

Declaration of Basic Principles of Justice for Victims of Crime and Abuse of Power 1985

The General Assembly,

Recalling that the Sixth United Nations Congress on the Prevention of Crime and the Treatment of Offenders recommended that the United Nations should continue its present work on the development of guidelines and standards regarding abuse of economic and political power, Cognizant that millions of people throughout the world suffer harm as a result of crime and the abuse of power and that the rights of these victim shave not been adequately recognized,

Recognizing that the victims of crime and the victims of abuse of power, and also frequently their families, witnesses and others who aid them, are unjustly subjected to loss, damage or injury and that they may, in addition, suffer hardship when assisting in the prosecution of offenders,

1. Affirms the necessity of adopting national and international measures in order to secure the universal and effective recognition of, and respect for, the rights of victims of crime and of abuse of power;
2. Stresses the need to promote progress by all States in their efforts to that end, without prejudice to the rights of suspects or offenders;
3. Adopts the Declaration of Basic Principles of Justice for

Victims of Crime and Abuse of Power, annexed to the present resolution, which is designed to assist Governments and the international community in their efforts to secure justice and assistance for victims of crime and victims of abuse of power;

4. Calls upon Member States to take the necessary steps to give effect to the provisions contained in the Declaration and, in order to curtail victimization as referred to hereinafter, endeavour:

   (a) To implement social, health, including mental health, educational, economic and specific crime prevention policies to reduce victimization and encourage assistance to victims in distress;

   (b) To promote community efforts and public participation in crime prevention;

   (c) To review periodically their existing legislation and practices in order to ensure responsiveness to changing circumstances, and to enact and enforce legislation proscribing acts that violate internationally recognized norms relating to human rights, corporate conduct, and other abuses of power;

   (d) To establish and strengthen the means of detecting, prosecuting and sentencing those guilty of crimes;

   (e) To promote disclosure of relevant information to expose official and corporate conduct to public scrutiny, and other ways of increasing responsiveness to public concerns;

   (f) To promote the observance of codes of conduct and ethical norms, in particular international standards, by public servants, including law enforcement, correctional, medical, social service and military personnel, aswell as the staff of economic enterprises;

   (g) To prohibit practices and procedures conducive to abuse, such as secret places of detention and *incommunicado* detention;

   (h) To co-operate with other States, through mutual judicial and administrative assistance, in such matters as the detection and pursuit of offenders, their extradition and the seizure of their assets, to be used forrestitution to the victims;

5. Recommends that, at the international and regional levels, all appropriate measures should be taken:

(a) To promote training activities designed to foster adherence to United Nations standards and norms and to curtail possible abuses;
(b) To sponsor collaborative action-research on ways in which victimization can be reduced and victims aided, and to promote information exchanges on the most effective means of so doing;
(c) To render direct aid to requesting Governments designed to help them curtail victimization and alleviate the plight of victims;
(d) To develop ways and means of providing recourse for victims where national channels may be insufficient;

6. Requests the Secretary-General to invite Member States to report periodically to the General Assembly on the implementation of the Declaration, as well as on measures taken by them to this effect;
7. Also requests the Secretary-General to make use of the opportunities, which all relevant bodies and organizations within the United Nations system offer, to assist Member States, whenever necessary, in improving ways and means of protecting victims both at the national level and through international co-operation;
8. Further requests the Secretary-General to promote the objectives of the Declaration, in particular by ensuring its widest possible dissemination;
9. Urges the specialized agencies and other entities and bodies of the United Nations system, other relevant intergovernmental and non-governmental organizations and the public to co-operate in the implementation of the provisions of the Declaration.

ANNEX

Declaration of Basic Principles of Justice for Victims of Crime and Abuse of Power

A. Victims of Crime

1. "Victims" means persons who, individually or collectively, have suffered harm, including physical or mental injury, emotional suffering, economic loss or substantial impairment of their fundamental rights, through acts or omissions that are

in violation of criminal laws operative within Member States, including those laws proscribing criminal abuse of power.

2. A person may be considered a victim, under this Declaration, regardless of whether the perpetrator is identified, apprehended, prosecuted or convicted and regardless of the familial relationship between the perpetrator and the victim. The term "victim" also includes, where appropriate, the immediate family or dependents of the direct victim and persons who have suffered harm in intervening to assist victims in distress or to prevent victimization.

3. The provisions contained herein shall be applicable to all, without distinction of any kind, such as race, colour, sex, age, language, religion, nationality, political or other opinion, cultural beliefs or practices, property, birth or family status, ethnic or social origin, and disability.

Access to justice and fair treatment

4. Victims should be treated with compassion and respect for their dignity. They are entitled to access to the mechanisms of justice and to prompt redress, as provided for by national legislation, for the harm that they have suffered.

5. Judicial and administrative mechanisms should be established and strengthened where necessary to enable victims to obtain redress through formal or informal procedures that are expeditious, fair, inexpensive and accessible. Victims should be informed of their rights in seeking redress through such mechanisms.

6. The responsiveness of judicial and administrative processes to the needs of victims should be facilitated by:
   (a) Informing victims of their role and the scope, timing and progress of the proceedings and of the disposition of their cases, especially where serious crimes are involved and where they have requested such information;
   (b) Allowing the views and concerns of victims to be presented and considered at appropriate stages of the proceedings where their personal interests are affected, without prejudice to the accused and consistent with the relevant national criminal justice system;
   (c) Providing proper assistance to victims throughout the legal process;
   (d) Taking measures to minimize inconvenience to victims,

protect their privacy, when necessary, and ensure their safety, as well as that of their families and witnesses on their behalf, from intimidation and retaliation;

(e) Avoiding unnecessary delay in the disposition of cases and the execution of orders or decrees granting awards to victims.

7. Informal mechanisms for the resolution of disputes, including mediation, arbitration and customary justice or indigenous practices, should be utilized where appropriate to facilitate conciliation and redress for victims.

Restitution

8. Offenders or third parties responsible for their behaviour should, where appropriate, make fair restitution to victims, their families or dependants. Such restitution should include the return of property or payment for the harm or loss suffered, reimbursement of expenses incurred as a result of the victimization, the provision of services and the restoration of rights.

9. Governments should review their practices, regulations and laws to consider restitution as an available sentencing option in criminal cases, in addition to other criminal sanctions.

10. In cases of substantial harm to the environment, restitution, if ordered, should include, as far as possible, restoration of the environment, reconstruction of the infrastructure, replacement of community facilities and reimbursement of the expenses of relocation, whenever such harm results in the dislocation of a community.

11. Where public officials or other agents acting in an official or quasi-official capacity have violated national criminal laws, the victims should receive restitution from the State whose officials or agents were responsible for the harm inflicted. In cases where the Government under whose authority the victimizing act or omission occurred is no longer in existence, the State or Government successor in title should provide restitution to the victims Compensation.

12. When compensation is not fully available from the offender or other sources, States should Endeavour to provide financial compensation to:

(a) Victims who have sustained significant bodily injury or impairment of physical or mental health as a result of serious crimes;

(b) The family, in particular dependants of persons who have died or become physically or mentally incapacitated as a result of such victimization.

13. The establishment, strengthening and expansion of national funds for compensation to victims should be encouraged. Where appropriate, other funds may also be established for this purpose, including those cases where the State of which the victim is a national is not in a position to compensate the victim for the harm.

Assistance

14. Victims should receive the necessary material, medical, psychological and social assistance through governmental, voluntary, community-based and indigenous means.

15. Victims should be informed of the availability of health and social services and other relevant assistance and be readily afforded access to them.

16. Police, justice, health, social service and other personnel concerned should receive training to sensitize them to the needs of victims, and guidelines to ensure proper and prompt aid.

17. In providing services and assistance to victims, attention should be given to those who have special needs because of the nature of the harm inflicted or because of factors such as those mentioned in paragraph 3 above.

B. Victims of Abuse of Power

18. "Victims" means persons who, individually or collectively, have suffered harm, including physical or mental injury, emotional suffering, economic loss or substantial impairment of their fundamental rights, through acts or omissions that do not yet constitute violations of national criminal laws but of internationally recognized norms relating to human rights.

19. States should consider incorporating into the national law norms proscribing abuses of power and providing remedies to victims of such abuses. In particular, such remedies should include restitution and/or compensation, and necessary material, medical, psychological and social assistance and support.

20. States should consider negotiating multilateral international treaties relating to victims, as defined in paragraph 18.

21. States should periodically review existing legislation and practices to ensure their responsiveness to changing circumstances, should enact and enforce, if necessary, legislation proscribing acts that constitute serious abuses of political or economic power, as well as promoting policies and mechanisms for the prevention of such acts, and should develop and make readily available appropriate rights and remedies for victims of such acts.

APPENDIX XIV

The Protection of Human Rights Act, 1993

ACT NO. 10 of 1994 [8th January, 1994.

CHAPTER I
PRELIMINARY

1. Short title, extent and commencement

(1) This Act may be called the Protection of Human Rights Act,1993.

(2) It extends to the whole of India.Provided that it shall apply to the State of Jammu and Kashmir only in so far as it pertains to the matters relatable to any of the entries enumerated in List I or List lll in the Seventh Schedule to the Constitutionas applicable to that State.

(3) It shall be deemed to have come into force on the 28th day of September, 1993.

2. Definitions

(1) In this Act, unless the context otherwise requires-

(a) "armed forces" means the naval, military and air forces and includes any other armed forces of the Union;

(b) "Chairperson" means the Chairperson of the Commissionor of the State Commission, as the case may be;

(c) "Commission" means the National Human Rights Commission under section 3;

(d) "human rights" means the rights relating to life, liberty,equality and dignity of the individual guaranteed by theConstitution or embodied in the International Covenantsand enforceable by courts in India.

(e) "Human Rights Court" means the Human Rights Courtspecified under section 30;

(f) "International Covenants" means the International Covenanton Civil and Political Rights and the International Covenanton Economic, Social and Cultural rights adopted by theGeneral Assembly of the United Nations on the 16th December, 1966 [and such other Covenant or Convention adopted by the General Assembly of the United Nations as the Central Governmentmay, by notification, specify"][1] ;

(g) "Member" means a Member of the Commission or of the State Commission, as the case may be;

(h) "National Commission for Minorities" means theNational Commission for Minorities constituted under section 3 of the National Commission for Minorities Act, 1992;

(i) "National Commission for the Scheduled Castes"means the National Commission for the Scheduled Castes referred to in Article 338 of the Constitution[2];

(ia) "National Commission for the Scheduled Tribes"means the National Commission for the Scheduled Tribes referred to in Article 338A of the Constitution[3];

(j) "National Commission for Women" means theNational Commission for Women constituted under section 3 of the National Commission for Women Act, 1990;

(k) "Notification" means a notification published in the official Gazette;

(l) "Prescribed" means prescribed by rules made underthis Act;

(m) "Public servant" shall have the meaning assignedto it in section 21 of the Indian Penal Code;

(n) "State Commission" means a State Human Rights Commission constituted under section 21.

---

1. Added by Act 43 of 2006.
2. Subs. by Act 43 of 2006.
3. Subs. by Act 43 of 2006.

(2) Any reference in this Act to a law, which is not in force in the State of Jammu and Kashmir, shall, in relation to that State,be construed as a reference to a corresponding law, if any, in force in that State.

CHAPTER II
THE NATIONAL HUMAN RIGHTSCOMMISSION

3. Constitution of a National Human Rights Commission

(1) The Central Government shall constitute a body to be known as the National Human Rights Commission to exercise the powers conferred upon, and to perform the functions assigned to it, under this Act.

(2) The Commission shall consist of:

(a) a Chairperson who has been a Chief Justice of the Supreme Court;
(b) one Member who is or has been, a Judge of the Supreme Court;
(c) one Member who is, or has been, the Chief Justice of a High Court;
(d) two Members to be appointed from amongst persons having knowledge of, or practical experience in, matters relating to human rights.

(3) The Chairperson of the National Commission for Minorities, [the National Commission for the Scheduled Castes, the National Commission for the Scheduled Tribes][4] and the National Commission for Women shall be deemed to be Members of the Commission for the discharge of functions specified in clauses (b) to (j) of section 12.

(4) There shall be a Secretary-General who shall be the Chief Executive Officer of the Commission and shall exercise such powers and discharge such functions of the Commission [except judicial functions and the power to make regulations under section 40 B][5], as may be delegated to him by the Commission or the Chairperson as the case may be.

(5) The headquarters of the Commission shall be at Delhi and

4. Subs. by Act 43 of 2006 for "The National Commission for the Scheduled Castes and Scheduled Tribes."
5. Subs. by Act 43 of 2006 for "as it may delegate to him."

the Commission may, with the previous approval of the Central Government, establish offices at other places in India.

4. Appointment of Chairperson and other Members

(1) The Chairperson and [the Members][6] shall be appointed by thePresident by warrant under his hand and seal;

Provided that every appointment under this sub-section shall be madeafter obtaining the recommendations of a Committee consisting of:

(a) The Prime Minister — Chairperson
(b) Speaker of the House of the People — Member
(c) Minister in-charge of the Ministry of Home Affairs in theGovernment of India — Member
(d) Leader of the Opposition in the House of the People — Member
(e) Leader of the Opposition in the Council of States — Member
(f) Deputy Chairman of the Council of States — Member

Provided further that no sitting Judge of the Supreme Court or sitting Chief Justice of a High Court shall be appointed except after consultation with the Chief Justice of India.

(2) No appointment of a Chairperson or a Member shall be invalid merely by reason of any [vacancy of any member in the Committee referred to in the first proviso to sub-section (1)][7].

5. Resignation and removal of Chairperson and Members[8]

(1) The Chairperson or any Member may, by notice in writing under his hand addressed to the President of India, resign his office.

(2) Subject to the provisions of sub-section (3), the Chairperson or any Member shall only be removed from his office by order of the President of India on the ground of proved misbehaviour or incapacity after the Supreme Court, on reference being made to it by the President, has, on inquiry held in accordance with the procedure prescribed in that behalf by the Supreme Court, reported that the Chairperson or the Member, as thecase may be, ought on any such ground to be removed.

6. Subs. by Act 43 of 2006 for "other members"
7. Subs. by Act 43 of 2006 for "vacancy in the Committee".
8. Subs. by Act 43 of 2006.

(3) Notwithstanding anything in sub-section (2), the President may, by order, remove from office the Chairperson or any Member if the Chairperson or such Member, as the case may be:

(a) is adjudged an insolvent; or
(b) engages during his term of office in any paid employment outside the duties of his office; or
(c) is unfit to continue in office by reason of infirmity of mind or body; or
(d) is of unsound mind and stands so declared by a competent court;or
(e) is convicted and sentenced to imprisonment for an offence which in the opinion of the President involves moral turpitude.

6. Term of office of Chairperson and Members[9]

(1) A person appointed as Chairperson shall hold office for a term of five years from the date on which he enters upon his office or until he attains the age of seventy years, whichever is earlier.

(2) A person appointed as a Member shall hold office for a term of five years from the date on which he enters upon his office and shall be eligible for re-appointment for another term of five years.

Provided that no Member shall hold office after he has attained the age of seventy years.

(3) On ceasing to hold office, a Chairperson or a Member shall be ineligible for further employment under the Government of India or under the Government of any State.

7. Member to act as Chairperson or to discharge his functions in certain circumstances

(1) In the event of the occurrence of any vacancy in the office of President may, by notification, authorise one of the Members to act as the Chairperson until the appointment of a new Chairperson to fill such vacancy.

(2) When the Chairperson is unable to discharge his functions owing to absence on leave or otherwise, such one of the Members as the President may, by notification, authorise in this behalf, shall discharge the functions of the Chairperson until the date on which the Chairperson resumes his duties.

9. Subs. by Act 43 of 2006.

8. Terms and conditions of service of Chairperson and Members

The salaries and allowances payable to, and other terms and conditions of service of, the [Chairperson and][10] Members shall be such as may be prescribed.

Provided that neither the salary and allowances nor the other terms and conditions of service of [the Chairperson or][11] a Member shall be varied to his disadvantage after his appointment.

9. Vacancies, etc., not to invalidate the proceedings of the Commission

No act or proceedings of the Commission shall be questioned or shall be invalidated merely on the ground of existence of any vacancy or defect in the constitution of the Commission.

10. Procedure to be regulated by the.Commission

(1) The Commission shall meet at such time and place as the Chairperson may think fit.

(2) Subject to the provisions of this Act and the rules made there under, the Commission shall have the power to lay down by regulationsits own procedure[12].

(3) All orders and decisions of the Commission shall be authenticated by the Secretary-General or any other officer of the Commission duly authorised by the Chairperson in this behalf.

11. Offices and other staff of the Commission.

(1) The Central Government shall make available to the Commission:

(a) an officer Of the rank of the Secretary to the Government of India who shall be the Secretary-General of the Commission; and

(b) such police and investigative staff under an officer not below the rank of a Director General of Police and such other officers no staff as may be necessary for the efficient performance of the functions of the Commission.

(2) Subject to such rules as may be made by the Central Government in this behalf, the Commission may appoint such other

10. Inserted by Act 43 of 2006.
11. Inserted by Act 43 of 2006.
12. Subs. by Act 43 of 2006.

administrative, technical and scientific staff as it may consider necessary.

(3) The salaries, allowances and conditions of service of the officers and other staff appointed under sub- section (2) shall be such as may be prescribed.

CHAPTER III
FUNCTIONS AND POWERS OF THE COMMISSION

12. Functions of the Commission

The Commission shall perform all or any of the following functions, namely:

(a) inquire, *suo motu* or on a petition presented to it by a victim or any person on his behalf [or on a direction or order of any court][13], into complaint of–
 (i) violation of human rights or abetment thereof; or
 (ii) negligence in the prevention of such violation, by a public servant;

(b) intervene in any proceeding involving any allegation of violation of human rights pending before a court with the approval of such court;

(c) visit, not withstanding anything contained in any other law for thetime being in force, any jail or other institution under the controlof the State Government, where persons are detained or lodgedfor purposes of treatment, reformation or protection, for the study of the living conditions of the inmates thereof and make recommendations thereon to the Government;

(d) review the safeguards provided by or under the Constitution or any law for the time being in force for the protection of human rights and recommend measures for their effective implementation;

(e) review the factors, including acts of terrorism, that inhibit the enjoyment of human rights and recommend appropriate remedial measures;

(f) study treaties and other international instruments on human rights and make recommendations for their effective implementation;

---

13. Inserted by Act 43 of 2006.

(g) undertake and promote research in the field of human rights;

(h) spread human rights literacy among various sections, of society and promote awareness of the safeguards available for the protection of these rights through publications, the media, seminars and other available means;

(i) encourage the efforts of non- governmental organisations and institutions working in the field of human rights;

(j) such other functions as it may consider necessary for the promotion of human rights.

13. Powers relating to inquiries.

(1) The Commission shall, while inquiring into complaints under this Act, have all the powers of a civil court trying a suit under the Code of Civil Procedure, 1908 (5 of 1908), and in particular in respect of the following matters, namely:

(a) summoning and enforcing the attendance of witnesses and examining them on oath;

(b) discovery and production of any document;

(c) receiving evidence on affidavits;

(d) requisitioning any public record or copy thereof from any court or office;

(e) issuing commissions for the examination of witnesses or documents;

(f) any other matter which may be prescribed.

(2) The Commission shall have power to require any person, subject to any privilege which may be claimed by that person under any law for the time being in force, to furnish information on such points or matters as, in the opinion of the Commission, may be useful for, or relevant to, the subject matter of the inquiry and any person so required shall be deemed to be legally bound to furnish such information within the meaning of section 176 and section 177 of the Indian Penal Code.

(3) The Commission or any other officer, not below the rank of a Gazetted Officer, specially authorised in this behalf by the Commission may enter any building or place where the Commission has reason to believe that any document relating to the subject matter of the inquiry may be found, and may seize any such document or take extracts or copies therefrom subject to the provisions of section 100, of the Code of Criminal Procedure, 1973 (2 of 1974), in so far as it may be applicable.

(4) The, Commission shall be deemed to be a civil court and when any offence as is described in section 175, section 178, section 179, section 180 or section 228 of the Indian Penal Code (45 of 1860). is committed in the view or presence of the Commission, the Commission may, after recording the facts constituting the offence and the statement of the accused as provided for in the Code of Criminal Procedure, 1973 (2 of 1974), forward the case to a Magistrate having jurisdiction to try the same and the Magistrate to whom any such case is forwarded shall proceed to hear the complaint against the accused as if the case has been forwarded to him under section 346 of the Code of Criminal Procedure, 1973.

(5) Every proceeding before the Commission shall be deemed to be a judicial proceeding within the meaning of section, 193 and 228, and for the purposes of section 196, of the Indian Penal Code (45 of 1860), and the Commission shall be deemed to be a civil court for all the purposes of section 195 and Chapter XXVI of the Code of Criminal Procedure, 1973 (2 of 1974).

(6) Where the Commission considers it necessary or expedient soto do, it may, by order, transfer any complaint filed or pending before itto the State Commission of the State from which the complaint arises, for disposal in accordance with the provisions of this Act[14];

Provided that no such complaint shall be transferred unless the same is one respecting which the State Commission has jurisdiction to entertain the same.

(7) Every complaint transferred under sub-section(6) shall be dealtwith and disposed of by the State Commission as if it were a complaintinitially filed before it.[15]

14. Investigation.

(1) The Commission may, for the purpose of conducting any investigation pertaining to the inquiry, utilise the services of any officer or investigation agency of the Central Government or any State Government with the concurrence of the Central Government or the State Government, as the case may be.

(2) For the purpose of investigating into any matter pertaining to the inquiry, any officer or agency whose services are utilised under sub- section (1) may, subject to the direction and control of the Commission,—

14. Inserted by Act 43 of 2006.
15. Inserted by Act 43 of 2006.

(a) summon and enforce the attendance of any person and examine him;

(b) require the discovery and production of any document; and

(c) requisition any public record or copy thereof from any office,

(3) The provisions of section 15 shall apply in relation to any statement made by a person before any officer or agency whose services are utilised under sub-section (1) as they apply in relation to any statement made by a person in the course of giving evidence before the Commission.

(4) The officer or agency whose services are utilised under sub-section (1) shall investigate into any matter pertaining to the inquiry and submit a report thereon to the Commission within such period as may be specified by the Commission in this behalf.

(5) The Commission shall satisfy itself about the correctness of the facts stated and the conclusion, if any, arrived at in the report submitted to it under sub-section (4) and for this purpose the Commission may make such inquiry (including the examination of the person or persons who conducted or assisted in the investigation) as it thinks fit.

15. Statement made by persons to the Commission

No statement made by a person in the course of giving evidence before the Commission shall subject him to, or be used against him in, any civil or criminal proceeding except a prosecution for giving false evidence by such statement;

Provided that the statement—

(a) is made in reply to the question which he is required by the Commission to answer; or

(b) is relevant to the subject matter of the inquiry.

16. Persons likely to be prejudicially affected to be heard

If, at any stage of the inquiry, the Commission—

(a) considers it necessary to inquire into the conduct of any person; or

(b) is of the opinion that the reputation of any person is likely to be prejudicially affected by the inquiry, it shall give to that person a reasonable opportunity of being heard in the inquiry and to produce evidence in his defence: Provided that nothing in this section shall apply where the credit of a witness is being impeached.

Chapter IV
Procedure

17. Inquiry into Complaints

The Commission while inquiring into the complaints of violation of human rights may:

(i) call for information or report from the Central Government or any State Government or any other authority or organisation subordinate thereto
  (a) if the information or report is not received within the time stipulated by the Commission, it may proceed to inquire into the complaint on its own;
  (b) if, on receipt of information or report, the Commission is satisfied either that no further inquiry is required or that the required action has been initiated or taken by the concerned Government or authority, it may not proceed with the complaint and inform the complainant accordingly;

(ii) without prejudice to anything contained in clause (i), if it considers necessary, having regard to the nature of the complaint, initiate an inquiry.

18. Steps during and after inquiry[16]

[The Commission may take any of the following steps during or uponthe completion of an inquiry held under this Act, namely:

(a) where the inquiry discloses the commission of violation of humanrights or negligence in the prevention of violation of human rights orabetment thereof by a public servant, it may recommend to the concerned Government or authority —
  (i) to make payment of compensation or damages to the complainant or to the victim or the members of his family as the Commission may consider necessary;
  (ii) to initiate proceedings for prosecution or such other suitableaction as the Commission may deem fit against the concerned person or persons;

16. Subs. by Act 43 of 2006.

(iii) to take such further action as it may think fit;

(b) approach the Supreme Court or the High Court concerned for such directions, orders or writs as that Court may deem necessary;

(c) recommend to the concerned Government or authority at any stage of the inquiry for the grant of such immediate interim relief to thevictim or the members of his family as the Commission may consider necessary;

(d) subject to the provisions of clause (e), provide a copy of theinquiry report to the petitioner or his representative;

(e) the Commission shall send a copy of its inquiry report togetherwith its recommendations to the concerned Government or authority andthe the Commission;

(f) the Commission shall publish its inquiry report together with the comments of the concerned Government or authority, if any, and the action taken or proposed to be taken by the concerned Government or authority on the recommendations of the Commission.][17]

19. Procedure with respect to armed forces

(1) Notwithstanding anything contained in this Act, while dealing with complaints of violation of human rights by members of the armed forces, the Commission shall adopt the following procedure, namely:

(a) it may, either on its own motion or on receipt of a petition, seek a report from the Central Government;

(b) after the receipt of the report, it may, either not proceed with the complaint or, as the cage may be, make its recommendations to that Government.

(2) The Central Government shall inform the Commission of the action taken on the recommendations within three months or such further time as the Commission may allow.

(3) The Commission shall publish its report together with its recommendations made to the Central Government and the action taken by that Government on such recommendations.

(4) The Commission shall provide a copy of the report published under sub- section (3) to the petitioner or his representative.

17. Subs. by Act 43 of 2006.

20. Annual and special reports of the commission

(1) The Commission shall submit an annual report to the Central Government and to the State Government concerned and may at any time submit special reports on any matter which, in its opinion, is of such urgency or importance that it should not be deferred till submission of the, annual report.

(2) The Central Government and the State Government, as the case may be, shall cause the annual and special reports of the Commission to be laid before each House of Parliament or the State Legislature respectively, as the case may be, along with a memorandum of action taken or proposed to be taken on the recommendations of the Commission and the reasons for non-acceptance of the recommendations, if any.

CHAPTER V
STATE HUMAN RIGHTS COMMISSIONS

21. Constitution of State Human Rights Commission.-

(1) A State Government may constitute a body to be known as the.................. (name of the State) Human Rights Commission to exercise the powers conferred upon, and to perform the functions assigned to, a State Commission under this Chapter.

(2) [The State Commission shall, with effect from such date as theState Government may by notification specify, consist of—

(a) a Chairperson who has been a Chief Justice of a High Court;

(b) one Member who is, or has been, a Judge of a High Court orDistrict Judge in the State with a minimum of seven years' experience as District Judge;

(c) one Member to be appointed from amongst persons havingknowledge of, or practical experience in, matters relating tohuman rights.][18]

(3) There shall be a Secretary who shall be the Chief Executive Officer of the State Commission and shall exercise such powers and discharge such functions of the State Commission as it may delegate to him.

(4) The headquarters of the State Commission shall be at such place as the State Government may, by notification, specify.

(5) A State Commission may inquire into violation of human rights only in respect of matters relatable to any of the entries

18. Subs. by Act 43 of 2006.

enumerated in List II and List III in the Seventh Schedule to the Constitution: Provided that if any such matter is already being inquired into by the Commission or any other Commission duly constituted under any law for the time being in force, the State Commission shall not inquire into the said matter: Provided further that in relation to the Jammu and Kashmir Human Rights Commission, this sub- section shall have effect as if for the words and figures" List II and List III in the Seventh Schedule to the Constitution", the words and figures" List III in the Seventh Schedule to the Constitution as applicable to the State of Jammu and Kashmir and in respect of matters in relation to which the Legislature of that State has power to make laws" had been substituted.

(6) [Two or more State Governments may, with the consent of a Chairperson or Member of a State Commission, appoint such Chairperson or, as the case may be, such Member of another State Commission simultaneously if such Chairperson or Member consents to such appointment:

Provided that every appointment made under this sub-section shall be made after obtaining the recommendations of the Committee referred to in sub-section (1) of section 22 in respect of the State for which a common Chairperson or Member, or both, as the case may be, is to be appointed.][19]

22. Appointment of Chairperson and [Members][19] of State Commission

(1) The Chairperson and other Members shall be appointed by the Governor by warrant under his hand and seal: provided that every appointment under this sub- section shall be made after obtaining the recommendation of a Committee consisting of:

(a) the Chief Minister— chairperson;
(b) Speaker of the Legislative Assembly- member;
(c) Minister in- charge of the Department- member; of Home in that State
(d) Leader of the Opposition in the member: Legislative Assembly

Provided further that where there is a Legislative Council in a State, the Chairman of that Council and the Leader of the Opposition in that Council shall also be members of the Committee: Provided also that no sitting Judge of a High Court or a sitting district judge

19. Subs. by Act 43 of 2006.

shall be appointed except after consultation with the Chief Justice of the High Court of the concerned State.

(2) No appointment of a Chairperson or a Member of the State Commission shall be invalid merely by reason of [any vacancy of any Member in the Committee referred to in sub-section(1).

23. [Resignation and Removal of Chairperson or a Member of the State Commission][20]

[(1) The Chairperson or a Member of a State Commission may,by notice in writing under his hand addressed to the Governor, resign his office.

(1A) Subject to the provisions of sub-section (2), the Chairperson orany Member of the State Commission shall only be removed from his officeby order of the President on the ground of proved misbehaviour orincapacity after the Supreme Court, on a reference being made to it bythe President, has, on inquiry held in accordance with the procedure prescribed in that behalf by the Supreme Court, reported that the Chairperson or such Member, as the case may be, ought on any such ground to be removed.][21]

(2) Notwithstanding anything in sub- section (1), the President may by order remove from office the Chairperson or any [Member][22] if the Chairperson or such [Member][23], as the case may be:

- (a) is adjudged an insolvent; or
- (b) engages during his term of office in any paid employment outside the duties of his office; or
- (c) is unfit to continue in office by reason of infirmity of mind or body; or
- (d) is of unsound mind and stands so declared by a competent court; or
- (e) is convicted and sentenced to imprisonment for an offence which in the opinion of the President involves moral turpitude.

24. Term of office of [Chairperson and][24] Members of the State Commission

(1) A person appointed as Chairperson shall hold office for a

20. Subs. by Act 43 of 2006.
21. Subs. by Act 43 of 2006.
22. Subs. by Act 43 of 2006 for "other member".
23. Subs. by Act 43 of 2006 for "other member".
24. Inserted by Act 43 of 2006.

term of five years from the date on which he enters upon his office or until he attains the age of seventy years, whichever is earlier.

(2) A person appointed as a Member shall hold office for a term of five years from the date on which he enters upon his office and shall be eligible for reappointment for another term of five years: Provided that no Member shall hold office after he has attained the age of seventy years.

(3) On ceasing to hold office, a Chairperson or a Member shall be ineligible for further employment under the Government of a State or under the Government of India.

25. Member to act as Chairperson or to discharge his functions in certain circumstances

(1) In the event of the occurrence of any vacancy in the office of the Chairperson by reason of his death, resignation or otherwise, the Governor may, by notification, authorise one of the Members to act as the Chairperson until the appointment of a new Chairperson to fill such vacancy.

(2) When the Chairperson is unable to discharge his functions owing to absence on leave or otherwise, such one of the Members as the Governor may, by notification, authorise in this behalf, shall discharge the functions of the Chairperson until the date on which the Chairperson resumes his duties.

26. [Terms and conditions of service of Chairperson andMembers of the State Commissions]

The salaries and allowances payable to, and other terms andconditions of service of, the Chairperson and Members shall be such as maybe prescribed by the State Government;

Provided that neither the salary and allowances nor the other termsand conditions of service of the Chairperson or a Member shall be variedto his disadvantage after his appointment.][25]

27. Offices and other staff of the State Commission

(1) The State Government shall make available to the Commission:

(a) an officer not below the rank of a Secretary to the State Government who shall be the Secretary of the State Commission; and

25. Subs. by Act 43 of 2006.

(b) such police and investigative staff under an officer not below the rank of an Inspector General of Police and such other officers and staff as may be necessary for the efficient performance of the functions of the State Commission.

(2) Subject to such rules as may be made by the State Government in this behalf, the State Commission may appoint such other administrative, technical and scientific staff as it may consider necessary.

(3) The salaries, allowances and conditions of service of the officers and other staff appointed under sub- section (22) shall be such as may be prescribed by the State Government.

28. Annual and special reports of State Commission

(1) The State Commission shall submit an annual report to the State Government and may at any time submit special reports on any matter which, in its opinion, is of such urgency or importance that it should not be deferred till submission of the annual report.

(2) The State Government shall cause the annual and special reports of the State Commission to be laid before each House of State Legislature where it consists of two Houses, or where such Legislature consists of one House, before that House along with a memorandum of action taken or proposed to be taken on the recommendations of the State Commission and the reasons for non-acceptance of the recommendations, if any.

29. Application of certain provisions relating to National Human Rights Commission to State Commissions

The provisions of sections 9, 10, 12, 13, 14, 15, 16, 17 and 18 shall apply to a State Commission and shall have effect, subject to the following modifications, namely:-

(a) references to" Commission" shall be construed as references to" State Commission";

(b) in section 10, in sub- section (3), for the word" Secretary General", the word" Secretary" shall be substituted;

(c) in section 12, clause (f) shall be omitted;

(d) in section 17, in clause (i), the words" Central Government or any" shall be omitted.

CHAPTER VI
HUMAN RIGHTS COURTS

30. Human Rights Courts

For the purpose of providing speedy trial of offences arising out of violation of human rights, the State Government may, with the concurrence of the Chief Justice of the High Court, by notification, specify for each district a Court of Session to be a Human Rights Court to try the said offences: Provided that nothing in this section shall apply if:

(a) a Court of Session is already specified as a special court; or

(b) a special court is already constituted, for such offences under any other law for the time being in force.

31. Special Public Prosecutor

For every Human Rights Court, the State Government shall, by notification, specify a Public Prosecutor or appoint an advocate who has been in practice as an advocate for not less, than seven years, as a Special Public Prosecutor for the purpose of conducting cases in that Court.

CHAPTER VII
FINANCE, ACCOUNTS AND AUDIT

32. Grants by the Central Government.

(1) The Central Government shall, after due appropriation made by Parliament by law in this behalf, pay to the Commission by way of grants such sums of money as the Central Government may think fit being utilised for the purposes of this Act.

(2) The Commission may spend such sums as it thinks fit for per- forming the functions under this Act, and such sums shall be treated as expenditure payable out of the grants referred to in sub-section (1).

33. Grants by the State Government'

(1) The State Government shall, after due appropriation made by Legislature by law in this behalf, pay to the State Commission by way of grants such sums of money as the State Government may think fit for being utilised for the purposes of this Act.

(2) The State Commission may spend such sums as it thinks fit for performing the functions under Chapter V, and such sums shall

be treated as expenditure payable out of the grants referred to in sub-section (1).

34. Accounts and audit

(1) The Commission shall maintain proper accounts and other relevant records and prepare an annual statement of accounts in such form as may be prescribed by the Central Government in consultation with the Comptroller and Auditor-General of India.

(2) The accounts of the Commission shall be audited by the Comptroller and Auditor-General at such intervals as may be specified by him and any expenditure incurred in connection with such audit shall be payable by the Commission to the Comptroller and Auditor- General.

(3) The Comptroller and Auditor-General and any person appointed by him in connection with the audit of the accounts of the Commission under this Act shall have the same rights and privileges and the au- thority in connection with such audit as the Comptroller and Auditor-General generally has in connection with the audit of Government accounts and, in particular shall have the right to demand the production of books, accounts, connected. vouchers and other documents and papers and to inspect any of the offices of the Commission.

(4) The accounts of the Commission, as certified by the Comptroller and Auditor- General or any other person appointed by him in this behalf, together with the audit report thereon shall be forwarded annually to the Central Government by the Commission and the Central Government shall cause the audit report to be laid, as soon as may be after it is received, before each House of Parliament.

35. Accounts and audit of State Commission

(1) The State Commission shall maintain proper accounts and other relevant records and prepare an annual statement of accounts in such form as may be prescribed by the State Government in consultation with the Comptroller and Auditor-General of india.

(2) The accounts of the State Commission shall be audited by the Comptroller and Auditor- General at such intervals as may be specified by him and any expenditure incurred in connection with such audit shall be payable by the State Commission to the Comptroller and Auditor- General.

(3) The Comptroller and Auditor- General and any person appointed by him in connection with the audit of the accounts of the State Com- mission under this Act shall have the same rights and

privileges and the authority in connection with such audit as the Comptroller and Auditor- General generally has in connection with the audit of Government accounts and, in particular, shall have the right to demand the production of books, accounts, connected vouchers and other documents and papers and to inspect any of the offices of the State Commission.

(4) The accounts of the State Commission, as certified by the Comptroller and Auditor- General or any other person appointed by him in this behalf, together with the audit report thereon, shall be forwarded annually to the State Government by the State Commission and the State Government shall cause the audit report to be laid, as soon as may be after it is received, before the State Legislature.

CHAPTER VIII
MISCELLANEOUS

36. Matters not subject to jurisdiction of the Commission

(1) The Commission shall not inquire into any matter which is pending before a State Commission or any other Commission duly constituted under any law for the time being in force.

(2) The Commission or the State Commission shall not inquire into any matter after the expiry of one year from the date on which the act constituting violation of human rights is alleged to have been committed.

37. Constitution of special investigation teams

Notwithstanding anything contained in any other law for the time being in force, where the Government considers it necessary so to do, it may constitute one or more special investigation teams, consisting of such police officers as it thinks necessary for purposes of investigation and prosecution of offences arising out of violations of human rights.

38. Protection of action taken in good faith

No suit or other legal proceeding shall lie against the Central Government, State Government, Commission, the State Commission or any Member thereof or any person acting under the direction either of the Central Government, State Government, Commission or the State Commission in respect of anything which is in good faith done or intended to be done in pursuance of this Act or of any rules or any order made thereunder or in respect of the publication by or under the authority of the Central Government, State Government, Commission or the State Commission of any report, paper or proceedings.

39. Members and officers to be public servants

Every Member of the Commission, State Commission and every officer appointed or authorised by the Commission or the State Commission to exercise functions under this Act shall be deemed to be a public servant within the meaning of section 21 of the Indian Penal Code (45 of 1860).

40. Power of Central Government to make rules

(1) The Central Government may, by notification, make rules to carry out the provisions of this Act.

(2) In particular and without prejudice to the generality of the foregoing power, such rules may provide for all or any of the following matters, namely :

(a) the salaries and allowances and other terms and conditions of service of the [Chairperson and Members][26] under section 8;

(b) the conditions subject to which other administrative, technical and scientific staff may be appointed by the Commission and the salaries and allowancesof officers and other staff under sub-section (3) of section 11;

(c) any other power of a civil court required to be prescribed under clause (f) of sub-section (1) of section 13;

(d) the form in which the annual statement of accounts is to be prepared by the Commission under sub- section (1) of section 34; and

(e) any other matter which has to be, or may be, prescribed.

(3) Every rule made under this Act shall be laid, as soon as may be after it is made, before each House of Parliament, while it is in session, for a total period of thirty days which may be comprised in one session or in two or more successive sessions, and if, before the expiry of the session immediately following the session or the successive sessions aforesaid, both Houses agree in making any modification in the rule or both Houses agree that the rule should not be made, the rule shall thereafter have effect only in such modified

26. Subs. by Act 43 of 2006 for "other members".

form or be of no effect, as the case may be; so, however, that any such modification or annulment shall be without prejudice to the validity of anything previously done under that rule.

40A. Power to make rules retrospectively[27]

The power to makerules under clause (b) of sub-section (2) of section 40 shall include the powerto make such rules or any of them retrospectively from a date not earlierthan the date on which this Act received the assent of the President, butno such retrospective effect shall be given to any such rule so as toprejudicially affect the interests of any person to whom such rule may beapplicable.

40B. Power of Commission to make Regulations[28]

(1) Subject to the provisions of this Act and the rules madethereunder, the Commission may, with the previous approval of the CentralGovernment, by notification, make regulations to carry out the provisionsof this Act.

(2) In particular and without prejudice to the generality of theforegoing power, such regulations may provide for all or any of the followingmatters, namely :

(a) the procedure to be followed by the Commission under subsection(2) of Section 10;
(b) the returns and statistics to be furnished by the StateCommission;
(c) any other matter which has to be, or may be, specified byregulations.

(3) Every regulation made by the Commission under this Act shallbe laid, as soon as may be after it is made, before each House of Parliament,while it is in session, for a total period of thirty days which may be comprisedin one session or in two or more successive sessions, and if, before theexpiry of the session or the successive sessions aforesaid, both Houses agree in making any modification in the regulations or both Houses agree that the regulation should not be made, the regulation shall thereafter have effect only in such modified form or be of no effect, as the case may be; so however, that any such modification or annulment shall be without prejudiceto the validity of anything previously done under that regulation.

27. Subs. by Act 43 of 2006.
28. Subs. by Act 43 of 2006.

41. Power of State Government to make rules

(1) The State Government may, by notification, make rules to carry, out the provisions of this Act.

(2) In particular and without prejudice to the generality of the foregoing power, such rules may provide for all or any of the following matters, namely:

(a) the salaries and allowances and other terms and conditions of service of the Members under section 26;

(b) the conditions subject to which other administrative, technical and scientific staff may be appointed by the State Commission and the salaries and allowances of officers and other staff under sub- section (3) of section 27;

(c) the form in which the annual statement of accounts is to be prepared under sub- section (1) of section 35.

(3) Every rule made by the State Government under this section shall be laid, as soon as may be after it is made, before each House of the State Legislature where it consists of two Houses, or where such Legislature consists of one House, before that House.

42. Power to remove difficulties

(1) If any difficulty arises in giving effect to the provisions of this Act, the Central Government may, by order published in the Official Gazette, make such provisions, not inconsistent with the provisions of this Act as appear to it to be necessary or expedient for removing the difficulty: Provided that no such order shall be made after the expiry of the period of two years from the date of commencement of this Act.

(2) Every order made under this section shall, as soon as may be after it is made, be laid before each House of Parliament.

43. Repeal and savings

(1) The Protection of Human Rights Ordinance, 1993 is (Ord. 30 of 1993) hereby repealed.

(2) Notwithstanding such repeal, anything done or any action taken under the said Ordinance, shall be deemed to have been done Or taken under the corresponding provisions of this Act.

Table of Cases

A.D.M. Jabalpur *v.* Shiv Kant Shukla, A.I.R. 1976 S.C. 1207,
A. K. Gopalan *v.* State of Madras, A.I.R. 1950 SC 27,
Abdul RehmanAntulay v.R.S. Nayak, A.I.R. 1992 S.C. 1630,
AjithKumar *v.* State of Assam, 1976 Cri.L.J. 1303,
Arvind Singh Bagga *v.* State of U.P., AIR 1985 S.C. 117,
Bhim Singh *v.* State of J &K, (1985) 4 S.C.C. 730,
Citizen for Democracy *v.* State of Assam, (1995) 3 S.C.C. 743,
D.K.Basu *v.* State of West Bengal, 1997(1) SCC 416,
D.P.Ghosh *v.* State of West Bengal, (1972) 2 S.C.C. 656,
Dr. Ram Krishan Bhardwaj *v.* Delhi, 1953 S.C.R. 708,
Francis Coralie Mullin *v.* Delhi, 981 S.C.R. (2) 516,
Golak Nath *v.* State of Punjab, A.I.R. 1967 S.C. 1643,
GovindPrasad *v.* State of West Bengal, 1975 Cri.L.J. 1249,
Gramophone Co. of India Ltd. *v.* Birendra Bahadur Pandey, A.I.R. 1984 SC 667,
Gunupati Keshav Ram *v.* Nafisul Hasan, A.I.R. 1954 S.C. 636,
Hussainara Khatoon (No. 1) *v.* Home Secretary, State of Bihar, A.I.R. 1979 S.C. 1360,
Hussainara Khatoon (No. 2) *v.* Home Secretary, State of Bihar, A.I.R. 1979 S.C. 1369,
Hussainara Khatoon (No. 3) *v.* Home Secretary, State of Bihar, A.I.R. 1979 S.C. 1377
In re Madhu Limaye, 1969 Cri.L.J. 1440,
Janardhan Reddi *v.* State of Hyderabad, A.I.R. 1951 S.C. 217,
Joginder Kumar *v.* State of U.P., (1994) 4 S.C.C. 260,
Jolly George *v.* Bank of Cochin, A.I.R. 1980 S.C. 470,
Kartar Singh *v.* State of Punjab, (1994) 3 S.C.C. 569,

K. Karunakaran *v.* T .V. Eachara Warrier, 1978 SCR (2) 209,
Keshavananda Bharathi *v.* State of Kerala A.I.R. 1973 S.C. 1461,
Kharak Singh *v.* State of U.P., 1964 S.C.R. (1) 332,
Khatri(II) *v.* State of Bihar, 1981 S.C.R. (2) 408,
Kishore Singh *v.* State of Rajasthan, 1981 S.C.R. (1) 995,
M.H. Hoskot *v.* State of Maharashtra, A.I.R. 1978 S.C. 1548,
M.P. Sharma *v.* Satish Chandra, 1954 S.C.R. 1077,
Maneka Gandhi *v.* Union of India, 1978 SCR (2) 621,
Miranda *v.* Arizona, 384 U.S. 436 (1966),
Munn v.I llinois, 94 U.S. 113 (1877),
Murli S. Deora *v.* Union of India, A.I.R. 2000 S.C. 40,
Nandini Satpathy *v.* P.L. Dani, 1978 S.C.R. (3) 608,
Neelabati Behera @ Lalita Behera *v.* State of Orissa 993 S.C.R. (2) 581
Nirmal Singh Kahlon *v.* State of Punjab, A.I.R. 2009 S.C. 984
Niyamavedi *v.* Central Bureau of Investigation, 1999(1) KLT 56
Olga Tellis *v.* Bombay Municipal Corporation, A.I.R. 1986 S.C. 180,
People's Union for Civil Liberties *v.* Union of India, A.I.R. 1990 S.C. 513,
Peoples' Union for Democratic Rights *v.* Police Commissioner, Delhi H.Q., (1989) 4 S.C.C. 730,
Peoples' Union for Democratic Rights *v.* State of Bihar, A.I.R. 1987 S.C. 355,
Prakash Singh *v.* Union of India, (2006) 8 S.C.C. 1,
Prem Shankar Shukla *v.* Delhi administration, 1980 S.C.R. (3) 85,
R. Rajagopal *v.* State of Tamil Nadu, (1985) 2 S.C.C. 431,
Ram Kumar *v.* State of Himachal Pradesh A.I.R. 1995 S.C. 1965,
Rudal Shah *v.* State of Bihar, A.I.R. 1983 S.C. 1086,
S.P. Saha *v.* M.S. Kochar, 1979 Cri.L.J. 1367,
Saheli *v.* Commissioner of Police, A.I.R. 1990 S.C. 513,
Sebastian M. Hongray *v.* Union of India, A.I.R. 1984 S.C. 1026,
Shalini Soni *v.* Union of India, 1981 S.C.R. (1) 962,
Sheela Barse *v.* State of Maharashtra, 1983 S.C.R. (2) 337,
Sher Singh *v.* State of Punjab, A.I.R. 1981 S.C. 625,
Smt. Shakila Abdul Gafar Khan *v.* Vasant Raghunath Dhoble, A.I.R. 2003 S.C. 4567,
State of Bombay *v.* Kathi Kalu, 1962 S.C.R. (3) 10,
State of Madras *v.* G.G.Menon, A.I.R. 1954 S.C. 517,
State of Maharshtra *v.* Ravikant S. Patil, (1991) 2 S.C.C. 373,
State of Punjab *v.* Ajaib Singh, 1953 S.C.R. 254,
State of West Bengal v.Subodh Gopal Bose A.I.R. 1954 S.C. 92,

Sunial Batra (1) *v.* Delhi Administration, A.I.R. 1978 S.C. 1575,
Sunil Batra *v.* Delhi Administaration, 1979 S.C.R. (1) 392,
Supreme Court Legal Aid Committee *v.* State of Bihar, (1990) 3 S.C.C. 482,
Surjeet Singh *v.* Jit Singh, 1998 Cri.L.J. 3562,
Tukaram *v.* State of Maharashtra, (1979) 2 S.C.C. 143,
T.V. EacharaVarier *v.* Secretary to the Ministry of Home Affairs, Government of Kerala, 1977 K. L. T. 335,
Vakil Prasad Singh *v.* State of Bihar, A.I.R. 2009 S.C. 1822,
Vijay Kumar *v.* State of J&K, 1982 S.C.R. (3) 522,
Zahira Habibulla *v.* State of Gujarat, A.I.R. 2004 S.C. 3114,
Unreported Cases,
Central Bureau of Investigation *v.* Murukeshan, (Crl) No(s).774/2011 of H.C. of Kerala),
Selvi *v.* State of Karnataka, Crl. Appeal 990/2010 S.C.,
Shukur Ali *v.* State of Assam, Crl. App. No. 546/2011 S.C.,

Bibliography

Books

Asish Kumar Das and P.K Mohanty, *Human rights in India*, Sarup & Sons, New Delhi (2007).

Bajwa.G.S, *Human Rights in India: Implementations and Violations,* Anmon publications, New Delhi (1995)

Bakshi, P.M., *The Constitution of India*, Universal law Publisher, New Delhi (10thEdn, 2010).

Basu D.D., *Crimial Procedure Code* (1973).

Brian Orend, *Human Rights : Concept and Context,* Oxford University Press (2002)

Clemens Neumann Nathan, *The Changing Face of Religion and Human Rights: A Personal Reflection,* Martinus-Nijhoff Publishers (2009).

David Braybrook, *Natural Law Modernized,* University of Toronto Press (2001).

David H. Bayley, *Police for the Future*, Oxford University Press (1994).

Dr. Reddy.G.B., *Judicial Activism in India,* Universal Law Books (2004).

Fernand De Varennes, *Asia-Pacific Human Rights Documents and Resources*, Vol.1, Martinus-Nijhoff Publishers (1998)

Frans Viljoen, *International Human Rights Law in Africa,* OxfordUniversity Press, New York (2007).

George Mukundi Wachira, *African Court on Human and Peoples' Rights: Ten years on and still no justice* (2008),Minority Rights Group International, London.

Gopal Bhargava, *Meaning and Source of Human Rights*, Kalpaz Publications (2003).

Halstead Peter, *The Comprehensive Guide to All Facts: Human Rights*, Hodder Arnold, London (2010).

Henry David Thoreau, *On the duty of Civil Disobedience*, Elegant Books (1842).

Ierodiakonou, *Topics in Stoic Philosophy*, Oxford Publishers (1999).

Jain M.P., *Indian Constitutional Law*, (5th edition, rep. 2006), Wadhwa Publications, Nagpur.

Janey Levy, *Iran and the Shia*, the Rosen Publishing Group (2009).

Jebagnanam Cyrill Kanmony, *Human Rights Violation*, Mittal Publications (2010).

Johannes Morsink, *TheUniversal Declaration Of Human Rights: Origins, Drafting & Intent*, University of Pennsylvania Press (1999).

Helmholz R.H. *et al.*, *The Privilege against Self-Incrimination: Its Origins and Development*, University of Chicago Press (1997).

John Stuart Mill, *Essays on Liberty*, Batoche Books Ltd, Canada (1973).

Justice Krishna Iyer V.R., *The Juristic Manifesto of the Human Person, Human Rights-A judges Miscellany*, B.R. Publishing Corporation (1995).,

Kelkar R.V., *Criminal Procedure*, Eastern Book Co., Lucknow (1998).

Krishna Iyer V.R., *Liberty- A Non-negotiable Value- The Dialectics and Dynamics of Human Rights in India: Yesterday, Today and Tomorrow*, Eastern Law House (1999).

Krishna Iyer V.R., *Human Rights and Inhuman Wrongs*, B.R. Publishing Co., New Delhi (1990).

M. Rishmawi, *The Revised Arab Charter on Human Rights: A Step Forward?*, Human Rights Law Review, Vol.(5) (2005).

Madhava Menon N.R., *Criminal Justice India Series: Kerala*, Vol.6, (N.R. Madhava Menon *et. al* eds. NUJS (2002).

Mashood A. Baderin, *International Human Rights and Islamic Law*, Oxford University Press (2nd Ed., 2005)

Muralidhar S., *Public Interest Litigation*, International Environmental Law research Center (1999)

Prakash Talwar, *Human Rights*, Gyan Books (2006).

Ramanatha Aiyer P., *Code of Criminal Procedure*, Modern publishers, Lucknow (1999).

Rhona Smith K.M., *Textbook on International Human Rights*, Oxford University Press, U.K. (3rdEdn, 2007).

Richard Falk A., *Human Rights Horizons: The Pursuit of Justice in a Globalizing World*, Roultledge, London (2000).

Sastry, T.S.N., *India and human Rights : reflection*, Concept Publishing Company (2005).

Seervai H. M., *Constitutional Law of India: A Critical Commentary*, vol. 1, 4th Edn.1991, Universal Law Publishing Co. Pvt. Ltd., Delhi.

Steven Greer, *European Convention on Human Rights: Achievements, problems and prospects,* Cambridge University Press (2006).

Steven R. Ratnerand Jason Abrams, *Accountability For Human Rights Atrocities In International Law: Beyond The Nuremberg Legacy*, Oxford University Press (2ndEdn, 2001).

Thomas Pine, *Rights of Man*, Elegant Books (1792).

UpendraBaxi, *Mambrino's Helmet? Human Rights for a Changing World*, Har-Anand Publication (1994).

U.N. Criminal Justice, *Use and Application of the Code of*

Information Network, *Conduct for Law Enforcement Officials, Including the Basic Principles on the Use of Force and Firearms*, Crime Prevention and Criminal Justice Division, United Nations Office at Vienna (1999).

High Commissioner for Human Rights, *Human Rights and Law Enforcement : Manual on Human Rights Training for the Police*, Professional Training Series No. 5 (1995).

Articles

Christof Heyna and Frans Viljoen, *The Impact of the United Nations Human Rights Treaties on the Domestic Level*, Kluwer Law International (2002).

Call Wellman, *Solidarity, the Individual and Human Rights*, Human Rights Quarterly, Vol. 22 (2000)

Gina Bekker, Recent *Developments in the African Human Rights System 2008-2009*, Human Rights Law Review, 9 (4), (2009)

Lammy Betten, *Current Development: European Community Law*, 50 Int'l & Comp. L.Q. (2001).

Lucio Martins Rodrigues, *Sixty years after the Universal Declaration : navigating the contradictions*, International Journal on Human Rights, Cidade University, Brazil, (2008).

Kalhan A., *et al.*, *Colonial Continuities: Human Rights, Terrorism, And Security Laws in India*, (2006), 20 Colum. J. Asian L. 93, fall 2006.

Kaur Jaskaran, *A Judicial Blackout: Judicial Impunity for Disappearances in Punjab, India,* Harvard Human Rights Journal, Vol.15 (2002)

Kolsky E., *Codification And the Rule of Colonial Difference: Criminal Procedure In British India* (2005), 23 law & hist. rev.; See also Kalhan. A *et al*, *Colonial Continuities: Human Rights, Terrorism, And Security Laws in India* (2006), Colum. J. Asian L. 93, fall (2006).

M. Rishmawi, *The Revised Arab Charter on Human Rights: A Step Forward?*, Human Rights Law Review, Vol.(5) (2005)

Michael Dennis. J., *Human Rights in 2002: The Annual Session of the UN Commission on Human Rights and the Economic and Social Council,* American Journal of International Law, Vol. 97, Issue 2 (2003).

Michael Dennis J. and David Stewart, *Justiciability of Economic, Social, and Cultural Rights: Should There be an International Complaints Mechanism to Adjudicate the Rights to Food, Water, Housing, and Health?* 98 A.J.I.L. (2004).

Michael Hor, *The Confessions Regime in Singapore,* Malayan Law Journal (1991).

Ralph Crawshaw, *Human Rights and Policing*, The Journal of Turkish Weekly (2005).

R.N. Mangoli and Ganapati M.T., *A Study of Human Rights Violation by Police in India,* International Journal of Criminology and Sociological Theory, Vol. 3 (2010)

Sicurelli, Daniella., *The European Union as a Model for the African Union—Effectiveness and Limits of European Norm Promotion,* Paper presented at the annual meeting of the International Studies Association's 50th Annual Convention "Exploring the Past, Anticipating the Future", New York, (Feb. 15-18, 2000)

Sunil Deshta and Kiran Deshta, *Philosophy of Right to life: A Movement from Rigidity to Flexibility*, Civil and Military Law Journal, Vol. 31, No. 3 (1995).

Venkata Rao R., *Custodial Violence and Judicial Response*, Vol. 7, Journal of the National Human Rights Commission, India (2008).

James Madison, *The Structure of the Government Must Furnish the Proper Checks and Balances between the Different Departments*; The Federalist Papers No. 51, Independent Journal, (1978).

Mohammed Amin Al-Midani, *The Enforcement Mechanisms of the Arab Charter on Human Rights and the Need for an Arab Court of*

Human Right, Regional Human Rights Mechanisms, The European Convention and the Arab Charter, International Conference, Bologna (Italy), (2008).

Reports

Asian Center for Human Rights, *Indian Human Rights Report 2009*
Asian Centre for Human Rights Report, *Torture in India 2009*
Asian Centre for Human Rights Report, *Torture in India 2010*
Asian Centre for Human Rights Report, *Torture in India* 2011.
Government of India, Third Report: National Police Commission (1980)
Justice V.S. Mallimath Committee on Criminal Justice Reform Report (2003)
Kerala State Human Rights Commission Annual Report 2006-07
Law Commission of India 48th Report
Law Commission of India 152nd Report
Law Commission of India 154th Report
Law Commission of India 180th Report
National Human Rights Commission Annual Report 1993-94.
National Human Rights Commission Annual Report 1994-95.
National Human Rights Commission Annual Report 1995-96.
National Human Rights Commission Annual Report 1997-98.
National Human Rights Commission Annual Report 1998-99
National Human Rights Commission Annual Report 1999-2000.
National Human Rights Commission Annual Report 2000-01.
National Human Rights Commission Annual Report 2001-02.
National Human Rights Commission Annual Report 2002-03.
National Human Rights Commission Annual Report 2003-04
National Human Rights Commission Annual Report 2004-05.
National Human Rights Commission Annual Report 2005-06.
National Human Rights Commission Annual Report 2006-07.
National Human Rights Commission Annual Report 2007-08
National Human Rights Commission Annual Report 2008-09.
National Human Rights Commission Annual Report 2009-10.
National Crime Records Bureau, Crimes in India 2010.
National Crime Records Bureau, Crimes in India 2011.
National Crime Records Bureau, Crimes in India 2012.
National Police Commission, Third Report 1980.
Reibero Commission Report (1996)
Soli Sorabjee committee Report (2006)

Statutes

Assam Police Act, 2007
Bombay Police Act,1951
Bihar Police Act, 2007
Chhattisgarh Police Act, 2007
Constitution of India
Criminal Law Amendment Act, 2013.
Criminal Procedure Code Amendment Act, 2005.
Criminal Procedure Code Amendment Act, 2008.
Criminal Procedure Code Amendment Act, 2010.
Criminal Procedure Code, 1973.
Haryana Police Act, 2007.
Himachal Pradesh Police Act, 2007.
Human Rights Commission of Sri Lanka Act, 1996.
Indian Evidence Act, 1872.
Indian Penal Code, 1861.
Juvenile Justice (Care and Protection of Children) Act, 2000.
Kerala Police Act, 1960
Kerala Police Act, 2011.
Karnataka Police Act, 1963.
Karnataka Police (Amendment) Act, 2012.
National Human Rights Commission of Nepal, 2000.
National Security Act, 1980.
Prevention of Terrorism Act, 2002.
Protection of Human Rights Act, 1993.
Punjab Police Act, 2007.
Rajasthan Police Act, 2007.
The Customs Act, 1962.
The Police Act, 1861.
The Railway Property (Unlawful Possession) Act, 1996.
The Terrorist and Disruptive Activities (Prevention) Act, 1985.
Sikkim Police Act, 2007.
Tripura Police Act, 2007.
Uttara Khand Police Act, 2007.

Conventions, Declarations, Protocols, Principles and Rules

American Declaration of Independence, 1776.
Basic Principles on the Use of Force and Firearms by Law Enforcement Officials, 1990.
Body of Principles for the Protection of All Persons under Any Form of Detention or Imprisonment, 1988.

Cairo Declaration of the Human Rights, 1990.
Constitutive Act of the African Union, 2000.
Convention on the Elimination All Forms Of Discrimination against Women, 1979.
Convention on the Rights of Child, 1989.
Declaration of Basic Principles of Justice for Victims of Crime and Abuse of Power, 1985.
Declaration of Rights of Man and of the Citizen,1789.
Declaration on the Elimination of Violence against Women, 1993.
First Optional Protocol to International Covenant on Civil and Political Rights
International Convention for the Protection of All Persons from Enforced Disappearance, 1992.
International Covenant on Civil and Political Rights, 1976.
Petition of Rights, 1628.
U.N.Code of Conduct for Law Enforcement Officials, 1979.
U.N. Convention against Torture and Other Cruel, Inhuman or Degrading Treatment or Punishment, 1984.
U.N. Declaration on the Protection of All Persons from Being Subjected To Torture and Other Cruel, Inhuman and Degrading Treatment or Punishment, 1975.
U.N. Declaration on the Rights of Child, 1989.
U.N. Rules for the Protection of Juveniles Deprived of Their Liberty, 1990.
United Nations Standard Minimum Rules for Non-Custodial Measures, 1990.
United Nations Treaty Collections.
Universal Declaration of Human Rights, 1948.
Virginia Declaration of Rights, 1776.

Newspapers and Periodicals

The Hindu (7 August, 2006).
Times of India (16 September, 2006).
The Hindu (4 April, 2008).
The Hindu (25 April, 2008).
The Hindu (26 April, 2010).
Frontline (29 January, 2011).

Websites

1. Amnesty International U.S.A., *Basics of Human Rights*, available at http://www.amnestyusa.org/research/human-rights-basics (Visited on May 22, 2011).

2. Constituent Assembly of India, Volume IX, 15 September, 1949, available at http://parliamentofindia.nic.in/ls/debates/vol9p35a.htm (Visited on December 17, 2010)
3. Constituent Assembly of India, Volume IX, 15 September, 1949, available at http://parliamentofindia.nic.in/ls/debates/vol9p35a.htm (Visited on December 17, 2010).
4. David Little, *The Nature and Basis of Human Rights*, United States Institute of Peace, available at http://www.usip.org/research/rehr/natbasis.html (Visited on January30, 2008)Cached (Visited on August 12, 2010).
5. Human Rights Features, *The Proposed Asian Human Rights Charter: No Rights at the End of This Tunnel,* 11 November, 2000, available at http://www.hrdc.net/sahrdc/hrfeatures/HRF27.htm (Visited on November 18, 2010)
6. J. Reghu, *Custodial Death of the Author of Play Called "Liberation (*2006), available at http://www.zcommunications.org/the-custodial-death-of-the-author-of-the-play-called-liberation-by-j-reghu (Visited on July 23,2011).
7. Joshi, G.P., Police Accountability in India, Commonwealth Human Rights Initiative, New Delhi, available at www.humanrightsinitiative.org/.../police/.../police_accountability_in_india.pdf*(Visited on May 14, 2010)*
8. Joshi, G.P., *Police Accountability in India: policing contaminated by politics,* Commonwealth Human Rights Initiative (2005), available at http://www.hrsolidarity.net/mainfile.php/2005vol15no05/2448/(Visited on February 22, 2011).
9. Kerala State Human Rights Commission, Annual Report, 2006-07 (2007), available at http://www.kshrc.kerala.gov.in/archives.htm(Visited on July 21, 2011)
10. Manoj Kumar Sinha, *Role of the National Human Rights Commission of India in Protection of Human Rights,* Internet publication, available at http://www.rwi.lu.se/pdf/seminar/manoj05.pdf (Visited on December 12,2010)
11. Mridushi, *National Human Rights Commission – Role in Human Rights Protection, Legal Information to Knowledge*, Jurisonline (2010), available at http://jurisonline.in/2010/03/national-human-rights-commission-%E2%80%93-role-in-human-rights-protection/ (Visited on June 3, 2011).
12. NareshMahipal, *The Protection of Human Rights Act 1993(No. X of 1994)*, Expert Column (2009), available at http://

expertscolumn.com/content/protection-human-rights-act-1993-no-x-1994 (Visited on January 14, 2011).

13. *National Human Rights Commission v. State of Gujarat,*Crl.M.P. No.10719/2003 in WP (Crl.) No. 109/ 2003,available at www.indiankanoon.org/doc/168922/?type=print (Visited on January 14, 2011)
14. *National Human Rights Commission* v. *State of Gujarat,*Crl.M.P. No.10719/2003 in WP (Crl.) No. 109/ 2003, available at www.indiankanoon.org/doc/168922/?type=print(Visited on January 14, 2011).
15. P.J. Alexander,Kerala *Police Bill,* 2010 *requires drastic changes to meet the standards* of *a legislation fitting for a modern democracy,* Asian Human Rights Commission, (2010), available at http://www.humanrights.asia/news/forwarded-news/AHRC-FST-053-2010/?searchterm (Visited on June 25, 2011).
16. Rahman, Azera, *U.P. police: The biggest violator of human rights,* Human Rights published, iGovernment, 2010, available at http://www.igovernment.in/site/police-biggest-violator-human-rights%E2%80%99-37465 (Visited on June 7, 2011).
17. S.L.P. (Criminal) Nos. 8485-87 of 2009, Supreme Court Judgment delivered on 25 October, 2010, available at http://www.indiankanoon.org/doc/1473938/(Visited on January 7, 2011).
18. *Selvi* v. *State of Karnataka,* Crl. Appeal 990 of 2010 Supreme Court of India (Arising out of SLP (Crl.) Nos. 10 of 2006 and 6711 of 2007), available at http://www.indiankanoon.org/doc/ (Visited on January 7, 2011).
19. *Shukur Ali* v. *State of Assam* (2011) INSC 195 (24 February 2011); In the Supreme Court, Crl. App. No. 546 of 2011 (arising out of S.L.P. (CRL.) No(s).679 of 2011), available at http://www.indiankanoon.org/doc/1470346/(Visited on May 22, 2011.)
20. Susan Waltz, *Who Wrote the Universal Declaration of Human Rights?* e Journal, USA (2008), available at www.heinonline.org (Visited on March 8, 2011)
21. Torture pictures, http://*www.gypsypalace.com* (Visited on March 8, 2011).
22. Torture pictures, http://frontlinepunjabiyouth.blogspot.com (Visited on March 7, 2011).

Index